The Complete Book of
Pickles and Relishes

The Complete Book of
Pickles and Relishes

LEONARD LOUIS LEVINSON

GARDEN WAY PUBLISHING CO.
Charlotte, Vermont

This book is for my mother
Sophie Levinson
and the memory of our spice-scented
kitchen at pickling time

Acknowledgments

From the first planning of this book, an integral source of practical, tested American pickling and relish recipes was the Agricultural Extension Services of the various states. They have had a great deal of experience in experimenting with the preserving of the food products of their farmers and many of them have continued to try out new methods, utensils, materials and varieties of produce when they become available.

To the many home economics and agriculture specialists across the land who have been so generous with their recipes and lore, I wish to express my thanks, not only generally, but also alphabetically, by states:

First, to the late Lavada Curtis, specialist in food preservation at Alabama Polytechnic Institute, Auburn; then to Mrs. Hazel C. Jordan, state home demonstration agent, University of Arkansas, Little Rock; George B. Alcorn, director of agriculture extension, and his staff, University of California, Berkeley, including M. A. Joslyn and W. V. Cruess for their instructions on pickling olives; Janina M. Czajkowski, extension nutritionalist, University of Connecticut, Storrs; Dr. R. A. Dennison and Forrest E. Myers, University of Florida, Gainesville; Nelle Thrash, head extension food preservation department, University of Georgia, Athens; Barbara Branthoover, former extension nutrition specialist, University of Idaho, Moscow; Dr. Norman F. Oebker, University of Illinois agriculture experiment station, Urbana; the late W. B. Ward, extension horticulturist, Purdue University, Lafayette, Indiana; Mrs. Jewel Graham, extension nutritionalist, Iowa State College, Ames; Estelle Fournet, specialist, food preservation, and Mrs. Irene M. Turner, specialist, nutrition, Louisiana State University, Baton Rouge; Dr. Andrew A. Duncan, Robert C. Wiley and Paul E. Nystron, University of Maryland, College Park; James W. Dayton and Kirby M. Hayes, University of Massachusetts, Amherst; Dr. Carl S. Pederson, New York State Experimental Station, Geneva, and Mrs. Lola T. Dudgeon, extension specialist in food and nutrition, Cornell University, Ithaca, N.Y.; Iola Pritchard and Marjorie Shearin, extension economists in food conservation and marketing, and Albert A. Banadyga, extension horticultural specialist, State College Station, Raleigh, N.C.; Louise W. Hamilton, nutrition specialist, Pennsylvania State University, University Park; Syvil D. Kaplan, extension specialist in foods and nutrition, University of Rhode Island, Kingston; Mrs. Marie S. Hindman, extension nutritionist, Clemson University, Clemson, S.C.; George I. Gilbertson, director of extension, State of South Dakota, Brookings; G. G. Gibson, former director, Texas Agricultural Extension Service, College Station; R. P. Davison, director, extension service, University of Vermont, Burlington; Inez M. Eckblad, extension food specialist, Washington State University, Pullman.

For information about pickle production and for recipes of dishes utilizing pickles I wish to thank Edward Guggenheimer, head of Bloch and Guggenheimer of Long Island City, N.Y.; Hal Nederman, formerly of H. J. Heinz & Co., now of the Dailey Pickle Co., Saginaw, Mich.; Oscar Rau, production manager, H. J. Heinz, Pittsburgh; Mary Hale Martin, director of home economics, Libby McNeill and Libby, Chicago; Hans J. Wolflisberg, president, and J. G. Crockett, group products manager, The Nestlé Company, White Plains, N.Y.; W. R. "Bill" Moore, secretary-treasurer, and John C. Smart, manager, marketing services, Pickle Packers International, Inc.; Marian Laylin, Elinor Ehrman, and Carolyn Dunn of Theodore R. Sills & Co., New York City; the Bernard Lewis organization, New York, representing the United Fresh Fruit and Vegetable Association; and A. M. Daniels, formerly of Anchor Hocking Glass Corp. of New York.

For pickling methods, my thanks go to Gladys Kimbrough, consultant to Ball Brothers Co., Inc., of Muncie, Ind.; Mrs. Zella Hale Weyant, consultant to Kerr Glass Mfg. Corp. of Sand Springs, Okla.; and the staff of Bernardine Bottle Cap Co. of Evansville, Ind.

Samuel Friedman, director of laboratories, New York City Dept. of Water, told me where I could learn the relative hardness of waters, important in pickling. I am grateful to friends like Miss Llewellyn Miller, not only for the use of her extensive library of culinary lore, but her "putting-up" deftness. And to orchestra leader Billy Mills, a West Coast pickling prize-winner who has been most gracious and generous with his recipes.

I wish to acknowledge with thanks the services of Mrs. Anita Fail, who acted as home economics consultant on this book, briefly but effectively.

It is not my custom to thank publishers for what they do in connection with books they publish—at least in print—but Fred Kerner took an interest in this book that was more than that of a publisher. From the start he collected and contributed recipes, especially exotic ones, which otherwise might not have found their way to these pages.

I am greatly indebted to all of the above named and again say "Thank you!"

LEONARD LOUIS LEVINSON

Preface

I have spent most of my adult life writing comedy for almost every medium of expression, but nothing I ever wrote evoked the smiles, grins, chuckles and outright laughter that greeted the announcement that I was writing a book about pickles.

Irving Stone writes about Michaelangelo, the talented stonecutter, and no one kids him. Morris West does a book about the Far East; it receives proper respect and no cracks. But my pickle project inspires a barrage of bad puns and shopworn jokes. (The fact that I had books about Casanova published during this same time didn't help, either.)

Perhaps this unkind levity left some psychic scar that slowed me down, because I started work on this book in 1956 and have been the despair of my publishers ever since.

Then again, I am sure I would have delivered a manuscript years ago, except that I took that word in the title (*"complete"*) too literally. I set out to absorb everything worth ascertaining about the subject, with the result that today I am such a treasury of pickle information that I not only know more than almost anyone else would want to know about pickles, but sometimes I have the feeling that I know more than I care to know, myself.

During this time (my Pickle Period), I wrote an article about commercial pickling for *Coronet* and learned how the wheels turned in the packing plants. (I had basic training as a boy in Pittsburgh, for whenever I was at loose ends during summer vacations, I'd wander across the river to H. J. Heinz's and go through the pickle works—mainly so I could lunch on the tray of samples they handed out at the end of the tour.)

After I wrote "The Peerless Pickle" article, I really got my teeth into the subject, if you will pardon the obvious pun. I began to haunt the shelves of the fancy groceries from the Farmers Market in Los Angeles to Fortnum & Mason's in Piccadilly, from Manganaro's in New York's Hell's Kitchen to Motta in Milan, and from Balzer's in L.A. to Berardo's in Rome. Not to mention the Vendôme in N.Y. and the places around Les Halles in Paris. Or, for that matter, Hudson's department store in Detroit and Harrod's in Knightsbridge. I am one of the few men in this world who can charge off a $5 bottle of Pickled Walnuts as a legitimate expense for income tax purposes.

I became a chutney cosmopolite and a raconteur of relish recipes. In London

I chivvied Jack Isow until he revealed a secret formula that brings the British beating a path to his Soho restaurant. In Italy I detoured on a journey from Milan to Turin to spend a highly pungent afternoon at Signor Ponti's vinegar works in Novara.

Recently I made another detour. On my way from Rome to N.Y., Alitalia set me down in Venice for a day so that I could induce Harry Cipriani to give me the exact description of the construction of a certain relish served at Harry's Bar. After watching the chef make it, I sat down and ate the whole batch. Ah, Venice is something more than canals!

Back in Manhattan, I became even more pickle-prone. I was so wrapped in the subject, a hostess had to bait me with some new way to serve pickles in her dinner before I would accept an invitation. Before long my friends ran out of ideas and I ran out of invitations.

But there were compensations. I was honored by the National (now International) Pickle Packers Association as the Pickle Writer of the Year. (I have the Golden Cucumber on my mantelpiece to prove it.) The Dil Pickle Club of Chicago made me an honorary member. Edward Guggenheim, the Long Island pickle plutocrat, sent me a year's supply of green dainties.

In addition, I bought and tested pickle products wherever I went. Those I couldn't sample on the spot, I sent to my apartment. Soon my refrigerator overflowed with strange jars partially filled with mysterious residues of pickling liquids I was still attempting to "crack."

I suppose the neighbors would have begun to complain, but the town house in which I had my apartment was condemned to be demolished and, one by one, the other tenants moved out.

I got my notice three months ago: Deadline, May 1. It was a severe blow. I couldn't possibly move all the material and research and correspondence and those jars, awaiting some gastronomic James Bond, to another place. Not without taking years to sort everything out again.

There was only one thing to do—stop collecting pickle lore and pickle recipes —stop eating and sleeping and thinking pickles . . . and start writing about them. I had hoped that the day would never come.

But it did and I have been writing ever since. Now, having finished the rest of the book, I am writing the preface. Just under the wire. Tonight the preface —tomorrow the wreckers.

It was a tough fight, but I made it. It didn't exactly take a house to fall down on me. But it was close.

LEONARD LOUIS LEVINSON

April 30, 1965

Contents

Acknowledgments 7
Preface 9
The Peerless Pickle 13
The Joy of Pickling 23
Equipment and Measures 33
Ingredients 41
Curing 68
Quick Process Pickle Recipes 93
Dill Pickles 96
Other Cucumbers 103
Mixed Pickles 116
Mustard Pickles 118
Relishes 128
Sweet Pickles 151
Fruit Pickles and Spiced Fruits 159
Pickled Vegetables 181
Pickled Eggs, Meats and Fish 200
Catsups 205
Bottled Sauces 213
Chutneys 219
Mincemeat 237
Fruit Butters 244
Put up and Put in the Refrigerator 246
Pickles and Condiments for Reducers 262
Around the World in a Pickle Barrel 268
Dishes with Pickles or Relishes as Ingredients 287
Showing Your Pickles 322
Index 325
The Author and His Book 336

The Peerless Pickle

(Updated from my article in *Coronet,* July, 1957)

He was president of a prosperous business, had plenty of money, a good reputation, civic honors, a lovely family and a beautiful home, but the man was unhappy and bitter. He brought his problem to a high-powered public-relations analyst.

"What's the use of working hard and becoming a success if I can't enjoy a little dignity and respect?" he asked. "I'm sick of being the butt of jokes and puns and gags wherever I go. Nobody will let me forget I run a pickle-packing plant. What can you do to build up my prestige or give pickles more stature and dignity?"

The consultant thought for a while before he replied.

"Nothing," he said. "The word 'pickle' is funny and there isn't enough money to convince the public otherwise. My advice is, since you can't lick 'em, join 'em. Kid yourself; lead the laughter; entertain the people with new pickle gags—and they'll love you."

That was in 1950 and the pickle plutocrat not only followed the expert's suggestion himself, but passed it on to the National Pickle Packers Association (now Pickle Packers International, Inc.). That trade group soon switched its traditionally reserved methods to a continuous high-comedy, low-pressure campaign with the result that the public now loves not only the merry pickle packer, but his piquant product as well.

Since then the pickle has fought its way up past the corn, the pea, the tomato and the bean to become America's No. 1 vegetable in popularity and dollar sales.

Although no one has ever taken a pickle census, still, by checking government, grower and industry figures, it can be predicted conservatively that in 1965 Americans will eat 7 billion pickles—467,500 tons of them—which is 4.8 pounds per person. This will add up to a national pickle bill of a cool $250,000,000.

Although the population of the U.S. has grown 54 per cent in the past 32 years, pickle production and consumption leapt 482 per cent and now pickles are served at least once a week in 9 out of 10 American homes. The total world output and intake, incidentally, would make a slippery girdle 10 pickles wide around the earth at the equator.

Much of this succulent success story can be traced to the way the pickle packers have used laughter to keep America pickle-privy.

"We've never been able to figure out what's so darn funny about pickles, but we're pleased about it, anyway," says William R. Moore, secretary of the processors association. H. L. Mencken once wrote that Americans found the sound of "p" and "k," as in Podunk and pickles, very amusing. Sam Levenson once said that the surest way to get a laugh was to talk about pickles. And the pickle packers have been keeping consumers conscious of their product by a well-timed stream of humorous publicity stunts.

Discovering a young grocer in the improbable town of Rolling Forks, Miss., with the improbable name of Dill L. Pickle, they brought him to Chicago for a hilarious Man-of-the-Year ceremony. Then one of the companies hired him as a traveling salesman to push pickle products.

Mississippi, it seems, is packed with Pickles, for during one Pickle Week another search revealed that the Carlos Pickle family of Smithville had the largest number of Pickles in one household—14 persons named Pickle. They were awarded all the pickles they could eat for 10 years and made honorary citizens of Dill City, Oklahoma.

The same year, the gherkin group selected the 82-year-old Earl of Sandwich as Man-of-the-Year, because his ancestor, the fourth earl, invented the sandwich and thereby helped popularize its inevitable accessory, the pickle. Lord Sandwich, on being informed of the award, said: "My distinguished ancestor would turn over in his grave if he knew about this. Nevertheless, I am both touched and amused by the honor."

Another headline stunt was the hiring of three former Air Force officers to make good on the boast that American bombardiers could drop a pickle into a barrel from the sky. The airmen plopped pickles from the fortieth floor of a Chicago hotel, aimed at a barrel on the sidewalk below, and came within 16 inches of the target. The latest pickle promotion had all the members of the association sending jars of pickles to the postmaster of Santa Claus, Indiana, at Christmas time.

From the hot pepper pickles of the Latin countries to the tiny salty finger-sized ones of Northern China, the preserved cucumber is an international favorite and almost every country has a distinctive favorite, from the English mustard pickle to the French sweet gherkin to the Jewish kosher dill. In India, bamboo shoots are pickled, and in the

Ozarks tiny green tomatoes are preserved with dill and garlic to resemble olives. Charles & Co., the Madison Avenue gourmet shop, carries almost a hundred different pickled products, including artichoke hearts, cantaloupe rind, water chestnuts, walnuts, pearl-sized Holland onions, tiny burr pickles stuffed with cherries and others with almond centers.

Ever since prehistoric times men have been preserving the cucumber in spices, salt brine and vinegar. It has been recorded that Cleopatra nibbled on them in the belief that they contributed to beauty and health. The Emperor Tiberius ate them every day, and they have been GI issue for the troops from the days of Julius Caesar and his legions, through the time of Napoleon, right up to the present. During World War II the government commandeered 40 per cent of the pickle output for the armed forces.

Americus Vespucius, before he became an explorer, was a pickle dealer in Seville. Samuel Pepys considered it worth recording in his famous diary when someone gave him "a gift of a glass of Girkins," and Dr. Samuel Johnson wrote in 1758, "received a present of pickles from Miss Pilcocks."

In Colonial America pickles were highly regarded as the only zestful, juicy vegetable available during the winter months. Washington and Adams were fond of them and Thomas Jefferson once wrote: "On a hot day in Virginia, I know of nothing more comforting than a fine spiced pickle, brought up troutlike from the sparkling depths of the aromatic jar below stairs in Aunt Sally's cellar."

The commercial processing of pickles in the U.S. began when the William Underwood Company went into business on a Boston wharf in 1821, preserving cucumbers, onions, cauliflower and red cabbage. The firm is still in business but only cans deviled ham and seafood today.

What is today the giant of the industry had its inception in Sharpsburg, Pa., when Henry John Heinz, the small son of Bavarian immigrants, began to sell his mother's horse-radish sauce from door to door. Soon he was supplying nearby Pittsburgh. In 1869 he opened a shop. The same year he began pickling sour onions and selling them by the barrel. Chowchow, mixed sour pickles and gherkins were added in 1871 and the prospering enterprise was moved to Pittsburgh 4 years later.

By 1893 Heinz was doing so well he exhibited his fancy pickle packs at the Columbian Exposition in Chicago. However, the display, in an obscure balcony location, drew few visitors until the resourceful pickle king had fake luggage checks printed and scattered about the grounds. These offered a free souvenir if they were returned to the Heinz exhibit.

The souvenir was a small plaster replica of a pickle, to be worn as a pin. It became one of the best-known trademarks in the world. The company has given away more than 69,000,000 little green pickle pins, and for many years the measure of the most of anything was "as many as Heinz has pickles."

Heinz packs 22 different varieties of pickle products, including some never sold in the U.S., such as very sour pickles for the English trade and specially spiced ones for Puerto Rico. In 1964 it sold well in excess of 50,000,000 jars, leading the field in both volume and dollars. Heinz is also the world's leading vinegar producer, but, while it is the biggest pickle packer, pickles are not the biggest Heinz seller—ketchup is.

The "crazy-busy season" in the pickle-packing industry is from May to October because that is when the cucumbers are popping up all over the land. A pickle begins life as a cucumber seed so tiny that there are 10,000 of them to a pound. A pound of seed, plus an acre of soil, water and sun, will yield a couple of tons of cucumbers. The seeds are of special pedigreed strains developed to produce straight, thin-skinned pickling cucumbers and are supplied to the grower by the packer, who contracts to take his whole crop.

The vegetable grows rapidly and is ready to pick within 60 days. At that time picking must be done quickly, for today's 3-inch cucumber is the day after tomorrow's 6-inch one and this is the only growing food where the premium price is paid for the smaller fruit. A bushel basket with 125 cucumbers brings around 50 cents while one filled with 1,000 gherkin-sized midgets is worth $2.50.

Twenty years ago a farmer raised an acre or two of cucumbers, and he and his kids could harvest the crop in a few days. Now growers plant from 500 to 3,000 acres and the picking problem is so serious that the packers have had to supply labor. Much of today's crop is harvested by Mexican nationals who are flown north in chartered planes. They also harvest sugar beets and cotton and are able to live well at home during the winter on their summer earnings, for the pickle picker now gets about half of the proceeds of cucumber sales. In a step toward automation, the University of Michigan has been trying to develop a picking machine but has not come up with a successful one yet. One solution would be to change the seed further, and they are working on a variety of cucumber which can be shaken from the vine when ripe. This would make a mechanical device more practicable and ease the labor burden.

After picking, cucumbers are used as either "green stock" or "salt" or "brine" stock. The green stock is the fresh cucumbers, which are shipped immediately to packing plants and processed as fresh cucumber pickles, quickles, overnight dills and pasteurized dills. These are washed, graded, packed in jars, surrounded by spiced or dill brine, capped, sterilized by heat, cooled, and are then ready to be eaten, 90 minutes after the process is begun.

The salt stock is processed at salting stations in the growing area, where the cucumbers are transformed into pickles by controlled fermentation. Salt is added gradually to the brine so that it permeates the cuke slowly until a 15 per cent solution is reached. These pickles now comprise the raw material used for all varieties except the fresh cucumber type and the pasteurized dills. They can be held in reserve at the salting stations until needed at the processing plants. Along the railway right-of-way from Chicago to Minneapolis there are miles of vats or pickle silos, each containing from 600 to 1,000 bushels of pickles. Salt stock is transported to the plants in special freight cars with wooden tanks and a company like Bloch and Guggenheimer of Long Island City will have a dozen or more tank cars shuttling between New York and Michigan constantly in order to keep up an inventory of a million dollars' worth of pickle products.

At the processing plant the salt stock is steam-treated in a desalting process which draws all but about 3 per cent of the salt from the pickle. It is then transformed into any of a number of varieties of sour, dill and sweet pickles. The latter are made by drawing off the vinegar from sour pickles and then placing them in a spiced and sweetened liquor for as long as 4 months.

Each section of the country has a different taste in pickle flavors. The New Englander likes spicy-sweet pickles and genuine dills, which are cured and finished at the same time, in a special salt solution seasoned with dill and spices, at the salting stations.

The South goes for candied and extra-sweet pickles, as well as extra-sour ones. The large cities of the North favor fresh-packed kosher pickles, strong on dill and garlic, which are the "new trend" in pickle styles. Also, because of the increase in outdoor eating and leisure time for picnics and travel, hamburger and hot dog relishes are now outselling the long-time leader, India relish.

The Midwest is still conservative in pickle taste, but the fresh-packed pickle is increasing in popularity. The West likes both the fresh kosher dills and sweet cucumber pickles. And everywhere there is an increase in the variety of pickles consumed. Where formerly people ate one ordinary type, today a refrigerator is not considered well stocked unless it contains 7 or 8 kinds of pickles and relishes.

This variety, as well as the versatility of the pickle, is the factor behind its pre-eminence, for eaters are enjoying pickles as an appetizer, as a regular vegetable course, and as an ingredient in other dishes, such as salads, cheese custard pie, beef stew, soups and even Yorkshire pudding.

Modern science has determined that Cleopatra was doing the right thing when she ate pickles for her health. A 3-year research project at Michigan State College by a team headed by Dr. F. W. Fabian, research professor of bacteriology, found that the process of pickling increases the amount of vitamin A in cucumbers and that pickles are a fine source of vitamin supply, since they also contain B_1 and B_2 and a considerable amount of the important vitamin C.

Thus Cleopatra, and all other pickle munchers, fortified the body against scurvy, beriberi and night blindness. Pickles also abound in calcium, phosphorus, iron and copper, and their salt content helps replenish the body's supply on hot days.

Pickles, with the exception of the sweet ones, are a boon to dieters, since they have practically no carbohydrates. One man, who slimmed down from over 300 pounds to 175, estimated that he ate 250 pounds of pickles in the process.

Most pickles are sold as a result of "impulse buying" which is induced by eye appeal, and therefore groceries and delicatessens make sure you are aware that they sell them by arranging mouth-watering displays. Stores push pickles because they're the grocer's pet; he makes more profit on pickles than on other vegetables. Some supermarkets devote as much as 100 feet of shelf space to their pickle parade.

And the pickle packers, always plugging their product, have come up with a new slogan: "Keep America Green—Buy Pickles!"

MORE ABOUT COMMERCIAL PICKLE-PACKING

It is popularly believed that pickles are made from young specimens of the ordinary garden variety of cucumber, which grows to enormous size and degree of toughness if left alone. This was once the case. But years ago pickle packers and university agriculturists joined forces to develop cucumbers especially adapted to pickle requirements.

Intensive and extensive soil studies and plant-breeding experiments had the desired result. Now commercially packed pickles are produced from pedigreed strains of pickle cucumbers which seldom grow far beyond maximum pickle size, even at the height of maturity, and which retain the tender, edible qualities essential for fine pickles.

This culture resulted in an improved cucumber whose qualities make possible tender, crisp, tasty pickles in place of the old varieties, which could not completely absorb the delicately spiced liquors responsible for real pickle flavors.

DISTRIBUTION OF SEED　In the spring, numerous field men go about the countryside to distribute pedigreed pickle seed to selected pickle growers in favorable growing regions. They represent the pickle packers and co-operate with growers to assure an ample yield of high quality.

GROWTH AND HARVESTING　A month and a half after the seeds are planted, the luxuriant vines and leaves of the plants have grown and the pickle cucumbers begin to appear. Up to that point cultivation may be prosaic enough, but from then on it is all watchfulness and excitement.

The cucumbers seem to grow overnight, and carefully timed, quick work by deft hands and sturdy backs is needed to gather the various required sizes at just the right time.

SALTING STATIONS AND "BRINE STOCK"　Aside from two exceptions described later, the newly harvested cucumbers first go to "salting stations," which are maintained by pickle packers right in the growing regions. Here they are thoroughly cleansed and carefully sorted. Then the selected cucumbers are immersed in a salt-water solution contained in wood vats, wherein they undergo a process of controlled fermentation.

The salt is added gradually according to precise formula, so that it permeates the pickles slowly, evenly and thoroughly. After weeks and even months of such curing, the pickles become known as "brine stock," which is then sent to the "finishing plant."

However, one kind of pickle which is not forwarded to the finishing plants but is finished right at the salting stations is the *genuine dill* pickle. At the salting station these pickles go immediately into a special salt solution flavored with dill and spices, and are cured and finished at the same time, entirely by a process of natural fermentation.

AT THE FINISHING PLANT　When the brine stock arrives at the finishing plant, the pickles are soaked in clear, cold water, then heated and soaked again, the treaments differing with various packers. This process "desalts" or freshens the pickles and restores crispness. The next step depends on the style of pickles to be made.

Processed dills are returned to a special brine-acid-dill-spice solution where, in a week, they absorb the flavor of the liquor.

Sour pickles are made in the same way, except that spiced sour vinegar takes the place of the dill solution.

Sweet pickles are made from sour pickles by first draining off the sour vinegar and then placing the pickles in vats or casks where sweet, spiced liquor, prepared according to recipe from sugar, spices and vinegar, is thoroughly circulated in and around the pickles.

FRESH PACKING   *Fresh cucumber pickles* and *pasteurized dills* are the exceptions to the salting station procedure. These are "fresh packed," which means that they are prepared entirely at the finishing plant from freshly picked cucumbers direct from the fields (called "green stock") and not from brine stock which has been cured at the salting station.

After sorting and washing, these cucumbers are put in cans or bottles and "preserved" by the same approved canning procedures which have made modern commercially canned foods of all varieties dependable.

COMMERCIAL PICKLE SIZES

Name	Length (inches)	Count per quart
Midgets #1	1¼	162
Midgets #2	to	112
Midgets #3	2	85
Gherkins #1	2	65
Gherkins #2	to	56
Gherkins #3	2¾	40
Medium	3 to 4	10 to 30
Large	4 and over	3 to 10

AFTER THE PICKLING IS OVER COOL CUCUMBERS AID TIRED EYES

"An old-fashioned rest cure for tired eyes uses cool, cool cucumbers to help freshen and effect serenity, as follows:

"Massage a skin softener such as vaseline or dry skin cream around the eyes using a circular motion at the temples. This relaxes tense muscles and counteracts the dryness that magnifies tiny wrinkles and crow's feet.

"Place two slices of cool cucumber peel over the eyes and lie down, feet higher than head.

"Five minutes will make a difference: 20 gives a dim-eyed you a clear-eyed view. The natural astringent qualities of the cucumber peel make the eyes sparkle, and the petroleum jelly massage reduces fatigue."

—New York *Post*

The following information is offered to serve as a guide for the home pickler on the amount of liquid required in jars of different kinds of pickles:

LIQUID CONTENT OF JARS AND BOTTLES OF VARIOUS COMMERCIAL PICKLED PRODUCTS

In proportion to the bulk of the pickled vegetables, sliced cucumbers, such as bread and butter pickles, pack fullest into the glass and require the least liquid. Next come the whole and long half slices of cucumber pickles, watermelon rind, midget gherkins and cucumber salad, followed by olives, spiced dainties and sweet mixed vegetables. Garden salad and baby gherkins require more liquid, and tiny treats and mixed pickles take almost 50 per cent pickling liquor.

Name of Pickle	Percentage of Liquid
Sliced, bread and butter	25%
Dills, long halves, watermelon rind, midget gherkins, cucumber salad	33⅓% to 35%
Olives, spiced dainties, sweet mixed vegetables	37% to 40%
Garden salad, baby gherkins	42%
Tiny treats, mixed pickles	46% to 48%

DICTIONARY OF COMMERCIAL PICKLES

DILL PICKLES Flavored primarily with dill, which is supplemented by mixed spices. They come in three varieties:

Genuine dill pickles. These are prepared entirely by the lengthy process of natural fermentation described above.

Overnight dill pickles. A "fresh fermented" variety of genuine dill pickles produced by stopping fermentation after only a day or two, by placing the pickles in cold storage. These pickles retain some of the flavor of the fresh cucumber along with the dill flavor. Like genuine dills, they are commonly sold in bulk.

Processed dill pickles. Started as regular brine stock, these are later finished in a dill solution. They have somewhat better keeping qualities than either the genuine or overnight dills.

SOUR PICKLES Brine stock pickles which have been finished in sour vinegar with spices. Besides *whole* sour pickles, here are other typical examples of sour pickle styles:

Sour mixed pickles. Produced by combining sour pickles with other sour pickled vegetables such as cauliflower, onions and peppers, all cut into small, convenient pieces.

Sour relish or piccalilli. Fine-chopped, sour pickles, sometimes packed alone and sometimes combined with other fine-chopped, sour-cured vegetables.

Chow-chow. Similar to sour mixed pickles except for the addition of a mustard sauce flavored with spices such as yellow and brown mustard seed, turmeric, garlic, cinnamon, cloves, ginger, nutmeg, cayenne, black and white pepper.

SWEET PICKLES   Sour pickles from which the vinegar has been drained. Then they are finished in sweet, spicy liquors which are added from time to time until the desired degree of sweetness is attained. A lengthy aging process follows. Sweet pickles are available in many varieties such as the following:

Sliced sweet pickles, chips, chunks or wafers. Plain sweet pickles cut crosswise into discs.

Candied chips. Extra-sweet, sliced sweet pickles.

Sweet dill pickles. Made from genuine or processed dill pickles instead of sour pickles and frequently cut lengthwise, as well as crosswise.

Mixed sweet pickles. Sweet pickles combined with other sweetly pickled vegetables such as cauliflower, onions, sweet pepper and green tomatoes.

Sweet relish or piccalilli. Finely chopped, sweet pickles sometimes combined with other finely chopped, sweet-pickled vegetables.

FRESH PACKED PICKLES (*Quickles*)   Pickles made from fresh, green cucumbers by the quick pasteurizing process rather than the long fermentation curing process of salting stations. Their flavor differs distinctly from that of salt brine-cured cucumbers. They are made into dills, sweets or relish and the following typical fresh packed pickle products:

Fresh cucumber pickles (quickles). Sometimes referred to as "bread and butter" style: these are fresh green cucumbers, cut crosswise and canned with a mildly spiced and sweetened solution.

Dill, Polish style pickles (quickles). Fresh, green cucumbers canned whole or sliced with a dill solution. The resulting flavor is a combination of the dill and the fresh cucumbers, approximately the same as overnight dills produced in bulk.

Vegetable relish (quickle relish). Fresh, green cucumbers and vegetables such as cabbage, red peppers, green tomatoes and green beans, spiced with mustard, turmeric, celery seed, and other pickling spices, canned with a sweetened liquor.

The Joy of Pickling

If you have read the preceding chapter you have a good idea of the commercial pickle-packing picture and you are aware that the shelves of your market are loaded with good, reliable pickle and relish products.

Then why go through all the work of pickling and relish-making at home?

There are several reasons:

To use up garden produce you have grown yourself, or have been given.

Family custom, handed down for generations.

Economic need to provide for large families at lowest cost.

Even the guilty feeling of having a shelf full of empty jars.

But today by far the best reason is pride in your kitchen craft and leisure time for this activity.

Many people rise to the challenge to make interesting, offbeat, zesty, tasty pickle products with a personal touch.

It is a gratifying hobby.

And although we have seen that the professional pickle packers were the target of hoots and jokes (which they have since turned to their advantage), everyone looks with respect at a home kitchen engineer who can turn out a mouth-watering pickle product. He or she has a slightly exalted position in the community; and if his output should win ribbons or prizes at fairs, festivals and other competitions, he is further honored and respected.

This book has been written with the home pickler in mind. Every effort has been made to provide you with everything a book can give you so that you can give your household a supply of the finest of pickles.

And not only pickles, but relishes and chutneys, krauts and butters, catsups and vinegars, marinades and sauces, etc.—in short, all of the food products which are prepared and preserved with vinegar or lemon juice or salt.

If it is made that way, I have tried to include a recipe for every category. If not, it is outside the province of this book.

A final word before we plunge into the mystique of pickling: whether working around the kitchen table and stove, or eating the outcome around the dinner table or barbecue—enjoy yourself!

But before you start clearing the decks for pickle-packing action, it is essential that you read a few rules.

IMPORTANT THINGS TO REMEMBER

SPEED   Plan your work to save time and steps. Have all equipment handy before you begin. Have jars clean and ready for use. Remember to fill the teakettle—you'll need plenty of boiling water. Sirup for fruits can be made in advance and reheated as needed.

But don't prepare too far in advance. When prepared food stands too long before being canned, its vitamin content may be lowered and, even worse, it may spoil. Prepare no more than you can handle in a single processing.

WASHING   Wash vegetables and fruits thoroughly unless otherwise directed. Dirt is the natural home of many organisms which cause spoilage. It will repay you to wash fruits and vegetables thoroughly. Use fresh water several times, if necessary. Cold water is preferred. Don't allow fruits and vegetables to remain in water longer than necessary for thorough cleaning. Use a brush to wash root vegetables. Scrub them thoroughly to remove all soil.

PEELING   Peel vegetables as thinly as possible.

To remove tomato and peach skins: Wash tomatoes and scald them for 1 minute. Plunge into cold water. With a sharp knife, core and slip off skin from blossom end. Use the same peeling method for peaches.

COLOR OF PEACHES AND PEARS   These fruits turn brown when exposed to air. To preserve color, drop them immediately into the hot sirup you are going to use in pickling them or into citric acid solution or into a vinegar and salt solution.

LIQUID   Don't open a jar to replace lost liquid; seal it as is.

SCREW BANDS   When jars have cooled overnight, remove screw bands that have a glass or metal disk underneath. Warm water run on top will help remove sticky sirup and release band.

COMMERCIAL JARS   Coffee, peanut butter, pickle and mayonnaise jars are not recommended for pickling.

COPPER, BRASS AND ZINC   Never use copper, brass or zinc utensils in canning. These metals form poisonous salts when they come in contact with certain foods. Iron darkens pickles.

WIRE BASKET   A wire basket is very useful for scalding tomatoes and peaches, for washing vegetables and for blanching vegetables in steam.

SPOILAGE If an odor which is not characteristic of the product is given off, the food should be burned or buried. Do not taste. Abnormal appearance of the food and clouding of the liquid are other indications of spoilage.

PICKLE POINTERS

These Do's and Don'ts come from the University of Idaho College of Agriculture and make valuable reading.

DO use modern-day pickle recipes. Grandmother's recipes may call for too much vinegar because the vinegar of 25 years ago had less acetic acid than today's. Then, variations in the strength of vinegar was the homemaker's biggest problem in pickling. Today you need not be plagued by uncertainty. Buy a standard 40- to 60-grain strength. This means that the vinegar contains 4 to 6 per cent acetic acid.

Distilled white vinegar is first choice for pickling. It safeguards the original color of the foods. You may prefer cider or malt vinegar for its mellow flavor and aroma even though the preserved foods may be slightly darkened. This is particularly true when making fruit pickles.

DO use pure granulated salt. Table salt has added lump-preventing materials that may be undesirable. Salt, when added to fruits and vegetables, draws out their juices, hardens the tissues and checks the action of organisms which may cause spoilage. If the salt solution is too weak, spoilage bacteria grow and cause soft or slippery pickles.

DO use soft water if possible. Large amounts of calcium and other salts found in many "hard" waters may interfere with the fermentation and pickling processes. High iron content in water may cause pickles to darken. If hard water must be used, boil and let stand 24 hours. See water section of Ingredients chapter.

DO use whole spices to give a clear, undarkened product. Use fresh spices and tie loosely in a bag to get the full flavor from them. Lift them out before packing the pickles. Use just enough sugar and spice to bring out the flavor of the pickle. White sugar gives a clearer color than brown, but some recipes call for brown sugar to give extra flavor.

DON'T use coloring agents. Well-selected cucumbers, properly processed, will be olive-green in color. This is the correct color for pickles, not bright green or blue-green. Don't heat cucumbers in a copper kettle to give a dark green color. Heating vinegar in copper produces poisonous copper acetate. Use enamelware, aluminum or stainless steel utensils. Don't add copper sulfate or vitriol.

Cucumbers suitable for pickling are firm and crisp with an even green color throughout and free from defects. Gather and brine them within 24 hours. Letting them stand too long between gathering and brining may cause hollow pickles.

In general, pickles keep better if sealed airtight for storage. Don't use zinc lids. The vinegar may unite with the zinc to form a poisonous compound.

Good cucumber pickles may be whole or in pieces of fairly uniform size. They have a clear, uniform olive-green color with no white or off-color spots and no soft or shriveled parts. The flavor is piquant and pleasing.

Here is a set of rules for pickling, preserving and canning that has been drawn up by the Georgia Agricultural Extension Service.

NINE STEPS TO SUCCESS

1. Use only fresh, sound fruits and vegetables of top quality.
2. Have equipment in good working order and know how to use it.
3. Have food, jars and everything used in canning thoroughly clean.
4. Work quickly, so as to can "freshness." This prevents deterioration.
5. Follow up-to-date directions backed by research.
6. Make sure jars are sealed airtight to keep out spoilage organisms.
7. Use boiling water bath for fruits, tomatoes, cucumber and sweet pickles.
8. Process hot enough and long enough to kill bacteria and other organisms so they will not "work" in the food and make it spoil.
9. Cool properly, then label and date jars. Store in a cool, dry, dark place unless otherwise directed. Allow several weeks to elapse before using so flavors can develop fully, unless otherwise instructed.

GLASS JAR EXPERT'S ADVICE

There must be something about a pickle that nudges the imagination and awakens the spirit of competition. How else can you explain the fact that year after year thousands of women pit their pickling skills against those of friend and foe in county and state fairs, church shows and club competitions?

According to a home economist who for 30 years read all requests for special recipes received by a large manufacturer of home canning supplies, the majority had to do with pickling. Some of these recipe requests came because the same type of pickle may have many different names. An ordinary mixed pickle may be known as End of the Garden, Garden's End, Hodge-Podge or what not, whereas what is chow-chow in one locality may be introduced as piccalilli in another.

There are dozens of versions of most recipes and every change of ingredient indicates that someone has used his or her imagination. In making pickles or relishes, change the amount and kind of spice, use more or less sugar, put in garlic or leave it out, but please, don't tinker with these rules:

1. Pickles should be processed 5 to 20 minutes in boiling water. The time depends upon the type of pickle and size of jar. Processing will not hurt the pickles but will kill most of the organisms which cause spoilage. It is particularly important when 2-piece metal caps are used. All brands depend upon vacuum for sealing. Vacuum depends upon applying enough heat to drive air from the jar.

2. Although some authorities recommend that jars be put into actively boiling water, this can cause breakage, particularly if the entire bottom surface of the jar fails to touch the water at the same instant. There is far less danger of breakage from thermal shock when jars are lowered straight down into steaming *but not boiling* water.

3. No matter how tightly a jar is sealed, gas pressure, which occurs when pickles are not heated enough to prevent fermentation, can break the seal. This permits some of the liquid to run out of the jar. Then the pickles begin to spoil.

4. Choose fresh small- to medium-sized (3 to 4 inches) pickling cucumbers. They should be firm and well formed.

5. Thoroughly wash and rinse cucumbers. Let them drain dry.

6. Use highgrade commercial vinegar. Acid strength appears on the bottle label. Unless the recipe calls for something different, use a vinegar of 5 per cent acid strength.

7. When possible, use pickling or dairy salt. However, table salt works all right in relishes.

8. When making extra-sweet pickles, start with a weak solution and add more sugar every day or two until the pickles are as sweet as you like. This installment plan helps prevent shriveling.

9. If pickles are to be left in brine or vinegar for several hours, put them into stoneware, enameled or glass containers. Brass, copper, iron, tin and zinc utensils are not for pickles. These metals can react with vinegar and salt to cause a change in color and flavor, and some of them may at times cause illness.

ADDITIONAL TIPS

• Follow the recipe exactly. Unless vinegar, sugar and salt are used in the proper proportions, pickles will not be of top quality. Too strong solutions produce soft, shriveled pickles; too weak ones may spoil.

• Use a large enamel pail or stone crock for brining. Copper and iron dishes may discolor the pickles.

• Use firm, fresh cucumbers of uniform size. They should be slightly underripe, rather than too ripe.

• Use the best vinegar and fresh whole spices, as old seasonings lack flavor. Unless specified, do not use ground spices, as they may darken the product.

• Spice bags should be thin and large enough so that juices can circulate and draw out the flavor of the spices.

• To peel a tomato, stick a sharp fork through the stem end. Plunge tomato into boiling water for a few seconds. Remove. With tip of knife, break the skin at the blossom end and peel back. Or hold the tomato over a flame, turning until the skin is blistered; then peel.

• To chop or mince onion, cut end slice from peeled onion; discard. Cut exposed surface into tiny squares to any desired depth. Cut crosswise into thin bits.

• To cut pineapple, slice horizontally into flat rounds, then peel. Remove core from each ring. Cut into wedges.

• Melon can be cut in a similar manner.

• Another method is to lop off the pineapple top and bottom, cut into quarters, core and peel lengthwise.

• To cut fresh mint, parsley, greens and so forth in small quantities: Wash and dry carefully on a towel. Then put sprigs in tumbler or glass and cut with scissors.

• A grape leaf may be placed in jars with pickles for décor and flavor.

• Do not use wire brushes or steel wool or washing soda for cleaning jars. Such things are likely to damage the glass.

• Always follow the manufacturer's instructions for filling, sealing, processing and testing the seal. Taking for granted that all home canning caps are alike and are used exactly the same way is a common cause of sealing failure.

PRESERVING TERMS DEFINED

BLANCHING OR SCALDING Dipping a vegetable in boiling water or steaming over boiling water for a definite length of time, then dipping product into cold water for easy handling and to stop cooking process. Used to remove some skins.

BOILING Heating water to the point that it rolls and bubbles from top to bottom.

PASTEURIZE To destroy bacteria by heating liquid to a temperature of 142° to 145°F for 30 minutes.

SIMMERING Heating food just below the boiling temperature (about 190°F).

STERILIZE To free from bacteria, yeast and mold. To sterilize, cover food containers with water, bring to boil, and boil steadily for 15 minutes. To prevent recontamination, leave containers in boiling water until ready to use.

PRECOOKING Cooking food in steam, boiling or simmering water or sirup for a given length of time before packing in jar for processing.

PROCESSING Cooking food after it is packed in the container.

HEAD SPACE Space between the food and the top of the jar, usually ½ inch. After liquid is added, there should be ¼-inch space between liquid and jar top.

SEALING Adjusting the lid on container to prevent air or bacteria from entering container.

WATER BATH A container to hold water and a rack for use in processing acid foods, such as tomatoes, berries and fruits. Jars or cans of food are placed upright on the rack in the boiling water. To process food in the water bath, water should be at least 2 inches above the tops of jars and should boil continuously for the required length of time.

A FEW WORDS ABOUT WORDS

"Pickle" has a well-documented history going back over a thousand years. Most authorities trace it to Middle English: *pykyl* or *pekille,* probably from Middle Dutch, meaning "that which is sharp, piquant, pricking." The Dutch *pikken,* "to prick" and the English (1550) *pick* "to pierce" are the most authentic ancestors. "Some have derived the word from the name of the supposed inventor of pickling," wrote the Rev. Walter W. Skeat in *A Concise Etymological Dictionary of the English Language.* "His name is variously given as Beukeler, Bökel and Pökel, a story in which it is hard to believe."

Anyhow, the word has the additional connotations these days of "being in a dilemma or in a sorry condition" and "being drunk." (In the 18th century, a young mischief-making boy was called a pickle; *Peregrine Pickle* is the title and profligate hero of Smollett's novel (1751); there was a Pickle Racket in New York City some years ago and gangsters took over the business until it was smashed and the ringleader was sent to prison. He was known as "Moishe Pickles.")

"Mustard" gets its name because the Romans soaked the seeds of this plant in "must" or new wine ("vino mustum").

Then there are "pimento" and "pimiento." The first is the name of the allspice bush, the second the fleshy vegetable we usually encounter curled up inside an olive.

The origin of "piccalilli" is obscure, but 150 years ago the Shakers were filling huge crocks with "Pickled Lily"—a combination of chopped vegetables, spices and vinegars.

In this book we refer to a whole celery plant as a "bunch" and a single branch or stick as a "stalk." The whole fruit of the garlic plant, sometimes called a "fist" or "bulb" is referred to here as a "cluster" while the individual kernel, bead or toe is called a "clove" of garlic.

PROCESSING IN BOILING WATER BATH

1. Place filled jars on wire rack in covered, deep kettle. (If no rack is available, folded chicken wire or wooden clothespins may be placed in the bottom of canner.)

2. Add enough boiling water to cover tops of jars by 1 inch; place over heat.

3. When water comes to a rolling boil again, start counting processing time. Keep water boiling steadily.

4. At end of processing time, remove jars; adjust seal by following instructions which come with jar lids. Place jars upright, well apart, on a cake rack or several thicknesses of cloth to cool. Keep out of draft.

5. The next day, test seal on jars. If jars are not sealed, store in refrigerator and serve food as soon as possible.

Processing times for pickling as given in the recipes are for altitudes less than 1,000 feet above sea level. At altitudes of 1,000 feet or more, you need to increase recommended processing times as follows:

Altitude (feet)	Increase in processing time (minutes)
1,000	1
2,000	2
3,000	3
4,000	4
5,000	5
6,000	6
7,000	7
8,000	8
9,000	9
10,000	10

SEALING JARS

Always follow manufacturers' instructions for sealing of jars, but here are general rules:

Fill jars as instructed, usually to within $\frac{1}{2}$ inch of top, then see that pickling solution covers material and is $\frac{1}{4}$ inch from top.

Wipe off any spilled food with a clean, hot, damp cloth. If the jar has a glass lid with a wire bail, push wire on top of lid so it fits into groove, leaving short wire up. Then jars are processed in boiling water bath, and after this has been done, push short wire quickly down to complete seal.

For kraut and other pickled products that are processed in water bath, where a metal screw band is used, screw band as tight as it will go, then turn back a quarter turn. (This is partial sealing.) Caution: If band is screwed too tight, jar may break. After food is processed, screw the band down tight at once. Never use a wrench to tighten jar lids.

STORAGE

• When thoroughly cooled, label correctly with name of recipe and date of packing.

• Store in a cool, dry, dark place.

• Pickles have a better blended, more mellow flavor when permitted to stand several months.

PICKLE FAILURES

If you follow directions carefully and use good quality fruits and vegetables, your homemade pickles and relishes should turn out well. Sometimes, however, they do not have the proper color or flavor, and you will want to know how to prevent this in the future.

Some of the common troubles encountered in pickle making, and their causes, are listed here.

Softening of Pickles This is usually due to spoilage caused by bacterial action. Softening may result when:
1. The brine used is too weak;
2. The strength of the brine is not kept up;
3. Pickles are not kept under the brine;
4. Vinegar is weakened too much;
5. The scum is not kept off the brine;
6. Pickles are boiled.

Shriveling of Pickles This often results when:
1. The vinegar, sugar or salt solution is too strong at the beginning

(use a weaker solution at first and gradually increase the strength);

2. Fruit is cooked too quickly in a strong sugar or vinegar solution, and not allowed to plump up.

Hollow Pickles This may result from:
1. Using faulty or old cucumbers;
2. Letting cucumbers stand too long between gathering and brining.

Dark Color in Pickles This could be the result of:
1. Using powdered spices;
2. Using too much spice;
3. Packing whole spices with pickles;
4. Using iron utensils or water containing iron;
5. Using iodized salt.

Faded Color in Pickles This is often caused by:
1. Not curing pickles;
2. Not heating unfermented pickles;
3. If beet pickles, using a poor variety for canning, or cutting the stem too close to the beet, so that it bleeds while cooking.

Equipment and Measures

A variety of utensils, some of which you already have, are required in the various processes of making pickles and relishes. Some, which you may have to buy or borrow, can be used for several different functions. I have listed the necessary equipment along with the varied steps in pickle-making.

For CURING or FERMENTING PICKLES, *glass jars, stone jars* or *crocks* are best, unless you intend to make large quantities, then *kegs* and *barrels* are needed. Latter should have 5-inch bungs, if possible, or loose-fitting covers. Jars and crocks need loose-fitting *covers,* preferably plates, and weights to hold covers down, preferably quart glass *jars* filled with water. Surface of wooden covers, and kegs and barrels (if practicable) should be coated with paraffin. Brick or stone weights can impart an undesirable flavor. Do not use resinous wood, such as pine.

For COOKING PICKLES, VINEGAR MIXTURES, RELISHES, etc., 2 or more 3- to 6-quart *preserving kettles,* of enamel, porcelain, agate (unchipped, uncracked), thick aluminum, stainless steel or glass. They should be large enough to simmer the ingredients without boiling over and, if the recipe calls for a rolling boil, should have three times the capacity of the recipe. Use open kettles unless otherwise specified. Fruits simmered slowly to extract the juices are cooked in covered pots or kettles. Do not use iron, copper, zinc or galvanized utensils, as the acids and salt brine used in pickling may form harmful chemicals.

For STERILIZING JARS BEFORE FILLING AND PROCESSING JARS AFTER FILLING, *1 large processing kettle, or metal can, or old-fashioned wash-boiler,* or one of the preserving kettles of large capacity can double, if it is not being otherwise used. This utensil should have a rack or false bottom or wire or hardwood platform inside, preferably with dividers so that jars do not touch and room so that water can circulate underneath the jars. There should be room for 2 inches of water above a quart jar and a cover to keep the steam in.

Also needed:

1 teakettle, for boiling water

Saucepans

2 long-handled wooden (or enamel or stainless steel) spoons, for stirring

1 slotted wooden spoon

1 long-handled wooden fork ("A hand in the brine spoils the batch.")

1 scum-skimmer ("Grease in brine will spoil the pickle, too.")

1 long-handled dipper or ladle with lip, for pouring (can double as scum-skimmer)

1 wide-mouthed funnel

1 sharp butcher knife, for slicing

1 sharp kitchen knife, for paring

1 vegetable peeler

1 wooden cutting and chopping board or block, or

1 wooden chopping bowl and "half-moon" mincer

1 food chopper or grinder, with fine, medium and coarse knives

1 small food mill

1 grater

1 or more stiff brushes to clean vegetables

1 enameled, footed collander or wire basket for washing, steaming and draining

1 sieve or wire strainer with nylon or nontarnish metal mesh

Mixing bowls for mixtures, overnight steeping, etc.

1 pair kitchen scissors

1 wavy-cut knife or cutter for pickle wafers

Set of measuring spoons and cups (latter in 1-cup, 1-pint and 1-quart sizes—glass preferable)

1 set household scales

1 cooking thermometer

1 clock with alarm, for timing

1 large calendar with plenty of white space, to note progress of pickling process

Cheesecloth and/or muslin, for covering crocks and making spice bags

Glass jars in ½-pint, pint and quart sizes, free of cracks, chips or other defects, with *caps,* glass preferable, that are "vinegarproof," and NEW *rubber seals*

1 jar-lifter or tongs

1 or more jar trays

Pot-holders or heatproof gloves

And lastly, don't forget

Labels.

STEAM PRESSURE CANNERS open a whole new world. Recipes are usually the same for ingredients, but time of processing differs. Follow the equipment manufacturer's instructions.

• The pickling kettle should be aluminum, enamelware, glass, or stainless steel. Copper utensils tend to turn pickles a peculiar shade of green; iron may turn them black.

• Be sure kettle is large enough so that pickles will not boil over.

• You will find that a long-handled wooden spoon and a wide-mouthed funnel make pickle preparation much easier.

• When brining pickles, use stone crocks, glass, pottery or enamel-lined pans—not metal.

• Select only perfect jars, no chipped or cracked ones, for packing pickles.

• Wash jars, glass lids, metal screw caps, rubber rings and funnel in hot soapy water; rinse well. *Never re-use rubber rings.* Use clean, new ones. Dip these into boiling water just before using.

• To sterilize, place clean jars, lids and caps in a deep kettle; cover with warm water. Boil, covered, 20 minutes. Remove from boiling water one at a time when ready to fill. If pickles are to be processed, it is not necessary to boil this equipment. Just be sure they are clean and hot.

• Before sealing, run clean knife blade around inside of jar to release air bubbles. Add more liquid if needed.

• Wipe sealing edges of jars free of food or liquid with clean paper towels or cloths before putting on lid.

• Because there are many types of lids and closures on the market, be sure to follow the manufacturer's instructions for sterilizing and sealing.

PICKLE THIEF MAKES OFF WITH 2,400-PECK CARGO

Three Oaks, Mich. (AP)—That fellow who picked a peck of pickled peppers was a piker compared to the slicker who snared 2,400 pecks of pickles from a Three Oaks concern recently.

The state police had the job of trying to catch the culprit on complaint of Jack Wineberg, owner of the Manhattan Pickle Company.

Mr. Wineberg discovered that his concern had lost 600 bushels of pickles.

Investigators say the thief apparently used dip nets to snare pickles from the vats, leaving some to float on water poured into the vats to give an illusion of full measure. The thefts were discovered by employes emptying vats for processing.

TABLES OF WEIGHTS AND MEASURES
(*All Level*)
LIQUID OR FLUID MEASURE

"A pinch," "dash," or "few grains" = less than ⅛ teaspoon
1 teaspoon = 60 drops = ⅓ tablespoon
1 dessert spoon = 2 teaspoons
1 tablespoon = 3 teaspoons = ½ liquid ounce
1 liquid ounce = 2 tablespoons = ⅛ cup
¼ cup = 4 tablespoons
⅓ cup = 5 tablespoons and 1 teaspoon
1 gill = ½ cup = 8 tablespoons
⅔ cup = 10 tablespoons and 2 teaspoons
¾ cup = 12 tablespoons
⅞ cup = 14 tablespoons
1 cup = 2 gills = ½ liquid pint = 8 liquid ounces = 16 tablespoons
1 pint = 2 cups = ½ quart = 4 gills = 16 liquid ounces = 32 table-spoons
1 quart = 2 pints = ¼ gallon = 4 cups = 32 liquid ounces = approx. 945 cubic centimeters = 57.75 cubic inches
1 gallon = 4 quarts = 8 pints = 16 cups = 231 cubic inches

DRY MEASURES

1 dry quart = 2 dry pints = ⅛ peck = 67.2 cubic inches
1 peck = 8 dry quarts = 16 dry pints
1 bushel = 4 pecks = 32 dry quarts = 2150.42 cubic inches

AVOIRDUPOIS WEIGHT

1 avoirdupois ounce = 28.35 grams
1 pound = 16 avoirdupois ounces = 453.6 grams
1 kilogram = 1000 grams = 2.2 pounds

According to Harry Schorr, who has spent most of his life in pickles, the perfect pickle packed in glass is characterized by some cloudiness in the brine.

This indicates that the seasonings have been completely saturated with the vinegar and hence have the most desirable flavor.

MEASURING VEGETABLES, FRUITS, ETC., FOR PICKLING
(*How to Relate Bulk to Weight*)

Since the weight in relation to bulk of any fruit or vegetable will vary according to size, shape, season, ripeness, variety and other factors, the following measures can only be considered approximate.

APPLES: 6 diced, sliced or chopped = 3 cups = 1 pound
  1 bushel, pickled or canned = 20 quarts = 48–50 pounds
APRICOTS: 8–14 whole = 3 cups = 2 cups, halved = 1 pound
  35–40 medium = 4 pints = 4 pounds
  3 cups, dried = 1 quart, cooked, drained = 1 pound
BANANAS: 1 large = 6 ounces = 4 ounces, peeled
  3 medium = 2–2½ cups, diced or sliced; 1¼ cups, mashed = 1 pound
  1 dozen = 4½ pounds, with skins = 3 pounds, without
BEANS, GREEN, SNAP, FRENCH: 2⅔–3⅗ cups = 1 pound
BEETS: 3½ cups, cooked, diced = 1 pound
BERRIES: 4 quarts make about 6 cups purée
  (Also see *strawberries*, which differ)
BROCCOLI: 1 bunch = 1½–2½ pounds
BRUSSELS SPROUTS: 3½ cups = 1 pound
CABBAGE: 3½ cups, shredded, or 4 cups, finely shredded = 1 pound
  1 medium head, shredded or finely chopped = 8 cups
  1 large, firm head, 7–8-inch diameter = about 2½ pounds
  1½ pounds, shredded, make 1 pint sauerkraut
  3 cups, cooked = 1 pound
CANTALOUPE: 6 pounds, trimmed and cubed, make 6 cups
CARROTS: 4 large, chopped and cooked = 3 cups = 1 pound
  2½ cups, sliced or diced, raw = 1 pound
  7 medium, grated, raw = 4 cups
  8 large, chopped, raw = 6 cups
CAULIFLOWER: 3⅔ cups cooked flowerets = 1 pound
CELERY: 1 stick or stalk = 1¼ ounces
  8–12 stalks = 1 pound
  1 large bunch, chopped = 1 quart
  4 cups, diced = 1 pound

CHERRIES: 3 cups, raw = 1 pound

2½ cups, pitted and stemmed = 1 pound

5–6 cups, pitted, make 1 quart

6–7 cups, with stones, make 1 quart

COCONUT: 5 cups, shredded = 1 pound

CORN: Kernels from 16–20 medium ears = 2 quarts

6 10-ounce frozen packages = 2 quarts

CRANBERRIES: 1–1½ quarts = 4–6 cups whole = 1 pound

3 quarts, whole, make 1½ quarts purée

2–2½ cups, ground = 1 pound

CUCUMBERS: 1 whole 6-inch = 8 ounces

1 peeled 6-inch =5–5½ ounces

2 large, sliced = 2 cups = 1 pound

3–4 medium, whole = 1 pound

12 medium, peeled and sliced = 8 cups

12 6-inch, sliced = 12 cups or 6 pints

50 medium, whole = 1 gallon = 6 pounds

50 3- to 4-inch, whole = 6–8 quarts = 9–12 pounds

75 2- to 3-inch, whole = 12 pints

100 very small, whole = 1 gallon = 6 pounds

CURRANTS: 2–2⅔ cups = 1 pound

DATES: 1 7¼-ounce package, pitted = 1½ cups

50–60, pitted = 2–3 cups, cut fine = 1 pound

FIGS: 1 cup, ground = ⅜ pound

12–18 = 2⅓–3 cups, chopped = 1 pound

GOOSEBERRIES: 2⅔ cups = 1 pound

6–8 cups make 1 quart

GRAPEFRUIT: 1 large = 1¾ cups broken pieces or ¾–1 cup juice

GRAPES: 2 cups, halved = 1 pound

6 pounds make 6 cups purée

LEMONS: 1 makes 2–4 tablespoons juice

12 make 2½ cups juice

1 large = ¼ cup juice and 1 teaspoon grated rind

LIMA BEANS: 2–3 cups, shelled = 1 pound

LIMES: 1 dozen make 1½–2 cups juice

MANGOES: 2–4 = 1 pound

MOLASSES: 1⅓ cups = 1 pound

1 cup replaces 1 cup sugar and ½ cup liquid

MUSHROOMS: 2 cups, canned, with liquid = 1 pound

MUSTARD: 1¼ cups, dry = ¼ pound, dry

  5 cups = 1 pound

NUT MEATS: 3–3½ cups, coarsely chopped = 1 pound

OLIVES: 135 "small" = 70 "mammoth" = 40 "colossal" = 32 "super-co-

  lossal = 1 pound

ONIONS: 1 medium, minced = ¾ cup

  2 medium, chopped or ground = 1 cup

  3 large or 4–4½ medium, diced = 2–2½ cups = 1 pound

  24 small, peeled and sliced = 4 cups or 1 quart

  12 medium, peeled and sliced = 5–6 cups

  2 cups, cooked = 1 pound

ORANGES: 1 makes 6–8 tablespoons juice

  1 large = ½ cup, diced = ½ cup juice

  1 dozen make 3–5 cups juice

PEACHES: 3–5, peeled and sliced = 2–2½ cups = 1 pound

  12–16, diced = 5 pints = 4 pounds

  1 bushel = 18–24 quarts = 48 pounds

PEARS: 4–5 medium = 2⅔ cups = 1 pound

  12–16 medium = 4–5 pints = 4 pounds

  1 bushel = 20–25 quarts = 48–50 pounds

PEPPERS: 1 large = 4 ounces

  4 large = 1 pound

  3–4 large, trimmed and chopped = 2 cups

  4–5 medium, diced = 2 cups or 1 pint

  6 large, trimmed and chopped = 4 cups or 1 quart

  12 medium, ground = 6 cups

  18, chopped = 7½ cups

PICKLES: 3–4 4-inch x 1¾ = 1 pound

  24 sweet, 2¾ x ¾ = 1 pound

PINEAPPLE: 1 medium, peeled and diced = 2½–3½ cups

  1 large, peeled and diced = 6 cups

  3¼ cups, raw = 1 pound

  1⅘ cups, canned = 1 pound

PLUMS: 12–20 prune plums = 1 pound

  1 bushel = 24–30 quarts = 50–56 pounds

PRUNES, DRIED: 30–40 = 4 cups, cooked, or 2⅛ cups, cooked and chopped

  = 1 pound

  60 medium, raw = 3 cups = 1 pound

RAISINS, SEEDED: 2½ cups = 2 cups chopped = 1 pound

RAISINS, SEEDLESS: 3 cups = 2½ cups, chopped = 1 pound
RHUBARB: 4–8 stalks = 1 pound
SACCHARIN: 1 ¼-grain tablet = 1 teaspoon sugar in sweetening power
STRAWBERRIES: 1 quart = 3 cups, hulled = 1 pint, crushed
  5 quarts make about 6 cups purée
SUGAR: 2 cups granulated = 1 pound
  2¼–2¾ cups brown, packed = 1 pound
  3½–4 cups powdered or confectioner's (4–4½ cups, sifted) = 1 pound
TOMATOES, GREEN: 10 large, sliced ½ inch thick = 4 quarts = 7 pounds
  8 quarts, whole = 10 pounds
TOMATOES, RED: 4 small to medium, sliced = 3 cups = 1 pound
  4 quarts, peeled and chopped = 3 quarts, canned = 8 pounds
  6 quarts, cored and sliced, with skins = 10 pounds
  44 medium = 11 pounds
  1 bushel = 15 to 20 quarts = 53 pounds
  2 cups, cooked or canned = 1 pound
WALNUTS, ENGLISH: 4 cups, chopped = 2½ pounds, unshelled
WATERMELON RIND: 10 pounds, trimmed, makes 3½–4 quarts
ZUCCHINI: 2¼ cups = 1 pound

Ingredients

Pickling cucumbers and other vegetables should be used as soon after harvesting as possible, preferably within 24 hours.

Choose fresh, good-quality fruits and vegetables free of blemishes and uniform in size. Imperfect and irregular fruits and vegetables can be cut up for relishes.

Fruits may be slightly underripe.

Wash all fruits and vegetables gently but thoroughly to remove dirt and grit, which could start bacterial action.

Cider vinegar can be substituted for distilled white vinegar, although its deeper color may cause a slight darkening of foods.

Use only fresh, whole spices for full flavor unless recipe specifies ground spices. Old spices may give a dusty flavor to pickles.

Use water as free from minerals as possible.

Use pure granulated salt rather than ordinary table salt when brining pickles. "Fillers" in table salt may cause cloudiness and darkening of pickles.

CUCUMBERS

The cucumber (botanical name: *Cucumis sativus*) is a fruit, like its cousins, the pumpkin, the melons and squash. Tomatoes, eggplants and peppers are also classified botanically as fruit.

The cucumber had spread from its origin in India both to the East Indies and to Europe before the year A.D. 1. It has been cultivated for 3,000 years, now, but still grows wild in the jungles of Asia.

Not all varieties of cucumbers are suitable for pickling. Those for table use are called "slicers." These garden and household varieties are frequently too large and tough-skinned. Through the efforts of the federal and state governments and the pickle packers, there is constant improvement in the types of cucumbers known as "pickles." They are thin-skinned and uniform in size and shape and resistant to the plant diseases that affect cucumbers.

Among the most popular pickling cucumbers are: Model, Producer, Ohio MR (Mosaic Resistant) No. 17, SR-6, Maine No. 2, Everbearing,

West India Gherkin, York State Pickling and Wisconsin SMR. Among the small varieties are: Niagara, Burpee Hybrid, Sensation Hybrid, and Sure Crop Hybrid. In Alabama, Kirby Stay Green, White Spine and Long Green are recommended varieties.

There is a flow of pickling cucumbers to all parts of the country that begins in the South, where crops mature early, and continues from May until September, plus some winter production from Florida and California.

Cucumbers for pickling become available for the housewife first from South Carolina and then North Carolina and Georgia in the middle of May, and by June or July the east shore of Maryland and northern Virginia have made their contributions. New Jersey cukes mature in July and August and, in the latter month, the prime Michigan and northern Indiana cucumbers arrive and the Illinois growers ship their long green crop. New York State starts sending its cucumbers to market in August and continues into September. The ones found in the market during the other months of the year are usually from the two glamour states, California and Florida.

Pickling cucumbers are a source of early income to farmers. The average yield is 150 bushels to the acre, with gross income of about $250 per acre, although if the produce hits the market when there is great demand and small supply, a grower may realize as high as $1,000 an acre. Of the $250, around half goes to the picker.

There is a technique to harvesting: Grasp the fruit near the stem and snap it from the vine with the thumb, or pinch off the stem with the fingernails. An efficient former picks his cucumber vines every 2 days since, in the warm growing season, "you can almost see the cucumbers growing."

MAXIMUM SIZES OF CUCUMBERS FOR PICKLING ACCORDING TO U.S. STANDARDS

U.S. No. 1	Up to $3\frac{1}{2}$ inches by $1\frac{1}{2}$
U.S. No. 2	Up to $5\frac{1}{2}$ inches by $1\frac{7}{8}$
U.S. No. 3	Up to 6 inches by $2\frac{1}{2}$

Cucumbers that stray from the straight and narrow are known as yellows, hollows, ball shapes, crooks, wasps and nubs.

For information regarding the growing of larger-than-garden-size cucumber acreage, contact your State Extension Service, which can give you the most suitable advice regarding type of seed, soil requirements, fertilizers, diseases and pests and cultivation in your locality.

SALT

All authorities agree that salt made especially for pickling is the best to use. After pickling salt, pure granulated salt is preferred. Dairy, cheese and kosher salts are also good but they are flaky (and sometimes known by that name) which means that while they are pound for pound as strong as the pure granulated salt, by measure—but not by weight— almost 1½ times as much is called for. All of the above have crystals that dissolve quickly and make clear brine, freer of scum than table or coarse salt. If your grocer or supermarket cannot supply you, they are available in feed- and farm-supply stores.

Neither table salt nor coarse salt is recommended for pickling. To prevent lumping, most table salts contain starch or carbonates or bicarbonates of sodium, magnesium or calcium. These chemicals interfere with the pickling process. Iodized salt may darken or cloud the brine. Coarse salt is also unsuitable, as it dissolves too slowly and cannot be distributed easily.

SUGAR

Granulated sugar is used for pickling, unless brown is specified or a darker color is desired. Since they differ in bulk, and sweetening power depends on weight, try to use weight measurements. Or see bulk-to-weight table.

WATER

Wherever possible, use soft water free of minerals, especially for pickling using the long process, as the minerals in hard water will interfere with the curing.

If your water supply is hard, plan in advance. Boil it, skim the scum, let it rest for 24 hours and when the sediment has settled to the bottom, ladle out from the top. If necessary, strain through several thicknesses of cloth.

Or use bottled distilled water.

The U.S. Geological Survey reports on the quality of water of cities and states in the U.S. Here, listed in order of softness and freedom from minerals, are the 100 best American towns and cities from the pickle maker's viewpoint:

Bogalusa, La.	Lake City, S.C.
Gulfport, Miss.	Hartsville, S.C.
Lufkin, Tex.	Camden, S.C.

Sherman, Tex.*
Greenville, S.C.
Mullins, S.C.
Pottsville, Pa.
Darlington, S.C.
Weymouth, Mass.
Yazoo City, Miss.
Bethlehem, Pa.
Hazelton, Pa.
Fitchburg, Mass.
Asheville, N.C.
Greenville, Miss.
Baton Rouge, La.
Ruston, La.
Gainesville, Tex.*
Greenwood, Miss.
Keene, N.H.
Shamokin, Pa.
Westfield, Mass.
Freeport, N.Y.
Palestine, Tex.
Nacogdoches, Tex.*
Riverton, Wyo.
Meridian, Miss.
Southbridge, Mass.
Bath, Me.
Rockland, Me.
Norman, Okla.
Coos Bay, Oreg.
San Francisco, Calif. (Hetch-Hetchy
   Reservoir, only)
Rumford, Me.
Worcester, Mass.
Portland, Oreg.
Biloxi, Miss.
Atlantic City, N.J.
Pascagoula, Miss.
Dunmore, Pa.
Berlin, N.H.
Hempstead, N.Y.

Cleburn, Tex.
West Memphis, Ark.
Boulder, Colo.
Bend, Oreg.
Bloomington, Ind.
Bristol, Conn.
Naugatuck, Conn.
Amsterdam, N.Y.
Hartford, Conn.
Norwich, Conn.
Springfield, Mass.
McComb, Miss.
Concord, N.H.
Manchester, N.H.
Everett, Wash.
Memphis, Tenn.
Taunton, Mass.
Brockton, Mass.
Woonsocket, R.I.
Boston, Mass.
Harrisburg, Pa.*
Paragould, Ark.
Rockville Centre, N.Y
Charlotte, N.C.
Charlottesville, Va.
Lynchburg, Va.
Auburn, Me.
Fall River, Mass.
New Bedford, Mass.
Glen Falls, N.Y.
Williamsport, Pa.
Missoula, Mont.
Bellingham, Wash.
Old Town, Me.
Utica, N.Y.
Albermarle, N.C.
Eugene, Oreg.
Salem, Oreg.
Seattle, Wash.
Oakland, Calif.*

* Cities with several sources of water, the softest being used for this list.

Little Rock, Ark.
Houston, Tex.*
Aiken, S.C.
Falls Church, Va.
Augusta, Me.
Kingston, N.Y.
New York, N.Y.
Pensacola, Fla.

Atlanta, Ga.
Salisbury, Md.
Sacramento, Calif.
Johnstown, Pa.
Carson City, Nev.
Tacoma, Wash.
Charleston, S.C.

According to the figures available, the latest of which were over 10 years old at time of publication, all of the above cities rate very high in water free of hardness and minerals. There is not too much difference between the 2 parts per million of Bogalusa and the 21 per million of Charleston.

HOW THE STATES RANK IN WATER FOR PICKLING

Here is a list of the States of the Union according to the state of their collective waters, beginning with the softest and most mineral-free:

Oregon
South Carolina
Maine
Massachusetts
New Hampshire
Connecticut
Rhode Island
North Carolina
Mississippi
Georgia
Arkansas
Washington
Hawaii
Maryland
New York
Vermont
Alabama
Delaware
Virginia
Louisiana
Tennessee
New Jersey

Pennsylvania
West Virginia
Alaska
District of Columbia
Kentucky
Missouri
Colorado
Minnesota
Michigan
California
Idaho
Montana
Florida
Oklahoma
Texas
Nevada
Ohio
Illinois
Wisconsin
North Dakota
Wyoming
Kansas

* Cities with several sources of water, the softest being used for this list.

Utah	New Mexico
Iowa	Nebraska
Arizona	South Dakota
Indiana	

State averages range from a low of 17 parts per million in Oregon to 299 in South Dakota.

20 WORST CITIES, WATERWISE, FOR PICKLING

Here are the places where the H_2O is so full of calciums, carbonates and other minerals that the use of tap water is not advised. A (w) after the city indicates that well water is responsible for the hardness. (If these conditions have changed since the government published its figures, the author will be happy to revise the list in the next edition.)

Sarasota, Fla. (w)	Ventura, Calif.
Oxnard, Calif. (w)	Sioux Falls, S.D.
Plainfield, N.J. (w)	Sioux City, Iowa
Peru, Ind.	Peoria, Ill. (w)
Estherville, Iowa	Lubbock, Tex.
Roswell, N.M.	Phoenix, Ariz.
Chickashaw, Okla.	Fort Dodge, Iowa
Carlsbad, N.M.	Culver City, Calif.
Salina, Kans.	Owosso, Mich.
Alexandria, La. (w)	Kokomo, Ind.

SEASONINGS

For many centuries pickles and relishes have been the appetite-sharpeners that have brought zest and savor to eating. Even kids who back away from anything resembling vegetables go for pickles and relishes.

In addition to the basic seasonings, salt and vinegar, there are scores of other unusual tastes which can be added to pickle products.

More than any natural vegetable, the pickled ones (especially cucumbers) offer a fertile field for the distribution of flavorings. They "take" whatever they are exposed to, and the more cut surface there is exposed— as in spears or chunks or slices—the quicker the flavor enters.

Put a small piece of very hot pepper in a jar of dill spears and in 2 weeks the mild spears will have taken on a peppery taste. With sweet pickles a few sprigs of mint will affect the taste and flavor. These are only 2 of many examples which could be cited.

Seasonings should be used with imagination and a frugal hand. For it is better to err on the skimpy side, and later add more if necessary, since it is impossible to subtract.

In purchasing and using seasonings:

Check for freshness before buying.

Buy small quantities at a time; keep containers tightly covered and away from heat; throw out old and weak flavorings.

If ground spices are called for, use a small hand peppermill for peppercorns; also one for fresh-ground cloves; and a small mortar and pestle to bruise, crack and grind seeds. (Ground spices will darken pickles but are specified frequently for relishes.)

Try to use fresh herbs in season. They will keep for days in tightly covered jars in refrigerator. Chop or crush them in mortar just before using.

When dried or powdered herbs are used in place of fresh, use only ¼ as much of the dried and ⅛ of the powdered.

Make cheesecloth or muslin bags (like tea bags) as spice bags for whole spices and herbs which are to be removed from the cooked mixture before packing.

In addition to the Dictionary of Pickling Seasonings and the Suggested Seasonings for Different Products which follow, see the chapters on sauces, chutneys, catsup and relishes, and the vinegar and mustard sections of this chapter.

DICTIONARY OF PICKLING SEASONINGS

Barks, beans, berries, blends, buds, bulbs, combinations, condiments, flowers, fruits, herbs, leaves, plants, powders, sauces, seeds and spices.

ALLSPICE, spice; whole or ground berry of allspice tree (Jamaica pimento). Nature's own blend, combining cinnamon, nutmeg, and clove flavors.

ANISE, herb; seed, and fresh and dried leaves; parsley family. Sweet, spicy taste and odor, adds licorice taste. Drop a few seeds in sweet pickles.

BALM (or *lemon balm*), herb; fresh and dried leaves; mint family. Sweet, lemon-mint scent and flavor.

BASIL (or *sweet basil*), herb; fresh and dried leaves and tender stems and essential oils; mint family. Highly aromatic, spicy flavor, between clove and licorice. Can be cooked for long periods.

BAY LEAF, dried leaf of sweet bay or laurel shrub or tree. Familiar strong, pungent smell; woodsy, almost bitter taste.

BORAGE, herb; fresh and dried leaves and flowers. The tender young leaves have a fresh, cool, cucumber flavor and can be cooked as spinach or greens.

BOUQUET GARNI, a blend of fresh or dried herb sprigs; tied with white thread, placed in soups and stews while cooking and removed before serving. See *seasoning blending*.

BURNET (or *salad burnet*), herb; fresh and dried leaves. Tender young leaves have distinct, delicate flavor, like cucumber.

CAPERS, flower buds of wild bushy herb; salted or pickled, bottled and used as condiment. Bitter, salty taste.

CARAWAY, herb; fresh leaves, roots and seedlike fruit; parsley family. Fresh young leaves have flavor similar to seed, but more delicate. Root is very sweet, more delicate than parsnips, and does not resemble taste of seed. Seed has spicy, aromatic flavor. Good in sauerkraut and pickled beets.

CARDAMOM, whole or ground seed of herb; related to ginger, although milder. Pleasant, pungent aroma and aromatic taste. $\frac{1}{8}$ teaspoon to 4 cups grapes.

CASSIA, whole bark and buds of a tree native to Burma and India that resembles cinnamon in flavor, but of an entirely different botanical family. There are numerous geographical varieties, varying in warmth, sweetness, pungency and color. Sold throughout United States as cinnamon.

CATSUP, condiment. "Catsup" is as near as the English language can come to a Chinese word meaning "brine of pickled fish." A sauce made with tomatoes, mushrooms or walnuts.

CAYENNE. See *pepper*.

CELERY, vegetable herb; fresh and dried leaves, fresh stalks and root, seed and salt. Every part is edible, useful. Seed frequently used in pickle recipes.

CHILI. See *pepper*.

CHILI POWDER, made from chili peppers and other spices in *mild* and *hot* flavors.

CHIVES, herb; fresh leaves, bulbs, salt; onion family. Young tender leaves have delicate onion flavor. Bulbs are pickled as tiny onions.

CHUTNEY, condiment; highly seasoned, sweet, pickled combination of tropical fruits, herbs, spices and nuts, with mango and raisins usually predominating.

CINNAMON (or *true cinnamon*), spice; aromatic inner bark, stick or ground, of cinnamon tree. More delicate than cassia. Practically all "cinnamon" sold in United States is cassia. For catsup, chili sauce, pickles.

CLOVES, spice; whole or ground dried unopened flower buds of clove tree. Spicy, aromatic, very warm taste. Pungent; use sparingly. For spiced fruits.

CORIANDER, whole or ground, dried seed of herb. Taste and smell reminiscent of orange, or, to some, mixture of lemon peel and sage. In sweet pickles and sauerkraut.

CRESS (or *land cress*), herb; fresh leaves; mustard family. Young leaves and stems have spicy, piquant taste like mustard plant or nasturtium leaves. See *water cress*.

CUMIN, whole or ground dried seed of herb; parsley family. Has aromatic flavor and warm, bitterish taste, somewhat like caraway seed, which it resembles in appearance. Ingredient of curry powder.

CURRY POWDER, condiment; combination of spices in powder or paste. According to different manufacturers' formulae, taste varies from fairly mild to very hot, depending on proportions of allspice, black pepper, red pepper, cayenne, ginger, cinnamon, cumin, cardamom seed, coriander seed, fenugreek, caraway seed, curry leaf, mustard seed, nutmeg, saffron, turmeric, white pepper and/or other spices used. Has pungent, tempting aroma. Known as "the salt of the Orient."

DILL, herb; fresh leaves, fresh or dried flowers or stalk tops, seed; parsley family. Pungent flavor.

FENNEL (also called *sweet anise, finocchio* or *sweet fennel*), herb; fresh and dried leaves and stalks, seeds, essential oil; parsley family. Pungent licorice taste. Popular in sweet pickles, sauerkraut and spiced peaches. Use like anise.

FENUGREEK, seeds of herb, allied to clover. Peculiar but pleasant aromatic odor, rather bitter taste. Use in mango and chutney recipes.

GARLIC, bulb; dried, powder, salt, oil. "The most pungent and wholesome member of the large onion family. Like all that is best, it must be used with care and discretion."—André L. Simon. For kosher and Polish pickles, vinegar.

GERANIUM, flower herb; fresh and dried leaves. There are many varieties, including apple, balm-scented, camphor-rose, lemon-scented, nutmeg, orange, peppermint, rose (the most popular) and spicy, each with the aroma and flavor of its name.

GHERKINS, condiment; small, prickly cucumbers after pickling.

GINGER, herb; dried whole and ground root and essence of semitropical plant. Aromatic and stimulating, sweet and spicy. Cracked ginger is small pieces of unground ginger. White ginger is the scraped peeled roots.

HERB, any fragrant plant with culinary or medicinal use.

HORSE-RADISH, fresh root of perennial herb of mustard family. Noted for pungency. Use sparingly.

JUNIPER BERRY, aromatic fruit of cedarlike shrub or tree. Tastes slightly bittersweet, with fragrant, spicy aroma. For sauerkraut, vinegar, pickled beef, venison and fish. Useful in many recipes aside from flavoring gin.

LEEK, herb; fresh bulbs or stalks; onion family. Mild onion flavor, strong fragrance.

LEMON, fruit; rind, juice, essential oil. Indispensable flavoring in preparing food. Substitute part lemon juice for vinegar in pickled and spiced fruits.

LIME, fruit; rind, juice, oil. Aromatic, tart flavor. ⅙ as much sugar as lemon. Good in blending other flavors.

MACE, spice; flakes or blades or ground, dried fleshy layer between kernel and outer husk of nutmeg. Same flavor as nutmeg, except stronger, more pungent.

MARJORAM (or *sweet marjoram*), herb; fresh and whole, crushed and powdered dried leaves; mint family. Has fragrant, spicy odor and warm, aromatic flavor. A less pungent substitute for sage. Use with discretion. For wild marjoram, see *oregano*.

MINCEMEAT SPICES, allspice, cinnamon, cloves and others.

MINT, herb; any of a number of different-flavored perennials, including curlyleaf, apple, apple-variegated golden, orange, spearmint, peppermint; fresh and dried leaves and flowering tops.

MIXED PICKLING SPICE. See index.

MUSHROOMS, edible fungi; alone or as a sauce add a distinctive flavor and negligible food value.

MUSTARD, herb spice; fresh leaves or greens, seed, powdered (flour), condiment. The lighter the seed, the milder the flavor. Dry mustard or mustard flour is pale yellow. When color is brighter, turmeric has been added. Prepared mustard or mustard sauce comes in a great variety of flavors and nationalities. More can be created by the addition of various spices. See *seasoning blending* in *vinegar section* of this chapter.

MYRTLE, leaves and seeds of shrub; can be used as substitute for bay leaf in marinades and stews.

NASTURTIUM (or *Indian cress*), flower; the word means "nose twist." Leaves and flowers used like water cress; seed pods, pickled, are similar to capers.

NUTMEG, spice; whole dried kernel of nutmeg tree. Best and strongest when freshly grated. Aromatic with spicy, almost bitter taste. Good for blending. See *mace.*

ONION *("The Kitchen Lily"),* bulb; young and green called green onion or scallion, has delicate flavor; matured bulbs are sun-dried. Also comes in dried flakes, powder, salt. Most white onions are milder than yellow or red.

OREGANO (or *wild marjoram),* herb; used same as marjoram, more pungent. Gives Latin flavor.

PAPRIKA. See *pepper.*

PARSLEY, herb; fresh, dried leaves. Contains more iron than spinach. Also a great deal of vitamins A and C.

PEPPER, BLACK and WHITE, spice; dried berries of vine that grows in East Indies and India. Black pepper is the whole ripe berry, cured; white pepper is the mature berry after the outer hull is removed and is milder than the black. Best grades are sun-dried rather than over slow fire. Freshest, best flavor comes when black peppercorns are ground in mill as needed. White pepper should be used where, in pickling, black specks are to be avoided.

PEPPER, RED, CAYENNE, CHILI, PAPRIKA, vegetable spices; dried whole, crushed and ground pods and seeds of ripe chili or red pepper pods of the capsicum family. Red pepper is made from the long red Mexican chili and is extremely hot and therefore should be used with great restraint. The crushed pepper, consisting of pod and seeds, is hotter than the ground pods. Cayenne pepper is the dried whole pod or ground powder of very small, very fiery chilies. Paprika is the ground dried pod and seeds of large sweet red peppers. It is rich in vitamins C and P, the latter a new one found in paprika. Sweet and pungent, paprika is also useful as a garnish because of its deep red color.

PICCALILLI, condiment; mixture of chopped green peppers, green tomatoes, onions, etc., highly seasoned and cooked slowly in vinegar.

PICKLES, condiment; cucumbers, small onions, cauliflowerets, and other vegetables and fruits pickled in salted vinegar bath; useful in sauces, salads and dressings.

PIMENTO, allspice, fruit of the allspice tree.

PIMIENTO, fleshy fruit of the Spanish pepper plant. Used fresh as vegetable, for stuffing; in mango pickling, relish; dried as paprika, cayenne or chili.

ROSEMARY, herb; fresh and dried leaves; mint family. Refreshing, spicy scent; piny flavor. Use with discretion.

SAFFRON, spice; dried stigmas of a crocus of iris family. Sweetish, aromatic odor, somewhat bitter taste. Expensive, but a small pinch goes a long way. Use for coloring as well as flavor.

SAGE, herb; fresh and whole and powdered dried leaves; mint family. About 500 varieties exist. Most used include common garden, cypress, Dalmatian, pineapple, rose, white. Very pungent, mildly astringent taste, therefore use sparingly. Do not cook long and do not use in foods to be frozen, as they will develop a bitter taste.

SALT, oldest, most indispensable seasoning and preservative. Brings out the natural flavor of almost every food. Herb salts include commercial blends such as Lawry's, also celery, charcoal, chive, curry, garlic, hickory, onion and smoked.

SAVORY, SUMMER and WINTER, herbs; fresh or dried leaves and flowering tops; mint family. Summer savory is a fragrant annual with flavor resembling thyme and a slight resin smell. The winter variety is a perennial with a stronger flavor. Used with horse-radish and sauerkraut.

SESAME (or *benne*), seed of a tropical herb; seeds and oil. Toasted, it has a flavor similar to that of roasted almonds.

SHALLOT (or *eschalot*), fresh or dried bulb or herb. A small brown brother of the onion, with a stronger but mellower, more subtle flavor and a shape like garlic.

SOY SAUCE, Chinese catsup, fermented juice of soybeans. Very salty.

SPICES, aromatic, often pungent plant substances used to season food and beverages.

SUGAR, the principal sweetening agent.

TABASCO SAUCE, fiery hot essence made from vinegar and small red peppers originally imported from the state of Tabasco, Mexico. Use very sparingly, a drop at a time.

TARRAGON (means *"little dragon"*), herb; fresh and dried leaves and flowering tops; aster family. Distinctive flavor. Used to flavor vinegars.

THYME (*pronounced "time"*), herb; fresh and dried whole and ground flowers and leaves; mint family. Strong, pungent, agreeable fragrance. There are varieties with lemon, orange and caraway scent and flavor. Most versatile herb. Use sparingly.

TRUFFLES, black underground fungus tuber. Use as garnish or seasoning for distinctive fragrance and flavor.

TURMERIC (also *tumeric*), spice; ground and whole rootstock of mild cousin of ginger. Has aromatic, warm flavor and beautiful yellow color. One pinch will color a big dish. Used in mustards, chow-chow pickles, etc.

VANILLA, spice; bean of climbing vine of orchid family. Stick and extract in alcohol are used.

VERBENA (or *lemon verbena*), herb; fresh or dried leaves. Fruit aroma and flavor like lime or lemon.

VINEGAR (*from French* vin *wine, and* aigre *sour*), dilute acetic acid, condiment and preservative. There are many commercial varieties: malt, cider, red and white wine, perry (pear), corn, distilled, herb and spice. To make your own herb and spice vinegars see vinegar section of this chapter.

WATER CRESS, herb; fresh leaves and stems; mustard family. Peppery, pungent, resembling nasturtium.

WINE, fermented juice of fresh, ripe grapes. There are many varieties: dry, sweet, semisweet, sour, in red, rosé and white. All except sweet wines can be made into vinegar. Burgundy and claret are best for pickling meats.

WORCESTERSHIRE SAUCE, condiment. Adds color and spice to all except sweet foods.

SUGGESTED SEASONINGS FOR DIFFERENT PRODUCTS

FRUIT PICKLE SPICES: Allspice, cider vinegar, cinnamon bark, cloves, lemon balm, lemon juice, grated lemon rind. For mango: fenugreek.

MEAT PICKLING SEASONINGS: Allspice, bay leaves, capers, cloves, mustard seed, paprika, peppercorns, tarragon.

MUSTARD SEASONINGS: Fresh and dried minced basil, capers, chervil, chili powder, curry powder, dill, garlic, horse-radish, lovage, marjoram, mushrooms, mustard seed, minced or powdered onion, oregano, paprika, parsley, rosemary, sage, tarragon, thyme, tomato paste, turmeric and cider, garlic, wine or tarragon vinegars.

PICKLES, SWEET and SPICED: Ground allspice, aniseed, caraway seed, cardamom seed, cassia buds, celery seed, cinnamon bark, cloves, coriander seed, fennel, ginger, mace, mint, mustard seed, nutmeg, turmeric.

SAUERKRAUT: Caraway seed, celery seed, dill seed, fennel seed, juniper berries, lemon mint, mustard seed, onion, parsley, savory.

TOMATO CATSUP SEASONINGS: Allspice, cayenne, celery seed, cinnamon, garlic, ginger, mace, chopped onion or onion salt, paprika, vinegar.

VINEGAR SEASONINGS: Allspice, balm, basil, bay leaf, borage, burnet, caraway seed, celery seed, chives, cinnamon, cloves, coriander seed, curry powder, dill seed or leaves, fennel, garlic, horse-radish, mace, marjoram, mustard seed, nasturtium seed and flowers, onion, peppercorns, rose geranium, rosemary, rose petals, rue, shallots, tarragon, thyme, verbena, water cress, cumin seeds, and chili peppers.

Every manufacturer or dealer in seasonings has his own formula and combination of spices for pickling—and they are usually excellent. However, if your do-it-yourself kick extends right down to mixing your own spices, here is a list you might consider. As usual, the ingredients are listed in order of their volume.

13 PICKLING SPICES

Allspice	Bay leaves
Mustard seed	Red pepper
Ginger	Chilies
Coriander seed	Dill seed
Black pepper	Mace
Cinnamon stick (or cassia buds)	Cardamom
Cloves	

This combination also adds distinctive flavor to gravies, sauces and stews. Try a tablespoon in boiled beets, cabbage, sauerkraut and with sauerbraten.

VINEGAR

Vinegar is both a preservative and a flavor. As a preservative for pickling purposes, it also lends one of the flavors that make the product appetizing.

It is one of the oldest food products known, is mentioned in the Bible and is one of the few food products that have come down, unchanged in essential form, from ancient times.

That is because it is almost a product of nature. The natural juice of fruit or grapes, on standing, yields to fermentation and, through nature's own chemistry, develops alcohol, which on exposure to the air is changed into acid. For example—sweet cider to hard cider to vinegar.

Commercial vinegars are divided into two general classes: fermented (cider and malt) and distilled (white vinegars). A commercial tarragon vinegar, such as Heinz's, is a blend of malt and white pickling vinegars with the herb added.

Originally vinegar was sold only in bulk, but Heinz, which began to manufacture the pickling liquid for its own packing use, was the first to market it in bottles.

When buying vinegar, check the label for percentage of acidity. Unless otherwise stated in recipes, use vinegar with 5% or 4 to 6% acidity. And, since you do not use great quantities and the difference between the highest price and the lowest is so little, buy quality vinegars for all recipes in this book.

APPLE CIDER VINEGAR (*Fermented*) In early Colonial days in the U.S., apples were abundant, but the demand for them was not equal to the supply; therefore much of the crop was used for apple cider, and a lot of this became vinegar by the process of nature. In that way cider vinegar became the kind universally used, since it required no special or costly equipment or ingredients.

Since certain species of apples are richer in juice and flavor than others, due to climatic and geographical factors, cider vinegar manufacture is concentrated in New York State; around Watsonville, California; Holland, Michigan; and Winchester in Virginia.

Giant screw and hydraulic presses extract the juice from millions of pounds of apples every year. The juice is pumped into storage tanks with a capacity of 20,000 gallons each. (In the proper fermentation of apple juice, the larger the quantity of juice in one receptacle, the better.) Here the juice is left to ferment naturally and after a period of months it becomes hard cider. It is filtered and sent through wooden pipes to generators where the alcohol in the cider is changed into acid by its contact with the oxygen in the air. The converted vinegar then goes through more wooden pipes into wooden storage tanks, where it ages and mellows.

WHITE VINEGARS (*Distilled*) These are produced by the distillation of alcoholic spirits from corn, rye and barley malt. The process is essentially the same as that used in the making of spirits for drinking and commercial purposes.

It begins with the mashing of the cereals—making a mash by grinding and adding water—which transforms it into malt sugar or maltose. Yeast is then added, causing the fermentation which changes the maltose into alcohol.

The alcohol is extracted by boiling the mash until the alcohol vaporizes and the vapor is forced into cool water, in which it condenses. As in the making of cider vinegar, oxygen transforms the alcohol into vinegar.

A favorite of North European countries, distilled vinegars are usually considered superior for preserving purposes because of the absence of any traces of vegetable matter and the fact that they will not discolor or darken the product. And white vinegars have high acetic strength that will preserve the pickled fruits and vegetables even after being somewhat diluted by the natural juices and liquids in the foods themselves.

MALT VINEGARS (*Fermented or Brewed*)   Made from cereals, such as barley, the grain is steeped in water at carefully regulated temperatures until it is soft; then it is drained and spread out on tile floors, where it begins to sprout. It is next dried and is brewed, along with crushed barley, in water, to produce a sweet liquid called "wort" which contains maltose.

Up to this point the process is quite similar to the one that produces beer and ale, or malt extracts.

The wort is processed until it ferments and produces alcohol. From now on the liquid is treated in much the same manner as distilled alcohol and turned into vinegar, this time with a bright golden color. It is considered the finest vinegar produced today. All of the aroma, pungency and delicate flavor of the malt remains in malt vinegar.

If, after this picture of the ramifications of the vinegar-producing processes, you still would like to essay a try at making your own, here is a set of directions worked out at the University of California:

HOW TO MAKE YOUR OWN VINEGAR

Vinegar has been defined as a condiment prepared from various sugary or starchy materials by alcoholic and subsequent acetic fermentation. It consists principally of a dilute solution of acetic acid in water, but also contains flavoring and coloring or extracted matter, fixed fruit acids, and salts, varying according to its origin. These additional substances give to vinegar its distinctive quality.

Vinegars are classified according to the material from which they are made and the methods of manufacture. Thus, there are cider, wine, peach, pear, orange and other fruit vinegars, and honey vinegar. Distilled vinegar, often called white vinegar (and sometimes erroneously white wine vinegar), is made by the acetic fermentation of dilute distilled alcohol.

PRINCIPLES OF VINEGAR MANUFACTURE: The manufacture of vinegar requires two fermentation processes. The first transforms the sugar of the fruit or juice into alcohol. This is brought about by yeast, a microscopic organism of the plant kingdom. The second changes the alcohol into acetic acid and is caused by vinegar bacteria.

The alcoholic fermentation must be complete before the acetic or "vinegar" fermentation is allowed to start, otherwise the yeast fermentation will be stopped by the acetic acid and unfermented sugar will remain in the vinegar. Such a condition results in weak vinegars of poor quality and low yields of acetic acid.

DIRECTIONS FOR MAKING VINEGAR IN THE HOME: Vinegar may be prepared on a small scale in the kitchen from many varieties of fruits and from waste peels and cores obtained in the preparation of fruits for canning or preserving. Honey may also be used.

PREPARATION OF THE JUICE: Pass apples, pears or pitted peaches through a small food grinder, using the coarse knife. Berries, grapes and other soft fruits may be crushed by hand or with a potato masher, without the use of a food chopper. Peels and cores may be mixed with an equal volume of water and boiled until soft. Honey should be diluted with 1 part fruit juice and 4 parts water, the fruit juice being necessary to furnish yeast food.

Press the crushed fruit or the boiled peels and cores through a double thickness of cheesecloth. To dilute juice of peels and cores, add ¼ pound of sugar per quart. Sugar should not be added to the juices of other ripe fruits or to honey.

YEAST FERMENTATION: To each quart of cooled juice add about ¼ cake of fresh yeast, which should be well broken up and thoroughly mixed with the juice. The juice must not be above 90°F when the yeast is added. Allow it to stand in a stone or glass jar with the lid off and the jar covered with a cloth until gas formation ceases; or allow the juice to ferment in a gallon jug or bottle of any suitable size, loosely plugged with cotton or covered with cloth. Fermentation usually takes 2 weeks.

VINEGAR FERMENTATION: When gas formation has ceased, separate the fermented liquid from the sediment. To each quart of this liquid add about ½ pint of good unpasteurized vinegar. Cover the jar or bottle with a cloth to exclude insects and allow it to stand in a warm place until the vinegar is strong enough to use. Separate it from the "mother of vinegar" and sediment, bottle it and cork tightly. Mother of vinegar is the white, rubbery mass of vinegar bacteria that often forms in vinegar.

Never add vinegar to the fresh juice, because it interferes with the yeast fermentation and will result in a weak vinegar. The vinegar must not be added until the yeast fermentation is complete. It will then cause the vinegar fermentation to proceed rapidly and will prevent the molding or spoiling of the fermented liquid.

Vinegar is corrosive. Do not use copper, zinc or iron utensils in handling it. *Galvanized ware is extremely dangerous to use, for the zinc coating dissolves and makes the juice or vinegar very poisonous.*

Unless you are able to determine the acidity of your homemade vinegar, and it runs about 5%, do not use it in pickling.

*And if the complications of making vinegar the California way have
thrown you, here is an old Jewish formula, so simple that it doesn't look
as if it would work. But try it if you will—you have little to lose.*

HONEY VINEGAR

1 quart strained honey
8 quarts warm water

Mix together and let stand in a warm place until fermentation ceases.
Seal in clean fruit jars. Makes, we are told, a white vinegar of good
quality.

HERBED AND SPICED VINEGARS

Seasoned vinegars are fun to put up, whether for using in pickling or
for cooking in general, probably because they are so easy and such a
challenge to your palate and blending ability.

Cider, malt, red and white wine, distilled and other vinegars all have
individual flavors. And almost all the herbs, spices, and seasonings will
blend with them, giving them mellowness as well as flavor. So any pickler
who cares to mix his own can certainly, with a little practice and dis-
crimination, achieve wonderfully subtle and unusual results with seasoned vinegars.

Fresh leaves: Place 1 packed cup minced and gently bruised leaves,
which have been washed and drained, and 1 pint vinegar, in jar with
tight cover. Let stand 1 to 2 weeks in warm kitchen or sun, shaking once
daily. Strain and bottle.

Dried leaves, crushed seed, or powder: 2 teaspoons to 1 pint hot vinegar, then proceed as with fresh leaves.

Seasonings for use in vinegars: allspice, basil, bay leaves, borage, burnet, capers, caraway, cardamom, cayenne, celery, chilies, chives, cinnamon, coriander, black cumin, curry powder (1½ ounces to pint), dill,
fennel, garlic (1 ounce minced to pint), geranium, horse-radish (2 tablespoons fresh-ground to pint), ginger, juniper berries, marjoram, mint,
mustard, onion, paprika, red peppers, white pepper, black peppercorns,
rosemary, shallot (2 ounces minced to pint), sorrel, spearmint, tarragon,
thyme.

Herb combination: allspice, basil, bay leaves, crushed cloves, dill seed,
marjoram, mint, rosemary, tarragon. Crush and blend in jar, add vinegar of choice, infuse for 2 to 3 weeks, filter and bottle.

Mint, spearmint, wintergreen or rose geranium can be used to make sweet vinegars by chopping and bruising 1 cup of fresh leaves and adding them to 1 pint cider vinegar and 1 tablespoon Sucaryl solution. Boil together for 5 minutes, then strain through fine strainer (or filter) into hot, sterilized bottles and cork tightly.

Tarragarlic vinegar: Place 2 cups tender tarragon leaves, washed, dried, and crushed, in wide-mouthed jar, pour 1 pint distilled vinegar over, add 2 crushed cloves and 1 split clove garlic. Keep in warm room 1 day, remove garlic, keep in warm place 2 weeks, shaking daily. Strain and bottle.

Blending different seasonings for infusing vinegars: Begin cautiously, mixing only 2 flavors together at first. After all, the vinegar provides a third one. Be guided by the rules for seasoning blending. Don't use too much of a strong seasoning (garlic, chives, tarragon, basil) with a milder one, or only the strong will come through. Try blending the different vinegars together, also.

SEASONING BLENDING In mixing together herbs and other flavors, new and unusual combinations can be achieved according to your own taste and the skill which you acquire from experience. There is one rule to remember—pick one leading flavor as the foundation for your blend and surround it with from 1 to 4 other, more subtle, seasonings. Never let 2 strong seasonings fight it out in a blend.

The "leading flavors" are the pungent, dominating herbs such as rosemary, sage, winter savory; then come sweet basil, peppermint, spearmint, sweet marjoram, tarragon, thyme and, of course, garlic.

Especially good in blends are chervil, chive, curled parsley, summer savory, lovage and celery. Then there are all the others with which to experiment. If you are extrasensitive in your blending, you can flavor your dishes with such unusual and pleasing combinations that only an expert could name the components.

Here if (excufe the curfivef) an old receipt from a Virginia lady'f manufcript cookbook:

RAFPBERRY VINEGAR

Meafure your Rafpberrief into a Bowl, and pour over them an equal Quantity of Vinegar.

The next Day take out the Fruit and add af much more to the Fame Vinegar. The Day following, remove the rafpberrief af before and again replace them with Frefh and on the fourth Day put to each Pint of Liquid a Pound of Loaf-fugar—place it in a Fkillet on a gentle Fire, Fimmer and Fkim it for a fhort Time when it will be ready to bottle for Ufe—Feal it down well.

9 SEASONS VINEGAR

1 teaspoon crushed dill seed
½ ounce dried marjoram
½ teaspoon black pepper
¼ teaspoon whole allspice
¼ ounce dried basil

¼ teaspoon whole cloves, crushed
¼ ounce curly mint
¼ ounce rosemary
¼ ounce dried tarragon
2 quarts cider vinegar

Blend herbs and spices; add to the vinegar and put in covered jar or crock for 3 weeks. Stir and mash every other day with a wooden spoon; after 3 weeks, strain, filter and bottle. Use sparingly in roasts, stews, meat and steak sauces.

SPICED VINEGAR No. 1

1 quart white vinegar
½ cup sugar
12 cloves
1 tablespoon crushed ginger
1½ tablespoons peppercorns
1-inch stick cinnamon

1 teaspoon finely ground horse-radish
2 cloves garlic, minced
1 teaspoon mustard seed
1 teaspoon mace
2 teaspoons salt

Place all ingredients in an enameled saucepan and slowly bring to a boil, then simmer gently for 20 minutes. Let stand until cold, then strain and bottle with airtight closure. Makes 2 pint bottles.

SPICED VINEGAR No. 2

1 quart vinegar
1 tablespoon allspice
1 tablespoon mace
1 tablespoon mustard seed

1 bay leaf
1 onion
1 tablespoon grated horse-radish
1 teaspoon salt

Combine all ingredients in pan, bring to a boil and simmer for 4 minutes. Strain and use cold.

SPICED VINEGAR No. 3

12 cloves
2-inch stick of cinnamon

Small piece of whole ginger
1½ pints vinegar

Put first three items in muslin or cheesecloth bag, place in vinegar and boil for 20–25 minutes, keeping lid on pot. Remove bag.
Use in place of straight vinegar, for pickling and chutneys.

HOT CHILI VINEGAR

24 red chili peppers
1 pint white vinegar

Cut peppers in half and place in quart bottle. Add vinegar and let stand for 2 weeks, shaking every day. Strain the vinegar through muslin or fine sieve and bottle in small bottles. Cork securely. Makes 1 pint.

MILD CHILI VINEGAR

2 ounces chili peppers
1 teaspoon salt
1 quart white vinegar

If peppers are large, cut in half lengthwise. Soak in vinegar, adding salt; shake every day for 10 days, then strain and bottle. Makes 1 quart.

ANOTHER CHILI VINEGAR

Fill bottles ¼ full of small dried chili peppers cut in half. Fill bottles with boiling cider or white wine vinegar; cork and store in cool place.

TEXAS A & M RECIPE FOR SPICED VINEGAR

3 cups vinegar
1 cup water
1½ cups sugar
1 tablespoon mustard seed

2 hot red peppers (if desired)
1 or 2 tablespoons mixed
    pickling spices

This spiced vinegar may be used over brined vegetables which have been freshened or it may be used in recipes for pickled beets, cucumbers and carrots made from fresh vegetables. This amount will cover about 4 quarts of well-packed vegetables.

Mix above ingredients and bring to boil. Pour while boiling hot over the vegetables. More or less sugar may be added as desired. Part honey or corn sirup could be substituted for sugar.

BASIL VINEGAR

Fill a glass jar loosely with bruised fresh basil leaves. Then fill the jar with distilled vinegar. Cover and leave in a cool place for 2 weeks. Then strain and bottle as usual.

Also pleasant for use in salads:

MINT VINEGAR

Proceed as with basil vinegar, substituting fresh, bruised mint leaves.

GARLIC VINEGAR

1 quart distilled vinegar
2 ounces garlic cloves, skinned and minced or crushed
¼ tablespoon salt

Combine. Pour into bottle; cork and store in cool place for 2 weeks, shaking bottle occasionally. Then strain and rebottle. Use sparingly in salads, as a little goes a long way.

A few leaves of basil may be added (optional).

CELERY VINEGAR

1 large bunch celery
1 quart vinegar
2 teaspoons celery seed

1 tablespoon sugar
1 teaspoon salt

Chop celery, including leaves and trimmed root, into small pieces. Place in bowl. Heat vinegar with other ingredients to boiling point and pour over celery. Let cool. Place in jar and put lid on. Leave for 12 days, shaking well every day. Strain, bottle and cork tightly. Makes 1 quart.

HORSE-RADISH VINEGAR

Place three good-sized horse-radish roots, freshly scraped, in a 2-quart jar or other container. Add ¼ teaspoon cayenne pepper, ½ teaspoon black pepper, ½ teaspoon celery seed. Pour 1 quart of vinegar over, cover tightly and steep for 10 days. Strain and rebottle.

HORSE-RADISH VINEGAR (Cooked)

1 quart white vinegar
1 cup grated horse-radish
1 teaspoon cayenne pepper

2 ounces fine-minced shallots or
   young onions
1 teaspoon salt

Heat vinegar to boiling point, place other ingredients in jar and pour vinegar over. Cover and put in a warm place for 2 weeks. Strain off vinegar, bring to a boil, bottle and seal airtight.

ONION VINEGAR

1 quart white vinegar
1 cup fine-chopped Spanish or white onions

Combine, cover and let stand for 2 weeks. Then strain and bottle. Fine for salads.

Shallot vinegar can be made by substituting 4 ounces of peeled and sliced shallots for the onions.

Here is an old-fashioned, old lady's recipe:

ROSE VINEGAR

1 cup rose petals, freshly gathered
White wine vinegar (about 1 quart)

Put petals in 1-quart jar. Cover with white wine vinegar. Place in sun for 2 weeks. Strain through paper filter. Bottle and cork. Delicious for salads.

The great name in English cookery books is that of Mrs. Beeton, who occupies a niche in British kitchens comparable to a combination of Fannie Farmer, Prudence Penny, Clementine Paddleford and your mother.

MRS. BEETON'S BRINE FOR PICKLING

½ pint vinegar
1½ pints water
½ pound salt

Heat together until salt is dissolved, then remove at once. Vinegar loses its preserving properties when boiled too long. Cool and use clear solution only. Makes about 1 quart.

"Then, too, I had trouble with the cookbooks. As I studied the recipes, I discovered the fateful word MEANWHILE. I was supposed to separate eggs, then beat them, MEANWHILE stirring something constantly. I was to melt butter, blend in flour and gradually add milk. MEANWHILE dicing or peeling something, and not forgetting to test the cake in the oven with a clean broomstraw. MEANWHILE I was theoretically tossing the salad.

"The most important lesson I learned was not to get in a panic when I saw MEANWHILE staring at me."

—*What Cooks at Stillmeadow,* by Gladys Taber

MARINADES

These are combinations of basting sauces and tenderizers and since they all have vinegar or wine as a basic ingredient, they belong here.

Although not usually classified as such, they are actually pickling fluids for the quick pickling of meats and fish.

COOKED MARINADE

½ cup fine-sliced onions
⅜ cup fine-sliced carrots
⅛ cup fine-sliced celery
2 cloves garlic, crushed
Bouquet garni:
  1 bay leaf
  1 sprig parsley
  1 sprig thyme (or 1 clove)

Dash pepper
½ teaspoon salt
3 pints red wine (or white wine for fowl or lamb)
½ pint vinegar

Brown all ingredients, except wine and vinegar, in a little olive oil. Add wine and vinegar; cook for ½ hour; cool.

Marinade may be re-used, but boil again and add more wine and vinegar every 2 days.

MARINADE FOR BEEF

1 onion, chopped
1 clove garlic
10 peppercorns
1 teaspoon thyme

6 juniper berries
½ teaspoon grated lemon peel
4 tablespoons olive oil
1 cup red wine vinegar

Grind onion and garlic in mortar, add pepper, thyme, juniper and lemon peel and pound into paste, adding oil little by little until it is all absorbed. Blend in vinegar until mixture is well homogenized.

Use to marinate beef by immersing in marinade, in snug container, the day before meat is to be used. Place in refrigerator and turn meat occasionally. Remove 1 hour before cooking. Makes more than a cup.

POT ROAST MARINADE

2 tablespoons sugar
2 teaspoons salt
1 teaspoon crushed cloves
½ teaspoon dried oregano
⅛ teaspoon cayenne pepper

2 cups red wine vinegar
Zest of 1 lemon, grated
½ cup olive oil
1 onion, grated

Mix sugar, salt, cloves, oregano and pepper in large bowl; then add enough wine vinegar to form a thick paste. Add grated lemon rind, blending well. Slowly pour in olive oil, blending by stirring vigorously, until the ½ cup is absorbed. Add onion and remainder of vinegar, again blending well.

Transfer to quart jar, seal and allow to "rest" at room temperature at least 12 hours; then store in refrigerator, where it will keep indefinitely. Makes 1½ pints.

For pot roasts and other baked meat, pour ½ of above recipe over meat in shallow pan and let stand at room temperature at least 5 hours, or overnight. Drain and cook meat according to favorite recipe, basting with the marinade liquid.

ROBERT'S BARBECUE MARINADE

1 pint oil
4 green onions, fine-chopped
15 peppercorns, crushed
3 cloves garlic, fine-chopped
1 tablespoon barbecue spices
¼ teaspoon basil
¼ teaspoon celery salt
1 sprig thyme
Salt to taste

Mix ingredients well in quart jar. Use to marinate shrimps, steaks, chops, liver, turkey steaks, chicken, quail or pheasant. Soak from 30 minutes to 1 hour, depending on size. Makes 1 pint.

HOT MEXICAN MARINADE AND BARBECUE SAUCE

1 cup olive oil
1 medium onion, fine-chopped
2 teaspoons chili powder or
4 dry Mexican chili pods
1 clove garlic, fine-chopped
1 bell pepper, fine-chopped
¼ teaspoon coriander
¼ teaspoon oregano
4 chorizo sausages, peeled and sliced
½ cup white vinegar
½ cup fine-sliced string beans
2 drops Tabasco (more if hot sauce is desired)
4 medium tomatoes, diced
2 tablespoons fine-chopped pimento
1 cup corn, cut from cob
1 cup clear stock
1 tablespoon fine-chopped parsley

Heat oil in heavy deep kettle. Add onion, chili powder, garlic, pepper, coriander, oregano and chorizo sausages and brown lightly. Add vinegar, string beans, Tabasco, tomatoes, pimento, corn and clear stock. Simmer 15 minutes. Sprinkle with parsley. Use hot or cold. Makes 4 cups.

HOT OR COLD MEXICAN BARBECUE SAUCE

4 strips bacon, fine-chopped
½ cup olive oil
1 medium onion, fine-chopped
1 green pepper in strips
1 teaspoon chili powder
1 clove garlic, fine-chopped
¼ teaspoon oregano

¼ teaspoon coriander
½ cup vinegar
15 ripe olives, pitted and sliced
1 avocado, peeled and diced
4 tomatoes, peeled and diced
1 cup clear stock or water

Sauté together bacon and olive oil in deep kettle. Add onion, pepper, chili powder, garlic, oregano and coriander, and brown lightly. Add vinegar, olives, avocado, tomatoes and clear stock. Simmer 20 minutes on slow fire. Makes 1 to 2 cups.

BARBECUED LAMB MARINADE

1 cup salad oil
1 cup dry white wine
15 peppercorns, crushed
1 tablespoon finely chopped mint leaves
6 cloves

1 tablespoon finely chopped parsley
1 stick cinnamon
1 twig rosemary
Salt

Mix together, blending well. Makes 1 pint.

BARBECUED POULTRY MARINADE

1 cup oil
1 teaspoon barbecue spices
½ cup white wine
1 tablespoon white vinegar

1 clove garlic, fine-chopped
10 whole peppercorns
¼ teaspoon basil
Salt to taste

Place all ingredients in a tightly sealed Mason jar and mix well. Soak pieces of poultry in this marinade for 20 minutes; then broil on charcoal. Makes 1½ cups.

WILD-GAME BARBECUE MARINADE

1 cup oil
½ cup red wine
½ onion, finely chopped
12 whole peppercorns, crushed
1 teaspoon smoked salt

2 cloves garlic, fine-chopped
¼ teaspoon oregano
¼ teaspoon basil
¼ teaspoon coriander
1 bay leaf

Shake all ingredients together in a tightly sealed Mason jar, mixing well. Soak wild game in this marinade. The size and age of game govern time required for marinating (from 20 minutes to 1½ hours), the older and larger, the longer. Makes over 1 cup.

BARBECUED RAINBOW TROUT MARINADE

½ cup olive oil
½ cup dry white wine
2 cloves garlic, fine-chopped
1 tablespoon barbecue spices
1 tablespoon salt

1 tablespoon crushed peppercorns
1 teaspoon celery salt
1 teaspoon Worcestershire sauce
1 teaspoon paprika

Mix all ingredients well. Useful also for any other fish to be barbecued. Makes 1 cup.

FISH BARBECUE MARINADE

1 cup oil
1 tablespoon barbecue spices or chili powder
1 teaspoon smoked salt (if chili powder is used)
Juice of ½ lemon

1 tablespoon fine-chopped parsley
¼ teaspoon oregano
¼ teaspoon basil
½ clove garlic
Salt to taste

Place all ingredients in quart Mason jar and shake well to blend. Makes 1 cup.

BARBECUED SHRIMP MARINADE

3 tablespoons barbecue spices
3 cloves garlic, fine-chopped
2 cups dry white wine
1 medium onion, sliced
1 medium bell pepper, sliced

1 tablespoon whole black peppercorns
1 tablespoon salt
1 cup water
1½ cups olive oil

Mix barbecue spices, garlic, wine, onion, pepper, peppercorns and salt well in large bowl. Add water and olive oil. Keep in refrigerator. Makes 1 quart.

Curing

The traditional way to make pickles is by curing in a salt and water solution until the raw cucumbers have been transformed into transparent pickles. This takes from 6 to 8 weeks. Then the "salt stock" is held until needed, after it is removed; the surplus salt in the cucumbers is withdrawn by soaking or light cooking. Next, vinegar, spices, sugar and other seasonings are added, depending on the type of pickle desired.

CUCUMBERS IN BRINE OR SALT PICKLES

Use whole cucumbers or gherkins. Wipe with clean cloth. Do not wash unless very dirty. Place in stone or glass jar. Completely cover cucumbers with cold brine strong enough to float an egg (2 cups of salt to 1 gallon water). Then cover with board or plate, held down by weight heavy enough to keep cover under brine. For each 2 gallons of cucumbers, use about 1 gallon of brine.

On following day, place 2 cups salt on the cover and allow to dissolve gradually. Do not place salt directly in brine as it may sink to bottom, resulting in too strong a brine at bottom and too weak at top.

Seven days later, place ½ cup salt on cover as before. Repeat ½ cup salt each succeeding week for 5 more weeks. Skim scum as it forms. This curing process requires 6 to 8 weeks, depending on size of cucumbers and temperature of room. Curing process is completed and cucumbers are ready for use when they contain no white spots and are an even olive-green color. If the cucumbers are kept well under the brine, and salt is added in the proportion indicated, it will not be necessary to exclude the air or seal in any manner. This is important. *One uncovered pickle may cause an entire batch to spoil.*

Also see Down Under Cucumbers in Around the World chapter.

SOAKING SALT PICKLES Brined cucumbers must be soaked to remove the excess salt before they are used for sweet or sour pickles. Soak pickles in equal parts of vinegar and water, or heat a little hotter than lukewarm in plain water, changing several times to remove excess salt.

SOUR CUCUMBER PICKLES, LONG PROCESS

After cucumbers have been brined and soaked as directed in brining instructions, use 1 gallon full-strength cider vinegar to ¾ peck (6 quarts) cucumbers. If spiced pickles are desired, a spiced vinegar should be made 3 weeks in advance.

SPICED VINEGAR Add to 1 gallon of vinegar ½ ounce (1 tablespoon) allspice, ½ ounce cloves, 1 stick cinnamon, 1 piece mace, 1 pound sugar for very sour pickle. Use 2 pounds sugar if sweeter pickle is desired. Granulated sugar is best. Tie spices loosely in clean, white muslin bag, drop in vinegar, add sugar and boil 15 minutes.

Set spiced vinegar aside for 3 weeks before removing the spice bag. After 3 weeks, remove spice bag and bring spiced vinegar to a boil.

Add cucumbers a few at a time, let boil 2 minutes. Stop cooking before cucumbers soften; remove pickles and place in sterile glass jars.

When all have been packed, bring vinegar again to a boil and pour over pickles in jars to cover completely. Seal jars with lids and leave screw bands permanently in place. Pickles should remain in spiced vinegar at least 6 weeks before using.

SOUR CUCUMBER PICKLES, SHORT PROCESS

Medium-sized cucumbers	1 cup salt
1 gallon cider vinegar	1 cup sugar
1 quart water	1 cup white mustard seed

After cucumbers have been brined and soaked as directed above, pack into sterilized jars.

Mix vinegar, water, salt, sugar and mustard seed; bring to boiling point. Pour hot mixture over cucumbers; seal at once.

SWEET CUCUMBER PICKLES, LONG PROCESS

After cucumbers have been properly brined from 6 to 8 weeks, soak in cold water overnight. Change the water twice the following morning. The cucumbers are now ready to be covered with spiced vinegar. To ½ gallon cucumbers use 1 quart of good apple cider vinegar. Add 1 cup of sugar and 2 teaspoons mixed pickling spices tied loosely in a cheesecloth bag. Bring the vinegar, sugar and spices to boil and pour over the cucumbers. Remove the spice bag to prevent discoloring the cucumbers.

On the following day pour off the vinegar, add another cup of sugar, bring to boil and pour over the cucumbers.

On the third day drain off the vinegar, add another cup of sugar, bring to boil and pour over the cucumbers. Allow the cucumbers to stand until they have a good flavor. If sweeter pickle is desired, another cup of sugar may be added. Usually 3 cups of sugar to 1 quart of vinegar will be sufficient.

For cucumber circles, the cucumbers may be cut into slices before the spiced vinegar is added.

Pack pickles into glass jars and cover with the same spiced vinegar after bringing it to boil. Seal, leaving screw bands permanently in place.

CHUNK PICKLES

25 large (about 6 pounds) cucumbers
3¼ cups salt
3 quarts water
1 quart vinegar

8 cups sugar
2 2-inch sticks cinnamon
2 blades mace
1 tablespoon whole cloves

Wash cucumbers; place in stone crock or jar; cover with cold brine made by dissolving salt in water; let stand 2 weeks.

Remove cucumbers from brine; wash; trim off stem ends; cut crosswise into 1-inch pieces. Cover with cold water; let stand overnight.

Drain; wash well. Combine remaining ingredients. Bring to boil. Pour immediately over cucumber chunks; let stand.

Repeat process 3 more mornings, reheating sirup each time.

Fourth morning, place cucumbers in jars; pour hot sirup over them; seal at once. Makes 8 pints.

NORTH CAROLINA MUSTARD PICKLE

2 ounces ground mustard
½ ounce turmeric
½ cup flour

1½ pounds brown sugar
1 cup vinegar

Rub dry items to a smooth paste with vinegar. Add ½ ounce of celery seed. Add gradually ½ gallon of vinegar. Cook until mixture thickens, stirring constantly.

This dressing may be poured over:

1 pint very small whole cucumbers which have been taken from brine and soaked overnight according to directions for soaking.
1 pint sliced brined cucumbers
1 pint small brined onions

3 sweet bell peppers, green, chopped, seed removed
3 sweet bell peppers, red, chopped, seed removed
1 pint green tomatoes, halved

Keep in large crock or jar for 6 weeks. Pack in small jars, using same dressing in which it has stood. Process packed jars 15 minutes. Makes 5 pints.

SAUERKRAUT

The Pennsylvania Dutch (German, really) are credited with introducing sauerkraut to the United States. Its health-giving properties have been recognized for 200 years. During the Civil War, in June of 1863, when the town of Chambersburg was captured by Southern troops, one of the demands made on the city fathers was for 25 barrels of sauerkraut. The local authorities thought the conquerors were joking, for in those days sauerkraut was prepared in the autumn and eaten in winter. But General Harmon of the Confederate forces explained that he was in earnest, since his men were suffering from scurvy and he knew sauerkraut was both a cure and a preventative.

The pleasant flavor and tartness of good sauerkraut adds zest to meals the year round. Sauerkraut ranks high among the list of foods valuable for vitamin C, which is necessary for healthy gums, strong teeth, and sturdy bones.

Apparently many homemakers like commercially made sauerkraut, for its production has increased tremendously in the last 25 years. At present, there are 110 kraut factories in the United States packing better than 200,000 tons of kraut, annually.

But many families enjoy good homemade sauerkraut. Here is the equipment needed:

Container for washing cabbage
Scales
Large knife for quartering cabbage
Kraut cutting board
Large enameled, stainless steel or aluminum pan
Large clean stone jars, crocks, or paraffined barrels, or quart jars. If it is necessary to paraffin the barrels, use a high-grade paraffin. Warm the container. Be sure it is thoroughly dry. Melt the paraffin and apply with a brush.
Large wooden tamper (optional)
Clean white muslin cloth or plastic cover
Round flat paraffined wooden cover or plastic bag
Weight to place on cover. Weight may be a jar filled with water.

QUANTITIES NEEDED 1 pound (2 cups) of salt for 40 to 50 pounds of cut cabbage; 45 pounds of cabbage for approximately 16 quarts of kraut (15-gallon crock).

GENERAL DIRECTIONS For making sauerkraut choose large, firm, well-ripened heads of cabbage. Let the cabbage stand at room temperature for a day to wilt. The wilting causes the leaves to become less brittle and less likely to break in cutting. Trim the outer leaves and wash the heads. With a large knife cut the heads in halves or quarters. Remove the core or cut it fine. To cut the kraut, use an ordinary kraut cutting board with blades set to cut shreds about the thickness of a dime. The setting of the blades may be varied, depending upon the individual preference for a very fine or a coarse cut.

Mix the salt and cabbage in a large enameled, stainless steel or aluminum pan and let the salted cabbage stand for 3 to 5 minutes. Then pack it in clean stone jars, crocks or paraffined barrels. With this method the shreds are less likely to break than they are when mixed with the salt and packed at once.

TO PACK IN PARAFFINED BARRELS OR STONE JARS   Packing is often the cause of unnecessary bruising and tearing of shreds and can result in a softening of the kraut. To pack the cabbage, you may prefer to use a large wooden tamper to force out the air and start the juice flowing. However, if cabbage and salt are mixed and allowed to stand in a pan a few minutes, you will have enough brine so that you can pack the cabbage by hand. Pounding is not necessary to draw the juice. Press the cabbage into the container until the juice comes to the surface.

Cover the cabbage with a clean white muslin cloth or plastic cover and then with a round paraffined cover of such size that it just fits snugly within the container. The size of the cover is very important. A plate, often used, exposes kraut and juice and allows growth of yeast and aerobic bacteria. Such organisms putrify the exposed kraut and the flavors spread throughout the barrel. Plastic covers are now commonly used for covering kraut. They should be larger than the diameter of the container. When the edges are carefully folded up along the sides of the container they form a bag. This may be filled with enough salt water to serve as a weight as well as to cover the kraut.

On top of the paraffined cover, place a weight of such size that the juice comes to the bottom of the cover, but not over it. The cloth should be moist but not covered with the juice. The weight needed to keep the juice at the proper height may vary, especially during the first few days of fermentation and with changes in temperature. Check the kraut often. If the juice level is too high, put a lighter weight on the cover, or, if there is not enough juice, use a heavier weight. For small containers, a bottle partly filled with water serves as a good weight. With this device you can pour out some of the water to lighten the weight or add water to increase it.

Room temperature of 68° to 72°F is recommended for fermenting cabbage, which is usually ready in 5 to 6 weeks. If it is kept at 75° to 85°F, fermentation will take place faster and at 85° the kraut will be ready for use in about 2 weeks.

Scum will soon form on the surface of the brine. It is important to skim it off every few days. Wash the cloth and cover or plastic bag and replace on kraut each time.

CANNING OF KRAUT, HOT PACK   If you serve kraut often and expect to use it all by the end of winter, you can store the kraut in the barrel or jar in a cold room; otherwise, kraut should be canned. Canning is simple and insures a good supply of kraut throughout the year. Since kraut requires little heating, the hot pack method is most efficient. To can kraut by this method, heat the cured kraut to between 160° and 165°F in its own juice. Add a little water; if necessary as much as $\frac{1}{3}$ water may be added to the juice if there is not enough liquid for canning. Pack in sterilized jars and seal immediately. Set the jars in a pan and cover with water at 150° to 155°F. Keep water at this temperature for 5 to 10 minutes and then remove the jars and air cool. If allowed to remain hot for a long period, the kraut softens and darkens in color. When canned and cooled properly the kraut is very much like the raw product in flavor and texture.

COLD PACK   The cold pack method is commonly used, although kraut is more successfully canned by hot pack methods. To can kraut by the cold pack method, warm the kraut to between 110° and 130°F in its own juice, pack into sterilized jars, partially seal, and process in a kettle of boiling water for 20 to 25 minutes. Remove jars, complete seal and put in a cool place so that they may cool as rapidly as possible.

QUART-JAR METHOD   After general directions above: When the cabbage and salt have been mixed and allowed to stand 3 to 5 minutes, fill quart jars so that the glass lid forces the cabbage down, leaving no air space. Partially seal jars to allow for the expansion of gases during fermentation. Fermentation starts within a day after packing, as you can usually see by the formation of gas bubbles on the surface. While high temperatures hasten fermentation, they may also cause spoilage. The best temperature for good quality kraut is 70°F or lower. During fermentation, some juice will run out of the jars. This runover is caused by the gases formed. In about a week or 10 days you may have to add more kraut to the jars. For this purpose it is well to provide an extra quart of kraut for every 4 quarts. At the end of 10 days seal the jars and allow the fermentation to continue. A month to 6 weeks or more is required for kraut to cure properly. If you are planning to use the kraut within a few weeks, it isn't necessary to process it in a boiling water bath. If you plan to store the kraut for a longer period of time, process the partially sealed jars in a boiling water bath. Process for 30 minutes. Remove jars and complete the seal.

WHAT HAPPENS IN THE CURING OF SAUERKRAUT Although many people have made kraut for years, few realize what happens in the typical curing process. When the cabbage is cut there are a great many bacteria, both desirable and undesirable, as well as yeasts and molds, on the cut shreds. The salt sprinkled upon the cabbage draws out the sugar, which is used by certain of the bacteria. They change the sugar to acids and other by-products. A typical mellowing of the cabbage takes place with these changes, resulting in the product we term sauerkraut (acid cabbage).

COMMON CAUSES OF SPOILAGE IN SAUERKRAUT

Off-flavors and off-odors develop when there is spoilage in sauerkraut. This is indicated by undesirable color, off-odors, and soft texture.

SOFT KRAUT Softness in sauerkraut may result from:
• Insufficient salt
• Too high temperatures during fermentation
• Uneven distribution of salt
• Air pockets caused by improper packing

PINK KRAUT Pink color in kraut is caused by growth of certain types of yeast on the surface of the kraut. These may grow if there is too much salt or an uneven distribution of salt, or if the kraut is improperly covered or weighted during fermentation.

ROTTED KRAUT This condition in kraut is usually found at the surface where the cabbage has not been covered sufficiently to exclude air during fermentation.

DARK KRAUT Darkness in kraut may be caused by:
• Unwashed and improperly trimmed cabbage
• Insufficient juice to cover fermenting cabbage
• Uneven distribution of salt
• Exposure to air
• High temperatures during fermentation, processing, and storage
• Long storage period

SAUERKRAUT (MEDIUM AMOUNT)

Wash, quarter, core and shred sound, hard cabbage. Weigh. Thoroughly mix ½ pound dairy or pickling salt with 20 pounds cabbage. Firmly pack into stone jar or tight keg. Cover with white cloth and dinner plate, or glass pie plate. Fill jar with water and use to hold plate under the brine, which forms as salt draws juice from cabbage. Remove scum each day. Sauerkraut is cured and ready to can in 2 to 4 weeks, depending upon the temperature at which it is kept. When properly cured, sauerkraut is yellow-white and free of white spots. Pack into hot, sterilized jars. If there is not enough juice to cover, add brine made by dissolving 2 tablespoons salt in 1 quart water. Process 30 minutes in boiling water bath.

SAUERKRAUT, FLORIDA QUICK METHOD (SMALL AMOUNT)

Select firm, crisp cabbage. Wash and shred finely. 1 pound of cabbage after shredding will pack into a pint jar. To 1 pound of cabbage add 2 teaspoons salt and mix thoroughly. Mix cabbage and salt in small amounts of 4 to 5 pounds at a time. Pack into pint jars. Place lid on, but do not seal tightly, as air must escape. Place jars in an enamel pan and store in a cool place. Fermentation will be complete in 8 to 10 days. When completed add enough brine (2 tablespoons salt to 1 quart of water) to cover kraut, wipe mouth of jar and seal. Process in boiling water bath.

Sauerkraut juice is a healthful drink and mixes well with an equal quantity of tomato juice.

LETTUCE KRAUT

Head lettuce of the Los Angeles or iceberg type may be made into kraut in the same manner as cabbage kraut. It is milder in flavor than that made from cabbage, and, if properly made, is an excellent product.

TURNIP SAUERKRAUT (SAUERRUBEN)

Select purple top variety turnips in perfect condition. Use young, sweet, juicy vegetables. Shred peeled turnips and, after thoroughly mixing with 4 ounces of salt for each 10 pounds of turnips, pack in stone crocks or glass jars. Press turnips down thoroughly and sprinkle salt liberally over them. Fit tasteless wooden or stone cover inside the jar and weight down with water-filled quart jar.

If the turnips are of prime quality, there should be enough juice to cover the top in about 24 hours. Allow to ferment at room temperature. It will take from 15 to 20 days for the fermentation to be completed. Keep product submerged in the brine to prevent discoloration and drying. Pack fermented turnips in glass jars and process as for sauerkraut.

Also see Chinese kraut in Around the World chapter.

SALTED PEPPERS

Remove stems, seeds and ribs. Pack in suitable-sized containers, nose down. Cover with brine made of 2 pounds of salt to 1 gallon of water. Suspend a cover over the peppers so as to hold them under the brine without crushing them. Continue to put salt on the cover until no more will dissolve.

If peppers are packed in containers that can be sealed, do not add extra salt. Fill jars with peppers, cover with brine and seal tightly. Before using the brine-cured peppers freshen them in cold water to remove excess salt. Peppers preserved this way may be stuffed or used for pickles.

SALTING OR BRINING
OF OTHER VEGETABLES

(Adapted from U.S. Department of Agriculture Farmers' Bulletin #1932, by John L. Etchells and Ivan D. Jones.)

Sauerkraut, made by salting cabbage, is well known and widely used. This section tells how to put up a number of other vegetables besides cabbage. It describes 4 different ways to salt or brine vegetables:

Method 1 (small amount of salt) is used for making sauerkraut from cabbage and makes a krautlike product when used with lettuce, turnips and rutabagas. Method 1 as used for snap beans and Method 3 (weak brine plus vinegar) give vegetables an acid flavor. They do not need to be soaked to remove the salt, but if the flavor is too tart, they can be rinsed well with water or soaked for a short time before being cooked.

Method 2 (large amount of salt) and Method 4 (strong brine plus vinegar) make products with a strong salty taste. Most people soak them 8 to 12 hours or overnight, using 1 gallon of clear water to a pound of vegetable, before they are cooked and served. This long soaking naturally reduces some of their food value. However, heavily salted or brined vegetables can be used without soaking if they are mixed with enough unsalted foods, such as meat, potatoes, carrots, turnips, onions or canned tomatoes, to make soup or stew. About ¼ pound of the salted vegetables should be used for each 2 quarts of soup or stew. Don't use any additional salt; the salted vegetables contain enough to flavor the whole dish.

Method 4 (strong brine plus vinegar) is particularly suitable for bulky vegetables. For example, peas or lima beans in the pods can be preserved in strong brine when a large volume of the vegetable must be processed promptly to prevent deterioration or loss.

Unless they are first blanched (scalded), some vegetables, such as mature snap beans, peas and lima beans, become firmer when salted or brined and will need to be cooked somewhat longer than fresh vegetables.

FIVE POINTS TO KEEP IN MIND

1. Follow directions exactly if you want a good product.
2. Weigh the vegetables carefully, and weigh or measure the salt as recommended in the directions.
3. Keep the vegetables covered with brine at all times to prevent the top layer from spoiling.
4. Keep the brine surface free from scum and insects.
5. Boil salted or brined vegetables vigorously for at least 15 minutes before eating or even tasting them. Throw away material that is soft or has a bad odor. This will prevent any possibility of botulinus poisoning.

EQUIPMENT AND SUPPLIES NEEDED Necessary supplies and equipment include: Containers, covers and weights; kitchen scales; measuring cup, spoons and jars (pint, quart and gallon); clean white cheesecloth; sharp knives, cabbage cutter; pure salt; and household vinegar. Glass jars are convenient to use in mixing and measuring brine as well as for containers.

For containers, use sound clean jars, crocks, wooden pails or kegs. Wooden containers should be paraffined inside, if possible, and should not be made of yellow or pitch pine because such woods give an unpleasant flavor to the vegetables.

For blanching, a 2-part steamer or a kettle and a wire basket will be needed. For processing, a large kettle that will hold several jars at a time is necessary.

LARGE CONTAINERS To hold vegetable material packed in large containers beneath the brine surface, a weighted cover is necessary. For a straight-sided container such as a crock, this may be a loose-fitting, latticed wooden cover, a plate, a small crock cover or a circular piece of board slightly smaller in diameter than the crock. It is best to use quart jars filled with water as weights.

WITH GLASS JARS Jars having small mouths and screw caps, such as 1- and 2-quart canning jars or 1-gallon mayonnaise or pickle jars, are convenient containers for salting vegetables. These jars are very well adapted for putting up small quantities of salted vegetables such as cabbage for kraut, and also are satisfactory for salting shelled peas, lima beans and cut corn. For these vegetables larger containers would not usually be practical. Not enough surplus vegetables are ordinarily available, and too much time and labor would be required to prepare enough fresh material to fill them.

In glass jars, loose covers and weights cannot be used to hold vegetables beneath the brine. Instead, after the material has been packed into the jar, 2 or 3 wooden strips, slightly longer than the width of the jar mouth, are slipped endwise into the jar and caught under the shoulder so the vegetables are held down under slight pressure.

The small wooden paddles often supplied with cups of ice cream are suitable for this use in ordinary fruit jars. Wooden tongue depressors, which can be bought at a drug store, or unpainted wooden garden labels, cut to the proper length, can also be used, particularly for jars having wider mouths.

SIZE OF CONTAINER TO USE   To have an idea of the size and number of containers needed for salting or brining the material on hand, see Table 1, which gives the estimated weights of different kinds of vegetables that can be packed in 1-quart, 1-gallon and 10-gallon containers. For other sizes the quantities will be proportionate to those given in the table.

Table 1   *Estimated weights of salted or brined vegetables that can be packed in containers of different sizes*

		Container		
Vegetable	Form	1-quart	1-gallon	10-gallon
Dry-salted by Methods 1 and 2:		Pounds	Pounds	Pounds
Cabbage	Shredded	2	8	80
Celery	Cut in pieces	1	4	40
Corn	Cut from cob	2½	10	100
Lettuce	Shredded	2	8	80
Lima beans	Shelled; blanched	2½	10	100
Okra	Cut in pieces	1	4	40
Peas	Shelled; blanched	2½	10	100
Rutabagas	Shredded	2	8	80
Snap beans	Cut; blanched	1½	6	60
Turnips	Shredded	2	8	80

Vegetable	Form	Container		
		1-quart	1-gallon	10-gallon
Brined by Methods 3 and 4:		Pounds	Pounds	Pounds
Beets	Whole	1½	6	60
Carrots	Whole	1½	6	60
Cauliflower	Cut in pieces	1	4	40
Cauliflower	Whole	—	—	30
Greens	Not blanched	½	2	20
Lima beans	In the pods	—	3	30
Okra	Whole	¾	3	30
Onions	Whole	1	4	40
Peas	In the pods	—	3	30
Peppers	Halved	1	4	40
Rutabagas	Sliced or diced	1½	6	60
Snap beans	Whole; blanched	¾	3	30
Turnips	Sliced or diced	1½	6	60

DRY-SALTING
METHOD 1

Small amount of salt (2½ to 5 per cent by weight)
Cabbage
Lettuce
Rutabagas
Snap beans (extra tender)
Turnips

PREPARING THE VEGETABLES Select fresh, sound, high-quality materials.
Trim off outside leaves of cabbage and lettuce heads. Wash and halve or quarter. Remove cores of cabbage.

Wash and trim root vegetables.

Wash snap beans thoroughly. Then blanch (scald) them for about 5 minutes in boiling water or, preferably, in live steam and cool promptly. Cut off ends and cut beans into short lengths.

SALTING PROCEDURE

1. Cabbage, lettuce, turnips and rutabagas: Shred with a sharp knife or cutter and pack in container such as crocks, kegs or wooden pails. Distribute the salt evenly over the vegetable while filling the container, allowing ¼ pound (4 ounces) of salt for each 10 pounds of vegetable. For volumes of the different grades of salt required for 10 pounds and other

quantities of vegetables when using 2½ per cent and larger proportions of salt, see Table 3. Pack firmly so that brine forms.

Snap beans (blanched): Use ½ pound (8 ounces) of salt to each 10 pounds of material and distribute evenly while packing firmly. Add 8 fluid ounces of vinegar for each 10 pounds of vegetable, or about 1½ tablespoons of vinegar for each pound, and distribute it evenly with the salt.

Small quantities of vegetables may be packed in glass jars of 1-gallon or smaller size, fitted with screw-type lids other than zinc. (Zinc may be affected by the salt and acid and make the product poisonous.) Mix the vegetables and salt in a large bowl or pan and pack in the small containers. For holding the vegetable under the brine in jars having small mouths, use wooden strips inserted inside the neck under the shoulder.

2. After the salt-vegetable mixture has been packed in large containers, put several layers of clean white cheesecloth on top of the material and tuck it inside, around the edge. On the cloth place a suitable cover and weight it down. Water drawn from the vegetable by the salt will form a brine that will rise above the cover. If the brine level is low in any container after it is packed, add 2½ per cent brine for cabbage, lettuce, turnips and rutabagas and 5 per cent brine for snap beans. The brine should cover the vegetable material. The amounts of salt and water to use in making these brines are given in Table 4.

3. Keep the packed containers at a temperature of about 70°F. An acid fermentation will start shortly after the material is salted and continue for about 2 weeks.

4. A shallow pan or folded newspapers should be put under glass jars of salted vegetables to catch the brine that usually runs over when gas is formed during fermentation. Near the end of the fermentation (in about 10 days) the brine level in the jars will drop noticeably (1 to 2 inches) and may go below the top of the packed material. If this occurs, add new 2½ per cent brine—5 per cent brine for beans—promptly; otherwise, the exposed material may spoil. When the brine level drops and bubbling stops, it is likely that the fermentation is about over.

REMOVING SCUM A white scum will appear on the brine surface within a few days. *Remove this scum repeatedly.* If allowed to remain and grow, it will not only use up the acid produced by the fermentation but will give off a bad odor and may spoil the food.

To remove scum, take the weight and cover off the large containers, being careful to avoid mixing the scum with the brine. Lift the cloth carefully so that the scum is held on it and the brine surface is left clean.

Wash cloth, cover and weight, and replace them. If scum develops very rapidly, it should be removed every other day.

If scum forms on the brine surface of small containers, such as glass jars, skim it off with a spoon. If the brine level is low and the scum cannot be reached readily, add brine of the correct strength (2½ or 5 per cent); the scum will float on the surface and can be easily removed.

REPACKING AND HEAT TREATING   It is desirable, after a fermentation period of about 10 days, to repack material that was salted in large open containers into smaller containers that can be sealed and will not require further frequent attention. Pack clean glass jars tightly with the vegetables, and fill to within ½ inch of the top with brine from the original container. If there is not enough of this brine, make more by adding 1 ounce of salt to a quart of water.

The jars should then be heat-processed in a boiling water bath. If using jars having 2-piece all-metal tops, seal tightly before placing them in the water bath; the metal bands should not be disturbed afterward. First tighten tops having screw caps and rubber rings, then turn back ¼ turn. Put the jars in a kettle of hot water. The water should be deep enough to cover the tops. Heat the water to a boil and keep it boiling. Leave pint jars in the bath for 25 minutes and quart jars for 30 minutes after boiling begins; then remove the jars and tighten the caps of those having rubber rings.

For vegetables packed originally in small jars, remove the cheesecloth and wooden crosspieces at the end of a 10-day period. Press the food down firmly with a spoon to release trapped gas bubbles. Then add brine, made as described, to within ½ inch of the top and put on the lids. Process the jars in a boiling water bath without repacking.

This processing is not intended to take the place of cooking. Its purpose is to prevent undesirable changes in the food during storage at ordinary room temperatures.

METHOD 2

Large amount of salt (up to 20 per cent by weight)
  Celery
  Corn
  Lima beans (shelled)
  Okra (cut)
  Peas (shelled)

PREPARING THE VEGETABLES   Select fresh, tender material carefully graded for high quality.

Boil corn 10 minutes to set the milk; then cut from the cob, but not too close.

Shell lima beans and peas.

Wash celery and okra thoroughly, and cut crosswise into short lengths.

For best results, peas, lima beans and celery should be blanched (scalded) in boiling water or preferably in steam for about 5 minutes before being salted.

SALTING PROCEDURE

1. Pack vegetables firmly into the containers, mixing evenly 1 pound of salt for each 5 pounds of vegetables.

2. Put several layers of clean white cheesecloth and a weighted cover on top of the mixture. If the brine formed from salt and vegetable juice is not enough to rise an inch or more above the vegetables after weighting, add strong brine (2¼ pounds salt per gallon of water) until it covers them.

When packing directly into small jars place several layers of cheesecloth on top of the salted material, and hold it under the brine with wooden crosspieces. Add brine if necessary. Screw the caps on loosely so that the gas which will form can escape.

3. For a better product, salted vegetables may be repacked in smaller containers that can be sealed for prolonged storage. This transfer cannot be made until fermentation, indicated by bubbling, has stopped. The bubbling may continue for a month. Look at the containers from time to time, and when bubbling has stopped, repack the material in small jars, fill up with strong brine, and seal.

Material that was packed originally in small jars does not need repacking. When bubbling has stopped, remove cheesecloth and crosspieces, fill jars to the top with strong brine, and seal.

Processing in a boiling water bath is not necessary in this method.

BRINING

METHOD 3

Weak brine (5 per cent) plus vinegar

Snap beans	Mustard greens
Beets	Turnip greens
Beet tops	Kale
Carrots	Rutabagas (sliced or diced)
Cauliflower (cut)	Turnips (sliced or diced)

PREPARING THE VEGETABLES Select fresh, tender, high-quality materials. In general, prepare the vegetables as for table use by trimming and cleaning. Wash greens several times to remove all traces of grit.

The snap beans should be washed thoroughly and may be left whole or cut in pieces. They should be blanched 5 minutes in boiling water, or preferably in steam, and cooled promptly. The best beans for brining are the tender varieties used for canning.

Wash carrots and beets, but do not slice them. Cut cauliflower into pieces or break into flowerets.

BRINING PROCEDURE

1. Pack the vegetable material firmly in clean containers until they are nearly full. Place on top of the vegetables several layers of clean white cheesecloth and tuck it in around the edge. On the cloth place a weighted cover.

2. Prepare enough 5 per cent brine to cover the vegetable material. The amount needed will be about half the volume of the vegetables packed. In each gallon of water dissolve ½ pound of salt (about ¾ cup of granulated, or a full cup of flake or medium) and 1 cup of vinegar (strength 4 to 5 per cent acetic acid).

3. Pour the brine over the vegetables until it comes up over the weighted cover. Keep containers in a cool place.

REMOVING SCUM Remove the scum that appears on the brine surface continuously, following the directions given in Method 1.

REPACKING AND HEAT TREATING After a fermentation period of about 10 days, repack the fermented material in smaller containers for processing in a boiling water bath. Pack clean screw-topped glass jars tightly with the vegetables and fill to within ½ inch of the top with brine from the original container; if necessary, make more 5 per cent brine, as described. Follow directions for processing given for Method 1.

METHOD 4

Strong brine (15 per cent) plus vinegar

Cauliflower (whole)
Lima beans (in pods)
Okra (whole)
Onion (preferably silver-skin type)
Peas (in pods)
Peppers

PREPARING THE VEGETABLES Select fresh, tender material of high quality and wash carefully.

Overmature peas, lima beans and okra will not make satisfactory brined products.

Remove any dry skin from onions.

Cut off and discard stalk and outer leaves of cauliflower. When brining cauliflower in glass jars, cut it into small pieces.

Cut peppers in half and remove core and seeds.

Use okra whole.

BRINING PROCEDURE

1. Pack the vegetables firmly in containers. *Keep a record of the weight of the material packed.* Put on top of the vegetables several layers of clean white cheesecloth and a weighted, solid cover (do not use slats or a latticed cover in this method).

2. Prepare a strong brine as follows: Dissolve 1½ pounds of granulated salt (2½ cups of granulated or 3¾ cups of flake or medium) in 1 gallon of water to which has been added 1 cup of vinegar. The amount of brine needed will be about half the volume of the vegetables packed.

3. Pour the brine over the vegetables until it comes up about 2 or 3 inches over the weighted cover. Be sure that enough weight has been put on to keep the vegetables under the brine.

4. In order to maintain the brine strength, extra salt must be placed on the cover; otherwise the brine will become diluted as juice is extracted from the vegetables. For every 10 pounds of vegetable packed and brined, weigh out 2 pounds of salt (or measure out 3 cups of granulated or 4½ cups of flake or medium salt). Place the salt carefully on the cover, under the surface of the brine, where it will dissolve gradually. Don't let salt slip off the edge, because this would make the brine too strong at the bottom.

5. Store the brined vegetables in a cool place, and keep the brine level above the cover with weights, or by adding more 15 per cent brine when necessary.

6. Keep the brine free from insects and scum.

REPACKING Fermentation may cause bubbling for several weeks. After this has stopped, repack the brined vegetables in small glass containers with tight-fitting caps (not zinc). Before repacking lima beans or peas, remove them from the pods. Pack the material firmly in the jars and fill them to the top with brine from the original container. If there is not enough of this brine, make up some new 15 per cent brine, as described. After filling the jars, put on and tighten the tops. Rubber rings or rubberized types of seals are not necessary. It is not necessary to heat the jars in a water bath.

SALT TABLES

The relation between weight of salt (pound or ounce) and volume of salt in common household measures (cup, tablespoon or teaspoon) is shown in Table 2. In this table, as elsewhere in this book, the volume measurements are in level teaspoons, tablespoons and cups.

Tables 3 and 4 summarize the information given about the amounts of salt needed for preserving vegetables by the 4 methods described.

Table 2 *Equivalent weights and volumes of different grades of salt used in dry-salting and brining*

Amount of salt recommended	Equivalent in granulated salt	Equivalent in flake (dairy) or medium salt
Weight:		
1 ounce	1 tablespoon & 1 teaspoon	2 tablespoons & 1½ teaspoons
½ pound	¾ cup	1 cup & 2 tablespoons
1 pound	1½ cups	2¼ cups
Measure:		
½ cup	5 ounces	3½ ounces
1 cup	10 ounces	7 ounces

RECIPE TO PRESERVE A HUSBAND

In choosing a husband, women should first be careful of their selection. Do not choose too young or too green and take only such as have been raised in a good, moral atmosphere.

When you have decided on selection, turn your thoughts to domestic use. Some wives insist on keeping husbands in a pickle, while others are constantly getting them in hot water. This only makes them sour, hard and sometimes bitter.

Even the poorest varieties can be made sweet, tender and good by garnishing them with patience, spicing them with smiles and flavoring them with kisses.

For a finished product, husbands should be wrapped in a mantle of kindness, kept warm with the fire of devotion and served with peaches and cream.

Husbands prepared this way will keep for years.

Table 3   *Amounts of salt to add to 1 pound and 10 pounds of fresh vegetables in dry-salting*

Per cent salt by weight	Volume of salt required for 1 pound fresh material		Salt required for 10 pounds of fresh material		
				On a volume basis	
	Granulated salt	Medium or flake (dairy) salt	On a weight basis	Granulated salt	Medium or flake (dairy) salt
2½	2 teaspoons	1 tablespoon	4 ounces	Scant ½ cup	¾ cup
5	4 teaspoons	2 tablespoons	8 ounces	Slightly over ¾ cup	Slightly over 1 cup
10	2 tablespoons & 2 teaspoons	4 tablespoons	1 pound	1½ cups	2¼ cups
15	4 tablespoons	6 tablespoons	1½ pounds	2½ cups	3¾ cups
20	5 tablespoons & 1 teaspoon	½ cup	2 pounds	3 cups	4½ cups

Table 4   *Amounts of salt and water required to prepare brines of different strengths*

Strength of brine per cent	Amount of salt to water				
	Ounces per quart	Ounces per gallon	Pounds per gallon	Cups of salt per gallon	
				Granulated	Flake or medium
1	½	1¾	¹⁄₁₀	⅙	¼
2½	1	3½	¼	⅓	½
5	1¾	7½	½	¾	1
10	4	16	1	1½	2¼
15	6¼	25	1½	2½	3¾
20	9	36	2¼	3½	5¼
26	12	48	3	4¾	7

SALT-BRINED BEANS

Thick, meaty, but tender green beans are best for pickling. Wash them thoroughly and cut fine, lengthwise. Mix thoroughly with salt, using 2½ tablespoons salt for 4 pounds beans. Pack tightly into quart jars, fill with clear water, and cover loosely with lids. Set in a cool, dark place (70° or lower) to ferment. When fermentation is complete, in 2 weeks or less, no more bubbles come off and the beans have a pickled aroma. At this point, wipe jars, screw lids down, and store in a cool, dark place. 4 pounds beans make about 3 quarts.

To serve, lift beans out of jar, discarding any sediment that has collected. Cook till tender, and flavor, to serve as a vegetable; or use the cooked beans in a vegetable salad, combining them with raw onions or beets or other vegetables.

Try them alone, cold, with French dressing.

OLIVE PLUMS

Green plums
Baking soda
Brine

Gather green plums before they begin to change color. Wash them and put them into a weak (1 cup salt to 12 pints water) brine for 24 hours. Drain, and put them into similar weak brine, only adding 1 teaspoonful of baking soda for each gallon of water. Bring to boil. Plums will turn to olive-green color. Pack at once in hot, sterilized jars. Fill to overflowing with boiling brine; seal at once. Let stand 8 weeks before using.

CURING OLIVES

When I lived in Laurel Canyon it was still a wild and picturesque spot, although it was about a mile or so from Hollywood Boulevard. There I had three beautiful old olive trees which not only provided gold and gray beauty all year long, but a green harvest of olives in the fall.

If you are lucky enough to have olive trees but are without facilities for pressing the fruit into oil, here is how to cure them.

Olives should mature on the tree until full size and should be harvested before they change to the dark, ripe color.

Unless you want to put them up "run-of-the-tree," grade them according to size, dropping them into buckets of water. Keep tree drops or culls separate and, after processing, give these jars to the neighbor you like least at Christmas.

Wash olives well and place in containers, stone crocks preferably, or tight wooden kegs. Fill to covering with a solution in following proportions:

1 ounce pickling salt	2 ounces soda lye
1 ounce lime	1 gallon water

Place plate or board to fit loosely over olives to hold them under. Lye-lime treatment is necessary to extract bitterness from olives. (Anyone who has tried to eat an olive from the tree can testify to his surprise at the taste.) Keep in lye-lime solution for 8 to 10 hours, stirring olives frequently.

Solution changes color of olive to yellowish green and should be allowed to penetrate flesh of olive almost to the stone. Penetration can be seen if tip of a large olive is cut off. It is marked by a dark ring in the flesh. When the ring has gone ⅔ the way to the pit, process is complete and olives must be removed at once. If lye goes to pit, olives will not be good.

Once out of lye bath, put olives in cold water for 3 or 4 hours, stirring occasionally and changing water 3 or 4 times, so that all traces of lye-lime solution are washed away. To test, slice several olives and press red litmus paper against exposed flesh. If any trace of lye remains, litmus paper will turn blue and more washing will be required.

Next, olives are to be brined in solution with the following proportions:

2 ounces pickling salt
1 gallon water

Bring brine to boil, cool and pour over olives.

Next day, drain olives and cover with new boiled and cooled brine solution, but made with 4 ounces of salt to the gallon.

Following day, drain olives and cover again with boiled and cooled brine made of 8 ounces of salt to 1 gallon of water. Let the crock rest in a cool place for 24 hours.

Now you have cured olives. Pack them in jars, fill to overflowing with the brine and adjust jar lids. Process in a simmering water bath (180°F) for 30 minutes. Tighten jars if necessary and store in cool, dark place.

However, if you want a fermented olive, with the flesh yellowish green clear through, go back in the above recipe to where the olives were free of the lye solution.

FERMENTED OLIVES Put lye-free olives back in crock, cover with brine made in proportions of 1 pound of salt to 9 pints of water ("brine to float an egg"), keep submerged with lid or plate and weight; skim scum as it appears; and allow to ferment for 3 or 4 weeks.

Although the above appears to be long drawn out, here is an even more thorough set of directions, as issued by the College of Agriculture, University of California.

PREPARATION OF RIPE OLIVES

1. *The fruit:* Use firm, freshly picked olives ranging from the straw-yellow to light pink stage of maturity. Black olives are too ripe and will usually give a soft pickled product. The Mission and Manzanillo varieties are best for the beginner; the Ascolano and Sevillano are very difficult to pickle successfully by the ripe process.

2. *Container:* To hold the olives during pickling, use a stoneware crock (jar) or a wooden tub. A barrel cut in half makes 2 suitable pickling tubs. Never use a zinc bucket or other metal container.

3. *First lye:* Prepare a lye solution containing 2 ounces of ordinary flake or granular lye (caustic soda) to each gallon of water. A convenient method of preparing the solution is to note the contents of the can (usually 12 ounces) and add the contents to the required amount of water. When the lye is well dissolved in the required amount of water, add enough to the olives to cover them well.

Caution: Lye is corrosive to skin and clothes. Have at hand a cup of vinegar and rinse hands in it to neutralize any lye present on the skin, then rinse in water. Dab vinegar on any lye solution that may get on the clothes.

Stir once an hour and occasionally cut several olives with a knife and note the penetration of lye; as the lye enters the olive the flesh is turned to ·a yellowish color.

Allow the lye to remain until the skins of all the olives are well penetrated, and the lye has entered the flesh to a depth of about 1/32 inch or less. The time required varies with the temperature, the variety and the lye concentration. Usually 4 to 5 hours is required. The purpose of the first lye is to facilitate the darkening of the olives; if the lye penetrates too deeply the color will fail to darken properly.

When the desired penetration has been attained, remove and discard the lye solution.

4. *Darkening of color:* Rinse the olives once with water; discard the water and leave the olives exposed to the air to darken. Twice a day for

4 days cover the olives with water, stir, discard the water and leave exposed to air.

5. *Second lye:* Prepare a new lye solution of 1 ounce of lye per gallon. Cover the olives with it and allow to penetrate about halfway to the pit. This will require about 3 or 4 hours. Remove the lye and discard it. This lye is also to facilitate the darkening.

6. *Second exposure:* Rinse once in water and expose to the air for 24 hours, stirring occasionally during this exposure.

7. *Third lye:* Prepare another lye solution of 1 ounce of lye per gallon. Place on the olives and allow to penetrate to the pit—about 4 to 6 hours is usually required. The purpose of this lye is to destroy the natural olive bitterness and must be allowed to completely reach the pit. This is judged by cutting several olives with a knife and noting depth of penetration. If the lye fails to reach the pits in 15 hours, prepare and apply a fresh lye of ¾ ounce of lye per gallon until it reaches the pits.

8. *Third exposure:* Rinse olives in water and expose 24 hours to darken the color still further.

9. *Washing:* Cover olives with water. Change the water twice a day for a week. The olives should now be free of the taste of lye. Absence of lye or its presence in the olives is easily detected by taste; the amount present is harmless to the taster.

10. *Brining:* Prepare a brine of about ¼ pound of salt per gallon (that is, 4 ounces per gallon or 1 pound to 4 gallons of water). Cover the olives with this brine for 2 days. They are then ready to serve.

11. *Storage:* To keep the olives for several weeks replace this brine after 1 week with a fresh brine of 8 ounces of salt to the gallon of water (1 pound to 2 gallons of water). Store in this brine 1 week. Replace it with a fresh brine of 12 ounces of salt to the gallon (3 pounds of salt to 4 gallons of water). Change this brine once every 3 weeks until the olives are consumed, each time preparing a fresh brine of 3 pounds of salt to 4 gallons of water (or ¾ pound to the gallon).

The olives will shrivel somewhat in this brine and are too salty to eat. Therefore, soak them in water overnight before serving. A weaker brine than the above is extremely dangerous, even if the olives are stored in open containers. Take no changes—use the brine as directed.

Home canning of olives is difficult and is not recommended.

CALIFORNIA "GREEN-RIPE" OLIVE PROCESS If a dark color is not considered essential, the olives can be pickled in a simpler manner than that given above.

Prepare a lye solution of 2 to 2½ ounces of lye per gallon of water.

Place it on the olives and allow it to go completely to the pits; this will usually take 8 to 12 hours. Discard the lye. Cover the olives with water. Change it 3 times a day until the olives are free from lye. Preserve in brine as directed in the first recipe.

The ripe olives pickled in this way are usually of better flavor than those pickled by the first recipe but are uneven and light in color, usually yellow to gray. Green olives become olive-green in color and are excellent prepared this way.

PREPARATION OF SPANISH PROCESS GREEN OLIVES   Green olives are pickled by fermentation in brine in much the same manner as cucumber pickles.

1. Use olives that have reached full size but which are still green to straw yellow in color. Sevillano and Manzanillo varieties are best. The Ascolano and Mission usually do not ferment satisfactorily on a small scale.

2. Prepare a lye solution of $2\frac{1}{2}$ ounces of lye to the gallon of water. This is equivalent to about 1 pound to 5 gallons of water. Be sure that the lye has dissolved. Stir well before using.

3. Cover the olives with this lye solution in a wooden tub or stoneware jar and allow it to stand, with occasional stirring, until the lye has penetrated halfway or $\frac{2}{3}$ way to the pit. Cut samples of the olives frequently with a knife to observe the depth of penetration of the lye. Penetration to the depth given requires ordinarily 5 to 7 hours.

4. Discard the lye. Cover the olives immediately with cold water. Pour this water off and replace it at once with fresh, cold water. Change this water 4 or 5 times a day for 2 days.

5. Place the olives in a barrel or small keg and fill the container completely with brine containing 1 pound of salt to each gallon of water. Also add $\frac{1}{2}$ pint of vinegar, about 1 pint of imported or domestic Spanish olive brine, or 1 pint of sound dill-pickle brine from a grocery, and $\frac{1}{2}$ pint of corn sirup, to each 5-gallon keg or larger container. Mix well.

6. Seal the container completely except for $\frac{1}{4}$-inch opening to allow escape of gas. When gas evolution has ceased, seal the small opening. Keep the barrel filled with brine at all times. The brine used for filling should be $7\frac{1}{2}$ per cent salt (10 ounces of salt to the gallon of water). If the barrel is stored in a warm room, the olives should be ready for consumption at the end of about 6 months. When the barrel is opened, add to each 5 gallons of olives about 1 quart of vinegar. Transfer the olives and brine to glass-top jars and seal. Do not use zinc-top jars. No further treatment is necessary.

PREPARATION OF GREEK PROCESS OLIVES

1. Use black ripe olives of Mission or Manzanillo varieties. The Sevillano and Ascolano varieties are not very suitable because they are deficient in oil. Use ¾- or ½-ground rock salt of good quality; this is a medium-coarse crushed salt; ice cream salt will do.

2. For containers use lug boxes, either 50- or 25-pound size, lined with ordinary burlap. Mix 5 pounds of the salt with each 10 pounds of olives placed in box.

3. Stir well once a week; this can be done by pouring the olives from one box to another. Brine forms and is allowed to seep away.

4. After about 6 weeks the olives should be ready to use. They will be somewhat shriveled and will have lost most of their bitterness.

To keep them, add a few handfuls of the coarse crushed salt, a little olive oil to coat them, and stir the olives occasionally. They should be eaten before they have completely dried or molded.

Quick Process Pickle Recipes

Quick pickles are made from fruits or vegetables which have not been through a brining process. Some of the recipes call for an overnight soaking in salt water, often called an overnight brining. The ingredients are sometimes soaked in brine water to give them crisp texture. Some are soaked a few hours in ice water and are given the name of ice-water pickles. Sour and sweet cucumber and mixed pickles made the quick way will not produce as high-quality a product as the cured product gives. Fruit pickles and certain relishes are rarely made from brined products, hence they belong to the quick pickle process.

QUICK PICKLING VINEGAR   The quick pickling method uses distilled white vinegar both as a flavoring and as a preservative. This short-cut method does away with much that is tedious and time-consuming in traditional recipes. Instead, fresh vegetables and fruits are cleaned and cut; then, without brining, they're popped into the preserving kettle, where they simmer in less liquid and for a shorter time than pickles ever did before. Look at the label for an acidity of 5 per cent. This is a concentration strong enough to make a good preservative, yet delicate enough not to override other flavors.

DELUXE CUCUMBER PICKLES

6 quarts sliced cucumbers	6 cups sugar
6 medium-sized onions, sliced	1/4 teaspoon cayenne pepper
1 cup salt	1 package mustard seed
6 cups vinegar	1 tablespoon celery seed

Combine cucumbers, onions and salt and allow to stand 3 hours. Drain well.

Make sirup by boiling vinegar, sugar, and spices 5 minutes. Add drained cucumber and onion slices. Heat to simmering. Do not boil. Pack hot in sterilized jars. Seal. Yield: about 10 pints.

QUICK CUCUMBER PICKLES

4 quarts small cucumbers
    (2- to 2½-inch)
½ cup salt
4 quarts water
4 teaspoons whole mixed
    pickling spice

1 pint water
2 pints vinegar
3 cups sugar

Wash and rinse cucumbers. Let soak in brine made of the salt and water for 10 to 12 hours. Rinse in 2 changes of fresh water.

Put spices into cheesecloth bag. Place cucumbers and spice bag in solution made of remaining ingredients and cook at slow boil for 10 minutes. Remove spice bag. Pack cucumbers into jars and fill with hot pickle solution. Seal at once. Makes 4 quarts.

CRISP LITTLE CUCUMBERS

8 quarts small cucumbers
1 cup sugar
1 cup salt
½ cup ground or prepared
    horse-radish

1 tablespoon dry mustard
1 gallon cider vinegar

Wash and dry cucumbers. Blend together remaining ingredients, mixing thoroughly. Pack cucumbers in sterilized jars; pour liquid over, filling to very top; seal. Should be ready in 3 weeks. Makes 8 quarts.

OLD VERMONT SWEET CUCUMBER PICKLES

Large cucumbers
Salt
Vinegar

Maple sirup, dark
Stick cinnamon
Cloves

Peel cucumbers, cut in quarters and remove seeds. Cover with salt water and let stand overnight.

Drain and cover with fresh water to which enough vinegar is added to make it taste a little sour. Cook until the cucumbers are tender. Drain.

Make a pickling sirup, to taste, of vinegar, dark maple sirup, stick cinnamon, and cloves. Boil this together until it has developed the taste desired. Then put the drained cucumbers into the sirup and heat to boiling point. Remove the cucumbers and pack them in jars. Continue cooking the sirup until desired thickness is reached, then pour over cucumbers, filling jars to the top. Seal. On standing, the cucumber takes up the sweetness of the surrounding sirup.

Below is a quick way to pickle cucumber slices, from Alabama's State Extension Service.

FRESH SOUR CUCUMBER SLICES

Select medium-sized cucumbers. Peel and slice thin. Sprinkle each gallon of slices with 1 cup of salt. Let stand for 12 hours. Drain out the salt water, drop the slices into glass jars, cover with pure, cold cider vinegar, and seal.

BASIC SPICED VINEGAR

This advice comes from the state of Washington.

This sirup is basic for quick pickles. By varying the amount of sugar you can make either sour or sweet pickles. You can add different spices and herbs to suit your taste. You'll use this sirup to make quick cucumber pickles, pickled vegetables, and fruits. For fruit pickles you will use the sweet spice vinegar.

2 quarts vinegar
Salt to taste
Spice bag:
   1½ teaspoons allspice
   1½ teaspoons cloves
   ½ stick cinnamon
   ½ piece mace

(Other spices or herbs which may be used: mustard seed, turmeric, garlic, ginger, celery seed, horse-radish, cassia buds, to taste.)
Sugar: 1 cup for sour pickles, 2 cups for medium pickles, 4 to 6 cups for sweet pickles.

Boil the sugar, vinegar and spices for 15 minutes. Cool, cover and set aside for 2 weeks or more before removing spice bag. Use an earthenware or glass jar for holding the product. Spiced vinegar that is used soon after making needs more spice.

Dill Pickles

QUICK DILLS

4 pounds 4-inch cucumbers
(1 gallon)
6 tablespoons salt
3 cups vinegar

3 cups water
6 heads dill or ¾ cup seed
1 teaspoon peppercorns
Garlic (optional)

Wash and cut cucumbers in half, lengthwise.

Combine salt, vinegar and water and bring to a boil.

Pack cucumbers into hot jars. Distribute dill and peppercorns, and garlic, if desired, among jars. Pour in boiling pickle solution, adjust lids. Process in boiling water bath for 10 minutes. Store in cool, dark storeroom. Makes 3 quarts, or about 7 pints.

If you like a sweet dill pickle, use basic spiced vinegar.

FRESH-PACK DILL PICKLES

This formula comes from Gladys Kimbrough, consultant to Ball Brothers, the Muncie, Indiana, jar manufacturer.

17–18 pounds 3- to 5-inch pickling
cucumbers
2¼ cups pure granulated salt
2 gallons cool water
6 cups vinegar
9 cups water
¼ cup sugar

2 tablespoons mixed pickling
spices
⅓ cup mustard seed
7 cloves garlic (optional)
21 heads of dill (green or dry) or
1 cup dill seed
7 small pods hot pepper

Wash thoroughly, rinse and drain cucumbers. Cover with brine made of 1½ cups salt and 2 gallons cool water and let stand overnight. Rinse and drain cucumbers.

Mix vinegar, 9 cups water, remaining salt, sugar, mixed spices (tied in cloth bag), and heat to boil. Keep hot.

Pack cucumbers to within ½ inch of top of quart fruit jars. Put 2 teaspoons mustard seed, 1 clove garlic, 3 heads of dill or 1 generous tablespoon dill seed and 1 pod of pepper in each jar. Cover cucumbers with the hot pickling liquid. Put lid on jar; screw band tight. Process 20 minutes in boiling water bath. Makes 7 quarts.

TO PICKLE CUCUMBERS IN DILL
(Seventeenth-century recipe)

Gather the tops of the ripest dill and cover the bottom of the vessel, and lay a layer of Cucumbers, and another of Dill until you have filled the vessel within a handful of the top.

Then take as much water as you think will fill the vessel, and mix it with salt and a quarter of a pound of allom to a gallon of water and poure it on them and press them down with a stone on them and keep them covered close. For that use I think the water will be best boyl'd and cold, which will keep longer sweet, or if you like not this pickle, doe it with water, salt and white wine vinegar, or (if you please) pour the water with salt upon them scalding hot which will make them ready to use sooner.

DILL PICKLES, LONG METHOD

35 to 40 cucumbers (3- to 4-inch)	1½ cups salt
Dill, green or dry	2 cups vinegar
3 tablespoons mixed spices	2 gallons hot water

Wash and dry cucumbers. Put a layer of dill and ½ the spices in a stone jar. Add cucumbers. Put a layer of dill and the remaining spices on top of the cucumbers.

Add the salt and vinegar to the hot water. Stir until salt dissolves. Cool brine. Pour over cucumbers. Cover with dinner plate or glass pie plate. Fill jar with water and use it to hold plate below brine. Keep at even temperature (68° to 72°F) 2 to 4 weeks. Remove scum each day.

The pickles are ready for packing in jars when well flavored and of even color throughout. There should be no white spots. Pack the pickles into hot jars. Make new brine, or strain brine in which pickles were cured. Boil 5 minutes. Pour over pickles. Process pints and quarts for 10 minutes in boiling water bath.

A THOUGHT FOR TOMORROW

"Authors of imaginative fiction sometimes advance the idea that super-health in the future will be accomplished by eating nothing more than nutritive essences concentrated into a capsule. For health, the digestive organs need the nutritive elements plus the right kind of bulk necessary for normal elimination. The celluloses and hemicelluloses in pickles contribute to dietary bulk requirements and aid elimination."

—Pickle Packers Association

DILL PICKLES, SHORT METHOD

35 to 40 cucumbers (3- to 4-inch)
3 tablespoons mixed spices
¾ cup sugar
½ cup salt

4 cups vinegar
4 cups water
Dill, green or dry

Wash, dry and cut cucumbers into halves, lengthwise. Add spices (tied in bag), sugar, salt, vinegar, to water. Simmer 15 minutes.

Put head of dill into each hot, sterilized jar. Pack pickles. Heat brine to boil. Pour over pickles. Cover pickles with dill. Process pints and quarts 15 minutes in boiling water bath.

DILL PICKLES—KOSHER TYPE

Follow recipe for long or short method dill pickles. Add 1 clove garlic, 1 bay leaf, ½ teaspoon mustard seed, 1 piece red pepper to each jar.

In Pittsburgh, my family made pickles before H. J. Heinz did, but only for home consumption. I had 5 aunts and their homemade dill pickles were the pride of their families. However, they never agreed on the methodology of pickle making, although they followed the same basic steps. But their refinements and variations were as individual as they were in other ways.

AUNT ANNIE'S DILL PICKLES

3 sprays dill
12 young cucumbers (4 to 5 inches)
1 quart water

½ cup salt
2 cups vinegar
1 teaspoon sugar
1 pod hot pepper

Put ½ of a dill spray into bottom of each of 3 sterilized quart jars. Scrub cucumbers and place four in each jar.

Dissolve salt and sugar in water and vinegar.

Divide pepper pod among 3 jars, top with remaining ½ sprays of dill and fill jars with the brine. Seal and store in cool place for about 4 weeks, to ripen. Makes 3 quarts.

AUNT MARY'S DILL PICKLES

3 quarts small uniform-sized cucumbers
6 grape leaves
6 slices peeled horse-radish root

6 sprays dill
3 pints vinegar
3 pints water
½ cup salt

Wash cucumbers well. Into bottom of 3 sterilized quart jars place 1 grape leaf, 1 slice horse-radish and 1 spray of dill.

Pack cucumbers into jars as tightly as possible; add another spray of dill, slice of horse-radish root and 1 grape leaf to each jar. Combine vinegar, water and salt. Pour into jars to cover cucumbers.

Cover jars with lids only half closed. Store in warm place 2 to 3 weeks. Add new brine (vinegar, water and salt mixture) when necessary, to keep cucumbers covered.

Remove scum as soon as it forms. When gas ceases forming (in 2 to 3 weeks), tighten lids and seal. Makes 3 to 4 quarts.

AUNT RACHEL'S DILL PICKLES

Wash 20 to 25 medium cucumbers. Let stand in cold water overnight. Drain. Pack in sterilized quart jars. Add to each quart the following seasonings:

2 garlic cloves	Then heat together:
¼ dry red pepper	3 quarts water
2 whole black peppers	1 quart vinegar
Plenty of dill heads	1 cup salt

Pour hot over packed pickles in jars. Seal. Makes 6 to 8 quarts, depending on size of cucumbers.

AUNT ELLA'S KOSHER DILL PICKLES

½ bushel small, firm cucumbers	1 pound salt
½ bunch dried dill	5 garlic cloves, sliced
3 gallons water	½ pound mixed pickling spices

Wash cucumbers carefully and place in large stone crock. Distribute dill evenly.

Make brine of remaining items and add to cucumbers, covering them completely. Then cover cucumbers with inverted dish weighted down with quart jar of water or a clean, heavy stone. Store at room temperature. Pickles may be eaten after third or fourth day, but well-done pickles need a week or longer.

When pickles are ready, refrigerate to halt pickling process. Makes about 10 quarts.

PICKLED GREEN TOMATOES

Follow recipe for Aunt Ella's Kosher Dill Pickles, using ½ bushel small, firm green tomatoes in place of cucumbers, and omitting dill.

AUNT BETSY'S SWEET DILLS

1 gallon dill tomatoes or cucumber rings
6 garlic cloves
3 cups cider vinegar
1 cup tarragon vinegar

10 cups granulated sugar
Spice bag:
  ½ cup whole allspice
  ½ cup peppercorns or 6 hot red peppers

Cut the dill tomatoes or cucumbers into rings about ¼ inch thick and let drain well. Place in a stone jar. Peel and distribute garlic. Tie spices in a bag and boil together with the vinegar and sugar. Pour over the rings, cover and set in a cool, dry, dark place. Stir well each day for about 10 days. Pack pickles into jars, cover with liquid and seal airtight. Store in a cool, dark, dry place.

DILL GREEN TOMATOES

40 to 50 medium green tomatoes
¾ cup (2 ounces) whole mixed pickle spices
Fresh or dried dill

1 pint (2 cups) vinegar
1 pound (1½ cups) salt
2 gallons water

Wash and drain the green tomatoes. Place half of the pickle spices and a layer of dill in a 5-gallon crock or stone jar. Fill the crock with tomatoes to within 4 or 5 inches of the top. Mix the vinegar, salt and water well and pour over the vegetable. Place a layer of dill and remaining pickle spices over the top.

Cover with a heavy plate and weight it down to hold the tomatoes under the brine. Use only enough brine to cover the plate, for as the liquid is drawn from the vegetable the crock may overflow.

Keep tomatoes at room temperature (about 70°F), and each day remove scum that forms over the top. Let tomatoes ferment until well flavored with dill and clear throughout, with no white spots when cut. In about 2 to 3 weeks the pickles are ready to use. Makes 4 to 5 quarts.

To store: Pack the cured tomatoes in hot, sterile quart glass jars. Strain the brine, bring to boil and pour over tomatoes to top of jar. If desired, add ¼ cup vinegar to each quart. Seal tightly.

WITH GARLIC: Add ½ pound garlic to preceding recipe. To prepare garlic, break the clusters open and separate the cloves. Remove the thin brown skin from each garlic clove. Add a few garlic cloves with the first layer of dill and pickle spices. Fill the crock with alternate layers of tomatoes and garlic cloves to within 4 or 5 inches of the top. Continue as in preceding recipe.

DILL CUCUMBERS

In the preceding recipe, substitute 40 large or 50 medium cucumbers for the green tomatoes and proceed with the same routine. Makes about 4 quarts.

DILL TOMOLIVES

4 pounds tiny firm green tomatoes
1 clove garlic, peeled and quartered
2 sprays dill

1 pint water
½ pint vinegar
¼ cup salt

Wash tomatoes and pack, whole, in hot, sterilized quart jars. In each jar place ¼ clove garlic, and ¼ spray of dill. Boil water, vinegar and salt for 1 minute and pour over the tomatoes. Seal at once. Ready in 4 to 5 weeks. Makes 2 quarts.

These may be served instead of olives—even in martinis. Small gherkin cucumbers may be pickled this way, also.

DIFFERENT DILL TOMATOES

5 quarts small, firm green tomatoes
5 stalks celery
3 small green peppers, seeded, cored and in strips
5 large sprays dill

1 quart water
1 quart vinegar
1 cup salt
5 cloves garlic (optional)

Pack tomatoes into sterilized quart jars, scattering 1-inch sections of a stalk of celery in each. Divide strips of pepper among the jars, add sprays of dill or put them in first.

Bring water, vinegar and salt to a boil and continue boiling for 5 minutes. Pour boiling brine over the tomatoes and seal. Should be ready to eat in 4 or 5 weeks. If "kosher" flavor is desired, pack a clove of garlic in each jar. Makes 5 quarts.

Marian Tracy, in her book The Peasant Cookbook, *says, "In most countries the food in the markets is seasonal unlike our year-round plenty. Because this is so, they have their own ways of achieving a fresh or acid contrast to their daily foods. One touch, surprising to many Americans but somehow very good, is to serve large dill-flavored pickles as we would serve a salad."*

The slightly fuzzy surface of green beans holds dust and particles of soil, which harbor harmful bacteria. This is why it is necessary to be extra careful to wash thoroughly even clean-looking beans.

DILL BEANS

4 pounds fresh, pencil-slim green beans

¾ cup salt dissolved in 4 quarts cool water

5 cups 5%-acid-strength vinegar

5 cups water

3 tablespoons salt

2 tablespoons mixed pickling spice

2 or 3 cloves garlic

1 head of dill or 1½ teaspoon dill seed per jar

1 teaspoon mustard seed, per jar

1 small hot pepper or a few drops of Tabasco, per jar (optional)

Wash, rinse and drain beans. Make brine of ¾ cup salt and 4 quarts cool water. Cover beans with brine and let stand 3 or 4 hours. Rinse and drain beans. Taste beans. If too salty, rinse and drain again.

Mix vinegar, 5 cups water, 3 tablespoons salt, spice and garlic (crush garlic and tie with spices in bag). Bring mixture to boil and keep hot, but not boiling, while packing beans upright in jars with dill, mustard seed and pepper. Beans should come to within about ½ inch of top of jar. If beans are too long, trim. Reheat pickling liquid to boiling and pour over beans. Be sure beans are well covered. Put lid on jar; screw band tight. Process 10 minutes in boiling water bath. Makes 6 or 7 pints.

DILL CAULIFLOWER

Substitute 4 pounds cauliflower broken into very small flowerets for the green beans in the preceding recipe. Makes a delightful addition to the appetizer tray.

PICKLE POINTERS: *When making dills, keep these points in mind: Use right amount of salt. In a brine too weak, tomatoes spoil; in a brine too strong, they shrivel. Have enough brine to cover well and keep tomatoes pushed under, or they're likely to mold and get slippery. Remove scum from top of brine every day or pickles may spoil.*

Other Cucumbers

Ripe cucumbers are large and sound; firm, not soft.

RIPE CUCUMBER PICKLES

12 ripe cucumbers
½ cup salt
1½ cups sugar
4 tablespoons mixed pickling
    spices, in bag

½ cup water
4 cups vinegar

Wash and dry yellow-ripe cucumbers. Cut as desired, trimming off seeds. Sprinkle with salt. Let stand 18 hours. Rinse. Drain.

Add sugar, spices and water to vinegar. Heat to boiling. Add cucumbers. Simmer 15 minutes. Pack hot cucumbers into hot sterilized jars. Heat sirup to boiling point. Pour, boiling hot, over pickles; seal at once. Makes 4 to 5 pints.

SUN GLOW SPEARS

12 large ripe cucumbers
6 large onions
1 cup salt
4 quarts water
3 cups vinegar
1 cup water

2 cups sugar
2 tablespoons white mustard
    seed
2 teaspoons celery seed
2 teaspoons turmeric

Pare cucumbers, slice in quarters lengthwise, cut off seeds. Soak cucumbers and sliced onions overnight in brine made of salt and water. Drain well.

Combine remaining ingredients and cook for 5 minutes. Add vegetables; heat to boiling, place in hot, sterilized jars and fill with liquid. Makes 6 pints.

U. S. Grant, commander of the Union Army, during the campaign in Virginia frequently breakfasted on a cup of coffee and a sliced cucumber in vinegar. He won the war.

GOLDEN GLOW MIX

3 quarts ripe cucumbers
6 medium onions
1 sweet green pepper
1 hot red pepper
¼ cup salt
3½ cups sugar

1 pint vinegar
1 teaspoon turmeric
15 whole cloves
⅛ cup mustard seed (2 table-
    spoons)

Peel, seed and dice cucumbers and fine-cut onions and pepper; combine and cover with salt. Let stand for 3 hours.

Wash and drain. Add water to cover and bring to a boil. Drain again.

Combine sugar, vinegar, turmeric, cloves and mustard seed. Add vegetables and boil for 30 minutes. Pour into hot, sterilized jars and seal. Makes 4 or 5 pints.

DOWN EAST RIPE CUCUMBER PICKLE

1 peck ripe cucumbers
Salt
3 pounds brown sugar
3 pints vinegar

Spice bag:
    1 level tablespoon whole cloves
    1 3-inch stick cinnamon
    2 tablespoons mustard seed

Peel cucumbers, remove seeds and cut into 3-inch pieces. Soak in brine overnight (½ cup salt to a gallon of water).

Next morning drain and wash. Drain again.

Make a sirup of the sugar and vinegar and cook for 20 minutes. Add spice bag and cucumbers and simmer until cucumbers are clear. Don't cook too fast. While still hot, put into sterilized jars and seal. Makes 8 to 10 pints.

The proportions in the recipe below are for each quart of pickles.

ICE WATER PICKLES

1 quart cucumbers
1 small onion, sliced
1 tablespoon mustard seed
¼ cup diced celery or
    1 teaspoon celery seed

1 cup vinegar
1 tablespoon salt
1 cup sugar
¼ teaspoon curry powder

Soak cucumbers, sliced lengthwise, in ice water for 2 hours. Remove, drain and pack in hot, sterilized jars with sliced onions, mustard seed and celery seed or diced celery. Heat vinegar, to which salt, sugar and curry powder have been added, and when boiling pour over cucumbers and onions. Seal. Makes 1 quart.

ICICLE PICKLES

3 pounds 4-inch cucumbers, cut
  into eighths lengthwise
6 small onions, quartered
6 5-inch pieces celery
1 tablespoon mustard seed

1 quart distilled white vinegar
1/4 cup salt
2 1/2 cups granulated sugar
1 cup water

Wash, cut cucumbers; soak in ice water 3 hours.

Drain; pack in clean pint jars. Add 1 onion, 1 piece celery and 1/2 teaspoon mustard seed to each jar.

Combine vinegar, salt, sugar and water; bring to boil. Pour solution over cucumbers, filling jars to 1/2 inch from top. Immediately adjust covers as jar manufacturer directs. Process in boiling water bath for 10 minutes. Makes about 6 pints.

CUCUMBER OIL PICKLES

100 medium cucumbers
3 onions, peeled
2 cups salt
1 gallon cold water
4 cups sugar
2 tablespoons peppercorns

4 tablespoons mustard seed
4 tablespoons celery seed
1 cup water
4 cups vinegar
1 cup olive oil

Wash, dry and thin-slice cucumbers and onions. Dissolve salt in the cold water. Add cucumbers and onions. Let stand 12 to 18 hours.

Drain. Taste cucumbers; if too salty, rinse well in cold water.

Add sugar, spices and water to vinegar. Boil 1 minute. Add cucumbers, onions and oil. Simmer until cucumbers change color, then bring to boil. Pack, boiling, into hot, sterilized jars; seal at once. Makes 15 quarts.

OLIVETTES

This is a Vermont home recipe. These pickles keep very well.

4 quarts medium-sized cucumbers
1/2 cup salt
1 1/2 pints water
1 tablespoon celery seed
1/4 cup mustard seed

1/4 to 1 teaspoon saccharin
  (optional)
1/2 cup olive oil
4 to 6 cups vinegar

Slice cucumbers, combine with salt and water, and let stand overnight.

Drain. Combine cucumbers with seasonings and olive oil. Pack into clean jars and fill to top with cold vinegar. Seal. Makes 4 quarts.

OLIVE OIL PICKLE SLICES (uncooked)

4 quarts thin-sliced medium or small cucumbers
1 quart thin-sliced onions
Salt
1 cup olive oil

¼ cup white mustard seed
¼ cup black mustard seed
2 tablespoons celery seed
1 quart white vinegar

Place cucumbers and onions in layers in a large bowl, sprinkling each layer with salt. Let stand for 5 hours; then drain well.

Mix olive oil and seeds in a saucepan and slowly stir in vinegar.

Pack cucumbers and onions into hot, sterilized jars, to within 1 inch of top. Pour the blended vinegar-oil mixture over to fill each jar to overflowing, distributing seeds equally. Seal and store in a cool, dark place for at least 2 weeks before using. Oil rises to the top and seals the pickles. To use, shake jar to distribute the oil. After jar has been opened, it must be stored in refrigerator. Makes 4 to 5 quarts.

For a hotter version, substitute ½ teaspoon crushed hot peppers for celery seed.

FRESH CUCUMBER MUSTARD PICKLES

6 pounds pickling cucumbers (3- to 5-inch)
⅔ cup chopped green pepper
1 pound (6 small to medium) onions
1½ cups chopped celery
¼ cup prepared mustard

4⅔ cups white vinegar
½ cup salt
3½ cups granulated sugar
2 tablespoons mustard seed
½ teaspoon turmeric
½ teaspoon whole cloves

Wash vegetables thoroughly, slice cucumbers, chop pepper, peel and slice onions and chop celery.

Blend mustard with a little vinegar. Add remaining vinegar and remaining ingredients. Cover, heat to boiling. Add vegetables. Cover, heat just to boiling point; then simmer while quickly packing 1 hot, sterilized jar at a time. Fill to ⅛ inch from top. Be sure vinegar solution covers vegetables. Seal each jar at once. Makes 9 pints.

FRESH CUCUMBER MUSTARD GHERKINS

6 pounds 2-inch whole gherkins may be substituted for the sliced 3- to 5-inch cucumbers.

MIXED MUSTARD PICKLES

Instead of sliced cucumbers, peppers, celery and onions in fresh cucumber mustard pickle recipe, use:

4 pounds 3- to 4-inch pickling cucumbers, cut into chunks
2 pounds (24) small onions, quartered

2 cups ½-inch carrot pieces
2 cups cauliflower flowerets
2 cups chopped sweet red pepper
1 quart 1½-inch celery stalks

Makes 11 pints.

One of the nicest taste sensations in the entire pickle department is provided by crunchy, toothsome mustard seeds, both white and black. Here is a recipe that gives you a plenitude of mustard seed.

MUSTARD SEED PICKLE

24 4-inch cucumbers
½ cup salt
3 medium onions, thin-sliced
1 cup mustard seed

1 tablespoon celery seed
1 teaspoon fennel seed
4 cups vinegar
½ cup olive oil

Wash and thin-slice, but do not peel, the cucumbers. Sprinkle with salt and let stand 3 hours. Drain. Add onions.

Mix spices, vinegar and olive oil.

Place pickles and onions in jars, cover with liquor and seal. Let stand in cool place for 3 or 4 weeks before using. Makes 4 quarts.

BILLY MILLS

During the Golden Years of radio, from 1940 to 1945, the most popular show on the air was "Fibber McGee and Molly," and its musical director, a droll and extremely capable conductor, was Billy Mills, rotund and toothbrush-mustached. Billy, it was revealed, could do something other than wave a stick at a studio full of musicians. He could pickle.

Remembering his prize-winning recipes, the author (who had collaborated with Don Quinn, the creator of the McGee show) wrote to Billy, requesting copies. Here is his reply:

"I see no reason why they shouldn't have another 'go 'round'—they were fantastically successful for me and if you can get any mileage out of the Relish and Bread and Butter Pickles, you are most welcome. They are both easy to make and are outstanding examples of old-time goodness . . . the only thing that is imperative is that the ingredients are of top quality and the formulas are not monkeyed with. I have experimented with them but always have to return to the basic formulas and proportions, as I find they are the best.

"About the Corn Relish, I discovered the recipe written in pencil on the margin of an old cook book, yellowed with age. It was almost unintelligible. The book belonged to my mother, and the recipe was probably given to her by her mother, as it had been passed down through generations. We came from Michigan and my mother put up this relish every fall during harvest time when the ingredients were plentiful. It keeps indefinitely and does not require refrigeration, although its flavor is enhanced if it is served chilled.

"I found this recipe in 1941 and made a batch of it to see if it was as good as I had remembered it as a boy back in Michigan. It was so good that a friend persuaded me to allow it to be taken and entered in the Los Angeles County Fair at Pomona. I thought so little of the idea that I didn't want to be bothered, so my friend entered it for me.

"I was away on a cruise at the time the judging was done and on my return found that the news services, Fair officials and publicity office were frantically trying to locate me because my Corn Relish had won first prize. Because of my connection with the Fibber & Molly show, the winning of a blue ribbon had great publicity potential.

"The success of the Relish gave me an idea—why not bottle it and send it out for Christmas? It seemed an ideal way to take care of those who 'had everything' and could be given nothing they already didn't have. Don Quinn drew me a label and I bought suitable containers and went ahead with the idea.

"This went on for several years, until the list got so large that I had to discontinue making it. At regular periods up until the present, I have made new batches and entered it in the Los Angeles County Fair. It always repeats and never has failed to win."

BILLY MILLS' CORN RELISH
"You've heard how it sounds—now see how it tastes!"

5 or 6 ears fresh, green corn (about 1 quart when cut from cobs)
3 cups ripe tomatoes, without seeds
1½ cups chopped green peppers (3 peppers)
¾ cup chopped sweet red pepper (1 small)
1 cup chopped, unpeeled green cucumber

1 cup chopped onion
Pickling solution:
1 cup sugar
1 pint vinegar
1 tablespoon salt
1 teaspoon celery seed
1 teaspoon mustard seed

Wash and drain vegetables. Cut corn from cob. Scrape cobs to get all of the milk from the kernels. Combine with all of the other prepared vegetables in a large pot or preserving kettle. Mix the pickling solution separately; pour over the vegetables; simmer for 1 hour and place in jars. Seal while hot to preserve flavor. Makes about 6 pints.

"After the success of the Corn Relish at the Los Angeles County Fair and several years of using it for Christmas presents," Bill Mills continued, "I decided to look around and try to find something different, as the novelty of the Relish was starting to wear off.

"I finally found the following recipe for Bread and Butter pickles, which turned out to be a worthy successor. I entered a batch in the County Fair and it also won first prize. I had a label made and sent out Bread and Butter pickles for several years. They are easy to make and are of superior quality. I still make them occasionally."

BILLY MILLS' BREAD AND BUTTER PICKLES
"Good alone or with somebody"

7 cucumbers, sliced	Pickling solution:
5 white onions, sliced	2½ cups white vinegar
1 green pepper, chopped	2½ cups granulated sugar
1 small sweet red pepper, chopped	1 tablespoon mustard seed
¼ cup salt	1 teaspoon celery seed
Cracked ice	¾ teaspoon turmeric
	¼ teaspoon powdered cloves

Prepare vegetables, mix in salt and cracked ice, put in cool place and let stand for at least 3 hours; drain.

Mix pickling solution. Add to drained vegetables in pot or kettle. Bring mixture to boiling point, remove vegetables to jars immediately and pour hot liquid over; seal. Makes about 6 pints.

Caution: If kettle is allowed to boil, pickles will become soft. Be sure mixture is only brought to a boil.

WARNING!

There was a young lady named Perkins,
Who was hooked on the habit of gherkins.
One day on a spree,
She ate 93
And pickled her internal workin's.

In addition to the Billy Mills recipe, here are 5 variations on what is probably the most popular sliced pickle in America, today. No one, however, seems to know how bread and butter pickles got their name.

BREAD AND BUTTER PICKLES No. 1

32 4-inch cucumbers (or 52 3½-inch)	5 cups sugar
8 small onions	1½ teaspoons turmeric
1 green pepper	½ teaspoon ground cloves
1 sweet red pepper	2 teaspoons mustard seed
½ cup coarse salt	2 teaspoons celery seed
	5 cups vinegar

Slice vegetables thin, add salt, cover with cracked ice and let stand 3 hours, stirring occasionally. Drain.

Combine rest of ingredients and pour over vegetables. Bring to a boil and pack into hot, sterilized jars; seal. Makes 8 pints.

BREAD AND BUTTER PICKLES No. 2

4 quarts (about 4 pounds) sliced cucumbers	4½ cups brown sugar
4 cups sliced Bermuda onions	1½ cups water
1 cup salt	3½ cups cider vinegar
9 cups water	1 teaspoon celery seed
½ vinegar, ½ water solution	4 teaspoons mixed pickling spices

Wash the cucumbers and cut in coarse slices crosswise. Peel the onions and cut in coarse slices crosswise. Place the cucumbers in one crock and the onions in another.

Prepare a brine by dissolving the salt in the water. Pour ½ the brine over the cucumbers and ½ over the onions. Let stand overnight.

Next morning drain both the cucumbers and the onions thoroughly. Combine the 2 in a cooking pot and cover with vinegar-water solution. Heat the vegetables in this for 10 minutes, making sure that the liquid never rises above the simmering point. Vegetables then should be tender —watch that they don't become too soft. Drain vinegar solution, pack vegetables in jars, cover with hot pickling sirup made by dissolving the brown sugar in the 1½ cups water and the cider vinegar; add spices and heat just to a boil. Seal at once. Makes 4 to 5 quarts.

BREAD AND BUTTER PICKLES No. 3

8 large cucumbers
8 small onions
2 large green peppers, cored and
   seeded
1 clove garlic
½ cup salt
2 quarts cold water

1 quart ice cubes
7 cups sugar
3 cups white vinegar
2 tablespoons whole mustard seed
2 teaspoons whole celery seed
2 teaspoons ground turmeric

Slice cucumbers, onions and green peppers very thin. Place vegetables and garlic clove in crock or enamelware pan and sprinkle with the salt. Add the cold water and ice cubes and let stand 2 hours. Discard garlic and drain.

Make sirup of remaining ingredients in large preserving kettle, add vegetables and stir well. Bring just to a boil; quickly remove vegetables and pack in hot, sterilized jars. Cover with sirup to ⅛ inch from top. Work out bubbles with scalded knife and seal at once. Makes 6 pints.

These bread and butter pickles have no onions:

BREAD AND BUTTER PICKLES No. 4

6 cups sliced cucumbers
12 cups water
½ cup salt
5 cups vinegar

3 cups sugar
1 teaspoon turmeric
2 teaspoons mustard seed
1 teaspoon celery seed

Wash cucumbers and cut into thin (⅛-inch) slices. Put them into a brine made of 8 cups water and the salt. Let stand for 3 hours, then carefully drain brine from slices.

Bring 3 cups of the vinegar and 3 cups water to a boil. Put drained cucumber slices into boiling water-vinegar solution; heat to boiling and simmer 8 minutes. Drain sliced cucumbers and discard solution.

Combine sugar with remaining 2 cups of vinegar and remaining 1 cup of water; add spices, bring to boil and simmer 10 minutes. Put drained cucumber slices into vinegar sirup and let stand 2 days.

Heat pickles and liquid to boil; quickly pack into hot, sterilized jars, filling them to top, and seal immediately. Makes 4 to 5½ pints.

BREAD AND BUTTER ICICLE PICKLES

4 quarts sliced medium (4–5 inch) cucumbers
6 medium onions, sliced
½ cup salt
1 quart cracked ice

3 cups cider vinegar
1 cup sugar
2 tablespoons mustard seed
1 teaspoon turmeric
2 teaspoons celery seed

Wash cucumbers thoroughly and slice thin; do not peel. Peel onions and slice thin. Mix cucumbers, onions and salt. Add cracked ice and let stand about 3 hours, then drain thoroughly. (The ice-salt mixture helps ensure crisp pickles.)

Combine remaining ingredients and bring to boil.

Add drained cucumbers and onions to hot pickling solution. Heat just to scalding point, stirring to ensure even cooking. Avoid overcooking pickles. Pack boiling-hot pickles in clean, hot jars; cover with sirup and seal promptly. Makes about 7 pints.

CRISP LUNCH PICKLES

25 to 30 medium-sized cucumbers
8 large white onions
2 large sweet peppers
½ cup salt
5 cups cider vinegar

5 cups sugar
2 tablespoons mustard seed
1 teaspoon turmeric
½ teaspoon cloves

Wash cucumbers and slice as thin as possible. Chop onions and peppers; combine with cucumbers and salt; let stand 3 hours and drain.

Combine vinegar, sugar and spices in large preserving kettle; bring to boil. Add drained vegetables; heat thoroughly but do not boil. Pack while hot into sterilized jars and seal at once. Makes 8 or 9 quarts.

CLEOPATRA'S CUCUMBER CHIPS

24 4- to 5-inch cucumbers
½ cup salt
1 tablespoon turmeric
7 cups vinegar
5 cups water
2 cups white sugar

Spice bag:
  ¼ teaspoon cloves
  1 tablespoon white mustard
    seed
  1 piece ginger root
  2 sticks cinnamon
  2 cups brown sugar

Wash, dry and cut slender cucumbers into thin (about ⅛-inch) slices. Thoroughly mix cucumbers and salt. Let stand 3 hours. Drain.

Add turmeric and 3 cups vinegar to 4 cups water. Bring to boil. Pour over cucumbers. Let stand until cold. Drain. (Taste cucumbers; if too salty, scald again.)

Add white sugar, spices in bag, and remaining 1 cup water to remaining 4 cups vinegar. Simmer 15 minutes. Pour over cucumbers. Let stand 12 to 24 hours.

Drain sirup into kettle. Add brown sugar. Heat to boil. Add cucumbers. Simmer 10 minutes.

Pack cucumbers into hot, sterilized jars. Heat sirup to boil. Pour, boiling hot, over cucumbers; seal at once. Makes 4 quarts.

OVERNIGHT CUCUMBER SLICES

10 pounds medium-sized
  cucumbers
1 cup salt

2¼ quarts vinegar
3 cups sugar
¼ cup mixed pickle spices

Wash and cut cucumbers into slices about ¼ inch thick. Mix slices and salt. Let stand overnight. In the morning drain and press out all the juice possible. Rinse once in cold water.

Combine vinegar, sugar and spices. Boil 1 minute. Add cucumbers and simmer 5 minutes. Pack cucumbers into hot, sterile jars to within 1 inch of top. Fill jars with the hot liquid to top; seal tightly. Makes about 4 quarts.

CUCUMBER SLICES AND ONION RINGS

Mix 2 quarts peeled and sliced small white onions with cucumbers and salt. Continue as in above recipe. Makes 5 to 6 quarts.

8-DAY PICKLE CHUNKS

10 medium cucumbers
8 cups sugar
2 tablespoons mixed pickling
  spices

5 teaspoons salt
4 cups cider vinegar

Cover cucumbers with boiling water; let stand overnight; drain. Repeat for 3 more days. On 5th day, drain and slice into ½-inch pieces.

Combine remaining ingredients, bring to boil and pour over cucumbers. Let stand 2 days. Next day, bring to boil, place in hot, sterilized jars and seal. Makes 5 to 7 pints.

84-HOUR CUCUMBER CHUNKS

Cucumbers	5 cups sugar
1½ cups salt	2 tablespoons mixed spices
1 gallon water	3 cups water
9 cups vinegar	

Wash, dry and cut into 1-inch pieces enough cucumbers to make 1 gallon. Put into enamelware kettle. Dissolve salt in 1 gallon water. Pour over cucumbers. Cover with dinner plate or glass pie plate. Fill a quart jar with water and use to hold plate below brine. Let stand 36 hours.

Drain. Pour 4 cups vinegar over cucumbers; add enough water to cover. Place over heat and simmer 10 minutes. Drain; discard liquid.

Add 2 cups sugar, spices in bag, and 3 cups water to remaining 5 cups vinegar. Simmer 10 minutes. Pour over cucumbers. Let stand 24 hours.

Drain sirup into another saucepan or kettle. Add remaining sugar. Heat to boil. Pour over cucumbers. Let stand 24 hours.

Pack pickles into hot, sterilized jars. Heat sirup to boil. Pour, boiling hot, over pickles; seal at once. If not enough sirup to cover pickles, add more vinegar. Makes about 4 quarts.

GRANDMOTHER'S PICKLES

8 cups sliced unpeeled cucumbers	3 cups sugar
2 cups sliced onions	2 teaspoons celery seed
3 green peppers, chopped	2 teaspoons turmeric
⅓ cup salt	1 3-inch cinnamon stick
2 cups vinegar	

Combine vegetables with salt and let stand for 1 hour. Drain.

Boil remaining ingredients together for ½ hour. Mix with vegetables. Pack into hot, sterilized jars and seal. Makes about 4 pints.

PETER PIPER PICKLES

2 quarts thin-sliced cucumbers	1½ pints vinegar
8 large onions, sliced thin	1 cup water
2 large sweet red peppers in thin strips	4 cups brown sugar
	3 teaspoons turmeric
2 cups salt	3 teaspoons mustard seed
12 whole cloves	2 sticks cinnamon

In kettle, mix cucumbers, onion and peppers in layers, alternating with generous sprinkling of salt; salt layer on top. Let stand 3 hours. Drain.

Bring remaining ingredients to a boil; add pickles; bring to a boil again, and put in jars. Makes 5 to 6 pints.

CURRY PICKLE CHUNKS

3 pounds 4- to 5-inch pickling
    cucumbers
1⅔ cups white vinegar
1 cup granulated sugar
1½ teaspoons curry powder

2 tablespoons mustard seed
1½ teaspoons celery seed
1 cup water
2 tablespoons salt

Wash cucumbers thoroughly, cut into chunks.

Combine remaining ingredients and mix well. Heat to boil. Add cucumbers. Heat just to boiling point; then simmer while quickly packing 1 hot, sterilized jar at a time. Fill to ⅛ inch from top. Be sure vinegar solution covers vegetables. Seal each jar at once. Makes 4 pints.

Mixed Pickles

SIMPLE PICKLE MIX

4 quarts cucumbers
1 quart onions
3 cups cauliflowerets
1 green pepper
3 cloves garlic
1/3 cup salt

Ice cubes
5 cups sugar
2 tablespoons mustard seed
1/2 tablespoon celery seed
1/2 tablespoon turmeric
1 quart cider vinegar

Thin-slice cucumbers and onions, break up cauliflower, cut pepper into 1/2-inch squares. Combine vegetables and garlic; add salt. Cover with ice cubes; mix well and let stand 3 hours. Drain well.

Combine remaining ingredients and pour over vegetables in large kettle. Bring just to boil, take out vegetables and place in hot, sterilized jars; cover with liquid. Makes 8 or 9 pints. Chill before serving.

MIXED PICKLES

4 cups cut cucumbers
2 cups cut carrots
2 cups cut celery
2 sweet red peppers
1 pod hot red pepper
1 cauliflower
2 cups pickling onions

1 cup salt
1 gallon water
4 tablespoons mustard seed
2 tablespoons celery seed
1½ cups sugar
5 cups vinegar

Wash, rinse, drain, seed and cut vegetables as desired. Dissolve salt in water. Pour over vegetables. Let stand about 18 hours. Drain.

Add seeds and sugar to vinegar. Boil 3 minutes. Add vegetables. Simmer until hot through; then bring to boil. Pack, boiling hot, into hot, sterilized jars; seal at once. Makes 4 or 5 pints.

See Danish pickle in Around the World chapter.

RUMMAGE PICKLE

2 quarts green tomatoes
1 quart ripe tomatoes
2 bunches celery
4 medium-sized onions
2 sweet green peppers
2 sweet red peppers
1 small hot red pepper

1 quart small green cucumbers
1 cup salt
1 quart vinegar
1 pound brown sugar
1 tablespoon mustard
1 tablespoon cinnamon

Trim all vegetables. Put them through food chopper, sprinkle with ½ the salt and allow to stand overnight.

Next morning, drain well and mix thoroughly with remaining salt and rest of ingredients. Allow to stand for 4 or 5 hours. Pack into jars; cover with liquid, adding vinegar if needed; process for 15 minutes and seal. Makes about 4 quarts.

TOMATO AND ONION PICKLES

1 gallon green tomatoes
6 onions
½ cup salt
1½ cups sugar
1 tablespoon mustard seed

1 tablespoon celery seed
1 tablespoon grated horse-radish
1 tablespoon allspice
1 tablespoon peppercorns
4 cups vinegar

Wash, drain and slice tomatoes. Peel and slice onions. Mix with salt. Let stand about 12 hours. Drain.

Add sugar, mustard and celery seed, horse-radish and allspice, in bag, to vinegar. Boil 5 minutes. Cool slightly. Add vegetables. Simmer 20 minutes. Bring to boil. Remove spice bag. Pack, boiling hot, into hot, sterilized jars; seal at once. Makes about 4 quarts.

CUCUMBERS AND ONIONS

2 pounds cucumbers
1 pound onions
¼ pound salt

Vinegar
1½ pints spiced vinegar

Scrub cucumbers, then slice and cut into small triangles. Thin-slice onions; mix together in bowl, cover with salt and leave for 24 hours.

Drain well. Put into jars, cover with plain vinegar for 24 hours.

Drain off and cover with the spiced vinegar. Store for 2 weeks before using. Makes about 3 pints. Recipe can be doubled or tripled.

Mustard Pickles

HOME PREPARED MUSTARD

2½ ounces powdered mustard
2 tablespoons sugar
2 teaspoons salt
4 tablespoons vinegar

1 teaspoon Worcestershire sauce
2 tablespoons olive oil
Dash Tabasco sauce

Blend mustard, sugar and salt. Add vinegar and remaining ingredients. Mix well, making a smooth paste.

See also Italian and Indian mustards in Around the World chapter.

MIXED MUSTARD PICKLES

1 medium cauliflower
3 green peppers
2 cups pickling onions
2 pounds green tomatoes
2 cups small cucumbers
4 cups unpeeled large cucumber slices, ⅛ inch thick
1 cup salt

6 cups water
6 cups vinegar
2 cups granulated sugar
2 teaspoons celery seed
4 tablespoons flour
¾ teaspoon turmeric
4 tablespoons dry mustard

Wash cauliflower; cut into small flowerets. Seed green peppers, cut in halves; slice crosswise ¼ inch thick. Scald and skin onions. Cut green tomatoes in eighths. Mix cauliflower, peppers, onions, tomatoes, cucumber slices; cover with a brine made of the salt and 4 cups of water. Let stand overnight; then bring to a boil in the brine.

Heat vinegar, sugar and celery seed. Mix the flour, mustard and turmeric with the remaining 2 cups of water. Add to hot vinegar mixture, stirring constantly.

Drain brine from vegetables. Add vinegar and mustard mixture to vegetables; cook for 20 minutes. Fill hot jars. Seal. Makes 7 pints.

SWEET MUSTARD PICKLES

3 large cucumbers	Salt
1 quart green tomatoes	Vinegar
3 heads cauliflower	1 ounce powdered turmeric
3 red peppers	4 ounces ground mustard
3 green peppers	2 cups flour
2 quarts small onions	8 cups sugar
1 quart small gherkins	3 quarts cider vinegar

If cucumbers are tender, they can be left unpeeled; cut into small chunks. Tomatoes should be cut into similar-sized pieces. Break cauliflower into flowerets; slice peppers into strips; peel onions. Gherkins are left whole. Put different vegetables each in a separate bowl and cover with a brine made of 1 part salt to 9 parts water; let stand overnight.

Drain the vegetables and cook each separately in salted water and vinegar (1 part vinegar to 2 parts water). Boil briskly until nearly tender (5 to 10 minutes according to vegetable). Drain well.

Make a paste of the turmeric, mustard, flour and sugar, adding the cider vinegar gradually until mixture is smooth. Bring to a boil and thicken, stirring constantly.

Combine all vegetables in large kettle; pour the liquid mixture, boiling hot, over; then bring all to a boil and keep boiling for 10 minutes. Pour into hot, sterilized jars and seal. Makes 10 to 12 quarts.

MUSTARD PICKLES WITH LIMA BEANS

1 head cauliflower	4 quarts water
1 quart small green tomatoes	1 cup sugar
3 green peppers	¾ cup flour
1 quart pickling onions	½ cup dry mustard
3 cups green lima beans	1 tablespoon turmeric
36 small (2-inch) pickling cucumbers	7 cups vinegar
	7 cups water
1 cup coarse salt	

Break cauliflower into flowerets, cut tomatoes into quarters, peppers into strips. Cover all vegetables with salt dissolved in 4 quarts of water and let stand overnight.

Drain, cover with boiling water and let stand 10 minutes. Drain again.

Combine remaining ingredients and boil until thickened. Add vegetables, boil until barely tender. Pack in hot, sterilized jars and seal at once. Makes 6 to 8 pints.

COMPANY MUSTARD PICKLES

1 quart (3) large cucumbers
1 quart green tomatoes
1 large cauliflower
1 quart button onions
1 quart small cucumbers or
gherkins
4 sweet green peppers

Salt
6 tablespoons dry mustard
1 tablespoon turmeric
2 tablespoons ground celery seed
1½ cups sugar
1 cup flour
2 cups vinegar

Chop large cucumbers, tomatoes and cauliflower into bite-sized bits; peel onions. Add gherkins and combine all vegetables in a large bowl. Cover with boiling, salted water (1 tablespoon salt to each quart of water). Let stand overnight and then drain well. Place vegetables in preserving kettle.

Then mix the spices, sugar and flour with enough of the vinegar to make a smooth paste. Gradually stir in remainder of vinegar, then pour mixture over vegetables. Bring to a boil slowly, stirring. Do not overcook. Pour into hot, sterilized jars, seal at once and store in dark, cool place. Makes 4 to 5 quarts.

MUSTARD BEANS

8 quarts green beans
Salt
6 cups sugar
1 cup flour

5 tablespoons dry mustard
1 tablespoon turmeric
6 cups vinegar

Cook beans in small amount of salted water until barely tender. Drain.

Mix dry ingredients together in pan. Add vinegar and bring to a boil. Add beans and again bring to a boil; simmer 5 minutes. Pack into hot, sterilized jars and seal at once. Makes 8 pints.

CUCUMBER ONION MUSTARD PICKLES

6 pounds 3- to 4-inch pickling
cucumbers
1 pound onions
1⅓ cups granulated sugar
½ cup salt
½ teaspoon turmeric

2 tablespoons cornstarch
1 teaspoon ground ginger
¼ teaspoon pepper
¼ cup prepared mustard
3 cups white vinegar
1 cup water

Wash cucumbers and onions thoroughly; peel onions; slice both. Combine dry ingredients in deep pot. Gradually stir in mustard, then liquids. Cover; bring to a boil. Add vegetables. Cover; heat just to boiling point;

then simmer while quickly packing 1 hot, sterilized jar at a time. Fill to ⅛ inch from top. Be sure vinegar solution covers vegetables. Seal each jar at once. Makes 7 to 8 pints.

CURRIED MUSTARD PICKLES

1 large head cauliflower	1 cup sugar
4 green peppers	3 tablespoons dry mustard
2 medium cucumbers	1½ tablespoons curry powder
⅓ cup salt	1½ teaspoons turmeric
1 quart water	1 quart white vinegar
¼ cup flour	

Trim the leaves from the cauliflower, separate into small flowerets, wash well and drain. Wash the peppers, remove stems and seeds and chop. Wash cucumbers and chop without peeling. Combine vegetables in a bowl, sprinkle with salt and add water. Cover and refrigerate overnight.

Transfer vegetables and liquid to a large saucepan or kettle and heat to boiling. Drain vegetables.

In a saucepan combine the flour, sugar, mustard, curry and turmeric. Gradually blend in the vinegar. Place over heat and cook, stirring until mixture thickens. Add vegetables and simmer for 10 minutes. Spoon into hot, sterilized jars, filling to within ½ inch of top. Seal. Makes about 2 pints.

MUSTARD PICKLE MEDLEY

36 1½- to 2½-inch cucumbers	1 gallon water
1 cauliflower	½ cup prepared mustard
2 cups pickling onions	1 tablespoon turmeric
3 sweet green peppers	2 to 3 cups sugar, to taste
3 sweet red peppers	2 cups spiced watermelon rind
1 cup salt	5 cups vinegar

Wash and drain vegetables. Cut half the cucumbers into ½-inch slices, cauliflower into small pieces. Scald and peel onions. Seed and cut peppers into small pieces. Dissolve salt in the water. Pour over vegetables including remaining whole cucumbers. Let stand about 12 hours. Rinse. Drain 1 hour.

Mix mustard and turmeric; add ½ cup water, a little at a time. Stir until smooth. Add sugar, watermelon rind and vinegar. Cook until sauce coats spoon. Add vegetables; simmer 15 minutes. Pack, hot, into hot, sterilized jars. Process pints or quarts 10 minutes in boiling water bath. Makes 4 pints.

MUSTARD CABBAGE

1 solid head cabbage	¼ teaspoon pepper
4 green peppers	1 quart cider vinegar
2 Spanish onions	5 tablespoons dry mustard
2 tablespoons salt	1 tablespoon turmeric
¼ teaspoon mace	Cayenne pepper to taste
¼ teaspoon allspice	

Fine-shred the trimmed and cored cabbage. Stem and seed the peppers; then slice them and onions very thin. Place in jar or crock in alternate layers, sprinkling with the salt, mace, allspice and pepper. Pour vinegar over, adding more if necessary to cover. Leave for 7 days with cover on, stirring occasionally.

Then drain off vinegar into pan, bring it to a boil, add the mustard and turmeric, which have been mixed into a smooth paste with a little cold vinegar, bring to a boil again and simmer 15 minutes. Add vegetables and cayenne pepper to taste and bring to boil again. Put in jars, cover tightly and hold 1 week before using. Makes 3 pints.

CHOW-CHOW

chow-chow (chou′ chou′), *n.* 1. a Chinese mixed fruit preserve. 2. *China, India, etc.* any mixed food, or food in general, or a meal. 3. a mixed pickle in mustard (orig. East Indian). 4. chow (def. 2). [Pidgin English]

 —*The American College Dictionary*

The only appreciable difference between mustard pickles and chow-chow seems to be that the first is in larger pieces than the second. Crosse & Blackwell, who label their chow-chow "The Original Mustard Pickle," further confuse the issue by selling it in other markets than the United States as "Piccalilli Pickle," its original name.

According to legend (the one on the C & B label), chow-chow was created for Napoleon by his distinguished chef, Signor Quailiotti, and when the Emperor went into exile at St. Helena, Quailiotti went to work for Crosse & Blackwell in London, where he re-created the condiment. The same recipe is used by the company today.

Word from the Nestlé Company, which recently bought C & B, is that when it was first imported into this country, most of the volume of chow-chow sales came from the upper Michigan peninsula, where the European tin miners bought it by the gross. Since then, of course, it has spread all over the country.

I have demonstrated what I consider remarkable restraint by not naming any of the succeeding recipes "Chattanooga Chow-Chow."

SOUR CHOW-CHOW

2½ pounds string beans	3 quarts cider vinegar
1 large head cauliflower	½ cup sugar
3 cups shelled limas	½ cup salt
3 cups corn	2 tablespoons celery seed
1 quart onions	2 tablespoons mustard seed
5 green peppers	½ pound ground mustard
2½ pounds green tomatoes	1 tablespoon turmeric powder

Cut the string beans in pieces; break the cauliflower into flowerets. Add the lima beans and corn and cook all 4 ingredients about 25 minutes. Chop the onions, peppers and tomatoes. Heat the vinegar and, when hot, add the sugar, salt and spices, which have been mixed together. Drain the water from the cooked vegetables and add to the hot vinegar. Then add the chopped vegetables and cook about 25 minutes, stirring constantly. Pour into hot, sterilized jars and seal.

GREEN TOMATO CHOW-CHOW

1 quart chopped green tomatoes	Spice bag:
1 quart chopped cabbage	1 tablespoon mustard seed
1 quart chopped green cucumbers	1 tablespoon celery seed
1 cup chopped onions	½ tablespoon stick cinnamon
1 cup chopped green peppers	½ tablespoon whole allspice
1½ quarts vinegar	½ tablespoon cloves
	1 cup sugar

Wash, trim and chop vegetables; measure each. Cover with brine made of ½ cup salt to 2 quarts of water. Let stand overnight.

Drain vegetables thoroughly to remove brine. Put spice bag with vinegar in kettle and simmer (do not boil) for 10 minutes. Add sugar and drained vegetables. Cook slowly, stirring often, until tender (about 1 hour). Pack into sterilized jars and seal. Makes 4 to 6 pints.

SWEET MIXED PICKLE CHOW-CHOW

2 medium heads cauliflower
2 medium green peppers
2 medium sweet red peppers
1½ pounds (9 medium) onions
2½ cups white vinegar
1½ cups water

1½ cups granulated sugar
3 tablespoons salt
1 tablespoon mustard seed
1 tablespoon celery seed
¼ teaspoon turmeric

Wash cauliflower; break into small flowerets. Cook in small amount of unsalted boiling water 5 minutes. Drain. Cut peppers into ¼-inch strips, peel and quarter onions.

Combine remaining ingredients; heat to boiling, covered. Add vegetables and boil, uncovered, 2 minutes. Quickly pack 1 hot, sterilized jar at a time, filling to ⅛ inch from top. Be sure vinegar solution covers vegetables. Seal each jar at once. Makes 3 to 4 pints.

PENNSYLVANIA CHOW-CHOW

1 pint sliced cucumbers
1 pint chopped sweet peppers
1 pint chopped cabbage
1 pint sliced onions
1 pint chopped green tomatoes
1 pint lima beans
1 pint cut green beans

1 pint sliced carrots
2 tablespoons celery seed
4 tablespoons mustard seed
1 quart vinegar
2 cups water
4 cups sugar
4 tablespoons turmeric

Soak cucumbers, peppers, cabbage, onions and tomatoes in salt water overnight (½ cup salt to 2 quarts water). Drain.

Cook lima and green beans and carrots until tender. Drain well.

Mix soaked and cooked vegetables with remaining ingredients and boil 10 minutes. Pack in clean, hot, sterile jars and seal. Makes about 8 pints.

The recipe above comes from the Pennsylvania State Home Extension Department, while the one below is from an Alabama state publication.

ALABAMA CORN CHOW-CHOW

2 quarts corn (16 to 20 medium ears)
1 quart cabbage
1 pint sweet red pepper
Salt
1 quart white vinegar

½ pound sugar
2 ounces ground mustard
2 tablespoons salt
2 tablespoons celery seed
3 tablespoons white mustard seed
1 tablespoon cloves (in bag)

Blanch ears of corn 2 minutes and drop into cold water. Cut from cob but do not scrape; measure. Shred cabbage; chop peppers. Put a layer of the vegetables in enameled pan or stone jar and sprinkle well with salt. Repeat until all the vegetables are used and the last layer is covered with salt. Let stand overnight. Drain well.

In separate kettle, put the vinegar and remaining ingredients. Heat to boiling, add the well-drained vegetables, and cook slowly until tender, about 20 minutes. Pack in jars. Process in a boiling water bath canner (212°F) for 10 minutes. Makes 5 or 6 pints.

POTTSFIELD PICKLE

2½ pounds onions	1 pint vinegar
2 pounds green tomatoes	½ teaspoon cloves
2 medium red peppers	1 tablespoon ground mustard
2½ pounds ripe tomatoes	1 cup sugar
¾ pound celery	½ teaspoon cinnamon
2 ounces salt	

Wash vegetables. Core tomatoes and seed peppers. Cut celery into 1-inch lengths and other vegetables into quarters. Run all through food chopper, using medium-coarse cutter. Place in kettle; stir in salt and let stand 10 to 15 minutes. Then add remaining ingredients. Mix well and simmer on low heat for 20 minutes or until the liquid content is quite low. Place in jars. Process in a boiling water bath canner (212°F) for 10 minutes. Makes 6 to 8 pints.

RAW-RAW CHOW-CHOW

2 large heads cabbage, trimmed	Salt
6 large onions, peeled	3 quarts vinegar
6 green pepper hulls	3 pounds light brown sugar
6 large cucumbers, peeled	2 tablespoons celery seed
6 large apples, cored	2 tablespoons white mustard seed

Put the first 5 ingredients through a coarse grinder. Salt well; let stand overnight. Also mix the remaining ingredients and let stand overnight separately.

Next morning, drain vegetables, add them to vinegar mixture; let stand 12 hours. Then, stir well, pack into sterilized jars, and seal. Makes about 5 quarts.

This product differs considerably from commercially made chow-chow. Recipe from Connecticut Agricultural College by way of University of California.

COLLEGE-BRED CHOW-CHOW

6 green peppers, mild
3 sweet red peppers (or hot peppers, if desired)
3 pounds button onions
2 cups salt
3 pounds small cucumbers
3 pounds small green tomatoes
3 pounds string beans

2 large cauliflowers
1 bunch celery
1/4 pound mustard
2 tablespoons turmeric
3 cups sugar
2 cups flour
4 quarts cider vinegar

Remove core and seeds from peppers and slice. Sprinkle with 1 cup salt and add enough water to cover. Let stand 24 hours. Treat sliced onions similarly in a separate bowl.

Drain brine from onions and peppers and add about 2 quarts of water to this brine. Cut remaining vegetables into moderate-sized pieces and parboil all the vegetables in this diluted brine about 5 minutes. Drain and discard liquid.

Make a paste by mixing mustard, turmeric, sugar and flour with a little cold vinegar; bring rest of vinegar to a boil and add to paste.

Stir for a few minutes to a smooth consistency, then pour over the drained vegetables and simmer slowly for 20 minutes. Pack scalding hot in jars, and seal. Makes 10 to 12 pints.

CURRIED CHOW-CHOW

1 large head cauliflower
4 green peppers
2 medium-sized cucumbers
1/3 cup salt
1 quart water
1 cup sugar

1/4 cup flour
3 tablespoons dry mustard
1 1/2 tablespoons curry powder
1 1/2 teaspoons turmeric
1 quart white vinegar

Trim leaves from the cauliflower and separate into small flowerets. Wash well; drain. Remove stems, seeds and ribs from peppers; wash and chop. Scrub cucumbers, but do not peel; chop. Combine vegetables in bowl and sprinkle with salt; then add water. Cover and refrigerate overnight.

Place vegetables and liquid in kettle or large saucepan and heat to boil. Drain vegetables.

In a saucepan combine sugar, flour, mustard, curry, turmeric; then gradually blend in the vinegar. Place over heat and cook, stirring until mixture thickens. Add vegetables and simmer for 10 minutes. Spoon into hot, sterilized jars, filling to within ½ inch of top, and seal. Makes 4 pints.

CHOW-CHOW RELISH

1 medium head **cabbage**	1½ quarts white vinegar
6 medium **onions**	2½ cups granulated sugar
6 green **peppers**	1½ teaspoons turmeric
6 sweet red **peppers**	1½ teaspoons ground ginger
1 quart green **tomatoes**	2 tablespoons mustard seed
(1½ pounds)	1 tablespoon celery seed
¼ cup pickling salt	1 tablespoon mixed whole
2 tablespoons prepared mustard	pickling spice

Wash vegetables. Chop cabbage, onions, peppers and tomatoes; mix with salt. Cover; let stand overnight; drain.

In kettle, mix mustard with small amount of vinegar; add remaining vinegar, sugar and spices. Simmer 20 minutes. Add vegetables; simmer 10 minutes. Continue simmering while quickly packing 1 hot, sterilized jar at a time. Fill to within ⅛ inch from top. Be sure liquid covers vegetables. Seal each jar at once. Makes 6 to 8 pints.

Use this relish within 6 months.

Relishes

Relishes consist of mixed chopped vegetables or fruits and spices, with or without mustard dressing. Better results are obtained by the use of salt-stock vegetables than by the use of fresh, but in the home it is usually more convenient to use the latter. The published recipes for making relishes are very numerous, and only a few of the more popular ones— 65 of them—will be given here.

A good relish has an attractive color and appetizing appearance. Most relishes are crisp, fairly uniform pieces of vegetables with a very small amount of liquid. The relish is moist but not watery.

This is the all-time favorite:

INDIA RELISH

3 pounds cucumbers, about 6 inches long	2½ cups sugar
	3 cups cider vinegar
3 pounds green tomatoes	⅓ cup white mustard seed
3 tablespoons salt	1 tablespoon celery seed
3 cups fine-chopped cabbage	½ teaspoon turmeric
2 to 3 medium onions	¼ teaspoon ground mace
3 to 4 large green peppers	½ teaspoon ground cinnamon
3 hot red peppers	

Choose fresh green cucumbers, tomatoes that have begun to turn whitish just before ripening, firm white cabbage, white onions and crisp fresh green and red peppers. Wash tomatoes and cucumbers very thoroughly. Remove a thin slice from stem and blossom ends of both and discard. Cut both into quarters. Put the cucumbers through the food chopper, using the coarse knife; then put the tomatoes through, letting them drop into a separate bowl. Stir ½ the salt into each vegetable. Invert a small plate on top of each, press down firmly and weight down. A small jar filled with wet sand makes a good weight. Let stand overnight.

Next morning turn each vegetable separately into a colander and press down firmly with the palm of the hand to force out as much of the brine as possible; combine the drained vegetables. Shred cabbage very fine; then cut across the shreds. Peel onions and quarter; wash peppers and remove stems, seeds and ribs from the green ones. Put through a food chopper separately, measuring each; there should be 1½ cups chopped onion and 2 cups chopped green pepper. Now combine all the vegetables. Place over low heat and slowly heat only to simmering, stirring gently from time to time. This heating makes the vegetables slightly tender. Now add sugar, vinegar and spices, mix well and reheat just to the boiling point. Pack into hot, sterile jars and seal immediately. Makes about 6 pints.

SWEET PICKLE RELISH

4 quarts green tomatoes	2 ounces mixed pickling spices
4 quarts onions	5 pounds sugar
24 sweet red and green peppers	2 quarts vinegar
2 bunches celery	

Cut and seed tomatoes; halve onions and peppers. Let tomatoes, peppers and onions stand overnight in salt water.

Next day, grind them with the celery. Squeeze out as much juice as possible.

Tie spices loosely in bag; bring sugar, vinegar and spices to a boil; then add ground, drained vegetables. Cook until onions are tender and mixture is clear. Remove spice bag. Pour into hot, sterilized jars and seal. Makes about 4 quarts.

PICCALILLI

2 quarts green tomatoes	¼ cup white mustard seed
⅜ cup salt	1 teaspoon celery seed
½ teaspoon pepper	1 pint vinegar
1 teaspoon dry mustard	2 green peppers
1 teaspoon cinnamon	2 cups chopped onions
1 teaspoon allspice	3 cups sugar
1 teaspoon cloves	

Chop tomatoes, sprinkle with salt and let stand overnight. Then drain well.

Combine spices and vinegar in a large kettle and bring to boil.

Seed and chop peppers. Add them, tomatoes, onion and sugar to kettle, bring to a boil again and simmer for 30 minutes, stirring occasionally. Pack into hot, sterilized jars, seal and stir. Makes 4 pints.

The following recipe from the Missouri Agricultural Extension Service differs considerably from commercially made piccalilli.

MISSOURI PICCALILLI

Use 12 pounds of green tomatoes, 2 or 3 sweet green peppers and 2 hot peppers, coarsely chopped or sliced. Sprinkle the cut tomatoes and peppers with 1 pint of salt, and cover with water and allow to soak overnight. Drain thoroughly, and heat until tender in the following mixture:

3 quarts vinegar	1 teaspoon ground cinnamon
4 cups sugar	2 tablespoons mustard (seed
1 teaspoon ground ginger	or ground)

Add 1 cup grated horse-radish, uncooked. Pack hot in glass-top jars, and seal. Allspice, cloves and 1½ pounds of sliced onions may be added to the recipe if desired, the onions being treated in the same manner as the other vegetables. Makes 10 to 12 pints.

ARKANSAS PICCALILLI

2 quarts green tomatoes	1 cup brown sugar
3 cups sweet green peppers	1 quart vinegar
1 cup cucumbers	2 tablespoons mixed pickling
½ cup onions	spice
½ cup salt	

Chop and combine the vegetables and mix with the salt. Let this mixture stand overnight.

Next morning, drain and press out all the liquid possible.

Mix sugar, vinegar, add cold to spices tied in bag. Place over heat; bring to a boil; add vegetables. Simmer slowly about 30 minutes, or until thick. Remove spice bag, pack into hot, sterilized jars, seal and store. Makes about 3 pints.

VEGETABLE RELISHES

ARTICHOKE RELISH

4 quarts Jerusalem artichokes, well scraped or peeled	2½ cups brown sugar
	1 teaspoon turmeric
4 large onions	4 tablespoons salt
2 tablespoons celery salt	1 tablespoon allspice
½ teaspoon red pepper	1½ pints vinegar

Grind artichokes and onions; mix all ingredients with the vinegar and simmer for 30 minutes, or until thick. Pack in sterilized jars and process at simmering, 10 minutes, in hot water bath. Makes about 8 pints.

THREE Cs RELISH

3 cups cabbage
1 tablespoon salt
1 cup chopped carrots
¾ cup cider vinegar
¾ cup water
3 tablepoons dry mustard

¾ cup sugar
1 tablespoon flour
3½ cups corn kernels (fresh, canned or frozen)
1 teaspoon celery seed
½ teaspoon mustard seed

Chop cabbage, put in bowl; add salt; mix well; let stand 1 hour and then drain well. Meanwhile cook carrots about 2 minutes; drain.

Heat vinegar and ½ cup of water to boiling point. Combine mustard, sugar and flour; add remaining water and mix to smooth paste. Stir in hot vinegar. Add cabbage, carrots, corn (which has been cooked if fresh), celery and mustard seeds; mix well and heat to boiling point. Place in hot, sterilized jars and seal. Makes about 2½ pints.

CUCUMBER RELISH

8 cups chopped cucumbers
1 cup chopped onions
2 cups chopped sweet red peppers
2 cups chopped sweet green peppers
1 tablespoon turmeric
½ cup salt

8 cups cool water
Spice bag:
    1 tablespoon mustard seed
    2 sticks cinnamon
    2 teaspoons whole cloves
    2 teaspoons whole allspice
1 to 2 cups brown sugar
4 cups vinegar

Wash and drain vegetables. Peel onions; remove seeds and ribs from peppers. Chop and measure all vegetables. Sprinkle with turmeric.

Dissolve salt in water. Pour over vegetables. Let stand 3 to 4 hours. Drain. Cover vegetables with more cool water. Let stand 1 hour. Drain.

Add spice bag and sugar to vinegar. Heat to boiling. Pour over vegetables. Let stand 12 to 18 hours.

Simmer until hot through. If too dry, add more vinegar. Bring to boil. Pack, boiling hot, into hot, sterilized jars; seal at once. Makes about 5 pints.

UNCOOKED CUCUMBER RELISH

12 large cucumbers   2 tablespoons salt
6 onions   3 cups sugar
6 sweet peppers   1 pint white vinegar

Chop the vegetables fine and sprinkle with the salt. Let stand 1 hour. Drain. Add the sugar and vinegar. Stir well and bottle cold. Makes 8 pints.

BEET RELISH

1 pint boiled beets   1/8 teaspoon white pepper
1 cup celery   2 tablespoons salt
1 pint cabbage   3/4 cup sugar
1 medium onion   1/2 cup beet juice
1 tablespoon horse-radish   1 3/4 cup vinegar
Dash red pepper

Chop beets, celery, cabbage and onion. Mix all ingredients in kettle and let them come to a good boil. Pack in sterilized jars and seal. Process 15 to 20 minutes at simmering point. Makes 3 pints.

HOT BEET RELISH

2 cups distilled white vinegar   2 quarts cooked beets
1 cup sugar   1 cup chopped onions
1 tablespoon salt   3 green pepper hulls
2/3 cup grated horse-radish

Heat vinegar; dissolve sugar and salt in it; add horse-radish and bring to boil.

Dice beets, chop onions and dice peppers. Add to vinegar mixture and simmer 20 minutes. Pour into hot, sterilized jars and seal. Makes 4 pints.

CABBAGE AND BEET RELISH

3 pints shredded cabbage   2 tablespoons salt
3 pints cooked, shredded beets   2 1/2 cups vinegar
1 cup chopped onion   1 cup sugar
3/4 cup grated horse-radish

Mix cabbage, beets, onion, horse-radish and salt in saucepan.

Heat vinegar, dissolve sugar in it and add to vegetables in saucepan. Place over heat and bring to boil; boil 12 minutes. Pack in hot, sterile jars; seal. Makes 6 or 7 pints.

CARROT RELISH

3 pounds carrots (12 medium)
5 medium green peppers
1 medium sweet red pepper
6 medium onions
2 tablespoons celery seed

¼ cup salt
6 cups sugar
6 cups distilled white vinegar
½ teaspoon cayenne pepper

Clean carrots, remove ribs and seeds from peppers, peel onions. Put all vegetables through food chopper, using coarse blade.

In kettle, heat spices, sugar and vinegar to boiling. Add ground vegetables and boil gently for 20 minutes. Pack while boiling into hot jars, filling to within ¼ inch of top. Be sure vinegar solution covers all vegetables. Seal each jar immediately. Process in a boiling water bath canner (212°F) for 15 to 20 minutes. Makes 4 pints.

CORN RELISH

9 cups fresh corn (12–15 large ears)
2 cups chopped onions
1 cup chopped green peppers
½ cup chopped red peppers

1 cup sugar
2 tablespoons salt
1½ tablespoons celery seed
1½ tablespoons mustard
3 cups cider vinegar

Cut corn from ears, but do not scrape. Combine corn, onions, peppers, sugar, salt, spices and vinegar. Bring to a boil. Cover and simmer 15 minutes, stirring occasionally to prevent scorching. Pour into hot, sterilized jars and seal. Makes about 5 pints.

OFF-THE-COB RELISH

20 medium ears corn
1½ cups sugar
1 cup diced green pepper
1 cup diced sweet red pepper
1 cup chopped onion
1 cup diced celery

1 tablespoon salt
2½ tablespoons mustard seed
1 teaspoon celery seed
½ teaspoon turmeric
2½ cups distilled white vinegar
2 cups water

Cook about 20 medium ears fresh-picked corn for 5 minutes in boiling water to cover. Dip in cold water and cut from cob. Chop peppers, onion and celery. Combine vegetables with remaining ingredients; simmer 20 minutes. Pack in hot jars, covering vegetables with the liquid and leaving 1-inch head space. Adjust lids; process in boiling water bath 15 minutes. Seal. Makes 6 to 7 pints.

ANOTHER CORN RELISH

18 large ears corn
4 large onions
2 green peppers
1 red pepper
1 cup brown sugar

¼ cup salt
3 tablespoons celery seed
3½ tablespoons dry mustard
1 quart vinegar

Cut kernels from corn, fine-chop onions and peppers and mix the vegetables. Add remaining ingredients and cook slowly for 20 minutes, stirring to prevent sticking. Pour into hot, sterilized jars and seal. Makes approximately 5 pints.

Also see index for Billy Mills' Corn Relish.

CELERY RELISH

4 bunches celery
2 medium green peppers
2 medium sweet red peppers
5 medium onions
2 cups white vinegar

½ cup water
2½ tablespoons salt
1¼ cups granulated sugar
2½ tablespoons mustard seed
½ teaspoon turmeric

Wash, prepare vegetables. Dice celery, seed and chop peppers, peel and chop onions.

Combine vinegar and water with remaining ingredients; heat to boiling point. Add vegetables. Simmer, uncovered, 3 minutes. Continue simmering while quickly packing 1 hot, sterilized jar at a time. Fill to ⅛ inch from top. Be sure vinegar solution covers vegetables. Seal each jar at once. Makes 5 pints.

HORSE-RADISH RELISH

1 cup grated horse-radish
½ cup vinegar, white
¼ teaspoon salt

Wash horse-radish roots thoroughly and remove the brown outer skin. (A vegetable peeler is useful for this.) The roots may be grated, or cut into small cubes and put through a food chopper or a blender.

Combine ingredients. Pack into clean jars. Seal tightly. Store in refrigerator. Makes about ½ pint.

PEPPER RELISH

18 red peppers, seeded
18 green peppers, seeded
1 hot pepper
15 red onions, peeled
Boiling water to cover
2 cups water

5 cups vinegar
4 cups sugar
4 tablespoons salt
5 tablespoons mustard seed
3 tablespoons celery seed
1 teaspoon flour

Grind all peppers and onions, using finest blade of food chopper. Cover with boiling water and let stand 10 minutes. Drain.

Heat water and 1 cup vinegar to boiling. Pour this over vegetables and let stand 4 minutes. Drain again, pressing firmly.

Add remaining 4 cups vinegar and other ingredients, mixing thoroughly. Seal in sterilized jars. Makes 8 to 10 pints.

QUICK PEPPER RELISH

12 red peppers
12 green peppers
12 medium onions
Boiling water to cover

2 cups vinegar
2 cups sugar
3 tablespoons salt

Chop vegetables; cover with boiling water; let stand 5 minutes. Drain well. Add remaining ingredients and boil for 5 minutes. Pour into hot, sterilized jars and seal immediately. Makes 6 or 7 pints.

PEPPER-ONION RELISH

1 quart onions
2 cups sweet red pepper
2 cups green pepper

1 cup sugar
1 quart vinegar
4 teaspoons salt

Chop onions and peppers finely. Combine all ingredients and bring slowly to boil. Cook until slightly thickened. Pour into hot, sterile jars. Fill jars to top; seal tightly. Makes 3 to 4 pints.

PEPPER-ONION HASH

1 cup chopped onion
1 cup chopped red pepper
1 cup chopped green pepper
2 tablespoons salt

2 cups vinegar
½ cup sugar
1 teaspoon celery seed

Sprinkle vegetables with salt; let stand 30 minutes; drain. Place in sterilized jars. Place remaining ingredients in a saucepan, bring to a boil, boil 5 minutes and pour over hash; seal. Makes 2 to 3 ½-pints.

SWEET RED PEPPER RELISH

7 cups finely chopped sweet red peppers

½ cup finely chopped onion

2 tablespoons salt

5 cups sugar

3 cups vinegar

Wash and drain thick-walled peppers; remove seeds and ribs; fine-chop pepper and onion and measure. Mix with salt. Let stand 3 to 4 hours. Drain. Add sugar and vinegar. Boil until thick. Pour, boiling hot, into hot pint or ½-pint jars. Put lid on jar; screw band tight. Makes 3 or 4 pints, 7 or 8 ½-pints.

RED AND GREEN PEPPER RELISH

4 large green peppers

4 large sweet red peppers

6 medium onions

2 teaspoons salt

2 cups sugar

2 cups vinegar

Use medium blade of food grinder to cut peppers and onions. Drain juice from vegetables. To them add the salt, sugar and vinegar; heat to boiling point and boil gently for 5 minutes. Put in hot, sterilized jars and fill to top. Seal immediately. Makes 4½ pints.

PENNSYLVANIA PEPPER RELISH

16 sweet red peppers

16 sweet green peppers

10 small onions

1 quart vinegar

1½ cups sugar

2½ teaspoons salt

Chop peppers and onions very fine; cover with boiling water and let stand 5 minutes. Drain off water; cover with new boiling water and let stand 10 minutes. Place in a muslin bag and allow to drain overnight.

Then combine vinegar, salt and sugar and bring to a boil. Add pepper mixture and cook for 20 minutes. Pour into hot, sterilized jars and seal. Makes 4 pints.

PEPPER POT HASH

16 red peppers

16 green peppers

3 small hot peppers

16 red onions

3 pints vinegar

4 tablespoons salt

3 cups sugar

Fine-chop peppers and onions. Cover with boiling water and let stand for 5 minutes; then drain.

Boil vinegar, salt and sugar. Add vegetables and bring to boil again. Seal at once in sterilized jars. Makes 12 pints.

PEPPER POT RELISH

5½ cups ground green and sweet
    red peppers
1 cup onions
Boiling water

¾ cup sugar
1 tablespoon salt
1½ tablespoons mustard seed
1 cup cider vinegar

About 12 large peppers, seeded and trimmed, will make 5½ cups. Three medium onions will yield 1 cup, ground. Cover vegetables with boiling water; cover with lid; let stand 20 minutes. Drain well. Add remaining ingredients and simmer 12 to 15 minutes. Seal at once in hot, sterilized jars. Makes about 3 pints.

GREEN TOMATO RELISH

6 quarts green tomatoes (36 to 40
    medium)
¼ cup salt
1½ quarts chopped onion
3 cups chopped green pepper

1½ cups chopped red sweet
    pepper
3 cups sugar
1½ quarts vinegar
2 tablespoons whole mixed pickle
    spices

Chop tomatoes, mix thoroughly with salt. Let stand overnight. Drain. Combine with chopped onions, green and red peppers, sugar and vinegar. Put spices loosely into a bag and place in tomato mixture. Bring to a boil. Boil gently with spices for 1½ hours, or until thickened, stirring frequently. Remove spice bag. Pour relish into hot, sterile jars. Fill jars to top, and seal. Store in a cool, dry place. Makes 8 to 10 pints.

UNCOOKED TOMATO RELISH

2 gallons ripe tomatoes
6 green peppers
6 sweet red peppers
4 medium onions
1 cup chopped cabbage
2 tablespoons celery seed

½ teaspoon red pepper
1 teaspoon ground cloves
4 teaspoons yellow mustard seed
5 tablespoons salt
1 cup sugar
1 quart cider vinegar

Scald and peel the tomatoes; seed peppers, chop all vegetables fine; add seasonings; mix well. Add the vinegar and allow to stand overnight. Next morning pack cold into sterilized jars, seal and process 15 minutes at 180°F, simmering temperature. Makes 10 to 12 pints.

TOMATO-CELERY RELISH

24 ripe tomatoes
2 green peppers
2 pimientos or sweet red peppers
1 chili pepper
3 onions
1 pint chopped celery

⅔ pound sugar
Spice bag:
12 cloves
2-inch stick of cinnamon
Small piece whole ginger
1 pint cider vinegar

Chop tomatoes, peppers and onions; mix with celery. Add sugar and spice bag to vinegar and heat until sugar dissolves. Add vegetables, bring to boil and simmer gently for 2 hours. Salt to taste, remove spice bag, put in jars and seal. Makes about 4 pints.

AUNT SALLY'S RADISH RELISH

1 pound radishes
½ pound celery stalks
1 cup sweet onions
2 hot red peppers
1 cup sugar

1 tablespoon mustard seed
2 teaspoons salt
1½ teaspoons dill seed
Vinegar to cover

Grind coarsely the radishes, celery and onions; seed peppers and dice. Combine all ingredients in kettle or pan and let stand 3 hours with vinegar to cover. Then bring to boil. Cook 10 minutes. Pour into hot, sterilized jars and seal. Makes 2 pints.

DOZEN VEGETABLE RELISH

3 medium carrots
1 head cabbage
1 pint green tomatoes
2 large onions
1 large green pepper
1 large sweet red pepper
2 bunches celery
1 pint large cucumbers
1 head cauliflower

25 tiny cucumbers
1 pint can red kidney beans
1 pint sweet corn
1 1-pound can large green peas
1 quart vinegar
4 tablespoons mustard seed
1½ pounds sugar
6 sticks cinnamon
1 tablespoon whole cloves

Chop carrots, cabbage, tomatoes, onions, peppers, celery and large cucumbers, which have been peeled. Parboil carrots and broken-up cauliflower a few minutes; scald small cucumbers in salt water. Mix all vegetables together and soak in strong salt water solution to cover, overnight. Drain.

Heat remaining ingredients, boiling gently for 10 minutes. Add the drained vegetables and salt to taste. Bring to a boil and pack in hot, sterilized pars. Seal. Makes 12 to 15 pints.

HURRY-UP VEGETABLE HASH

1 medium head cabbage	3 tablespoons salt
7 medium green peppers	1 tablespoon celery seed
7 medium carrots	1 tablespoon mustard seed
4 large onions	3 cups distilled white vinegar
1½ cups sugar	¾ cup water

Quarter and trim cabbage and peppers; peel and quarter onions. Put vegetables through food chopper, using coarse blade. Drain.

Combine rest of ingredients in large kettle; bring to a boil; add vegetables; simmer 5 minutes. Put vegetables into hot, sterilized jars, covering with vinegar mixture; seal at once. Makes 5 or 6 pints.

VEGETABLE CHOP

12 medium onions	6 cups sugar
10 green tomatoes	2 tablespoons white mustard seed
1 medium head cabbage	1 tablespoon celery seed
12 green peppers	1½ teaspoons turmeric
6 sweet red peppers	4 cups cider vinegar
½ cup salt	2 cups water

Trim and coarse-grind vegetables; mix well; sprinkle with the salt; let stand overnight. Rinse and drain.

Combine remaining ingredients; pour over vegetables and heat to boiling; simmer 3 minutes. Put in hot, sterilized jars; seal. Makes 6 to 8 pints.

VEGETABLE RELISH

10 medium green peppers	¾ cup water
1 pound (4) onions	1½ cups granulated sugar
1 pound (7 medium) carrots	3 tablespoons salt
1 pound (½ medium head) cabbage	1 tablespoon mustard seed
	1 tablespoon celery seed
2¾ cups white vinegar	

Wash vegetables; quarter peppers and onions, scrape carrots; put all through food grinder, using coarse blade. Drain.

Combine remaining ingredients in large kettle; bring to boil. Add vegetables; simmer 5 minutes. Continue simmering while quickly packing 1 hot, sterilized jar at a time. Fill to within ⅛ inch from top. Be sure vinegar solution covers vegetables. Seal each jar at once. Makes **5 to 6 pints.**

COMBINATION RELISHES

AMBER RELISH

12 ripe cucumbers
6 white onions
½ cup salt
1 quart vinegar
2 cups sugar

Spice bag:
¼ teaspoon cinnamon
1 teaspoon white mustard seed
1 teaspoon ground mustard
¼ teaspoon ground cloves
1 tablespoon turmeric

Peel and chop cucumbers and onions. Add salt and water to cover. Let stand 1 hour; drain off brine. Boil vinegar, sugar and spices, tied in a bag, together for 20 minutes. Add the vegetables to the prepared vinegar and cook slowly until vegetables are tender and yellow in color. Pack in sterilized jars and seal. Makes 5 to 6 pints.

BORDEAUX SAUCE No. 1
(Green Tomato-Cabbage Relish)

4 quarts chopped green tomatoes
  (24 to 28 medium-sized)
4 quarts sliced cabbage
3 cups onion, chopped
1 cup chopped sweet red pepper
¼ cup salt

1 teaspoon ground allspice
2 teaspoons celery seed
2 teaspoons mustard seed
1 pound brown sugar (2 cups
  firmly packed)
1 quart vinegar

Place layers of each vegetable in large bowl; sprinkle each layer with salt. Let stand overnight. Drain. Add remaining ingredients. Simmer 25 minutes or until there is just enough liquid left to moisten ingredients well. Pack into hot, sterile jars; fill to top; seal tightly. Makes about 4 quarts.

BORDEAUX SAUCE No. 2

2 quarts fine-chopped cabbage
1 quart fine-chopped green
  tomatoes
3 quarts fine-chopped sweet red
  peppers
3 quarts fine-chopped onions

1 pound sugar
¼ cup salt
1 quart vinegar
½ ounce mustard seed
¼ ounce celery seed
¼ ounce turmeric

Mix all ingredients and simmer for 2 hours. Ladle hot into sterilized pint jars; seal quickly. Store in a cool place. Makes about 8 pints.

One of the most famous names in Italian culinary circles is my friend Luigi Carnacina, and the next recipe is dedicated to him.

CÁRNACINA RELISH

12 red peppers
12 green peppers
12 medium-sized onions

1 pint vinegar
2 cups sugar
3 tablespoons salt

Chop peppers and onions, or put through meat grinder, using coarsest blade. Cover with boiling water. Allow to stand 5 minutes. Drain well and add remaining ingredients. Boil for 5 minutes. Pour into hot, sterilized jars and seal. Makes about 4 pints.

CURRY RELISH

4 cups chopped ripe tomatoes
8 cups chopped green tomatoes
3 cups chopped onions
1 cup chopped green peppers
1 cup chopped sweet red
   peppers
1 cup chopped cucumber
4 cups chopped cabbage
2 cups chopped celery
2 cups seeded raisins
½ cup salt

4 cups brown sugar
Spice bag:
   1 tablespoon celery seed
   1 tablespoon mustard seed
   2 teaspoons curry powder
   1 teaspoon ground ginger
   ½ teaspoon ground cloves
   1 tablespoon ground cinnamon
   2 cloves garlic
8 cups vinegar

Wash and drain vegetables. Scald, core and peel ripe tomatoes. Core green tomatoes. Peel onions; remove ribs and seeds from peppers. Chop and measure all vegetables. Add salt; mix thoroughly. Let stand 12 to 18 hours in a cool place. Drain. Add sugar; spices and garlic, in bag, to vinegar. Simmer 10 minutes. Add vegetables. Simmer 30 minutes. Bring to boil. Remove spice bag. Pack, boiling hot, into hot, sterilized jars; seal at once. Makes 10 to 12 pints.

MRS. JACK GRIMES' RELISH

2 medium heads cabbage,
   trimmed
9 large green peppers, cored
9 medium carrots
12 large onions

½ cup salt
5 cups cider vinegar
5 cups sugar
1 teaspoon celery seed
1 teaspoon mustard seed

Grind vegetables. Mix well with salt and let stand 2 hours. Drain; mix in vinegar, sugar, celery and mustard seeds. Pack in jars without cooking; seal. Makes about 6 pints.

Here is a universal American favorite.

DIXIE RELISH

1 pint chopped sweet red pepper
1 pint chopped sweet green
  pepper
Brine
1 quart chopped cabbage
1 pint chopped white onions
4 tablespoons yellow mustard
  seed

2 tablespoons celery seed
3 tablespoons salt
¾ cup sugar
1 quart cider vinegar
Strips of red pepper ¼ inch wide
  and 3 inches long

Soak whole peppers for 24 hours in a brine made of 1 cup salt to 1 gallon water.

Freshen in clear cold water for 1 to 2 hours; drain well. Seed and cut out ribs. Chop separately and measure vegetables; then mix. Add spice, salt, sugar and vinegar. Let stand overnight in covered crock or enameled pot.

Drain off vinegar and save. Garnish opposite sides of each sterilized jar with pepper strips. When these strips are neatly placed in vertical position, pack vegetable mixture in; then fill jars to overflowing with drained vinegar. Adjust lids; process 10 to 15 minutes in water bath at simmering. Makes about 2 quarts.

FARMER STYLE RELISH

1 quart medium-chopped green
  tomatoes
2 cups chopped sweet red
  peppers
2 cups chopped sweet green
  peppers
1 cup chopped onions

¼ cup salt
1 quart cider vinegar
1 cup sugar
2 teaspoons mustard seed
2 teaspoons celery seed
1 teaspoon white pepper

Mix vegetables and sprinkle salt through and over; let stand overnight; drain.

Heat vinegar with remaining ingredients to boiling point. Add vegetables slowly; simmer for 10 minutes. Pour into hot, sterilized jars, covering with vinegar, and seal. Makes about 5 pints.

If pickles were nickels,
The pay phones, I guess,
Would be in a terrible mess.

FRENCH PICKLE

2 quarts green tomatoes
1 sweet red pepper
1 green pepper
3 large onions
1 quart vinegar
2 cups white sugar

¼ cup salt
1 ounce mustard seed
1 ounce celery seed
1 teaspoon turmeric
2 quarts cabbage, chopped

Chop tomatoes, peppers and onions. Drain after chopping. Combine chopped vegetables with vinegar, sugar, salt, mustard seed, celery seed and turmeric in kettle and simmer 20 minutes. Let stand overnight.

Next morning combine with the cabbage. Pack into clean jars and seal. Makes 4 to 5 pints.

GARDEN SPECIAL

6 sweet peppers
1 quart onions
1 quart celery
1 quart water

4 quarts ripe tomatoes
3 tablespoons salt
2 tablespoons sugar

Dice peppers, onions and celery. Coarse stalks and leaves of celery may be used. Add water, and cook together for 20 minutes. Add tomatoes, which have been peeled and cut up; salt and sugar. Bring to boil, put into hot jars and process in boiling water bath: 30 minutes for pints, 40 minutes for quarts.

Flavor may be heightened by addition of fresh or dried basil, marjoram, summer savory or thyme, or a blend of these herbs. ½ to 1 teaspoon of a blend of these dried herbs for each batch is about right for most people. Makes about 5 quarts.

"I like pickled onions,
I like piccalilli,
Pickled cabbage is all right
With a bit of cold meat on Sunday night.
I can go termatoeses,
But what I do prefer
Is a little bit of cucumcu-cumcu-cum
A little bit of cucumber."
—Old English Music Hall Song

HOT DOG RELISH

2 cups onions	1 quart vinegar
2 cups cabbage	1 cup water
4 cups green tomatoes	½ tablespoon celery seed
6 sweet green peppers	1 tablespoon mustard seed
¼ cup salt	¾ teaspoon turmeric
3 cups sugar	3 ground sweet red peppers

Grind each vegetable with coarse blade. Measure. Sprinkle salt over them and let stand overnight. Rinse and drain. Combine remaining ingredients and pour over vegetables. Heat to boil and simmer for 3 minutes. Seal in hot, sterilized jars. Makes about 4 pints.

POP'S HOT DOG RELISH

2 pounds dill pickles	4 cups cider vinegar
2 pounds pickled cauliflower	½ cup sugar
1 pound pickled onions	1 teaspoon mustard seed
1 pound sweet red peppers	1 teaspoon celery seed
1 pound green peppers	1 teaspoon turmeric
1 pound carrots	1 teaspoon paprika
1 pound pimientoes	2 tablespoons salt
1 tablespoon dry mustard	

Wash and trim all vegetables. Chop into tiny squares, using medium or small blade of food chopper. Cover with boiling water; let stand for 5 minutes; drain well. Make a paste of the dry mustard with a little of the vinegar; then add remaining vinegar and all other remaining ingredients to vegetables; bring to a boil and cook 10 minutes, stirring occasionally. Pack into hot, sterilized jars and seal. Makes about 9 pints.

KENNEBUNK PICKLE

3 pounds green tomatoes	9 tablespoons salt
3 pounds red tomatoes	1½ quarts vinegar
1 medium head cabbage	4½ cups brown sugar
3 sweet red peppers	4½ sticks cinnamon
3 green peppers	1½ teaspoons whole cloves
1 quart onions	1½ teaspoons mustard seed
1½ bunches celery	

Fine-chop the vegetables. Add the salt and let stand overnight.

Drain; add vinegar and brown sugar. Mix well. Make a spice bag to hold remaining ingredients and boil all ingredients for 30 minutes. Remove spice bag and pour vegetables into sterilized jars. Seal at once. Makes 10 pints.

LANCASTER RELISH

1½ quarts fine-chopped ripe tomatoes
1½ quarts fine-chopped green tomatoes
1½ quarts shredded cabbage
1½ quarts chopped onions
3 sweet red peppers, trimmed and ground

2 large stalks celery, ground
½ cup salt
3 cups sugar
3 pints vinegar
½ teaspoon cloves
½ teaspoon cinnamon
½ cup mustard seed
½ cup prepared horse-radish

Combine vegetables and salt, mix thoroughly and let stand overnight. Drain.

Make a sirup by boiling sugar, vinegar and spices together for 10 minutes.

Add vegetables and horse-radish; cook gently for ½ hour. Pour into clean, hot jars and seal at once. Makes about 8 pints.

PHILADELPHIA RELISH

3 pounds green tomatoes
3 bunches celery
2 small cauliflowers
6 cucumbers
1½ pounds onions
1 small cabbage
¾ cup salt

2 quarts vinegar
Spice bag:
   1 tablespoon peppercorns
   1 tablespoon cloves
2 tablespoons mustard seed
½ pound sugar

Trim blossom ends of tomatoes, remove leaves from celery and cauliflowers, put all vegetables through coarse blade of food chopper or grinder and mix well. Put vegetables in large bowl, in layers, with 2 tablespoons salt over each layer. Let stand 24 hours. Mix well together, drain and squeeze out all moisture.

Heat vinegar with spice bag, mustard seed and sugar. Put in vegetables, bring to boil. Put in hot, sterilized jars and seal. Makes 6 to 8 pints.

SWEET RELISH

6 pounds (22 medium) green
  tomatoes
½ pound (3 medium) onions
1 large stalk celery
½ pound (2 medium) sweet red
  peppers
1⅔ cups granulated sugar

1¾ cups white vinegar
½ teaspoon ground cinnamon
½ teaspoon ground allspice
½ teaspoon turmeric
¼ teaspoon cayenne pepper
1½ teaspoons celery seed
3 tablespoons salt

Wash, trim vegetables. Quarter, remove stem end from tomatoes; peel onions, quarter peppers and put all vegetables through medium blade of food grinder. Drain excess liquid.

Bring sugar and remaining ingredients to boil. Add vegetables; simmer 10 minutes, stirring occasionally. Continue simmering while quickly packing 1 hot, sterilized jar at a time. Fill to ⅛ inch from top. Be sure vinegar solution covers vegetables. Seal each jar at once. Makes 5 to 6 pints.

SAVORY AUTUMN RELISH

2 quarts green tomatoes
1 quart ripe tomatoes
3 green peppers
3 red peppers
3 celery stalks
3 large onions
½ head of cabbage

1 peeled cucumber
3 pints mild vinegar
1 teaspoon ground mustard
1 teaspoon paprika
½ cup salt
4 cups brown or white sugar

Chop all vegetables, place in kettle in layers with the salt and let stand overnight. Next day drain and press out liquid.

Heat the vinegar, sugar and seasonings together, add the well-drained vegetables and boil gently for 1 hour, or until vegetables are transparent. Pour into hot, sterilized jars and seal. Makes about 6 pints.

WINTER RELISH

3 quarts green tomatoes
15 green peppers
6 sweet red peppers
12 onions
1½ cups salt
3 cups white vinegar

¾ cup white mustard seed
1½ cups celery
1½ cups granulated sugar
Vinegar
1 tablespoon mustard

Chop tomatoes, peppers and onions fine and combine with salt and 3 cups vinegar; let soak overnight. Drain. To this mixture add mustard seed, fine-chopped celery and sugar. Cover with vinegar and cook about 5 minutes. Add mustard, mix and immediately pour into hot, sterilized jars. Seal while still hot. Makes about 5 pints.

FRUIT RELISHES

APPLE RELISH

4 pounds apples	½ cup light corn sirup
3 quarts water	⅔ cup water
1¼ cups white vinegar	2 teaspoons whole cloves
1 cup sugar	1½ sticks cinnamon

Wash, pare, core and cut apples into eighths. Immerse in 3 quarts water and 4 tablespoons vinegar to prevent browning.

Combine sugar, corn sirup, rest of vinegar, ⅔ cup water, cloves and cinnamon, broken into pieces, in a saucepan; heat to boiling point. Drain apples and add; cover and boil 3 minutes, stirring occasionally. Fill hot, sterilized jars with fruit, cover with hot liquid and seal. Makes 4 pints.

This relish is served with roast duck, chicken or pork.

CHIQUITA BANANA RELISH

2 cups cider vinegar	Spice bag:
8 tablespoons sugar	1 tablespoon cloves
	2 teaspoons cinnamon stick
	2 teaspoons allspice
	16 ripe bananas

Combine vinegar, sugar and spices and cook until mixture begins to thicken, stirring only until sugar is dissolved.

Peel and cut bananas into ½-inch rounds and add to sirup. Boil hard for 2 minutes and pour into ½-pint sterilized jelly glasses and seal, or keep chilled until used. Makes 6 to 7 ½-pint glasses.

ELDERBERRY RELISH

3 pints ripe elderberries
1½ pints malt vinegar
½ pound sugar
1 tablespoon cinnamon

1 tablespoon allspice
1 tablespoon cloves
¼ tablespoon cayenne pepper

Measure the elderberries after stems have been removed; stew gently in the vinegar until soft. Sieve the pulp, add the sugar and spices and simmer until it begins to thicken. Pour while hot into hot bottles and seal. Makes about 1 quart.

SWEET MANGO RELISH

1 quart green mangoes
2 large onions
6 sweet red peppers
2 large hot peppers
1 tablespoon salt

1 tablespoon white mustard seed
1 tablespoon celery seed
4 cups sugar
1 cup vinegar

Peel mangoes, cut from seed, chop or put through coarse blade of food chopper; measure. Chop or grind onions and peppers. Combine all ingredients. Bring to boil and boil 10 minutes. Let stand overnight. Next morning cook until slightly thickened. Pack, boiling hot, into sterilized jars and seal. Makes 3 to 4 pints.

2 cups raisins also may be added if desired.

TOMATO-PEAR RELISH

2½ cups tomatoes or 1 No. 2 can
2½ cups fresh pears or 1 No. 2 can
½ cup green pepper
½ cup onion
1 cup sugar
½ cup vinegar

1 teaspoon salt
½ teaspoon ground ginger
½ teaspoon dry mustard
⅛ teaspoon cayenne pepper
¼ cup chopped canned pimiento

If fresh, chop tomatoes, dice pears, chop pepper and onion. Combine tomatoes, pears (use liquid of canned tomatoes and pears), green pepper, onion, sugar, vinegar, salt, ginger, mustard and cayenne pepper. Boil slowly for 1 hour, stirring occasionally, until somewhat thickened. Add pimiento; boil 3 minutes longer. Pack into hot, sterile jars; fill to top; seal tightly. Makes about 2 pints.

PEAR RELISH

6 pounds pears
3 green peppers
3 sweet red peppers
1 hot pepper

3 large onions
3 cups vinegar
3 cups sugar
1 teaspoon salt

Core, peel and grind pears through coarse food chopper and drain until excess juice is removed. Grind peppers and onions. Combine all ingredients, bring to a boil and boil 20 minutes. Pack into containers. Process in a boiling water bath canner (212°F) for 10 minutes. Makes about 5 pints.

PEPPER AND PEAR RELISH

3 quarts bell peppers
5 quarts pears
1 quart vinegar
4 cups sugar
5 tablespoons salt, or to taste

2 tablespoons turmeric powder
2 tablespoons black pepper
2 tablespoons dry mustard
1 tablespoon allspice

Trim, seed and grind peppers and pears coarsely; combine with vinegar and seasonings. Cook over slow heat until pears are tender. Fill sterilized jars with boiling hot relish. Seal, place jars in hot water bath and simmer 5 minutes. Makes about 8 pints.

TROPICAL RELISH

4 quarts prepared guavas
1½ pounds raisins
1 clove garlic (optional)
1 pound preserved ginger
¼ cup white mustard seed

1 teaspoon dried chili pepper
1 quart vinegar
5 cups sugar
⅛ cup celery seed
⅓ teaspoon salt

Cut blossom and stem ends from guavas; peel, if blemished, and remove seed. Put through food chopper with raisins, garlic, ginger, mustard seed and chili. Add remaining ingredients and boil mixture 30 minutes. Let stand overnight. If too thick, dilute with vinegar. Reheat, pack while hot into sterilized jars and seal. Store several weeks before using. Makes about 8 pints.

AUNT KATIE'S RELISH

24 ripe tomatoes
8 peaches
8 pears
8 apples
3 onions

2 cups cider vinegar
4 cups sugar
2 tablespoons salt
2 tablespoons mixed pickling
spices

Peel, trim, core, seed and fine-chop tomatoes, peaches, pears, apples and onions. Dissolve sugar in vinegar in large kettle, mix in all ingredients (spices in a cloth bag), bring to boil and simmer until relish is thick. Pour into hot, sterilized jars and seal. Makes 4 to 6 pints.

RAISIN RELISH

4½ pounds apples
2 pounds seedless raisins
1 large onion, chopped
4 cups brown sugar
6 cups vinegar

½ cup salt
1 ounce ground or grated ginger
1 ounce white mustard seed
1 ounce celery seed
¼ ounce red pepper

Peel, core and chop apples, put into enameled kettle or pan, add other ingredients and boil for 30 minutes. Seal in hot, sterile jars. Makes 4 pints.

NEW ENGLAND RHUBARB RELISH

2 quarts rhubarb
1 quart white onions,
peeled and sliced
4 cups brown sugar
1 cup cider vinegar
2 teaspoons salt

Spice bag:
1 clove garlic
1 tablespoon cinnamon
1 tablespoon ginger
1 tablespoon mixed pickling
spices

Cut rhubarb into ½-inch pieces, using all stalks up to 2 inches below leaves; do not skin. Cook all ingredients together until rhubarb is tender but not falling apart. Remove spice bag; pack into hot, sterilized jars and seal. Makes about 3 pints.

Sweet Pickles

The reason so many of the sweet pickle recipes take so long to make is that the sugar must be added gradually so that the pickles won't shrivel.

It has been difficult to herd all of the sweet pickle recipes into this one section because they are scattered about under other categories. Therefore consult the index for more of them.

SWEET PICKLE CHIPS

4 pounds 3- to 4-inch pickling cucumbers
1 quart cider vinegar
3 tablespoons salt
1 tablespoon mustard seed
6 cups granulated sugar
2⅓ cups white vinegar
2¼ teaspoons celery seed
1 tablespoon whole allspice

Wash cucumbers thoroughly; cut crosswise into ¼-inch slices. Combine with vinegar, salt, mustard seed and ¼ cup sugar in large saucepan; simmer, covered, for 10 minutes. Drain; discard liquid. Place cucumber slices in hot, sterilized jars.

Meanwhile, heat white vinegar, remaining 5¾ cups sugar and other ingredients together until sugar is dissolved and mixture reaches boiling point. Continue simmering while filling jars to within ⅛ inch from top of jar with sirup that covers vegetables. Seal each jar at once. Makes 5 pints.

SWEET CUCUMBER PICKLES

10 medium cucumbers
½ cup salt
2 quarts water
1 quart vinegar
2 cups sugar
2 tablespoons whole black pepper
1 stick cinnamon
¾ teaspoon mustard seed
½ teaspoon whole cloves

Wash cucumbers. Drain and cover with brine made of salt and water. Let stand 24 hours. Drain. Add remaining ingredients and heat to boiling point. Boil gently 3 to 4 minutes. Pack pickles in sterilized jars. Fill to overflowing with sirup and seal. Makes approximately 3 pints.

SWEET CUCUMBER ROUNDS

6 pounds medium cucumbers, sliced

Heavy brine (1 pound salt to 9 pints water)

Weak vinegar solution (1 part vinegar to 3 parts water)

6 cups white vinegar

4 pounds sugar

3 sticks cinnamon

2 tablespoons whole cloves

2 tablespoons dried ginger root

Cover cucumber slices with heavy brine in crock, weighing down the fruit below the surface. Keep in cool place 8 hours.

Drain cucumbers, wash and freshen them in several changes of cold water to remove salt. When well drained, cover with weak vinegar solution for 4 hours. Then add 2 cups vinegar and let stand overnight.

Drain and discard vinegar.

Heat together 2 pounds sugar, remainder of vinegar and all the spices in preserving kettle. Cover and simmer 1 hour. Cool and pour over drained cucumber slices. Allow to stand overnight.

Next morning, drain the sirup and add to it the remaining 2 pounds of sugar. Heat sirup to boil, add cucumber slices and cook together until cucumbers are sparkling clear and transparent. Remove from heat, cover and cool in sirup to plump slices before packing.

Transfer slices to jars, strain sirup and pour over to brim; use knife to remove air bubbles and seal. Makes about 5 pints.

ORANGE-FLAVORED PICKLE STRIPS

7 pounds cucumbers

1 gallon water

1 cup salt

3 quarts cider vinegar

5 pounds sugar

Spice bag:

4 tablespoons pickling spice

1 tablespoon whole fennel seed

3 tablespoons salt

1 cup orange juice

Slice cucumber into strips and soak for 24 hours in gallon of water, to which salt has been added.

Remove and wash pickles, then soak in clear water for 12 hours.

Drain and soak for 12 hours more in vinegar, in which sugar has been dissolved by stirring.

Then heat pickles and liquor, plus spice bag, additional salt and orange juice until liquor becomes sirupy, about 30 minutes.

Pack pickles in hot, sterilized jars, cover with liquor and seal. Makes 6 to 8 pints.

YELLOW CUCUMBER SWEET PICKLE

Thoroughly ripe cucumbers that have turned yellow can be treated in the same manner as the watermelon rind and made into excellent sweet pickles.

DOUBLE-SWEET WATERMELON RIND

3 quarts trimmed watermelon rind
Boiling water
10 cups granulated sugar
2 cups vinegar

½ teaspoon oil of cloves
½ teaspoon oil of cinnamon
1 small whole orange
1 lemon

Rind from firm watermelon is best. Trim off green skin and any red meat; cut into 1-inch cubes. Place in large saucepan; cover with boiling water; boil about 10 minutes, until tender but not soft. Drain well. Combine ½ of sugar, vinegar, seasonings in saucepan; bring to boil; pour over rind. Let stand overnight at room temperature.

Next day, drain sirup from fruit, add remaining sugar, heat to boiling and pour over rind again. Let stand overnight.

Third day, slice orange and lemon, quarter each slice and add to watermelon rind and sirup. Heat to boiling and place in hot, sterilized jars. Seal at once. Store in cool, dry place. Makes 4 to 6 pints.

PICKLED MELON

Use cantaloupe, Persian melon, honeydew, etc., removing rind and seeds and cutting fruit into slices to fit into quart jars. Cover with a sirup made of 6 parts sugar, 4 parts water and 1 part vinegar, which has been brought to a boil. Sirup should come to within ½ inch of top of jars. Seal, place in boiling water and process for 1 hour.

WATERMELON BALL PICKLES

10 cups watermelon balls
(3 pounds pink meat)
¼ cup salt
2 quarts cold water

3 lemons, sliced
4½ cups granulated sugar
2 tablespoons crystallized ginger

Cut balls from firm pink watermelon with scoop. Soak overnight in mixed salt and water. Drain and rinse in cold water. Add lemons, sugar and ginger. Add enough water to cover the fruit. Cook slowly until clear, about 20 minutes. Place fruit in hot, sterilized jars. Boil sirup until it threads. Pour over fruit and seal. Makes about 3 pints.

SPICED WATERMELON RIND

9 cups (3 pounds) cubed white
watermelon rind
5 cups water
2 tablespoons salt
5 cups sugar
2 cups cider vinegar

1 tablespoon whole cloves
1 tablespoon whole allspice
1 tablespoon coarsely chopped
stick cinnamon
1 lemon, sliced

Remove all green skin from rind (watermelons with thick rind make the best pickles). Cover watermelon rind with 4 cups of the water. Add salt. Let stand overnight. Drain. Cover with more cold water in saucepan. Cook, covered, over low heat until tender—about 2 hours. Drain.

Meanwhile, combine sugar, vinegar and remaining 1 cup of cold water. Tie spices and lemon slices in a cheesecloth bag. Drop into vinegar mixture. Boil 5 minutes. Then add watermelon rind and cook until rind is transparent—45 to 60 minutes. Remove spice bag. Pack rind and sirup into jars and seal. Makes 4 pints.

For a fancy pack, watermelon rind can be cut into various shapes with a small cooky cutter or by hand into diamond and other shapes.
Red, pink or green food coloring can add attraction, also.

SPICY WATERMELON PICKLES

2 quarts prepared watermelon
rind
½ cup salt
2 quarts water
2 cups vinegar
2 cups water

3 cups brown or white sugar
1 lemon, thinly sliced
1 stick cinnamon
1 teaspoon whole cloves
1 teaspoon whole allspice

Remove outer skin and any pink portions from rind. Cut into small pieces. Soak overnight in brine made of salt and the water. Drain and wash with fresh water; drain again. Simmer or steam in fresh water until tender. Make sirup of remaining ingredients and simmer 5 minutes. Add rind and cook until clear. Pack into hot, sterilized jars and fill with sirup. Seal immediately. Makes 2 quarts.

WATERMELON SWEET PICKLE

1 medium-sized watermelon
8 pounds sugar
4 cups vinegar

4 tablespoons whole cloves
4 sticks cinnamon

Trim green outer skin and pink flesh from watermelon rind. Cut into fairly small pieces. Place in large cooking pot, cover with water and simmer until tender.

Boil the sugar and vinegar and the spices (in a cheesecloth bag) for a few minutes. Then add watermelon rind and simmer until it is clear and transparent. Pack into hot, sterilized jars; fill to overflowing with sirup. Seal immediately. A 15-pound watermelon will yield about 6 pints.

4-DAY SWEET GHERKINS

7 quarts (about 5 pounds) 1½- to 3-inch cucumbers
½ cup salt, pure granulated
8 cups (2 quarts) sugar
6 cups (1½ quarts) vinegar
¾ teaspoon turmeric

2 teaspoons celery seed
2 teaspoons whole mixed pickling spice
8 1-inch pieces stick cinnamon
½ teaspoon fennel seed (optional)
2 teaspoons vanilla (optional)

First day, morning—Wash cucumbers thoroughly; scrub with vegetable brush. Stem ends may be left on if desired. Drain cucumbers; place in large container and cover with boiling water. Afternoon (6 to 8 hours later)—Drain; cover with fresh, boiling water.

Second day, morning—Drain; cover with fresh, boiling water. Afternoon—Drain; add salt; cover with fresh, boiling water.

Third day, morning—Drain; prick cucumbers in several places with table fork. Make sirup of 3 cups of the sugar and 3 cups of the vinegar; add turmeric and spices. Heat to boiling point and pour over cucumbers. (Cucumbers will be partially covered at this point.) Afternoon—Drain sirup into pan; add 2 cups of the sugar and 2 cups of the vinegar to sirup. Heat to boiling point and pour over pickles.

Fourth day, morning—Drain sirup into pan; add 2 cups of the sugar and 1 cup of the vinegar to sirup. Heat to boil and pour over pickles. Afternoon—Drain sirup into pan; add remaining 1 cup sugar and the vanilla to sirup; heat to boiling point. Pack pickles into clean, hot pint jars and cover with boiling sirup to ½ inch of top of jar. Adjust jar lids.

Process for 5 minutes in boiling water (start to count processing time when water returns to boil). Remove jars and complete seals if necessary. Set jars upright, several inches apart, on a wire rack to cool. Makes 7 to 8 pints.

"It seems curious that we should have two distinct names for what is essentially the same article," writes Basil Hargrave in Origins and Mean-

ings of Popular Phrases and Names *(London, 1911)*, *"for a gherkin is, of course, a cucumber of the small variety used for pickling. The explanation is that in the one case ('gherkins') we borrow the word, through the Dutch* agurkje, *from the Arabic* khirgar *and the Hindu* khivar, *all of which denote a cucumber; while in the other case ('cucumber') we take the name from the Latin* cucumis *(acc.* cucumerem). *The cucumber must have been known and used from very ancient times, for we learn from the Bible (Numb. xi.5) that it was enjoyed in Egypt before the exodus of the Israelites, and it is said to have been common in England during the reign of Edward III., but that in the War of the Roses it was allowed to go out of cultivation and was re-introduced from the Netherlands about 1538."*

9-DAY WONDER SWEET PICKLES

25 pounds 3-inch cucumbers
(½ bushel)
5 pounds pure salt
4 grape leaves

1 part white vinegar and 3 parts
water to cover
White sugar
Mixed pickling spices

1st day—Place washed pickles in crock, add 2½ pounds of salt, cover with water.

2nd day—Drain off water, cover with fresh water, add 1¼ pounds salt.

3rd day—Drain off water, cover with fresh water, add remaining 1¼ pounds salt.

4th day to 6th day—Every day drain off water and cover with fresh water.

7th day—Drain off water, prick blossom end of pickles. Into kettle put grape leaves and vinegar solution made with 1 part vinegar to 3 parts water. Add pickles to this solution and simmer 1½ hours. Return pickles and liquid to crock and let stand overnight.

8th day—Drain off liquid and weigh pickles. To every 7 pounds of pickles allow 3 pounds of sugar and 3 ounces spices. Boil in kettle for 5 minutes with the remaining vinegar. Pour boiling liquid over pickles and let stand overnight.

9th day—Drain off spiced vinegar, heat in kettle and bring to boil, pour over pickles again and let stand until cold. Pack cold in sterilized jars. Makes 25 pints.

11-DAY SWEET PICKLE CHUNKS

14 cucumbers, 5 inches long
Boiling water
1 quart vinegar
8 cups sugar

2 tablespoons mixed whole
pickling spices in bag
2 tablespoons salt

Wash cucumbers; pour boiling water over them and let stand overnight; drain. On 4 successive days, repeat the process: Add fresh boiling water; let stand overnight and drain.

On the 6th day, cut the drained cucumbers in ¼-inch slices. Combine vinegar, sugar, spices and salt; heat to boiling point. Pour over cucumber slices and let stand overnight. The next morning, drain the vinegar sirup, reheat and again pour over the cucumber slices. Repeat this process 3 more days. On the 11th and last day, pack cucumber slices in sterile jars. Heat the vinegar sirup to boil, remove spice bag and pour over the slices in the jars, filling them to the top. Seal immediately. Makes 6 pints.

14-DAY SWEET PICKLES

75 2- to 3-inch cucumbers
4 quarts water
2 cups salt
Boiling water

6 cups vinegar
8 cups sugar
2 tablespoons celery seed
2 tablespoons cassia buds

Cut cucumbers in half, lengthwise. Place in crock. Boil water and salt; cool; pour over cucumbers; cover; let stand 1 week.

8th day: Drain; cover with boiling water; let stand. 9th day: Drain; cover again with boiling water; let stand. 10th day: Drain; cover with sirup made of vinegar, 5 cups of the sugar and the seasonings, which has been heated to boiling point.

For next 3 days, drain off sirup, add 1 cup sugar, heat to boiling, pour over pickles. On the 14th day, drain, pack in hot, sterilized jars, pour boiling hot sirup over and seal. Makes about 12 pints.

PICKLE PYROTECHNICS
Breaking of a Jar Draws Fire Fighters to Kitchen

Cheyenne, Wyo. (AP)—A jar of pickles brought the Cheyenne fire department on the run recently.

Mrs. W. H. Tyler dropped the pickles. The jar broke and juice ran into a floor plug. It caused a short.

The firemen's report: one sticky floor, one inoperative floor plug.

Through the courtesy of the State of Arkansas, we have a new pickle recipe from Mrs. Jack Grimes of Little Rock.

23-DAY SWEET PICKLES

2 gallons (about 150) small cucumbers (12 pounds)
2 cups salt and 1 gallon water (brine to cover)

1 part water and 2 parts vinegar to cover
8 cups (2 quarts) cider vinegar
16 cups sugar
1 stick cinnamon

Put cucumbers, unwashed, in crock and cover with brine. Keep submerged with plate and weight. Leave for 12 days.

Drain and put in ice-cold water or cover with ice cubes for 24 hours.

Split cucumbers, regardless of size, lengthwise. Put in kettle and cover with water-vinegar solution. Bring to boil. Drain. Put back in crock.

Prepare sirup of 8 cups vinegar and 7 cups of the sugar. Add cinnamon, bring to boil and put over cucumbers. This should cover; if not, add more vinegar-sugar solution in above proportions.

For 9 days, each morning drain off sirup into pan, add 1 cup of sugar; bring to boil; pour back over cucumbers.

On final day, pack cucumbers in jars; boil sirup once more and immediately pour over pickles and seal. Makes about 10 quarts.

Fruit Pickles and Spiced Fruits

Pickles made of fruit usually will have a better flavor and be more plump when they are left standing in sirup for several hours after cooking before being packed and processed.

SPICED SLICED APPLES

6 cups sugar
2 cups distilled vinegar
4 sticks cinnamon, in small pieces

2 teaspoons whole cloves
5 pounds firm apples, peeled, cored and in thick slices

Place sugar, vinegar, spices in kettle and bring to boil. Add apples and simmer, uncovered, until apples are tender but not broken.

Pack slices in hot, sterile jars to within 1/4 inch of top; cover well with sirup. Seal at once. Makes 3 to 4 pints.

LITTLE PICKLED APPLES

1 quart cider vinegar
1 quart wine vinegar
4 pounds brown sugar

Spice bag:
  2 tablespoons whole allspice
  2 tablespoons whole cloves
  2 sticks cinnamon
12 pounds crab apples or small
    tart apples

Bring vinegars, sugar and spice bag to a boil and continue for 15 minutes, skimming off any scum.

Trim blossom ends of apples, wash and add to boiling liquid. Boil over low heat until apples are tender; remove, using slotted spoon, and pack into hot, sterilized jars. Reduce sirup until thick and pour over apples. Seal immediately. If apples are cored, cut cooking time so they will not lose shape. Makes about 8 pints.

PICKLED APPLE MÉLANGE

20 medium-sized apples	1 pound sugar
½ peeled onion	½ pound raisins
½ ounce mustard seed	2 ounces salt
6 chili peppers	1½ pints vinegar

Peel, core and cut up apples; chop onion. Make a spice bag of mustard seed and peppers. Place all ingredients in enameled saucepan and bring slowly to a boil, stirring until sugar is dissolved. Simmer gently until apples and onion are tender. Remove spice bag, pour into hot, sterilized jars. Fine with cold fowl or pork. Makes 4 to 5 pints.

PICKLED SLICED APPLES

6 pounds cooking apples	¾ pound sugar
2 ounces salt	¾ ounce ground ginger
¾ ounce turmeric	12 cloves
¾ ounce dry mustard	12 peppercorns
3 pints vinegar	10 shallots

Peel, core and slice apples and put in bowl in layers, sprinkling each layer with salt. Let stand for 24 hours; then drain.

Mix turmeric and mustard to a smooth paste with a little cold vinegar. Put rest of vinegar in pan with the sugar, spices and shallots. Bring to a boil and then stir in the turmeric mixture. Boil for 10 minutes, then add the apples and cook them until they are tender, about 15 minutes. Remove shallots and put in jars; seal. Makes 3 to 4 pints.

PICKLED LADY APPLES

3 pounds sugar	Spice bag:
2 cups cider vinegar	6 sticks cinnamon
	12 whole cloves
	6 pounds Lady apples

Fruit should be perfect, as it is left whole, unpeeled and unstemmed. Boil sugar and vinegar with spice bag for 10 minutes.

Steam apples over boiling water until tender, then put in hot, sterilized Mason jars and fill with boiling sirup and seal.

If apples are not steamed, boil sirup 4 minutes, add apples and cook until just tender. See that they do not become soft. Pack apples in jars, fill with sirup, and seal. Makes 6 pints.

Also see Scotch apple pickle in Around the World chapter.

PICKLED BANANA CHUNKS

4 cups sugar
1 cup white vinegar

Spice bag:
  1 teaspoon mace
  1 teaspoon cinnamon
  ½ teaspoon powdered cloves
9 large bananas

Boil spice bag with vinegar and sugar for 15 minutes.

Cut bananas in 4 pieces, crosswise. Boil them in sirup until they can easily be pierced with a toothpick or wooden skewer. Cool in sirup. Place all in jars and seal. Makes 3 pints.

PICKLED BANANA SLICES

1 pound brown sugar
¾ pint vinegar
1½ teaspoons powdered mace

1½ teaspoons cinnamon
¾ teaspoon powdered cloves
12 bananas

Boil the sugar with the vinegar and spices for 15 minutes.

Peel bananas and cut into ¼-inch slices. Put in liquid and cook until nearly tender. Drain fruit, put into jars, strain vinegar sirup and pour over. Seal. Makes 4 pints.

PICKLED BLACKBERRIES

3 pounds blackberries
½ pound lump sugar

Spice bag:
  8 cloves
  1½-inch stick cinnamon
  Small piece whole ginger
1 pint vinegar
1 pound granulated sugar

This requires 2 utensils. In one, cook the blackberries with the lump sugar and small amount of water. When sugar is dissolved, bring to a boil, then simmer.

Meanwhile, place spice bag in vinegar and boil for 20 minutes, keeping lid on pan. Add spiced vinegar, spice bag and granulated sugar to berries, stirring to dissolve the sugar; then simmer gently for 20 minutes, being careful to keep from breaking fruit. Take out berries with strainer and put into jars. Reduce sirup by ¼, take out spice bag and pour over berries. Seal. Makes 4 pints.

SPICED BLUEBERRIES

3 pounds sugar
1 pint diluted vinegar

Spice bag:
 1 tablespoon stick cinnamon
 1 tablespoon whole cloves
 1 tablespoon whole allspice
5 pounds blueberries, cleaned

Make a sirup of sugar, vinegar and spices in bag. Add cleaned berries to cooled sirup, heat slowly to simmering and simmer until done. Cool quickly; let stand ovrenight. Remove spice bag, pack berries into jars; heat sirup to boil and pour hot over berries. Seal and store. Makes 3 to 4 pints.

My father was in the liquor business in Portland, Oregon, San Francisco, Pittsburgh, Pennsylvania, and Los Angeles before and after Prohibition. During that doleful era, he operated fruit-packing plants all over California. I remember a brandied cherry formula of his that combined his two careers.

DAD'S VISCHNIK

1 gallon ripe black cherries (Bing, Tartarian, Black Republican)
Sugar
2 quarts grape brandy

Wash cherries, remove stems and put in large jug; cover with sugar; add the brandy. Store in a cool place for 6 weeks, shaking jug twice a week.

Use this cherry-flavored brandy, pouring from jug until it is gone. Then replenish with new brandy and half the sugar. Cherries should be replaced every 2 years, or when they become bleached out.

Straight bonded rye, bourbon or grain alcohol, according to taste, may be substituted for the brandy.

KIMMEL CHERRIES

4 pints cherries, stones removed
3 cups white distilled vinegar
8 cups white sugar

Cover cherries with vinegar and steep overnight.

Next day, drain. Place in deep bowl, add sugar, cover. Stir once a day for 9 days. Place in hot, sterilized jars; seal. Makes 4 pints.

QUICK PICKLED CHERRIES

½ pint vinegar
Spice bag:
  8 cloves
  2-inch stick of cinnamon
  Small piece whole ginger

1 pound sugar
2 pounds cherries, washed and
  stemmed

Boil vinegar for 15 minutes in covered pan with spice bag. Add sugar and when it is dissolved, remove spice bag. Meanwhile, pack cherries into jars, ¾ full. Pour boiling hot spiced vinegar over the cherries, filling the jars, and seal. Makes 2 to 3 pints.

COLD PICKLED CHERRIES

2 quarts pitted fresh red sour cherries (or 4 1-pound cans)
1 quart white vinegar
8 cups (2 quarts) sugar

Soak cherries overnight in cold water; drain; cover with vinegar; let stand at room temperature 1 week, stirring daily. Drain vinegar. Add sugar to cherries. Stir carefully until well mixed. Let stand at room temperature 1 week, stirring once or twice a day. Pack cherries and sirup into jars and seal. Serve as an accompaniment to meat. Makes 4 pints.

CHERRY PICKLES

Wash, drain and pit cherries. Cover with vinegar. Let stand 12 hours. Measure both cherries and juice and add an equal measure of sugar. Let stand 10 days in a cool place. Stir each day. Pack cherries into hot, sterilized jars. Heat sirup to boil. Pour, boiling hot, over cherries; seal at once.

OLIVE CHERRIES

2 quarts perfect Bing cherries
2 tablespoons salt

1 cup white distilled vinegar
4 tablespoons sugar

Wash cherries but do not remove stems. Pack in 4 hot, sterilized pint jars. Make sirup of remaining ingredients; bring to a boil and pour over cherries, dividing equally in jars, filling to top with cold water; then seal. Let stand 4 weeks before using.

SALTED CHERRIES

1 quart large dark red cherries
½ cup vinegar
1 tablespoon salt

Wash slightly underripe cherries, leaving stems on. Place in quart jar. Dissolve salt in vinegar and add to cherries; fill jar with cold water; seal immediately. Nothing is heated. Let stand 4 months before opening. Use like olives.

CRAB APPLE PICKLES

1 gallon crab apples
5 cups sugar
2 sticks cinnamon
1 tablespoon allspice

½ tablespoon cloves
3 cups water
4 cups vinegar

Wash, rinse and drain apples. Do not remove stems. Run large needle through each apple. This will not keep the skins from cracking but will usually prevent apples from bursting.

Add sugar, spices (in bag) and water to vinegar. Boil until sugar dissolves. Cool. Add apples and simmer until tender. Let stand 12 to 18 hours in a cool place. Pack apples into hot, sterilized jars. Heat sirup to boiling point. Pour, boiling hot, over apples. Process pints and quarts 10 minutes in boiling water bath. Makes 3 to 4 quarts.

PICKLED CRAB APPLES

7 pounds uniform-size crab apples
1 quart cider vinegar
1 cup water
3½ cups sugar

Spice bag:
1 ounce whole cloves
1 tablespoon whole allspice
1 tablespoon mixed pickling spices

Wash apples, remove blossom end.

Combine vinegar, water, sugar and spice bag in large, open kettle. Bring to a boil rapidly. Allow sirup to cool, then add apples. Put back over heat and bring to a boil slowly; otherwise the skins will break. Cook for about 5 minutes. Remove kettle from heat, remove spice bag, and let apples stand in sirup overnight. Pack apples cold in hot, sterilized jars, pour cold sirup over and seal. Let stand before using. Makes 4 to 6 pints.

SPICED CRAB APPLES

12 pounds crab apples
1 quart vinegar
1 quart sugar

Spice bag:
  1 stick cinnamon
  1 tablespoon cloves
  1 teaspoon allspice
  1 teaspoon mace

Wash apples, pierce each one. Make sirup of remaining ingredients. Bring to boil; then cool. Add crab apples and heat slowly so as not to burst the fruit. Bring to a boil, remove and allow to cool overnight. Remove spice bag. Pack crab apples into clean, sterilized jars; fill to within ½ inch of top with sirup. Seal and process 20 minutes at simmering temperature (about 180°F).

SPICY CRAB APPLES

4 pounds crab apples
4½ cups sugar
1 quart vinegar

2 sticks cinnamon
½ tablespoon whole cloves

Choose firm, ripe crab apples, free from blemishes. Do not pare; leave the stems attached.

In a kettle large enough to contain the fruit, combine sugar, vinegar and spices. Bring slowly to a boil and cook for 5 minutes. Add fruit, again bring to a boil, then turn down heat and cook slowly until apples are tender. Allow fruit to stand in sirup overnight. The next day, drain off the sirup and cook it until it is the consistency of honey. Pack fruit into 1-pint sterilized jars and fill with sirup. Seal. Makes 4 or 5 pints.

SWEET AND SPICY CRAB APPLES

5 pounds small crab apples
Water to cover
5 cups sugar
1¼ cups cider vinegar
1½ cups liquid from apples

1 stick cinnamon
2 teaspoons whole cloves
1 tiny piece ginger root
1 blade mace

Wash crab apples and only remove blossom ends. Do not peel. Use only enough water to cover fruit, bring to a boil and cook 5 minutes longer. Drain and save liquid.

Place remaining ingredients in kettle and cook for 5 minutes; then add crab apples. Cook very slowly until tender. Fruit should be almost transparent. Remove and pack immediately into hot, sterilized jars, covering with hot sirup. Seal at once. Makes about 5 or 6 pints.

Peaches and Seckel pears may be put up the same way.

SPICED CRANBERRIES

2 quarts cranberries	2 tablespoons ground cinnamon
1⅓ cups vinegar	1 tablespoon ground cloves
⅔ cup water	1 tablespoon ground allspice
6 cups sugar	

Wash and inspect cranberries. Place in large kettle and add remaining ingredients. Cook slowly over low fire for 45 minutes. Pour into hot, sterilized glasses and seal. Makes 6 to 8 ½-pints.

SPICED FRESH CURRANTS

7 pounds currants	Spice bag:
5 pounds brown sugar	2 tablespoons cinnamon
1 pint vinegar	2 tablespoons cloves

Inspect currants, wash, drain and remove stems. Put into preserving kettle or pan with remaining ingredients and bring to boil. Reduce heat and cook slowly for 1½ hours, remove bag and put in jars. Makes about 8 pints.

A good relish for game:

SPICED DRIED CURRANTS

4 quarts dried currants	Spice bag:
1 quart vinegar	1 teaspoon cinnamon
6 cups brown sugar	1 teaspoon allspice
	1 teaspoon cloves
	1 teaspoon nutmeg

Clean currants and place in enameled pan. Add vinegar, sugar and spice bag. Simmer steadily for 1 hour, stirring frequently.

Cool, remove spice bag and seal in jars. Makes about 5 quarts.

SPICED CURRANTS AND RASPBERRIES

2 pounds red raspberries	2 pounds sugar
2 pounds currants	1 cup vinegar
2 tablespoons ground cinnamon	1 teaspoon salt
1 tablespoon ground cloves	

Weigh the fruit after washing, remove imperfect pieces and stem currants. Mix all ingredients, bring to a rapid boil and cook 20 minutes, stirring constantly. Fill the boiling fruit into hot, sterilized pint jars; cool; seal tightly. Makes about 4 pints.

FIGKLES

1 gallon figs	1 tablespoon cloves
5 cups sugar	1 tablespoon allspice
8 cups water	2 sticks cinnamon
3 cups vinegar	

Wash, drain and peel firm-ripe figs. If preferred unpeeled, pour boiling water over figs and let stand until cold.

Add 3 cups of the sugar to water. Boil until sugar dissolves. Cool. Add figs. Boil slowly 30 minutes. Add remaining sugar, vinegar, spices, in bag. Boil until figs are clear. Let stand 12 to 24 hours in a cool place.

Heat to simmering. Pack, hot, into hot, sterilized jars. Process pints and quarts 30 minutes at simmering in hot water bath. Makes 3 to 4 quarts.

LOUISIANA PICKLED FIGS

5 quarts figs	Spice bag:
1 quart water	1 tablespoon cinnamon
3 pints sugar	1 tablespoon cloves
1 pint vinegar	1 teaspoon allspice
	1 teaspoon mace

Select firm, ripe figs, scald with soda solution (1 cup of soda to 6 quarts boiling water). Drain and rinse. Cook figs until tender in 1 quart water and 1 pint sugar.

When figs are tender, add remaining 2 pints sugar, vinegar, spice bag, and cook until figs are clear and transparent. If sirup is not thick, remove figs and continue boiling until it is almost as thick as a preserve sirup. Allow figs to stand in this sirup overnight.

On the following morning, pack fruit into jars, cover with sirup and process pint or 12-ounce jar in a water bath for 15 minutes at boiling or 30 minutes simmering at 180°F. Makes 8 to 10 pints.

PICKLED DATES

3 pounds dates	1½ ounces mixed pickling spices
¾ pound brown sugar	2¼ pints vinegar
Salt to taste	

Stone dates, cut them in halves and pack in hot, sterilized jars.

Put other ingredients in pan and bring to boil, then pour over dates. Cool, seal and do not open for 3 months. Makes about 4 pints.

PICKLED STUFFED DATES

2 pounds fresh dates
1 quart malt vinegar
1 teaspoon allspice

Remove stones from dates. Cavities may be stuffed with fine-chopped raisins if desired. Place in hot, sterilized jars, heat vinegar to boiling point, add the spice and pour over dates while hot. Seal and put away for 1 week before using. Makes about 2 pints.

SPICED ELDERBERRIES

5 pounds elderberries
3 pounds sugar
1 pint diluted vinegar

Spice bag:
   1 tablespoon stick cinnamon
   1 tablespoon whole cloves
   1 tablespoon whole allspice

Clean and inspect berries. Make sirup of sugar, vinegar and spices in bag, bring to boil, then cool. Add berries to cooled sirup, heat slowly to simmering point and simmer until berries are tender. Cool quickly; let stand several hours or overnight. Remove spice bag. Pack berries in jars. Heat sirup and pour, hot, over berries; seal and store. Makes 4 pints.

Spiced huckleberries may be made the same way.

SPICED TOKAY GRAPES

10 pounds Tokay grapes,
   stemmed
8 cups sugar
2 cups white vinegar

Spice bag:
   1 teaspoon nutmeg
   1 teaspoon ginger
   1 teaspoon cinnamon
   1 teaspoon cloves

Cut grapes in halves and remove seeds. Boil sugar, vinegar and spice bag 5 minutes. Add grapes and cook until thick. Remove spice bag; pour into hot, sterilized jars and seal. Makes about 8 pints.

SPICED CONCORD GRAPES

10 cups Concord grapes
5 cups sugar
½ teaspoon ground allspice

2 teaspoons ground cinnamon
½ teaspoon ground cloves
1 cup vinegar

Wash, drain, stem and measure grapes. Press to separate pulp from skins. Save skins. Cook grapes until soft. Press through sieve to remove seed. Mix skins, pulp, sugar, spices and vinegar. Boil almost to jellying point. The mixture, when dipped out on a spoon, will come off in thick drops and the last 2 will "sheet" together or combine. Pour, boiling hot, into hot, sterilized jars; seal at once. Makes 4 or 5 pints.

SPICED BERRIES. Use blueberries, cranberries, currants, elderberries. Wash, drain and measure hard-ripe berries. Follow recipe for spiced Concord grapes, but do not press berries to remove skins and seeds.

GUAVA SWEET PICKLE

3 quarts prepared guavas
Spice bag:
  1 tablespoon allspice
  3 dozen whole cloves
  2 large sticks cinnamon
  ½ cup preserved ginger, or
    4 pieces of fresh ginger root

½ teaspoon salt
3 cups brown sugar
1 cup white sugar
1 cup vinegar

Select large, meaty guavas. Cut them into halves and scoop out center; measure. Place pulp in preserving kettle; add spice bag and other ingredients and let stand 3 to 4 hours. Then cook until fruit is tender and sirup-heavy. Time required depends on type of guavas used. Seal, boiling hot, in hot, sterilized jars. Water-bath pints for 10 minutes, quarts 15 minutes. Makes about 2 quarts, or 3 to 4 pints.

SPICY LEMON PICKLE

1 pound lemons
3 tablespoons salt
4 tablespoons crushed red pepper

1 teaspoon paprika
¼ teaspoon garlic powder
3 cups vegetable oil

Quarter lemons; roll each quarter in salt. Place in a quart jar. Cover and let stand at room temperature 4 days. Add red pepper, paprika and garlic. Heat oil. Pour hot oil over lemons. Cool. Cover and let stand at room temperature 4 days longer. Makes 1 quart.

SPICED MANGOES

8 pounds ripe mangoes
4 pounds sugar
1 pint vinegar

1 cup water
2 tablespoons whole cloves
2 sticks cinnamon

Wash and peel fruit and slice from seed. Weigh it.

Make a sirup of the vinegar, water and sugar, with spices tied loosely in a cheesecloth bag and slightly pounded. Add prepared fruit and boil until fruit just begins to look clear. Allow to stand until next morning. Heat to boil again and seal in sterilized jars. Makes about 5 pints.

PICKLED MANGOES

12 slightly underripe mangoes
1 quart white vinegar
Spice bag:
  1 ounce mustard seed
  1 ounce ginger
  1 ounce horse-radish
  12 peppercorns

1 clove garlic, minced
1 tablespoon salt
4 ounces sugar

Cut mangoes into slices, peeling and stoning, and pack into jars.

Bring all the remaining ingredients to a boil and boil for 20 minutes. Remove spice bag and pour vinegar while hot over mangoes. Seal and let stand 1 month before using. Makes 3 to 4 pints.

SPICY PRESERVED ORANGE SLICES

8 seedless oranges
4 cups sugar
1 cup vinegar

½ cup water
10 whole cloves
2 sticks cinnamon

Slice oranges about ¼ inch thick; discard ends. Cover with water in saucepan and simmer, covered, 1 hour or until tender. Drain.

Boil sugar, vinegar, water and spices 5 minutes. Add oranges and simmer about 1 hour until slices are well glazed. Pack slices in jars; fill with hot sirup; cool; seal with paraffin.

Serve with poultry, duck, goose, venison, etc. Makes 3 pints.

SWEET SPICED PAPAYA PICKLES

Use freshly picked, sound, firm, ripe fruit. Peel and cut in sizable uniform pieces. Remove seeds or not, as preferred. Weigh; for every pound of papaya add 1 pound of sugar. Sprinkle over fruit and allow to stand for a few hours or until sugar is dissolved. If not enough liquid is drawn from the fruit to cover well, add water sufficient to cover.

Place over heat, bring to a boil and boil 15 minutes or until fruit is clear and transparent.

When sirup is thick and heavy, remove fruit and add ½ to ¾ cup of vinegar for each pint of sirup, and whole spices as follows: 1 tablespoon whole cinnamon, 1 teaspoon each of cloves and allspice tied loosely in a cheesecloth bag and lightly pounded. Boil 10 minutes, then add papaya and cook another 10 minutes. Remove from heat and let stand overnight.

Bring to boil again, transfer fruit to hot, sterile jars, cover with hot sirup and seal at once.

CROCKED BRANDIED PEACHES

8 quarts peaches
Sugar
4 cups brandy

Select firm, unblemished peaches, peel and weigh them. Use half their weight in sugar.

In a large crock place a layer of peaches, then a layer of sugar, pouring some of the brandy over each layer. Continue until the ingredients are used. Cover the crock with a clean cloth and place a lid on top. Set aside in a cool place and let stand for 2 or 3 months before using.

JARRED BRANDIED PEACHES

2 cups white vinegar	½ teaspoon oil of cloves
5 cups white sugar	24 small peaches
2 sticks cinnamon	4 or 5 ounces brandy
2 teaspoons cassia buds	

In kettle, mix all ingredients except peaches and brandy. Bring to a boil.

Drop peaches in boiling water; remove skins; add to mixture and boil 5 minutes. Put stick of cinnamon in each pint jar. Put peaches in and pour mixture over. Add 1 ounce brandy and seal. Makes 4 or 5 pints.

STAGGERING QUESTION . . .

"The kind of quiz show which I am eminently fitted for comes up pretty soon. It will be run by a distillery called Brown-Forman, makers of strong boozes. As you may know, distilled strong boozes are aged in wooden barrels made of white oak and charred. These barrels cost about $25 apiece. Each can be used for only one filling of booze apiece. After that, there is hardly any use for the barrels. For many years, the distillers have been selling them to pickle companies for 25 cents apiece, a social and economic comedown indeed.

"The quiz the distillers will soon launch, with big cash prizes, will be to find what to do with these barrels and make more than a quarter apiece. I've got a million ideas. I'll pay 50 cents a barrel, for instance, and just eat the tender, ripe inside part."

—From "Dream Street," Robert Sylvester's
syndicated column in the New York *Daily News*

PICNIC PEACHES

10 pounds firm cling peaches
Whole cloves
10 cups sugar
5 cups cider vinegar
2½ cups water

Spice bag:
  8 long sticks cinnamon
  3 tablespoons whole allspice
  2 tablespoons whole cloves

Pour boiling water over peaches and let stand until skins come off easily; dip in cold water and peel. Stick 4 cloves in each peach.

Make sirup of sugar, vinegar and water by boiling in covered kettle with spice bag for 5 minutes. Add peaches a few at a time, cover and cook gently 10 minutes or until fruit is just tender. Cool and let fruit stand in sirup overnight.

Drain; pack fruit into hot, sterilized jars. Bring sirup to boil, remove spice bag and pour to overflowing over fruit. Seal at once. Makes about 5 quarts.

CLOVE-STARRED PEACHES

15 firm ripe medium peaches
1 tablespoon finely chopped
  candied ginger
½ cup finely chopped citron
¼ cup finely chopped glacé
  lemon peel
½ teaspoon ground ginger
½ teaspoon ground cinnamon
½ teaspoon ground nutmeg

½ teaspoon ground coriander
  seed
60 whole cloves
4 cups sugar
2 cups cider vinegar
6 tablespoons water
1 stick whole cinnamon,
  2 inches long

Rub fuzz from 12 of the peaches with a coarse towel. Wash and wipe dry. Cut a segment from one side of each peach large enough to remove the pit.

Peel, pit and chop the remaining 3 peaches very fine. Mix with ginger, citron, lemon peel and ground spices. Pack into peach cavities. Replace peach wedges and either sew in place with strong thread or fasten with toothpicks. Stick 4 cloves in each peach.

Combine 1½ cups sugar with the vinegar, water and whole cinnamon sticks in a large saucepan or kettle. Mix well. Bring to boil, cover and boil 5 minutes.

Add one layer of peaches and simmer 10 minutes or until peaches are thoroughly hot. Remove from sirup and place in large bowl. Repeat until all the peaches have been heated.

Bring sirup to boil again and pour over peaches. Cover and let stand 5 hours.

Remove peaches from sirup and add 1 cup more of the sugar to the sirup. Bring to boil, add peaches and cook 10 minutes or until peaches are thoroughly hot. Cover and let stand overnight (at least 8 hours).

Drain off sirup, mix with remaining sugar and bring to boiling point. Add peaches and simmer 5 minutes. Pack into hot, sterilized jars, filling to within ½ inch of top with sirup. Seal at once. Wait 6 weeks before using. Makes 5 to 6 quarts.

CHOCK-FULL-OF-NUTS PEACHES

16 freestone peaches, peeled	1 teaspoon cinnamon, ground
8 tablespoons slivered blanched almonds	7 cups sugar
	2½ cups water
4 tablespoons shredded coconut	1½ cups white vinegar
2 tablespoons honey	18 cloves, in bag

Carefully remove stones from stem end of peaches, leaving them whole. Mix almonds, coconut, honey and cinnamon and fill peach cavities.

Blend sugar, water, vinegar and bag of cloves in saucepan and bring to a boil.

Pour carefully over peaches, which have been arranged, open end up, in large kettle. Place over heat and simmer until peaches are barely cooked through, about 10 minutes. Remove peaches carefully to hot, sterile pint jars, packing 4 to a jar. After discarding clove bag, pour boiling sirup over, filling almost to top, and seal. Makes 4 pints.

TO BLANCH ALMONDS: Cover whole nuts with boiling water, let stand 5 minutes, drain and slip skins off. Almonds can be slivered easily when they are soft after blanching.

For a crisp nut or nut slivers, brown lightly in a 350°F oven, stirring frequently.

A stick with a crosspiece about 1 foot in length nailed to its end is frequently used for turning the vines to locate cucumbers; it has the double advantage of saving the operator from excessive stooping and serving as a protection against poisonous snakes in localities where they are found.

PEACH PICKLES

24 peaches (about 4 quarts)   2 cups water
4 cups sugar   3 cups vinegar
Spice bag:
  1 piece ginger root
  2 sticks cinnamon
  1 tablespoon allspice
  1 tablespoon cloves

Clingstones are best for pickling, but freestone peaches may be used. Wash, drain and peel hard-ripe fruit.

Add 2 cups sugar, spice bag and water to the vinegar. Boil until sugar dissolves. To this sirup add one layer of peaches at a time; simmer until hot through, about 5 minutes, then remove from sirup to bowl. When all peaches have been heated, bring sirup to boil. Pour over peaches. Let stand 3 to 4 hours.

Drain sirup into kettle; add 2 cups sugar. Boil until sugar dissolves. Cool. Add peaches. Let stand 12 to 24 hours in a cool place. Pack peaches into hot, sterilized jars. Add remaining sugar to sirup. Boil until sugar dissolves. Pour, boiling hot, over peaches. Process pints and quarts 10 minutes in boiling water bath. Makes about 4 quarts.

The sugar is added in small amounts to avoid shriveling.

SWEET PICKLED PEACHES

25 pounds peaches   1 ounce cloves
1 gallon vinegar   3 sticks cinnamon
10 pounds granulated sugar

Select ripe, firm peaches, absolutely sound. Peel as smoothly as possible.

Boil vinegar, sugar, and spices in bag, for 5 minutes. To boiling vinegar add ¼ of peaches at a time; allow them to remain for 1 minute, but not until soft; remove from fire, place in large jar or crock, and when all have been scalded, pour over them sufficient boiling vinegar solution to cover well. Seal with hot paraffin; let stand for 6 weeks before packing in jars. Remove the spice bag after 3 weeks. Process packed jars for 15 minutes in boiling water bath. Makes about 11 quarts.

PICKLED PEACHES

3 quarts sugar   2 tablespoons whole cloves
2 quarts vinegar   16 pounds (about 11 quarts)
7 2-inch pieces stick cinnamon   peaches, small or medium

Combine sugar, vinegar, stick cinnamon and cloves. (Cloves may be put in a clean cloth, tied with a string, and removed after cooking if not desired in packed product.) Bring to a boil and let simmer, covered, about 30 minutes.

Wash peaches and remove skins, dipping the fruit in boiling water for 1 minute, then quickly in cold water. To prevent pared peaches from darkening during preparation, put them immediately into cold water containing 2 tablespoons each of salt and vinegar per gallon. Drain just before using.

Add enough peaches for 2 or 3 quarts at a time to the boiling sirup and heat for about 5 minutes. Pack hot peaches into clean, hot jars. Continue heating in sirup and packing peaches into jars. Add 1 piece of stick cinnamon and 2 or 3 whole cloves (if desired) to each jar. Cover peaches with boiling sirup to ½ inch of top of jar. Adjust jar lids.

Process in boiling water for 20 minutes (start to count processing time after water in canner returns to boiling). Remove jars and complete seals if necessary. Set jars upright, several inches apart, on a wire rack to cool. Makes 7 quarts.

SPICED PEACHES (Small Amount)

3 pounds peaches
1½ cups vinegar
3 cups sugar

6 sticks cinnamon
12 whole cloves

Remove skins from peaches.

Boil vinegar and sugar and drop peaches into liquid, a few at a time. Cook until tender. Transfer peaches to hot, clean jars. Add cinnamon and cloves to hot sirup and boil for a few minutes. Pour sirup over the peaches and seal jars. Makes 3 pints.

GINGER PEARS

2 pounds Kieffer pears
2 ounces green ginger root

2 pounds sugar
Grated rind and juice of 2 lemons

Peel, core and fine-chop pears.

Scrape and chop ginger. Put all ingredients in deep kettle and simmer over a low flame, until quite thick, almost 2 hours. Pour into hot, sterilized glasses and seal tops with paraffin. Makes about 2 pints.

PICKLED SECKEL PEARS, UNPEELED

8 pounds pears	8 cups sugar
Spice bag:	1 quart vinegar
10 2-inch pieces stick	1 pint water
cinnamon	
2 tablespoons whole cloves	
2 tablespoons whole allspice	

Wash pears and remove blossom end. Cover with water and boil 10 minutes. Drain. Prick the skins.

Bring spices, sugar, vinegar and water to a boil and boil about 5 minutes. Add pears and boil about 10 minutes or until tender. Let stand in sirup overnight.

Next morning, remove spice bag. Bring sirup and pears to boil. Pack into clean, hot, sterile jars and seal. Makes about 8 pints.

PICKLED SECKEL PEARS, PEELED

2 quarts sugar	Spice bag:
1 quart vinegar, white	2 tablespoons cloves, whole
1 pint water	2 tablespoons allspice, whole
4 sticks cinnamon, 4 inches long	8 pounds (4 or 5 quarts) Seckel
	pears
	8 2-inch pieces cinnamon

Combine sugar, vinegar, water and first cinnamon; add cloves and allspice tied in clean, thin white cloth. Bring to boil and simmer, covered, about 30 minutes.

Wash pears; remove skins and all of blossom end; the stems may be left on if desired. (To prevent peeled pears from darkening during preparation, put them immediately into cold water containing 3 tablespoons each of salt and vinegar per gallon. Drain just before using.)

Add pears to boiling sirup and continue simmering for 20 to 25 minutes. Pack hot pears into clean, hot pint jars; add 1 2-inch piece cinnamon per jar and cover with boiling sirup to ½ inch of top of jar. Adjust jar lids.

Process in boiling water for 20 minutes (start to count processing time as soon as water in canner returns to boil). Remove jars and complete seals if necessary. Set jars upright, several inches apart, on a wire rack to cool. Makes 7 to 8 pints.

KIEFFER PEARS are also frequently used for making fruit pickles. To pickle Kieffer pears: Use 12 pounds Kieffer pears and reduce vinegar to 3 cups in recipe above. Wash the pears; peel, cut in halves or quarters; remove hard centers and cores. Boil pears for 10 minutes in water to cover. Use 1 pint of this liquid in place of the pint of water in recipe above. Finish in the same way as Seckel pears. Makes about 8 pints.

SPICED PEARS

3½ pounds medium ripe pears
  (14 to 16)
Vinegar-water (1 quart water plus
  1 tablespoon vinegar)
2½ cups granulated sugar
1¼ cups white vinegar

1 cup water
Spice bag:
  2 teaspoons whole ginger
  2 tablespoons whole cloves
  7 3-inch cinnamon sticks

Wash, peel and core pears. Place immediately in vinegar-water to prevent browning.

Combine sugar, vinegar, 1 cup water; bring to boil. Add spices tied in bag. Cover. Boil 5 minutes.

Drain pears; add to sirup. Cover. Simmer 5 minutes or until soft but still firm. Remove spice bag.

Fill clean, hot jars with pears. Add sirup to 1 inch from top of jar. Adjust covers as jar manufacturer directs. Process in boiling water bath 15 minutes. Makes 3 to 4 pints.

In Portuguese, quince is marmelo; *and originally, when marmalade was introduced, it applied only to quince marmalade. Later the name marmalade was used for many varieties.*

SPICED QUINCES

7 pounds quinces
6 cups sugar
2 cups vinegar

½ ounce cinnamon
1 ounce whole cloves

Wash and peel quinces.

Combine other ingredients and boil until thickened. Add the quinces and cook until fruit is tender. Pour into sterilized jars and seal. Makes about 7 pints.

PICKLED WALNUTS

Walnuts should be picked about midsummer, before the shells have formed and while they are still in the green stage. Pierce each nut in several places with a pin or larding needle. Place nuts in a large crock and cover with a brine made of salt and water, using ½ cup salt to every quart of water. Allow nuts to stand in this brine for 1 week. Remove the nuts and drain thoroughly. Place nuts in a large kettle and cover with fresh brine made in the same proportions. Simmer gently for 30 minutes. Remove from brine and place in a sieve to drain. When dry, arrange on a flat surface until they turn black. This will take several days. Fill hot, sterilized jars about ⅔ full of walnuts and cover with the following pickle:

1 quart cider vinegar	1 tablespoon salt
2 tablespoons black pepper	1½ teaspoons allspice
1 tablespoon ginger	¼ teaspoon cayenne pepper

Bring to a boil and cook for 10 minutes. Seal jars at once.

MOCK OLIVES (Green Plums)

Small green plums, picked before the stones have formed, can be pickled as imitation olives. Dissolve ¼ pound salt in 1 quart water and pour this over plums. Let stand 3 days. Drain and dry plums, pack in jars and cover with spice vinegar No. 2. Cover tightly and keep in dark, dry place for 3 months before using.

CLOVE-STARRED PRUNES

Try these with chicken dishes.

2 pounds prunes	1 cup vinegar
Whole cloves	2 large sticks cinnamon, broken
1 pound brown sugar	

Wash prunes and soak overnight. In morning insert 2 whole cloves in each prune.

Boil sugar, vinegar and cinnamon together for 5 minutes. Place prunes in sirup. Simmer for 2 hours. Pack in hot, sterilized jars; seal. Makes 3 pints.

SPICED PRUNES

15 large dried prunes	1 teaspoon whole cloves
1 cup sugar	1 3-inch cinnamon stick
½ cup water	½ teaspoon ginger root
½ cup vinegar	

Wash the prunes and cover with cold water. Let stand overnight.

In the morning, cook slowly until tender, in the same water. Set aside to cool.

Combine the sugar, water, vinegar and spices and boil for 5 minutes. Place cooled prunes in a sterilized jar and pour the hot sirup over them. Cover tightly and let stand for 3 weeks before using.

PICKLED STRAWBERRIES

6 quarts ripe strawberries	2 cups white vinegar
Powdered cinnamon	5 cups white sugar
Powdered cloves	

Inspect strawberries, discarding overripe ones. Put a layer in bottom of a large stone jar. Sprinkle a little cinnamon and cloves; then succeeding layers of berries and spices until all the berries are used.

Bring vinegar and sugar to boil; skim and pour over berries. Let stand overnight.

In morning drain off sirup and bring to boil. Pour over the berries as before and let stand overnight again.

Third morning, boil berries and sirup together for 20 minutes. Seal in jars. Makes 6 pints.

PINEAPPLE STICKS

2 medium pineapples	2 tablespoons whole cloves
¾ cup white vinegar	1 2-inch stick cinnamon
3½ cups sugar	1 lemon, sliced thin

Top, peel and cut pineapple into wedges 3 inches long by ½ inch wide.

Heat vinegar in preserving kettle, adding sugar, spices and lemon. When vinegar sirup boils, add pineapple sticks, cover and simmer for 15 minutes, or until fruit becomes transparent. Remove fruit to hot, sterile ½-pint jars and cover with boiling, strained sirup. Green mint or red cinnamon coloring may be added. Seal immediately. Makes 4 ½-pint jars.

SPICED PINEAPPLE SLICES

4 medium pineapples
2 cups granulated sugar
½ cup water

⅔ cup white vinegar
20 whole cloves
1 6-inch cinnamon stick, broken

Cut pineapple into ¼-inch slices crosswise; pare, remove eyes. Cut out cores.

Combine remaining ingredients; heat to boiling point. Add pineapple; simmer 40 minutes. Continue simmering while quickly packing 1 hot, sterilized jar at a time. Fill to ⅛ inch from top. Be sure vinegar solution covers fruit. Seal each jar at once. Makes 4 pints.

PINEAPPLE PICKLE BITS

12 pounds fresh pineapple
7 cups vinegar
7 pounds white or brown sugar

Spice bag:
  12 whole cloves
  12 peppercorns
  3 sticks cinnamon

Peel, core and cut pineapple into small pieces.

Put vinegar, sugar and spice bag in kettle, bring to boil and boil for 10 minutes. Add fruit and boil until tender and well seasoned, about 30 minutes. Strain fruit out, continue boiling sirup for 5 minutes. Put fruit in hot, sterilized jars, cover with boiling sirup and seal. Makes 8 pints.

Pickled Vegetables

The Jerusalem artichoke (Helianthus tuberosus) *is not an artichoke and does not come from Jerusalem. It is a species of native American sunflower which develops delicate tubers on its roots. These are like small knotty potatoes and suggest the flavor of the true artichoke, which is called globe artichoke.*

JERUSALEM ARTICHOKE PICKLES

1 gallon small Jerusalem
  artichokes
1 cup salt
1 gallon water
2½ cups sugar

1 clove garlic
1 tablespoon turmeric
3 tablespoons mixed pickling
  spices
8 cups vinegar

Scrub, rinse and drain artichokes. Dissolve salt in the water. Pour over artichokes. Let stand 18 hours. Rinse. Drain.

Add sugar, garlic, turmeric, spices (in bag) to vinegar. Simmer 20 minutes.

Pack artichokes into hot, sterilized jars. Heat sirup to boiling. Pour, boiling hot, over artichokes. Process 15 minutes in boiling water bath. Makes 4 quarts.

PICKLED WHOLE ARTICHOKES

10 pounds small Jerusalem
  artichokes
2 large sliced onions
2 cups sugar
¼ pound mustard

4 tablespoons turmeric
4 tablespoons mixed pickling
  spice
1 cup salt
3 quarts vinegar

Scrub artichokes well. Pack in jars with sliced onions. Mix sugar, mustard and turmeric together and add spices and salt. Dissolve dry ingredients well in vinegar, place in kettle and bring to boil. Pour hot over artichokes. Seal and process 10 minutes at simmering point in hot water bath. Makes 4 to 5 quarts.

VINEGAR-BRINED BEANS

14 to 15 pounds green (snap) 1½ cups vinegar
beans   1 cup salt
1½ gallons water

Wash beans; remove tips and strings. Leave whole or cut in 1-inch pieces. Cover with enough boiling water and let stand 5 minutes. Cool promptly by dipping in cold water. Pack beans in a 3-gallon crock or stone jar to within 4 or 5 inches of the top. Cover beans with 2 or 3 layers of thin, white cloth and tuck the edges down against the inside of the jar. Cover with a plate or paraffined board that fits loosely inside the jar. Weight with a glass jar filled with water.

Mix the water, vinegar and salt; stir until salt is dissolved. Pour brine over beans until it just covers plate or board. Keep at room temperature, about 70°F.

Remove scum every few days, and each time wash plate, cloth and weight. Let beans ferment for about 2 weeks.

To store, pack beans snugly in clean jars to within 1 inch of top. Fill jars with brine to within ½ inch of top. If there is not enough brine, make additional by recipe above.

Set jars in a kettle of cold water; water should come to shoulder of jar. Bring water slowly to boiling point, then remove jars. Wipe off jar rims and adjust lids. Boil jars, 25 minutes for pints, 30 for quarts, in a boiling water bath (be sure water covers jars). Remove jars; complete the seals. Makes about 10 quarts.

SOUR BEANS

Wash and string wax beans. Cook in boiling salted water until tender. Drain, pack in jars or crocks. Cover with cider vinegar, measuring amount. Add ½ cup of sugar for each quart of vinegar used. Season with salt, pepper and mustard seed, to taste. Sealing not necessary.

DILLED GREEN BEANS

4 pounds green beans, well washed, Crushed hot red pepper
with ends trimmed off   5 cups distilled vinegar
Mustard seed   5 cups water
Dill seed   ½ cup salt
Garlic cloves, halved

Cut beans in proper length to fit either pint jars or ½ pints. Rinse jars in hot water and stack beans in jars lengthwise.

For each pint jar add ½ teaspoon whole mustard seed, ½ teaspoon dill seed, 1 clove garlic cut in two, ¼ teaspoon crushed red pepper. If ½-pint jars are used, halve the amount of seasonings in each jar.

Combine vinegar, water and salt in saucepan and heat to boiling. Pour boiling solution over beans, filling to within ½ inch of top of jar. Adjust lids according to manufacturer's directions and process in boiling water for 5 minutes. Place jars on rack in large kettle filled with boiling water, 1 or 2 inches above tops of jars. Cover. When water returns to rolling boil, begin timing and process for 5 minutes.

Remove jars from kettle and tighten lids if necessary. Set jars upright on rack to cool.

Store in cool place for 2 weeks to develop full flavor.

There are other dilled bean recipes in the Dill Pickle chapter.

PICKLED BEETS

3½ pounds beets (24 small)
1 cup liquid from cooking beets
2 cups white vinegar
1¼ cups granulated sugar
2 tablespoons salt

Spice bag:
  6 whole cloves
  1 3-inch cinnamon stick
½ pound onions (3 medium), sliced

Remove beet tops, leaving roots and 1-inch stem. Wash beets; cover with boiling water; cook until tender. Drain, keeping 1 cup cooking liquid. Remove skins; slice beets.

Combine cooking liquid, vinegar, sugar and salt. Add spice bag to vinegar mixture. Heat to boiling point, covered. Add beets and sliced onions. Simmer 5 minutes. Remove spice bag. Continue simmering while quickly packing 1 hot, sterilized jar at a time. Fill to ⅛ inch from top. Be sure liquid covers beets. Seal each jar at once. Makes 4 pints.

Also see beetroot in Around the World chapter.

The man from Colorado entered the Carnegie Delicatessen in midtown Manhattan and was bewildered by the many strange dishes on the menu. His waiter offered to serve him a typical delicatessen dinner.
"Just leave it all to me," said the waiter.
"Okay, go ahead," the Westerner told him.
After the meal, the waiter asked him how it had been.
"Just dandy," replied the customer. "Only one thing—there was no green vegetable."
"Is that so," said the waiter. "The pickle was maybe poiple?"

BEET PICKLES

1 gallon small beets
2 cups sugar
1½ teaspoons salt
2 sticks cinnamon

1 tablespoon allspice
1½ cups water
3½ cups vinegar

Wash and drain beets. Cover with boiling water. Cook until tender. Remove skin, stem and root ends.

Add sugar, salt, spices and water to vinegar. Simmer 15 minutes. Pack beets into hot, sterilized jars. Heat liquid to boil. Pour, boiling hot, over beets. If not enough liquid to cover, add more vinegar. Process pints and quarts 30 minutes in boiling water bath. Makes 3 to 4 quarts.

For pickled carrots, follow recipe for beet pickles, using small carrots.

SWEET BEET PICKLES

10 pounds beets
4 cups vinegar
4½ cups sugar

1 tablespoon mixed pickling
spices

Beets about the size of golf balls are just right for pickling. See that taproots and skin are unbroken (to prevent leakage of color when beets are cooked). Trim stems to about 4 inches from the beets; wash carefully, rubbing with the hands; do not scrub with brush. Let water run over the washed beets to rinse thoroughly. Pack beets into an aluminum or enamelware kettle and add cold water to cover to a depth of 2 inches. Heat to boiling; reduce heat to simmer, cover, and cook until just tender (30 to 45 minutes, depending on age and size of beets). Drain off liquid, cool slightly and slip skins off. Slice, quarter, or leave beets whole.

Heat vinegar, sugar and spices just to scalding: then add beets and heat until steaming hot. Pack into hot, sterile jars, filling to within ½ inch of top with the pickling solution. Seal. Makes about 5 pints.

PICKLED HONEY BEETS

2 quarts small beets
1½ cups vinegar
1 cup honey
1 cup water
1 teaspoon salt
1 teaspoon ground allspice

Spice bag:
  2 teaspoons broken cinnamon
  2 teaspoons whole cloves
  2 teaspoons white mustard
    seed
2 cups onion rings

Cook beets and peel them.

Combine vinegar, honey and water; add salt and allspice. Add spice bag to vinegar sirup. Simmer 5 minutes. Add beets and onions and simmer 20 minutes. Remove spice bag, pack in hot, sterilized jars and seal at once. Makes 5 pints.

PICKLED CABBAGE

2 medium heads cabbage	2 cups cider vinegar
Salt	8 cups water
2 green peppers	1 bay leaf
2 cups sugar	1 4-inch stick cinnamon

Wash cabbage, shred, drain and let stand overnight in brine made of 1 part salt to 9 parts water. In morning, drain and squeeze water out of cabbage. Fine-cut green pepper and add to cabbage.

Combine sugar, vinegar and water, add spices, bring to boil; boil for 5 minutes. Pack cabbage in hot, sterilized jars; pour boiling hot pickling liquid over. Seal and do not use for at least 3 weeks. Makes 4 quarts.

PICKLED RED OR WHITE CABBAGE

3 large cabbages	Spice bag:
Salt	1 ounce whole cloves
2 quarts wine vinegar	1 ounce mace
1 cup brown sugar	1 ounce allspice
½ cup white mustard seed	1 ounce peppercorns
	1 ounce celery seed
	1 stick cinnamon

Trim off outer leaves, core and shred cabbage. Place in a bowl, generously salting each layer. Cover and stand in a cool place for 24 hours. Drain thoroughly and place cabbage in sun for 2 or 3 hours, or drain in a bag for 6 hours. The cabbage should be dry. Then pack into jars.

Put remaining ingredients into kettle, bring to boil and boil 5 minutes. When cool, remove spice bag and pour over cabbage. If more liquid is needed, add vinegar, after dividing boiled liquid evenly. Cover and store in cool place. Makes 8 to 10 pints.

From The Art and Mystery of Curing, Preserving and Potting All Kinds of Meats, Game, and Fish; *also* The Art of Pickling and the Preservation of Fruits and Vegetables, *adapted as well for the wholesale dealer as all housekeepers. By a Wholesale Curer of Comestibles. London: Chapman and Hall, 1864.*

RED CABBAGE
(A recipe from Halton Castle)

Take two middle-sized close-knit red cabbages, just when the frost has seasoned them, strip them of all superfluous leaves, cut them across in slices nearly a quarter of an inch thick, and scatter finely beaten bay or rock salt over them when laid in large dishes and covered with cloths; so let them lie twenty-four hours. Next drain the cabbage on a sieve and let it remain until the next day, still covered over. Put it into one jar that will contain it without pressure, and strew as you proceed pretty plentifully the following mixture amongst and finally upon the cabbage:

Allspice, coarsely beaten	1 ounce
Gingre, sliced	1½ ounces
Black peppercorns	1 ounce
Bay leaves, shred	½ ounce
Laurel leaves, shred	½ ounce

Now pour pure cold best London pickling vinegar into the jar, and take care that the cabbage is perfectly covered, and to the depth of an inch or more. Make up the jar with a bung, and secure it with resin or pitch. In a month you will have perhaps the best article of its kind to be found anywhere, its excellency consisting in its flavour, its colour, and crispness.

OLD-FASHIONED PICKLED RED CABBAGE

Prepare cabbage by shredding, sprinkling well with salt and standing in cool place for 24 hours. Then drain thoroughly and place in sun for 3 hours. Cover cabbage with vinegar, then pour off vinegar, measure, and add ½ cup sugar for each quart; season with pepper, celery seed, allspice, mace and cinnamon to taste. Boil liquid 5 minutes, then pour over cabbage, which has been packed into crock or crocks. Cover and store in cool place.

PICKLED RED CABBAGE

3 heads red cabbage	8 or 10 small onions
Salt	2 or 3 sweet red peppers
Cloves	Vinegar

Wash the cabbage thoroughly; drain. Cut in chunks or as for slaw with a cabbage slicer. Place in a stone jar which has a cover. Cover with salt. Stir and turn the cabbage every hour or so. At the end of 24 hours, drain off the water. Arrange in layers with cloves, onions and very small red peppers or strips of sweet red pepper. Pour vinegar over to cover. Lay a clean cloth over the jar and place its lid on. Let stand in a cool place for 1 month. Makes about 20 servings.

SWEET PICKLED CARROTS

10 pounds small carrots (5 or 6 dozen)	Spice bag:
1 quart **vinegar**	1 tablespoon stick cinnamon
1 quart **sugar**	1 tablespoon whole cloves
	1 tablespoon whole allspice
	1 tablespoon mace

Boil young carrots until skins slip. Slip skins, slice or leave whole. Make spiced sirup of remaining ingredients and pour boiling hot over carrots. Let stand overnight, then bring to boil and boil 5 minutes. Remove spice bag. Pack in jar, cover with spiced sirup; seal; store.

PICKLED CAULIFLOWER No. 1

2 cauliflowers	2 tablespoons white mustard seed
2 cups pickling onions	1 tablespoon celery seed
1 cup salt	1 hot red pepper
1 cup sugar	3 cups white vinegar

Wash, drain and cut cauliflower into 1- or 2-inch pieces. Scald, cool and peel onions. Mix salt and vegetables. Add enough cool water to cover. Let stand 18 hours. Rinse. Drain. Taste; if too salty, soak 1 hour in cold water to remove some of the salt.

Add sugar, seed and pepper to vinegar. Boil until sugar dissolves. Add vegetables. Boil 10 minutes, or until barely tender. Pack, hot, into hot, sterilized jars. Heat liquid to boiling. Pour, boiling hot, over pickled vegetables; seal at once. Makes 4 to 5 pints.

PICKLED CAULIFLOWER No. 2

1 quart vinegar	8 whole cloves
2 tablespoons mustard seed	4 sticks cinnamon
1 cup sugar	2 heads cauliflower

Simmer all ingredients except cauliflower together for 15 minutes.

Meanwhile wash cauliflower, cut away all leaves and break into uni- form flowerets. Blanch by putting them into kettle of boiling water, turn off heat and let stand 2 minutes. Drain and put flowerets into jars. Pour hot sirup over, straining out spices, and seal. Makes 3 to 4 quarts.

PICKLED CAULIFLOWER No. 3

2 pounds cauliflower
3 cups chopped onions
1 cup chopped sweet red pepper
½ cup salt

1½ cups white vinegar
2 cups sugar
2 tablespoons mixed pickling
   spice, in bag

Break cauliflower into flowerets, chop onions and pepper. Sprinkle with salt and let stand overnight; rinse with fresh water and drain.

Put vinegar, sugar and spices into kettle and boil 5 minutes. Remove from heat, add vegetables; mix well; let stand 2 hours. Return to heat, bring to boil, reduce heat and simmer for 15 minutes. Remove spice bag and pack in hot, sterilized jars. Makes 4 pints.

Also see pickled cauliflower, Syrian style, in Around the World chapter.

EGGPLANT PICKLE

6 eggplants
Chopped onions
Spice bag:
   ½ teaspoon allspice
   ½ teaspoon cloves
   ½ teaspoon whole white
      peppercorns
   1-inch cinnamon stick

1½ cups cider. vinegar
5 cups sugar
1 cup water

Peel and chop the eggplants, adding ⅓ as much chopped onion. Cover with lightly boiling salted water, boil quickly for 5 minutes; drain, cover with cold water; drain again.

Put spice bag in enameled pan with vinegar, sugar and water; bring to boil. Add eggplant and onion mixture; simmer until sirup is thick and vegetables tender; remove spice bag; fill hot, sterilized jars; seal. Makes 4 to 5 pints.

MARINATED MUSHROOMS

1 pound mushrooms
4 tablespoons olive oil
1 clove garlic
2 quarts white vinegar

Spice bag:
   3 peppercorns
   4 cloves
   2 bay leaves
   2 sage leaves
Salt

Clean mushrooms; trim stems, parboil for 1 minute in hot water. Remove and drain thoroughly on a napkin.

Heat olive oil, brown garlic and remove. Pour in vinegar. Add spice bag and salt to taste. Bring to a boil and boil for 1 minute. Add mushrooms immediately. Reduce flame and cook over very low flame for 30 minutes.

Drain and cool mushrooms. Place in jars, fill with vinegar mixture, which has been brought to boil again; seal. Makes 2 quarts.

PICKLED MUSHROOMS

1 pound young mushroom caps	1 teaspoon salt
Vinegar	2 blades mace
¾ onion	½ teaspoon white pepper
1 teaspoon ground ginger	

Wash mushrooms in salt water, rub or scrape clean and put in pan. Pour in enough vinegar to cover; add remaining ingredients and cook slowly, until mushroom caps shrink. Remove them and pack in jars, pouring strained hot vinegar mixture over them. Cover, cool and seal. Makes 1 pint or 2 ½-pint jars.

Also see Syrian pickled mushrooms in Around the World chapter.

PICKLED OKRA

In each pint jar place following seasoning:	1 garlic button
½ teaspoon mustard seed	1 or 2 pods hot pepper
½ teaspoon celery seed	1 teaspoon salt

Use small okra pods (3 to 4 inches long). Blanch okra in boiling water for 1 minute. Place okra, stem end down, in jars. Cover with vinegar and leave ½ inch head space. Put on lids and process for 30 minutes in 185°F water bath.

DILL PICKLED OKRA

2 pounds young whole okra	⅔ quart water
Celery leaves	1⅔ cups white vinegar
4 cloves garlic	2 tablespoons salt
4 sprigs dill	

Scrub okra and pack into pint jars with a few celery leaves, clove of garlic and sprig of dill in each jar.

Heat water, vinegar and salt to boiling point and pour over okra; seal. **Let stand 1 month before using. Makes about 4 pints.**

PICKLED ONIONS

2 quarts onions
½ cup salt
1 quart cold water
4 cups white vinegar

2 tablespoons mixed pickling
  spices, tied in bag
1 cup sugar
Red pepper pods
Bay leaves

Select fresh, tender pickling onions which are sweet and flavorful. Wash and clean, then cover with scalding water and let stand for 2 minutes. Transfer onions at once to cold water and peel.

Make solution of the salt and cold water. Pour over onions and let stand overnight or longer. Drain. Rinse with cold water and drain again. Be careful to remove all brine which may have accumulated on onions.

Mix vinegar, pickling spices and sugar. Simmer for 10 minutes. Pack onions into hot, sterile jars, add small red pepper pod and bay leaf to each jar, bring vinegar mixture to a quick boil, and pour over onions. Seal at once. Makes 4 pint jars.

And here is a different recipe for double the quantity:

ONION PICKLES

1 gallon pickling onions
1 cup salt
2 cups sugar
3 tablespoons white mustard
  seed

2 tablespoons grated horse-radish
6 cups white vinegar
Small red peppers
Bay leaves

Scald onions 2 minutes in boiling water. Dip in cold water. Drain and peel. Sprinkle with salt. Add cool water to cover. Let stand 12 to 18 hours. Rinse. Drain.

Add sugar, seed and horse-radish to vinegar. Simmer 15 minutes. Pack onions into hot, sterilized jars. Add 1 each, pepper and bay leaf, when jar is ½ filled. Heat pickling liquid to boiling. Pour, boiling hot, over onions; seal at once. Makes 3 or 4 quarts.

For lamb or veal:

MINTED ONION RINGS

2 cups cider vinegar
2 tablespoons sugar
1 cup fresh mint leaves or
  2 tablespoons dried

Green food coloring
2 cups onion rings
2 pimientos

Combine vinegar and sugar in saucepan; add mint leaves in spice bag. Heat gently for 10 minutes; remove from fire; add coloring. Add onions, which have been sliced thin, and pimientos, which have been cut in thin strips. Heat to boiling point. Pack onions into hot, sterilized jar, make sure liquid covers, and seal. Makes about 1 pint.

PICKLED GREEN PARSLEY
(From *The English House-Keeper*, by Mrs. Raffald, 1769)

Take a large quantity of curled Parsley, make a strong Salt and Water to bear an Egg, put in your Parsley, let it stand a Week, then take it out to drain, make a fresh Salt and Water as before, let it stand another Week, put it in Spring Water, and change it every Day for three Days, then scald it in hard Water till it becomes Green, take it out and drain it quite dry, boil a Quart of distilled Vinegar a few Minutes, with two or three Blades of Mace, a Nutmeg sliced, and a Shalot or two; when it is quite cold, pour it on your Parsley, with two or three Slices of Horseradish, and keep it for Use.

PEPPERS

The small pointed varieties of peppers, such as the chili verde and yellow wax chili, are very hot. Like garlic, a small amount of them goes a long way.

The large chili pepper and green pepper are less pungent in flavor and they can be used either as a seasoning or as a vegetable.

Before using any of the small hot peppers, remove the stem and seeds, then chop.

To pickle hot peppers, pack them whole in a hot, sterilized jar; add 1 teaspoon salt and 1 clove garlic and cover with boiling vinegar. Seal jar and let stand in refrigerator for 2 weeks before using. Use chopped peppers as condiment, in cocktail dips, deviled eggs or sandwich fillings.

The vinegar in which they have been pickled can be used where a hot effect is desired.

Try dropping a small, hot pepper in a bottle of French dressing, let stand 2 weeks, then use.

PICKLED PEPPERS No. 1

1 gallon peppers	1 clove garlic
1½ cups salt	1 tablespoon horse-radish
1 gallon water	1 cup water
2 tablespoons sugar	5 cups vinegar

Wash and drain Hungarian or other long red, green or yellow peppers. Cut 2 small slits in each pepper. Dissolve salt in 1 gallon water. Pour over peppers. Let stand 12 to 18 hours. Rinse. Drain.

Add sugar, garlic, horse-radish and 1 cup water to vinegar. Simmer 15 minutes. Remove garlic.

Pack peppers into hot, sterilized jars. Heat pickling liquid to boiling. Pour, boiling hot, over peppers; seal at once. Makes 4 quarts.

PICKLED PEPPERS No. 2

1 quart water	1 tablespoon salt
1 quart white vinegar	6 garlic cloves
¾ cup firmly packed brown sugar	12 medium green peppers,
6 tablespoons salad oil	trimmed and cut into eighths

Combine water and vinegar in a saucepan; bring to a boil.

Place 2 tablespoons sugar, 1 tablespoon oil, ½ teaspoon salt, and a garlic clove in each of the jars. Pack peppers into jars. Pour in hot vinegar liquid. Seal jars securely. Let stand at room temperature at least a week, turning jars occasionally to distribute flavorings. Makes 6 pints.

PICKLED PEPPERS No. 3

4 pounds sweet red peppers	1 cup vinegar
Boiling water to cover	1 cup olive oil
Ice water	

Seed the peppers and either cut into strips or leave whole. Blanch in boiling water, let stand 2 minutes. Drain and cover with ice water. Drain again and put in hot, sterilized jars. Boil vinegar for 2 minutes, add oil, and when it boils again, pour over peppers and seal. Makes about 2 quarts.

CABBAGE-STUFFED PEPPERS

6 sweet red peppers	1 tablespoon whole yellow
½ head cabbage	mustard seed
½ tablespoon salt	2 cups vinegar

Remove stems and cut off tops of peppers and remove the seeds without breaking the shells. Cut cabbage fine as in slaw, and add to it the salt and mustard seeds. Mix thoroughly and place in peppers, pressing in tightly. Place tops on pepper cases and fasten them down with toothpicks. Place them upright in stone jar and cover with cold vinegar. Place cover over jar and put away in cool place until ready to use. May be kept several months before using.

PICKLED SWEET RED PEPPERS

Wash outside of peppers and wipe them dry. Cut top off stem end and remove seeds. Cut into thin strips with scissors, or into long ribbons, working around and around the pepper. Scald well; then drop into ice water to crisp. Drain. Put the peppers into clean, hot jars; fill to overflowing with hot sirup made in the proportions of 1 cup sugar to 2 cups vinegar; seal immediately.

PRESERVING PIMIENTOS

4 pounds sweet red (pimiento) peppers	Ice water
	1 cup vinegar
Boiling water to cover	1 cup olive oil

Seed the peppers and either cut into strips or leave whole. Blanch in boiling water, let stand 2 minutes. Drain and cover with ice water. Drain again and put in hot, sterilized jars. Boil vinegar for 2 minutes, add oil, and when it boils again, pour over peppers and seal. Makes about 2 quarts.

PICKLED PIMIENTO PEPPERS

16 to 20 large pimiento peppers	1½ cups sugar
3 cups vinegar	½ teaspoon salt

Wash, stem and seed peppers, cut into strips, cover with boiling water and let stand 3 minutes. Drain well; pack in hot, sterilized jars.

Boil remaining ingredients 5 minutes and pour over peppers, filling jars to overflowing. Seal at once. Makes 4 pints.

A foreigner once commented, You Americans are strange. You devote only one day out of the year to your fathers and mothers, and an entire week to pickles."

PUMPKIN

Here are two ways to turn pumpkins into pickles.

PICKLED PUMPKIN

4- or 5-pound pumpkin
Salt
1 pint vinegar
½ pint maple sirup
2 cloves

¼ teaspoon ground ginger
6 peppercorns
1 bay leaf
1 clove garlic

Peel and seed the pumpkin and cut into small cubes. Sprinkle with salt and let it stand 2 or 3 hours.

Meanwhile make a sirup of the remaining ingredients.

Wash salt off pumpkin, pack into hot, sterilized jars and pour the sirup over it. Seal at once and store. Makes 5 pints.

PETER'S PICKLED PUMPKIN

1 pint vinegar
4 pounds sugar
Spice bag:
  1 teaspoon whole cloves
  1 tablespoon broken stick
  cinnamon

5 pounds pumpkin, pared and cut
in 1-inch cubes

In saucepan place vinegar, sugar and spice bag. Heat to boiling and boil 5 minutes. Pour over pumpkin, which has been put in preserving kettle. Cook pumpkin in sirup 5 minutes or until tender. Place in jars, cover with vinegar sirup and seal. Makes 5 pints.

For a radish pickle see Japanese pickled radishes in Around the World chapter.

TOMATOES

Tomatoes have been used as food by the Indians of Mexico since prehistoric times. The cultivated tomato probably evolved from wild species growing on the slopes of the Andes mountains. The Italians, early in the 16th century, apparently were the first Europeans to eat tomatoes. Sometimes called "love apples," they were grown later for ornament in the gardens of England, Spain, and mid-European countries. Perhaps because the plant is a member of the nightshade family, tomatoes were for many years considered poisonous. In 1812, probably owing to French influence, tomatoes were used as food in New Orleans. Another 20 to 25 years elapsed before the northeastern states grew them for food, although records show that Thomas Jefferson cultivated them in Virginia as early as 1781.

CHERRY TOMATO PICKLES

2 pounds small green cherry tomatoes	1 teaspoon mustard seed
2 heads of dill	1 teaspoon mixed pickling spices
1 small clove garlic	1 small hot red pepper
1 thumbnail-sized piece of horse-radish	1 cup white vinegar
	1 teaspoon salt
	2 cups water

Hard green tomatoes are best. Wash, dry and remove stems.

Place seasonings in hot, sterilized quart jar. Pack jar tightly with tomatoes. Combine vinegar, salt and water; bring to boil and pour over tomatoes, filling jar to overflowing. Seal at once. Makes 1 quart.

Gherkins or burr cucumbers may be pickled in the above manner, as well as any other small green and red tomatoes.

TOMATO COCKTAIL PICKLES

1 gallon small green tomatoes	4 cups vinegar
1 cup sugar	Dill
1½ tablespoons salt	Small hot peppers
2 or 3 cloves garlic	Bay leaves
2 tablespoons mixed spices	Mustard seed
4 cups water	

Cherry or plum tomatoes are best for this pickle, but tiny regular tomatoes can be used. Wash, rinse and drain tomatoes.

Add sugar, salt, garlic, spices (in bag) and water to vinegar. Simmer 15 minutes.

Pack tomatoes into hot, sterilized jars with 1 head dill (green or dry), 1 pepper, 1 small bay leaf and 1 teaspoon mustard seed. Pour hot pickling liquid over tomatoes. Process pints and quarts 30 minutes at simmering, or 15 minutes in boiling water bath. Makes 4 quarts.

SPICED GREEN TOMATOES

6 pounds small whole green
tomatoes
4 pounds sugar
1 pint vinegar

½ tablespoon mace
1 tablespoon cinnamon
½ tablespoon cloves
½ tablespoon allspice

Small green Italian or plum tomatoes are suitable for this pickle. Scald and peel.

Make a sirup of the sugar, vinegar and spices. Drop in the whole tomatoes and boil until they become clear. Pour into trays, cool quickly and pack cold into jars. Strain sirup and pour over them; process for 15 minutes at simmering point. Makes about 4 pints.

GREEN TOMATO PICKLE SLICES

15 pounds fresh green tomatoes
1 cup salt
2 quarts boiling water
2 cups cider vinegar

5 cups sugar
Spice bag:
  2 sticks cinnamon
  ⅓ cup cloves

Slice tomatoes and place in layers in large bowl or crock, sprinkling with the salt. Let stand overnight; drain in morning; then pour boiling water over and let stand 20 minutes. Drain again.

Place vinegar and sugar and spice bag in enamel or stainless steel kettle and boil together for a few minutes. Pour over tomatoes and let stand overnight.

Next day, pour off sirup and bring to a boil. Pour over tomatoes again and let stand overnight.

Next morning place all in kettle; cook until tomatoes are transparent and fill hot, sterilized jars with the tomato slices. Remove spice bag from sirup and boil until quite thick; pour over tomatoes to top of jars and seal. Makes 4 quarts.

GREEN TOMATO AND ONION SLICES

½ peck green tomatoes (4 quarts
  or 8 pounds)
Salt
12 large white onions
3 teaspoons white mustard seed
2 teaspoons dry mustard
1 teaspoon allspice

1 teaspoon whole cloves
1 teaspoon celery seed
1½ tablespoons turmeric
2 dozen small cayenne peppers
½ pound brown sugar
Cider vinegar

Slices tomatoes as thin as possible, using vegetable cutter. Put in crock or jar, sprinkling each layer with salt. Let stand overnight; then drain carefully. Put into preserving kettle, add the onions, which have been sliced as thin as the tomatoes, then all of the spices. Boil together for 3 hours, skimming off scum when necessary. Shortly before removing from fire, add the sugar. Place in hot, sterilized jars or stone crock, covering with sufficient vinegar. Hold for at least 3 months before using. Makes 5 to 6 pints.

Also see Swedish green pickled tomatoes in Around the World chapter.

GREEN TOMATO SLICES

Wash and cut 12 firm green tomatoes into ½-inch slices. Sprinkle with 1 tablespoon salt. Let stand 1 hour. Drain.

Boil ½ cup sugar, 1 cup vinegar, 1 cup water 5 minutes.

Pack tomatoes into hot jars. Pour hot liquid over tomatoes. If not enough to cover, add 1 tablespoon vinegar to each jar and fill with boiling water. Process pints and quarts 20 minutes in boiling water bath.

Tomato slices are used for frying and for pies.

This is a New York State specialty:

GREEN TOMATO RACHEL PICKLES

2 quarts green tomatoes (18 medium small)	½ teaspoon celery seed
3 tablespoons salt	1 teaspoon turmeric
2 cups vinegar	3 cups sliced onions (1 pound)
⅔ cup dark brown sugar	2 large red peppers, trimmed and chopped
1 cup granulated sugar	1 hot green or red pepper, chopped
3 tablespoons mustard seed	

Slice tomatoes and thoroughly mix with the salt and let stand about 12 hours. Drain.

Heat the vinegar, sugars and spices to the boiling point. To the hot vinegar sirup add the sliced onions and boil gently for 5 minutes. Add the drained tomatoes and the chopped peppers, bring slowly to boil and simmer for 5 minutes. Stir occasionally with a wooden spoon. Pack into hot, sterilized jars and fill to the top. Seal immediately. Makes 9 ½-pints.

GINGER TOMATOES

6 pounds green tomatoes
2 pounds red tomatoes
5 pounds granulated sugar

3 lemons, sliced
1 teaspoon whole cloves
3 pieces ginger root

Scald and peel tomatoes and cut in quarters. Place in kettle, add sugar, lemons and spices. Bring to a boil; reduce heat and cook slowly until mixture is thick. Pour into hot sterilized glasses and seal. Makes 15 to 18 6-ounce glasses.

RIPE TOMATO PICKLE

24 firm ripe tomatoes
6 hot red peppers
6 green peppers
12 onions
2 cups sugar
4 ounces salt

1 large stick cinnamon, broken
1 teaspoon whole cloves
1 ounce mustard seed
½ ounce celery seed
6 cups vinegar

Peel tomatoes, trim and slice all vegetables; add remainder of items; boil for 1 hour. Pour into hot, sterilized jars and seal. Makes 4 quarts.

TOMATO CHUNKS

Wash, drain and remove stem end from slightly ripe tomatoes and cut into 1-inch chunks. Measure. For each quart of chunks, make sirup of ¾ cup vinegar, ½ cup brown sugar, 1 teaspoon whole mixed spices in bag, 1½ teaspoons salt. Boil 5 minutes. Add tomato chunks. Boil 5 minutes; remove spice bag. Pack, boiling hot, into hot, sterilized jars; seal at once.

A few slices of onion may be added if desired.

DILL ZUCCHINI SLICES

1 quart white distilled vinegar
1 cup sugar
¼ cup salt
2 teaspoons celery seed
1 tablespoon dill seed

1 teaspoon ground mustard
4 quarts sliced, unpeeled zucchini
1 quart sliced onions

In saucepan, bring vinegar, sugar, salt, seeds and mustard to boil.

Place zucchini and onions in preserving kettle. Pour boiling vinegar mixture over; let stand 1 hour.

Place over heat, bring to boil, cook 3 minutes. Pack in hot, sterilized jars immediately; seal. Makes 6 to 7 pints.

ZUCCHINI PICKLE

4 pounds zucchini	2 teaspoons celery seed
1 pound small white onions	2 teaspoons turmeric
½ cup salt	2 teaspoons dry mustard
1 quart cider vinegar	2 teaspoons mustard seed
2 cups sugar	

Cut unpeeled zucchini into very thin slices, like cucumbers. Peel onions and slice thin. Cover with water and add salt. Let stand 1 hour; then drain.

Combine remaining ingredients, bring to boil and pour over vegetables. Let stand 1 hour. Return to heat, bring to boil and cook 3 minutes. Pack in sterilized jars, seal at once. Makes about 4 pints.

Among the Pennsylvania Dutch it is traditional at every meal to serve seven sweets and seven sours. Try it sometime and see if your company isn't impressed. Here is a suggested list:

Sweets	Sours
Watermelon rind	Dilled beans
Pear butter	Sauerkraut
Spiced cherries	Pickled green tomatoes
Sweet mixed pickles	Pepper relish
Clove-starred peaches	Pickled beets
Pineapple spears	Mixed mustard pickles
Nutty chutney	Pickled cauliflower, Syrian style

Pickled Eggs, Meats and Fish

EGGS

Sometimes it is well to make some pickled eggs when egg prices are very low. It is one way of conserving eggs. They can be served as a meat substitute, can be prepared into deviled eggs, served as creamed sour eggs or used as garnishes.

PICKLED EGGS

18 eggs
2 cups white vinegar
1½ quarts water
2 teaspoons salt

Spice bag:
1 small dry red pepper
1 tablespoon mixed pickling spices

Simmer fresh eggs for 30 minutes until hard boiled. A slow cooking process makes the eggs more tender.

Make pickling solution of remaining ingredients and when boiling add peeled eggs and bring to a boil again.

Pack into hot, sterilized jars. Cover completely with pickling solution and seal immediately.

Eggs may be pickled with beets for color. They may also be colored by adding fruit coloring to pickling solution.

SIMPLE PICKLED EGGS

16 hard-boiled eggs, peeled
½ ounce black peppercorns
½ ounce whole ginger

½ ounce allspice
1 quart vinegar

Pack eggs in wide-mouthed jars. Boil spices in vinegar for 10 minutes; then pour, boiling, over eggs. Cool and seal.

PEPPERED PICKLED EGGS

12 eggs
1¾ pints white vinegar
20 peppercorns

Pinch of cayenne pepper
Coriander seeds

Hard-boil the eggs, peel them, put them in a pickling jar, pour over them the vinegar, which has been boiled for 10 minutes on a gentle heat, together with the peppercorns, the cayenne pepper and if possible some coriander seeds.

Leave them uncovered for 48 hours, then close the pickling jar.

Eggs preserved like this make an excellent hors d'oeuvre, very quickly prepared, very useful if you have to serve a meal unexpectedly.

MUSTARD PICKLED EGGS

6 eggs
1 pint spiced vinegar
1½ teaspoons mustard flour
1½ teaspoons cornstarch

1 teaspoon sugar
½ teaspoon turmeric
1 teaspoon salt

Place eggs in boiling water and boil for 10 minutes. Put into cold water and remove shells. Pack into jars. Put spiced vinegar in saucepan; add mustard and cornstarch, which have been mixed smooth into a paste with a little of the vinegar. Also add sugar, turmeric and salt. Stir well until it boils, then pour over eggs and seal.

MEATS

HOME-CORNED BEEF

8 quarts cold water
3 pounds pickling salt
1 ounce sodium nitrate
2 tablespoons brown sugar

1 tablespoon mixed whole spices
20 bay leaves
10 pounds lean brisket of beef
8 to 10 cloves garlic (optional)

Combine all ingredients except meat and boil 8 minutes. Place meat in stoneware crock fitted with tight cover. Add 8 to 10 cloves of garlic if desired, pour pickling solution over meat as soon as it is cold, then weight meat down with heavy plate or rock, or if possible, a wooden board which fits inside crock. Cover top with double layer of muslin tied securely around crock and store in cool place for 2 weeks.

CORNED BEEF IS MISNOMER—*There is no corn in corned beef. The product got its name from the corn-sized bits of salt once used in the preserving process.*

PICKLED PIGS' FEET

Scald, scrape and clean feet thoroughly. Sprinkle with salt and let stand 4 hours. Wash feet well in clean water, place them in kettle of hot water and cook until tender, but meat still adhering to bones. Pack feet in clean jars. Fill jars to within ½ inch of top with boiling spiced vinegar. Process in hot water bath 90 minutes.

SPICED VINEGAR:

2 quarts vinegar
1 small red pepper
2 tablespoons grated horse-radish

1 teaspoon black pepper
1 teaspoon whole allspice

Mix well together, bring to boil and pour over pigs' feet.

AUNT ANNETTA'S PICKLED TONGUE

It is the pickling which gives a beef tongue its red color and distinctive flavor.

¼ teaspoon sodium nitrate
2 quarts warm water
1 cup salt
2 teaspoons mixed pickling spices

2 tablespoons sugar
2 cloves garlic, sliced
½ teaspoon paprika
1 beef tongue

Dissolve sodium nitrate in ½ cup of the warm water; add remaining water, salt, spices, sugar, garlic and paprika. Place in stone crock or large bowl, but do not use metal or enamel container. Place tongue in this mixture and weigh down dish or bowl with heavy weight to keep tongue under liquid. Let stand 3 weeks, turning tongue every second day.

Wash tongue thoroughly, cover with hot salt water and simmer until tender, allowing 1¼ hours for each pound. When cool enough to handle, skin and remove bones, etc., at root. Chill in refrigerator until ready to use. Makes 8 to 12 servings.

PICKLED TONGUE SLICES

1 ox tongue
Salt
Pepper

Whole cloves
Stick cinnamon
Vinegar

Wash tongue; cover with boiling water and cook slowly until tender. Remove and, when completely cooled, skin and trim off fat and roots.

Slice cold tongue very thin and pack into pint jars adding for each jar 1 teaspoonful of salt, 1/4 teaspoon fresh-ground black pepper, 1/2 teaspoon whole cloves and 1/2 cinnamon stick.

Fill to top with vinegar and screw on lid.

SEAFOOD AND FISH

PICKLED OYSTERS

100 large oysters	9 blades mace
Salt	3 bay leaves
2 cups vinegar	1 large hot red pepper broken
24 black peppercorns	into small pieces
24 whole cloves	

Put oysters and their liquor in a porcelain-lined pan, add salt to taste and bring slowly to scalding point. Do not allow the liquor to boil. Take out oysters, just at their plumpest and before the edges begin to curl; set aside to cool.

Strain liquor; return to pan; add vinegar, spices and pepper; bring to boiling point; cool. When almost cold, pour over oysters. Cover oyster jar, place in cool spot overnight.

Next day put in sterilized jars, seal and store in cool place. Makes about 5 pints.

PICKLED TROUT

Trout	Bay leaf
Allspice	Vinegar
Mustard seed	Water
Onion	

Clean trout, leaving heads and tails on. Fry gently but not very well in oil. Pack into hot, sterilized jars, adding to each jar 1/2 teaspoon allspice, 1/2 teaspoon mustard seed, 1 small onion, thinly sliced, and 1 bay leaf. Fill jars with 3 parts vinegar to 1 part water, cap and let stand.

Also see fresh pickled fish in Fresh chapter, and Japanese pickled fish in Around the World chapter.

PICKLED PICKEREL

1 pickerel	1 tablespoon sugar
2 onions, sliced	½ lemon, sliced
1 teaspoon whole black pepper	White vinegar
1 teaspoon whole allspice	1 tablespoon capers

Cut fish into small fillets; cover with water. Add onions, pepper, allspice, sugar and lemon. Boil until fish is nearly done; then add vinegar to equal amount of liquid remaining. Boil till done; add capers and seal in hot, sterilized jars.

Pike or crappies may be used instead of pickerel.

Catsups

Catsup is smooth, thick enough to prevent separation and yet not so thick that it will not pour. Chili sauce is about the same thickness as catsup, but it is not smooth as it is made of chopped, unstrained ingredients.

TOMATO CATSUP

12 pounds ripe tomatoes
3 large onions
2 sweet peppers, seeded
½ clove garlic (optional)
Spice bag:
   1 3-inch stick cinnamon
   1 teaspoon black peppercorns
   1 teaspoon allspice berries
   1 tablespoon whole cloves
   1 hot pepper pod
   1 teaspoon celery seed or
     fennel seed

1 cup light brown sugar (or
   ½ cup brown and ½ cup white)
1½ cups vinegar
1½ tablespoons salt
1 tablespoon paprika
1 tablespoon dry mustard

Peel and chop tomatoes, onions and peppers. Add garlic if used. Cook slowly until soft. Put through fine sieve. Simmer for 30 minutes. Add spice bag and remaining ingredients. Simmer 2 or 3 hours, until very thick, stirring frequently. Remove spice bag; strain into hot, sterilized jars and bottle. Makes 4 to 5 pints.

TOMATO CATSUP, KITCHENETTE STYLE

3 quarts seasoned tomato purée
2 teaspoons paprika
½ to 1 cup sugar

2 cups vinegar
Cayenne pepper, spices and salt to
   taste

If there is no purée available, add onion and peppers to canned tomatoes, boil until thick, then strain and measure. Mix all ingredients. Boil until as thick as wanted. Pour, boiling hot, into hot, sterilized jars; seal at once. Makes 5 pints to 3 quarts.

This recipe is from the Heinz vinegar instruction booklet.

OUR OWN HEINZ'S TOMATO KETCHUP

1 cup Heinz Distilled White Vinegar	1 teaspoon celery seed
1½ teaspoons whole cloves	8 pounds tomatoes (32 medium)
1½ teaspoons broken stick cinnamon	1 cup onions, peeled and sliced
	¼ teaspoon cayenne pepper
½ teaspoon whole allspice	½ cup granulated sugar
	4 teaspoons salt

Combine first 5 ingredients in saucepan. Bring to a boil; then remove from heat. Let vinegar stand to absorb spices.

Wash and cut tomatoes into quarters; combine with sliced onions and cayenne pepper. Simmer uncovered, 20 minutes, stirring occasionally to prevent sticking. Press through a sieve. Combine sugar and hot tomato juice in a large kettle. Cook, uncovered, stirring frequently until volume is halved, about 1 hour, 15 minutes.

Strain vinegar; discard spices. Combine salt with spiced vinegar; add to boiling tomato mixture. Continue boiling, uncovered, 30 minutes longer or until thick; stir constantly. Quickly pour into hot, sterilized jars. Fill to ⅛ inch from top. Seal each jar at once. To help retain color, wrap jars individually in brown paper before storing. Makes 2 pints.

If this recipe is doubled, a longer cooking time will probably be required, and a slightly darker product may result.

HOT TOMATO CATSUP

1 peck ripe tomatoes (8 quarts or 16 pounds)	Spice bag:
	1 tablespoon whole allspice
10 medium onions	1 medium stick cinnamon
½ clove garlic	1 tablespoon whole mace
2 bay leaves	1 tablespoon black peppercorns
2 sweet red peppers, seeded and sliced	1 tablespoon celery seed
	1 tablespoon whole cloves
6 small hot red peppers	2 cups vinegar
¾ cup brown sugar	Salt to taste

Dip tomatoes in boiling water and skin; cut into small pieces. Slice onions thin. Add garlic, bay leaves, sweet peppers and hot peppers. Boil all together until they are soft. Press through a strainer. Add brown sugar and mix. Add spice bag. Boil until ingredients are reduced to ½ their bulk. Add vinegar and salt. Boil again until catsup has reached desired consistency, remembering that it will get a little thicker as it cools. Bottle at once in hot, sterilized bottles that have necks wide enough for easy pouring. When caps are in place, dip top of each bottle in melted paraffin for an airtight seal. Makes 6 to 8 pints.

SEASONED TOMATO PURÉE

4 quarts chopped tomatoes	3 sweet peppers
6 onions	2 cups chopped celery
3 carrots	Salt and pepper to taste

Wash, chop and measure firm ripe tomatoes. Steam or simmer until soft. Press through fine sieve. Cook until thick. Chop other vegetables. Cover with boiling water and cook until soft; press through sieve, and add to the tomato pulp. Reheat and pour into hot, sterilized jars. Process 45 minutes in boiling water bath. Makes 3 quarts.

MAINE CATSUP

State-of-Maine folk like a sour catsup.

8 quarts strained tomatoes	4 teaspoons dry mustard
1 quart vinegar	1 teaspoon ground cloves
½ cup brown sugar	1 teaspoon ginger
6 tablespoons salt	½ teaspoon black pepper

Combine and simmer until quantity is reduced by ½. Pour into hot, clean bottles. Makes about 3 pints.

GARDEN CATSUP

2 pounds ripe cucumbers, peeled and chopped	1 cup sugar
1 cup chopped onions	2 tablespoons mustard seed
2 green peppers, chopped	1 tablespoon celery seed
2 cups vinegar	1 tablespoon salt

Put cucumbers, onions, peppers in a preserving kettle, cover with water and cook until tender. Put remaining ingredients in another kettle and boil 2 minutes. Add vegetable mixture and cook until catsup is clear. Seal in sterilized jars. Makes 2 or 3 ½-pints.

Sourpuss: Someone who was weened on vinegar.
—Left Handed Dictionary, Jr.

In case your catsup wins so many compliments that someone offers to back you in a factory to make it commercially, here is a recipe which is used in the industry:

COMMERCIAL TOMATO CATSUP FORMULA

600 gallons (2,400 quarts) tomato pulp, specific gravity 1.022
300 pounds sugar
50 pounds salt
8 pounds paprika
2 pounds garlic

12 ounces mace
10 ounces cinnamon, broken and sifted
12 ounces cloves, without heads
13 ounces cayenne pepper
16 gallons 100-grain vinegar

Place the whole spices in spice bag. Cook, dissolving the sugar in tomato a little at a time. Add the salt at the end. Cook down to 200 gallons. Makes 1,828 regular 14-ounce bottles.

VEGETABLE AND FRUIT CATSUPS

APPLE CATSUP

4 pounds tart apples
2 cups cider vinegar
3 cups sugar
1 teaspoon salt

Spice bag:
  6 whole cloves
  6 whole allspice berries
  6 peppercorns
  Small stick cinnamon
  2 teaspoons mustard seed

Peel, core and dice the apples and put in covered pan without water. Steam on slow heat until apples are soft. Press through a sieve or food mill. Add vinegar and sugar to juice and whatever pulp is pressed through, discarding pulp left in sieve. Put mixture in saucepan and add salt and spice bag. Simmer 20 minutes. Remove spice bag and bottle the sauce while hot. Seal immediately. Makes about 4 pints.

GRAPE-APPLE CATSUP

Substitute 2 pounds of Concord or other slip-skin grapes for half of the apples; wash grapes and remove stems; then proceed as above.

BLACKBERRY CATSUP

4 pounds ripe blackberries
2 pounds light brown sugar
2 cups vinegar

Spice bag:
  2 teaspoons cloves
  2 teaspoons cinnamon
  1 teaspoon whole allspice

Cook all ingredients until very soft, about 2 hours. Remove spice bag, put in bottles or jars and seal. Makes 2 to 3 pints.

CRANBERRY CATSUP

This is an English recipe. Also see anchovy catsup in Around the World chapter.

2 pounds cranberries
1½ cups water
1½ cups vinegar
1 teaspoon cloves

1 teaspoon allspice
½ teaspoon mace
1 stick cinnamon
2 cups brown sugar

Combine all ingredients except sugar. Simmer until fruit is soft. Rub through sieve. Add sugar and cook until thick. Seal in sterilized jars. Makes 1 pint.

ZESTY CRANBERRY CATSUP

4 pounds cranberries
1 pound onions
3 cups water
7 cups sugar
3 cups vinegar

1 tablespoon powdered cloves
1 tablespoon cinnamon
1 tablespoon pepper
1 tablespoon allspice
1 tablespoon salt

Cook cranberries and onions in water until tender; then pass through sieve. Add remaining ingredients and boil until thick. Seal in sterilized jars or bottles. Makes 4 ½-pints.

CUCUMBER CATSUP

2 quarts ripe cucumbers
  (ground)
1 cup onion
1 red pepper, chopped
4 cups vinegar

2 cups sugar
1 teaspoon cinnamon
1 teaspoon cloves
1 teaspoon salt
⅛ teaspoon black pepper

Mix vegetables together, add enough water to prevent sticking. Cook slowly, stirring often, until tender. Add remaining ingredients and cook until thick. Pour into sterilized jars; seal. Makes 2 to 3½ pints.

GOOSEBERRY CATSUP

5 pounds gooseberries
4 pounds sugar
1 tablespoon cinnamon

1 tablespoon cloves
1 tablespoon allspice
3 cups cider vinegar

Wash and trim gooseberries; drain and put in preserving pan or kettle with remaining ingredients. Bring to boil and simmer 2 hours. Pour into sterilized bottles or jars; seal. Makes 3 to 4 pints.

RED GOOSEBERRY CATSUP

5 cups red gooseberry pulp
3 cups sugar
1 cup cider vinegar

1 tablespoon ground mace
1 tablespoon ground cinnamon

Mix together and simmer until consistency of catsup. Pour into sterilized bottles or jars; seal. Makes about 3 ½-pints.

GUAVA CATSUP

Slice washed guavas in preserving kettle. Add enough water to prevent scorching and cook until tender; then put through coarse sieve to remove seed.

To each quart pulp add ½ level tablespoon each of salt and ground mustard; ½ tablespoon each whole pepper, allspice, cinnamon, cloves and celery seed; 1 small piece dried ginger and 2 small hot peppers (tied loosely in bag); 1 clove garlic, chopped very fine. Simmer until very thick, then add 1 to 1½ cups strong cider vinegar and 1 cup sugar and cook again until thick and smooth. Let stand overnight. Reheat to boil; pour into clean, hot jars and seal while boiling hot.

LEMON CATSUP

12 large lemons
4 tablespoons white mustard
   seed
1 tablespoon turmeric
1 tablespoon white pepper
1 teaspoon cloves
1 teaspoon mace

2 tablespoons granulated sugar
2 tablespoons fresh grated
   horse-radish
1 shallot, minced fine
2 tablespoons salt
Dash cayenne pepper

Grate rind of lemons and use that and juice. Mix all ingredients together and allow to stand in a cool place for 3 hours. Then bring to a boil and cook 30 minutes. Pour into a crock, cover tightly and allow to stand for 2 weeks, stirring well every day. Strain and fill hot, sterilized bottles and seal. Makes 2 pints.

This is a delicious seasoning for fish sauces, fish soups and game.

MUSHROOM CATSUP

7 pounds mushrooms	Ground ginger
½ pound salt	Powdered mace
Allspice	Cayenne pepper

Wipe mushrooms clean and put in a large jar, sprinkling layers and top with the salt. Stir at least 3 times each day for 3 days. Then cook very gently on stove or in low oven until juice flows out. Strain liquid through cloth, but do not squeeze mushrooms. Return liquid only in jar and add for each quart 1 tablespoon each of allspice and ginger and 1½ tablespoons each of mace and cayenne. Place jar in pan of boiling water and cook over very low flame for 3 hours. Cool and strain several times through fine cloth or muslin, before bottling. If sediment remains, sauce will not keep.

GREEN TOMATO CATSUP

3½ pounds green tomatoes	Spice bag:
2 large or 3 small sweet green peppers	½ stick cinnamon
	1 teaspoon whole cloves
2 medium onions	1 teaspoon allspice
Salt	1 teaspoon celery seed
1 pint vinegar	4 ounces sugar
	½ tablespoon dry mustard
	Salt and pepper to taste

Remove blossom ends from tomatoes, and stems and seeds from peppers, and chop them and onions; mix together, sprinkle with salt and let stand 3 hours. Drain and put vegetables in pan or kettle with vinegar, adding spice bag. Simmer until soft and rub through sieve. Put purée back into pan, which has been rinsed. Add sugar and mustard, which have been mixed into a smooth paste with a little cold vinegar; season mixture to taste and simmer slowly for 1 hour, adding more vinegar if the catsup looks too thick. Makes about 4 pints.

One test for the mumps is to suck a pickle, and if you scream, you've got them.

PEACH CATSUP

7 pounds tomatoes
7 ripe peaches
2 pounds brown sugar

1 pint strong vinegar
½ ounce cloves
1 ounce cinnamon

Cook tomatoes and peaches to a pulp. Strain. Add remaining ingredients and boil 2 hours. Pour into hot, sterilized bottles or jars and seal. Makes 4 or 5 pints.

WALNUT CATSUP

Young tender green walnuts are needed for this catsup. Prick each walnut several times with a large needle; then place them in a stone crock or earthenware pan. For every 25 walnuts, add 1 tablespoon of salt. Cover with cold water. Place a cover on the crock and allow to stand for 2 weeks, stirring the walnuts once every day. Drain off this water into a kettle and set aside. Cover the walnuts with hot vinegar and crush the nuts to pulp. Then strain through a fine sieve. Combine this juice with the water in the kettle. Measure it and for every quart of the liquid, add:

2 tablespoons white pepper
2 tablespoons ginger
1 tablespoon cloves
1 tablespoon nutmeg

⅛ teaspoon cayenne pepper
1 small onion, chopped fine
1 teaspoon celery seed (tied in bag)

Boil all together slowly about 1 hour. Allow mixture to become cold before bottling and sealing.

Bottled Sauces

ANCHOVY SAUCE

1 pound salted anchovies
½ teaspoon ground mace
½ teaspoon cayenne pepper

1 pint cold water
2 ounces (4 tablespoons) vinegar

Pound anchovies in a mortar until smooth, then pass through a sieve. What does not pass through, put into a pan, add the water (or liquor in which anchovies had been bottled), the mace and cayenne and simmer gently for 30 minutes. Strain liquid and mix with anchovy purée. Rinse pan, put mixture back in, bring to a boil, add vinegar, simmer for 10 minutes longer. Take off fire, cool until cold and bottle. Makes about ½ pint.

AUNT JENNIE'S BARBECUE SAUCE

4 cups tomato catsup
½ cup water
1 cup lemon juice
2¼ cups meat stock
2 tablespoons sugar

¼ cup Worcestershire sauce
1 teaspoon paprika
2 tablespoons onion flakes
1 tablespoon salt

Combine and blend all ingredients. Bring to a boil. Pour at once into hot, sterile pint jars. Seal immediately and process 45 minutes in water bath or in a pressure cooker at 240°F (10 pounds pressure). Makes about 4 pints.

CHILI SAUCE, KITCHENETTE STYLE

2 onions
1 red or green sweet pepper
2 quarts canned tomatoes
½ to 1 cup sugar
Salt to taste

1 teaspoon mustard seed
1 tablespoon mixed spices
1 teaspoon celery seed
1 cup vinegar

Peel onions; remove ribs and seeds from pepper; chop. Mix all ingredients, except spices and vinegar. Boil until thick. Add spices, in bag, and vinegar. Boil until as thick as wanted; remove spice bag. Pour, boiling hot, into hot, sterilized jars; seal at once. Makes 3 to 4 pints.

In its very handy little booklet, "Pickling the Easy Way," the Heinz company offers the following savory recipe:

HEINZ'S CHILI SAUCE

1½ cups Heinz Distilled White Vinegar	5½ pounds tomatoes (22 medium)
2 teaspoons whole cloves	1 cup granulated sugar
1 teaspoon broken stick cinnamon	1 tablespoon chopped onion
	½ teaspoon cayenne pepper
1 teaspoon celery seed	1 tablespoon salt

Combine first 4 ingredients. Bring to a boil; then remove from heat. Set aside.

Now, wash, peel and quarter tomatoes; combine ½ of them, ½ cup sugar, onion, and cayenne pepper in deep kettle. Boil vigorously, stirring frequently, 30 minutes. Stir in remaining tomatoes and sugar. Boil vigorously, stirring frequently, 30 minutes longer.

Strain vinegar mixture and discard spices. Add spiced vinegar and salt to boiling tomato mixture. Stirring constantly, continue boiling for 15 minutes or until desired consistency is reached. Pour immediately into hot, sterilized jars, filling to ⅛ inch from top. Seal each jar at once. To help retain color, wrap jars individually in brown paper before storing. Makes 1¾ to 2 pints.

If this recipe is doubled, a longer cooking time will be required and a slightly darker product may result.

Verjuice of apple was in constant use in England until the last century when its place was taken by a squeeze of lemon juice. It is really sharp (hard) cider, not a vinegar. The distilling was of interest, for it could account for the apparent mildness of some of the pickles made.

"To distill verjuice for pickles: Take three quarts of the sharpest verjuice and put in a cold still and distill it off very softly; the sooner it is distilled in the spring the better for use."

The best verjuice was made of crab apples.

"Gather crabbs as soon as the kernels turn blacke, and lay them in a heap to sweat and take them into troughs and crush with bettles [a heavy wooden mallet]. Make a bagge of coarse hair-cloth and fill it with the crabbs, and presse and run the liquor into Hogsheads."

—*Compleat Hosewife*, 18th century

Mrs. Ada Nellis, of Palatine Bridge, N.Y., is very famous in food circles as an outstanding maker of pickle products.

MRS. NELLIS' CHILI SAUCE

8 pounds skinned ripe tomatoes, fine-chopped
6 medium onions, fine-chopped
6 seeded green peppers, fine-chopped
1½ cups sugar
2 tablespoons salt
1 quart vinegar
¼ cup whole cloves
¼ cup allspice
4 sticks cinnamon

Combine chopped tomatoes, onions and green peppers in large kettle. Add sugar, salt and vinegar. Tie spices securely in a cheesecloth bag and place in kettle. Cook mixture slowly until thick, about 2½ hours, stirring occasionally. **Makes 3 pints.**

APPLE CHILI SAUCE

4 pounds (16) tomatoes
4 pounds (16) apples
1 pound (4 medium) onions
1 pound (5 or 6) sweet green and red peppers

Spice bag:
   2 tablespoons whole allspice
   1 tablespoon whole cloves
   1 stick cinnamon, broken
2 cups cider vinegar
1 cup sugar
2 tablespoons mustard seed
1 tablespoon salt

Peel and stem tomatoes, peel and core apples, peel and slice onions, stem and seed peppers. Fine-chop all or put through food grinder. Place in kettle with spice bag and cook, uncovered, for 1½ to 2 hours, stirring frequently. Then add vinegar, sugar, mustard seed and salt and cook until quite thick. Taste while cooking; if sharper flavor is desired, add small quantity dry mustard and/or pepper. Pour into hot, sterilized jars and seal. **Makes 5 to 6 pints.**

PICKLED PEPPER SAUCE

Wash small hot red and green peppers. Make 2 or 3 small slits in each. Pack into bottles, and cover with cider vinegar. Cork and stand in cool place 3 weeks before using. As the sauce is used, add more vinegar.

Use in other sauces and with beans and seafood.

This way to make chili sauce comes from the Texas Agriculture Service:

TEXAS CHILI SAUCE

1 gallon chopped ripe tomatoes
2 cups onion
2 cups sweet red pepper
1 cup brown sugar
3 cups vinegar
3 tablespoons salt

Spice bag:
 1 teaspoon whole cloves
 1 teaspoon allspice
 2 teaspoons cinnamon
 1 clove garlic
 1 hot red pepper (optional)

Chop and combine vegetables. Add spice bag to vegetables. Cook rapidly, stirring often to keep from sticking. When the vegetables have cooked to about ½ the original amount, add the sugar, vinegar and salt. Boil rapidly for 5 minutes, stirring constantly. Pour into hot, sterilized jars; seal and store. Makes 5 to 6 pints.

PERUVIAN SAUCE

24 red, ripe tomatoes
3 large onions
3 green sweet peppers
1 pod hot pepper
6 tart apples
1 clove garlic (optional)

3 cups brown sugar
1 tablespoon salt
1 tablespoon allspice
1 tablespoon mustard seed
1 teaspoon ground cinnamon
3 cups vinegar

Wash and drain vegetables. Scald, core and peel tomatoes. Peel onions; remove seeds and ribs from sweet peppers. Core and pare apples. Chop apples and vegetables. Add sugar. Boil until thick. Add spices and vinegar. Boil until as thick as wanted. Pour, boiling hot, into hot, sterilized jars; seal at once. Makes about 6 pints.

Large green tomatoes may be substituted for ripe ones in the above recipe; however, the color is likely to be rather dull.

An outstanding sauce-relish from the University of Idaho laboratory:

POWWOW SAUCE

12 Winesap or Jonathan apples
9 onions
12 tomatoes
3 green peppers
1 quart vinegar

½ teaspoon ground cloves
3 cups brown sugar
2 teaspoons salt
1 teaspoon cinnamon
1 teaspoon ginger

Core, trim and wash unpeeled apples, peeled onions, tomatoes and green peppers. Put through the food chopper. Add all other ingredients and simmer 1 hour. Seal while hot.

RED HOT SAUCE

24 long hot red or green peppers
12 red, ripe tomatoes
4 cups vinegar

1 cup sugar
1 tablespoon salt
2 tablespoons mixed spices

Wash and drain vegetables. Remove seeds from peppers. Core tomatoes. Chop vegetables. Add 2 cups vinegar. Boil until soft. Press through sieve. Add sugar, salt and spices, in bag. Boil until thick. Add remaining vinegar. Boil 15 minutes, or until as thick as wanted. Pour, boiling hot, into hot, sterilized jars; seal at once. Makes 4 to 5 pints.

Rubber gloves should be worn to prevent hands from being burned when seeding peppers.

In Arkansas, as well as neighboring Louisiana, they like a dash of hot condiment with their food.

ARKANSAS TABASCO SAUCE

3 dozen hot red peppers
1 clove garlic, chopped
1½ teaspoons horse-radish

1 tablespoon sugar
½ teaspoon salt
1 cup cider vinegar

Cover peppers with water. Add garlic and cook until soft. Put peppers and garlic through a sieve. Add horse-radish, sugar, salt and vinegar to the peppers. Simmer for about 5 minutes, or until blended. Pour into hot, sterilized jars, seal and store. Makes 5 or 6 pints.

GREEN TOMATO SAUCE

6 pounds green tomatoes
3 pounds onions
1 pound brown sugar
1 tablespoon black pepper

1 tablespoon mustard
1½ tablespoons salt
1 quart vinegar

Slice tomatoes and onions and put in preserving kettle with seasonings; pour vinegar over all and cook for 4 hours over slow heat, stirring occasionally. Put mixture through a sieve, return to kettle and bring to a boil again. Pour into hot, sterilized jars and seal. Makes about 6 pints.

VICTORIA SAUCE

8 cups chopped rhubarb
½ cup chopped onion
1½ cups chopped raisins
3½ cups brown sugar
½ cup vinegar

1 teaspoon salt
1 teaspoon ginger
1 teaspoon cinnamon
1 teaspoon allspice

Wash, chop and measure rhubarb and onion. Then mix with raisins, sugar and vinegar. Boil slowly until thick. Add spices about 5 minutes before removing sauce from heat. Pour, boiling hot, into hot, sterilized jars; seal at once. Makes 7 or 8 ½-pints.

This rhubarb condiment goes well with meats.

Also see Around the World chapter for beefsteak sauce.

Chutneys

Until I began to collect recipes, I never knew how many different materials could be used in making chutneys. Without trying very hard a collection of 40 different kinds has been assembled in this book. And since the variety is so great, let us lead off with one called . . .

JUST PLAIN CHUTNEY

6 apples, peeled and sliced	1½ pints cider vinegar
1 large jar preserved ginger	2 tablespoons cinnamon
1 pound raisins	4 tablespoons salt
1 pound dates	1 pound figs
1 pound currants	1 tablespoon allspice
1 pound citron and orange peel	4 ounces ground onion
3 chili peppers	1 ounce ground garlic
1½ pounds brown sugar	

Cut up all fruits and peppers.

Boil sugar and vinegar ½ hour. Add all other ingredients and simmer until thick. Seal in sterilized jars. Makes 4 to 5 pints.

HINTS ON THE MANUFACTURE OF CHUTNEYS AND PICKLES

From The Warren Hastings Book of Indian Condiments *Containing 100 Original Recipes of Chutneys and Pickles collected in the old "John Company" Days and including many used by Warren Hastings. (Calcutta: Thacker, Spink & Co., 1917)*

Cleanliness is the first thing to be observed. See that your servants or coolies wash their hands properly, and be careful that they have no sores. If they have on rings make them take them off.

Never weigh any fruit or other ingredient till they have been peeled and stoned.

All ingredients should be ground with vinegar. On no account must water be used.

When there is no particular quantity of vinegar mentioned for use, always use a small quantity at the beginning and make up by adding more when bottling.

When it is mentioned in any recipe to strain after boiling, it means to strain and reject the ingredients that have been boiled with the vinegar.

In boiling always use a slow fire, as too much heat destroys the flavour.

When peeling mangoes or any fruit use silver knives, a very good substitute is tank oyster shells rubbed on a stone till a hole forms, the size of a pice, but when neither are obtainable and a steel knife has been used, in such a case a bowl of water should be kept alongside and the fruit thrown into it immediately they are peeled.

When pricking limes, plums, etc., either make pins out of bamboos or use babool (acacia) thorns. Never use needles or pins.

When goor or brown sugar is mentioned in a recipe the former should be procured if possible as it makes a great difference in the flavour, but it should always be dissolved in vinegar and strained.

All chutneys put in jars to be exposed to the sun should get a stir every second or third day so as to get even heat.

After corking bottles always put sealing wax over them to prevent any air getting in, as used corks cannot be relied on.

APPLE CHUTNEY

3 pounds green tomatoes (10 to 12 medium)	1½ tablespoons salt
	1½ teaspoons pepper
1¼ pounds red apples (4 medium)	1½ teaspoons ground cinnamon
	¾ teaspoon ground cloves
3 medium sweet red peppers	2½ cups granulated sugar
4 medium onions	2 cups white vinegar

Wash fruit and vegetables. Trim and quarter tomatoes. Core and quarter unpeeled apples. Seed and quarter peppers; peel and quarter onions. Put fruit and vegetables through coarse blade of food grinder.

Combine salt and remaining ingredients; heat to boil. Add fruit and vegetables. Simmer, stirring occasionally, for 30 minutes. Continue simmering while quickly packing 1 hot, sterilized jar at a time. Fill to ⅛ inch from top. Seal each jar at once. Makes 6 pints.

ALL-DAY APPLE CHUTNEY

36 cooking apples
3 pounds onions
3 pounds brown sugar
1/2 pound seedless raisins
2 ounces mustard seed

1/4 pound salt
2 quarts white vinegar
1 ounce ground ginger
1 small chili pepper, fine-chopped

Grind apples and onions or chop very fine. Add other ingredients and mix well together in preserving kettle. Bring to boil, lower heat to minimum and simmer all day, until you have dark pulp. Makes 8 to 10 pints.

APPLE AND BANANA CHUTNEY

2 pounds apples
3/4 pound onions
1/2 pound raisins
1 dozen bananas
2 ounces salt

1 teaspoon cinnamon
1 teaspoon ground ginger
1 ounce curry powder
1 pint vinegar

Peel and core apples, chop them and onions finely, cut raisins in half, peel bananas and slice into disks.

Put the salt, sugar and spices in the vinegar, bring to a boil and add the fruit. Simmer gently for 2 hours, stirring frequently to prevent the bananas from burning. When the mixture is thick and the fruit tender, place in hot, sterilized jars and seal tightly. Makes 3 to 4 pints.

APPLE AND TOMATO CHUTNEY

3 pounds apples
3 pounds tomatoes
1 pound onions
1 quart vinegar

1 pound sugar
1 tablespoon white pepper
2 tablespoons ground ginger
4 tablespoons salt

Peel and core apples, slice them and the tomatoes thinly, fine-chop the onions and put in bowl with vinegar for 24 hours. Place in kettle, add salt, sugar and spices, bring to a boil and simmer until the fruit is tender, about 1/2 hour. Put in jars while hot and seal. Makes about 5 or 6 pints.

BLUEBERRY CHUTNEY

2 pounds blueberries
½ pint vinegar
¼ pint chili vinegar
¼ pound onions
¼ pound seedless raisins
3 ounces brown sugar

1 teaspoon mustard
½ teaspoon powdered ginger
½ teaspoon cinnamon
Pinch each of grated nutmeg, salt,
    cayenne pepper

Put blueberries and two vinegars into pot or kettle and mash fruit to a pulp. Fine-chop onions and raisins or put through food mincer. Add them and remaining ingredients and simmer together until thick. Pour into jars or pots and cool; then cover. Makes about 2 pints.

RED CABBAGE AND BEET CHUTNEY

2 pounds red cabbage
½ pound onions
2 pounds beets, raw
3 ounces salt

1 pound sugar
2 ounces peppercorns, in bag
2 ounces mustard seed
1 quart vinegar

Fine-chop cabbage and onion; peel and cut beets into very small dice. Put remaining ingredients into pan; bring to a boil; then add vegetables and simmer gently until very tender. Remove peppercorns. Put in bottles or jars while hot; seal. Makes 2 or 3 pints.

CHIQUITA CHUTNEY

1 pound Spanish onions
½ pound dates
6 bananas
1½ cups vinegar
¼ pound crystallized ginger

1 teaspoon salt
1 teaspoon curry powder
½ pound seedless raisins
2 cups juice from canned fruit

Chop onions, stone and chop dates and put them and bananas through fine food chopper or potato ricer, into pan; add vinegar, simmer for 20 minutes. Add remaining ingredients and cook until thick. Pour in jars and seal. Any canned fruit juice will do. Makes 3 pints.

CRANBERRY CHUTNEY

1½ cups seedless raisins
1 pound dates, pitted
6 cups whole cranberry sauce
    (canned cranberry sauce may be
    used)
1 cup sugar

1 cup vinegar
½ teaspoon ginger
½ teaspoon cinnamon
½ teaspoon allspice
¼ teaspoon cloves
¼ teaspoon salt

Chop raisins and dates. Combine all ingredients and cook slowly until thick, 20 to 30 minutes. Stir occasionally. Place in hot, sterilized jars and seal. Makes 4 pints or 8 8-ounce jelly glasses.

QUICK CRANBERRY CHUTNEY

1½ pounds whole cranberry sauce
¾ pint vinegar
½ pound brown sugar
¼ pound seedless raisins

¼ pound blanched almonds, chopped fine
1 teaspoon garlic salt
1 teaspoon ground ginger
½ teaspoon red pepper

Mix all ingredients in kettle; boil slowly, stirring occasionally, until fairly thick. Pour mixture into hot, sterilized jars and seal immediately. Makes 3 ½-pints.

DRIED FRUIT CHUTNEY

½ pound dried apples
½ pound dried peaches
½ pound dried apricots
½ pound dates
½ pound seedless raisins
2 cloves garlic, fine-chopped

1 pound sugar
1 tablespoon allspice
1 tablespoon salt
Pinch of cayenne pepper
1½ pints vinegar

Soak dried apples, peaches and apricots overnight in water; drain; cut into small pieces; stew until soft in part of the water drained off, cooking apples longer than peaches or apricots.

Put dates and raisins through food chopper or grinder; add garlic and remaining ingredients to fruit, in kettle. Cook for 30 minutes, until chutney is thick and soft, stirring frequently so mixture will not stick to bottom. Pour into jars, cool and cover. Makes 4 or 5 ½-pints.

GOOSEBERRY CHUTNEY

3 pounds gooseberries
½ pound seedless raisins
4 onions
1¾ pounds brown sugar
1½ teaspoons crushed mustard seed

½ teaspoon cayenne pepper
¼ teaspoon turmeric
2 tablespoons salt
1½ pints vinegar

Chop onions, place all ingredients in kettle, bring to a boil and cook over low flame for 2 hours. Gooseberries should be pulp. If vinegar boils away, replace. Pour into hot, sterilized jars and seal. Makes about 4 pints.

SMOOTH GOOSEBERRY CHUTNEY

1 quart green gooseberries
¾ pound seeded raisins
3 medium onions
½ pound brown sugar
2 tablespoons mustard seed

2 tablespoons ground ginger
2 tablespoons salt
½ teaspoon cayenne pepper
Pinch of turmeric
1 quart vinegar

Fine-chop gooseberries, raisins and onions. Put in enameled pan, add remaining ingredients, heat slowly and simmer for 1 hour. Strain through coarse sieve and seal in jars. Makes about 3 pints.

GUAVA CHUTNEY No. 1

3 pounds tamarinds
2 quarts vinegar
3 quarts prepared guava shells
2 pounds raisins
1 pound green ginger, chopped
2 pods chili pepper, dried
1 pint chopped pimiento
2 cloves garlic

½ pound onions
1 tablespoon ground allspice
1 tablespoon ground cloves
1 tablespoon ground cinnamon
1 tablespoon salt
¼ cup white mustard seed
¼ tablespoon pepper
¼ cup celery seed

Remove fibrous hulls from tamarinds and soak pulp in vinegar, stirring often to dissolve pulp from seed. When pulp is dissolved, run through fruit press or colander to remove seed. Put guavas, from which seeds have been removed, through food chopper, using coarse blade. Put raisins through same chopper. Chop green ginger, peppers, pimiento, garlic and onions with finest blade. Mix all ingredients and simmer 40 to 50 minutes. Let stand overnight. Reheat to a boil. Pour into hot, sterilized jars and seal at once. Makes about 6 pints.

GUAVA CHUTNEY No. 2

5 quarts guavas
2 pounds seeded raisins
1 pound onions
1 clove garlic
6 cups sugar
2 quarts vinegar

2 tablespoons salt
2 tablespoons cinnamon
2 tablespoons cloves
1½ tablespoons dry mustard
1½ tablespoons powdered sugar
3 small hot peppers

Put guavas through sieve to remove seeds. Boil until smooth and thick. Put raisins, onion and garlic through food chopper. Add these and sugar, vinegar and seasonings. Cook until thick, stirring constantly, and let stand overnight. Reheat and seal boiling hot. Store for several weeks before using. Makes 6 to 7 pints.

KUMQUAT CHUTNEY

1 pound kumquats
1½ cups sugar
1 cup water
2 pounds rhubarb
2 onions, large
2 green peppers
2 cloves garlic
½ cup citron
4 teaspoons dried ginger root
6 cups vinegar
6 cups dark brown sugar
2 cups sliced celery

1 cup raisins
Grated peel and juice of
   2 oranges
1 teaspoon pepper
1 teaspoon curry powder
1 teaspoon cinnamon
1 teaspoon allspice
1 teaspoon powdered ginger
4 teaspoons salt
2 tablespoons Worcestershire
   sauce

Wash the kumquats in hot water; cut in half, lengthwise; remove seeds, place in large pan. Add white sugar and water, mixing well; simmer for 40 minutes. Cut rhubarb in 1-inch pieces; fine-chop onion; seed and chop green peppers, mash or mince garlic and slice citron and ginger root into slivers. Add all these and remaining ingredients to simmering mixture; mix well, stirring occasionally; continue to simmer for 1¼ hours more, then taste. If desired, add more ginger, pepper and cayenne for a hotter chutney. Continue to simmer for ½ hour more, or until chutney is thick. Pour into hot, sterilized jars and seal. Makes 5 pint jars.

BURGLAR AGAIN OUTWITS PICKLE TRAP IN YONKERS

Yonkers, Aug. 4—For the second time this year, William Polinsky's pickle trap has failed to catch a thief. Last night again, a burglar stole $20 from his little grocery at 101 Ashburton Avenue.

Mr. Polinsky rigged the trap with two five-gallon glass jars, each filled with pickles and brine. Every night at closing, he has carefully set the open jars on a trap door leading from the basement, in the hope that when an intruder opened the door he would be surprised by pickles.

But last night, for the second time since June, a burglar scaled a back fence, forced his way into the basement, went up the stairs and somehow opened the door without upsetting the jars. As a burglar stopper, Mr. Polinsky is beginning to despair of pickles.

LOQUAT CHUTNEY

5 cups loquats (measure after
    preparing)
2 large onions, chopped
1 clove garlic, chopped fine
1 large apple, peeled, cored
    and chopped
1½ cups seedless raisins
2 ounces green ginger, peeled and
    cut fine

4 cups brown sugar
1 red pepper, finely chopped
1 teaspoon salt
1 teaspoon cloves
1 teaspoon allspice
1 teaspoon nutmeg
2 cups cider vinegar

Prepare loquats by removing stem ends and stones, then cutting in small pieces. Prepare all other ingredients. Put all together in saucepan or pot and cook slowly until soft and thick. Put in sterilized jars and seal immediately. Makes about 6½ pints.

GREEN MANGO CHUTNEY

20 large green mangoes
5 cloves garlic
6 hot chili peppers
1 quart malt vinegar
10 ounces currants

5 ounces raisins
3 ounces pitted dates
5 tablespoons salt
6 cups sugar
3 ounces green ginger

Peel and chop mangoes (do not grind). Grind garlic and peppers and add, with ½ cup of the vinegar, to mangoes. Clean and chop currants, raisins and dates; mix with another ½ cup vinegar. Add to mango mix. Let stand 36 hours.

Mix salt, sugar and ginger with remaining vinegar and add to mango mixture. Cook until desired thickness is reached, about 4 hours. Stir often to prevent burning. Put into hot, sterilized jars and cap or cover with paraffin. Makes approximately 8 pints.

RIPE MANGO CHUTNEY

10 large firm ripe mangoes
½ pint seeded raisins
½ pint vinegar
½ pint lime juice
1½ cups brown sugar
2 chili peppers or
    ½ teaspoon dried

2 cloves garlic, grated
1 onion, chopped fine
1 tablespoon mustard seed
1 tablespoon celery seed
1 tablespoon fresh ginger root,
    chopped fine
1½ tablespoons salt

Pare and cut the mangoes in small pieces. Put all ingredients together in a crock or bowl. Cover and let stand overnight. Cook next morning for 3 hours. Seal in sterilized jars. Makes 4 pints.

If fresh ginger root is not available, use ground ginger.

MANGO CHUTNEY

6 quarts vinegar	1 tablespoon ground nutmeg
10 pounds brown sugar	1 tablespoon ground cinnamon
16 pounds ripe mangoes	1 tablespoon ground allspice
½ pound preserved ginger	½ pound citron peel
½ pound onions	1 pound currants
2 teaspoons minced garlic	1½ pounds seedless raisins
2 teaspoons celery seed	½ pound blanched almonds
2 teaspoons chili pepper	

Peel and slice mangoes; fine-chop ginger and onions; chop chili pepper, seeds and all; chop citron peel and almonds. Bring vinegar and brown sugar to a boil over brisk heat and add mangoes about ¼ at a time so that mixture keeps boiling. Then boil for 10 minutes more; add ginger, onion and garlic and boil 1 hour longer. Add remaining items and boil 1 hour more over low heat. Pour, boiling, into hot, sterilized jars and seal at once. Makes 10 to 12 pints.

If mangoes are very sour, use more sugar and less vinegar.

MINT CHUTNEY

4 ounces mint leaves	Pinch of salt
¾ cup seeded raisins	1 teaspoon lemon juice
½ cup seedless raisins	2 tablespoons tomato sauce
1 tablespoon brown sugar	

Wash, dry and fine-chop mint and raisins. Add remaining ingredients in kettle, heat and stir well until thick and juicy. Place in small jars and seal. Makes about 1 pint.

Try this with cold lamb.

PERSIMMON CHUTNEY

6 pounds ripe persimmons	1 ounce salt (2 tablespoons)
1 pound onions	½ teaspoon cayenne pepper
1 clove garlic	1 quart spiced vinegar

Skin, core and slice persimmons; mince onions; place in enameled kettle. Add seasonings and spiced vinegar and cook until thick, between 1 and 2 hours. Cool. When cold put in jars and seal. Makes about 6 or 7 pints.

PAWPAW CHUTNEY

3 pounds pawpaw
1 pound green cooking apples
1 pound tomatoes
1 pound seedless raisins
2 ounces peeled garlic

6 chili peppers
1 pound sugar
1½ pints white or cider vinegar
1 tablespoon salt
1 ounce scraped ginger

Pawpaws should be just underripe and weighed after removing skin and seeds. Peel and core apples and skin and trim tomatoes before weighing. Remove seeds from chili peppers. Put these ingredients through food mill or mincing machine, then add remaining ingredients and boil slowly for 2 hours. Pour into jars and let stand until next day before sealing. Makes 4 to 6 pints.

From Zelda Hale Weyant of Sand Springs, Oklahoma, consultant to the Kerr glass jar firm, comes this recent recipe.

PEACH CHUTNEY

1 medium onion
1 small clove garlic
1 cup seedless raisins
8 cups diced peaches
2 tablespoons chili powder
1 cup chopped crystallized
   ginger

2 tablespoons mustard seed
1 tablespoon salt
1 quart vinegar
2¼ cups brown sugar

Put onions, garlic and raisins through food chopper, using fine blade. Peel, dice and measure peaches. Mix peaches with all the remaining ingredients. Add the onion-raisin mixture. Mix well.

Simmer 1 hour, or until deep brown and rather thick.

Pack while hot into sterilized Kerr (or other) jars and seal at once. Makes 3 to 4 pints.

At a recent Fine Foods Fair at the Coliseum in New York, I encountered a new relish at the G. S. Raffetto booth. It was called Chut-Nut. No attempt was made to imitate the East Indian condiment, which usually is dominated by a mango base (because not much else in the way of fruits was available in India when chutney was first produced).

Melons and raisins seem to dominate Chut-Nut, which is intended to accompany a wide variety of dishes in addition to curries . . . such as canapes, with cottage cheese, French dressing, along with scrambled eggs and for meats, blended with horse-radish for boiled beef and with mint jelly for lamb.

Rather than be rebuffed (and rightly so) if I asked the Raffetto people for their recipe secrets, I have constructed a version of my own for you, calling it

NUTTY CHUTNEY

1 pound mixed melon rind
½ pound mango
1 teaspoon alum (see note)
2 tablespoons salt
Vinegar, about 1 quart
1 tablespoon mustard seed
1 teaspoon celery seed
½ cup preserved ginger
2 cups white sugar
1 cup brown sugar

1 cup chopped raisins
1 cup tiny black currants
½ cup chopped black walnuts (or English walnuts, or slivered almonds)
¼ cup thin lemon rind, chopped
1 teaspoon powdered cinnamon
1 teaspoon powdered cloves
1 teaspoon powdered allspice

Prepare melon rind: peel outer skin and all but thin layer of fruit, then cut into small pieces and place in water to cover with alum and salt, then cooking until almost tender.

NOTE: To skip the alum, soak in brine (1 part salt to 8 parts water) overnight; then drain; cover with cold, clear water and boil until pieces are tender.

If pickled melon rind and canned mangoes are used, forget preparation above.

Weigh drained fruits, cover with vinegar and let stand 2 or 3 hours. Drain off vinegar, set fruit aside and add enough vinegar to what you have to make 1 quart.

Pound the seeds together and place them, with all the remaining ingredients, in preserving kettle with the vinegar, stirring until sugar is dissolved, after the mixture has been brought to a boil. Add fruits, after they have been diced into shreds and bits, and boil quickly until rind is clear and tender and the sirup is thick.

Let stand overnight. In morning, test for flavor, adding more seasoning or sugar as necessary. Bring to a boil again and pour into hot, sterilized jars; seal. Makes 4½ pints.

You, too, can become a pickling detective. Read the list of contents on any pickle, relish or chutney label. (Remember the ingredients are given in the order of their quantities.) Try a spoonful for taste, marking down the characteristics you recognize. Then look carefully at the product; spread out a bit on a plate; identify the various components (keep tasting); pierce the secret of the juice or liquid.

Then find in this book a comparable recipe and substitute the ingredients and quantities you have identified and use the method given for the printed recipe. Try your new version, but be sure to save some of the product you are trying to duplicate. When you have bottled your new version (or better still, when you have the batch in the kettle, ready to bottle) compare yours with what you are trying to copy. Maybe you'll be delighted with your detective work. Maybe you can correct your product by seasoning. Or maybe you'll know how to get a more accurate duplication next time. Make notes, the kind you can read later on. And be consoled—Holmes didn't become a Sherlock in a day.

INDIANA PEACH CHUTNEY

3½ pounds peaches
4 ounces green ginger root, diced
3½ cups sugar
1½ cups vinegar
4 tablespoons Worcestershire sauce
2 large cloves garlic, minced
1 cup chopped onion
¾ cup lime juice
¾ teaspoon ground ginger
1 pod chili, crushed
½ cup white raisins
½ cup seedless raisins
Red, yellow and green food coloring

Peel and slice peaches ¼ inch thick. Cover with brine made of 2 tablespoons salt to 1 quart water and let stand 24 to 36 hours. Drain.

Cook ginger in water to cover until almost tender. Drain; reserve water.

Mix 4 tablespoons of reserved ginger water, sugar, vinegar, Worcestershire sauce and garlic. Bring to a boil. Add peaches.

Cook slowly until peaches are clear. Remove peaches from sirup. Add cooked ginger and remaining ingredients.

Cook until onions are soft, and mixture is of desired thickness.

Return peaches to sirup. Add food coloring to get a rich brown tone. Return to heat and bring to a boil. Pour into hot sterilized jars; seal. Makes 2½ pints.

NOTE: The best chutney is made with green ginger root. This is available in Chinese and Spanish markets in large cities. Though less potent, crystallized ginger may be substituted. Soak in water to cover until sugar crystals are dissolved; dice. Use soaking water as substitute for that in which the green ginger is cooked.

MARYLAND PEACH CHUTNEY

7 pounds firm fresh peaches
  (enough for 4 quarts)
1 pint cider vinegar
2 pounds dark brown sugar
½ cup grated onions
2 pounds seedless raisins
5 apples, pared and diced
2 tablespoons white mustard
  seed

¼ cup scraped ginger root
  (or 3 tablespoons ground ginger)
1½ tablespoons salt
2 tablespoons paprika
1 tablespoon cumin powder
Grated rind and juice of 2 lemons

Peel and cut peaches in slices about ¾ inch thick. Cover with vinegar and brown sugar. Set aside.

Combine all remaining ingredients and cook over low heat, stirring constantly, until the mixture is thoroughly blended.

In a separate saucepan, cook the peach mixture for several minutes or until peaches are tender but still hold their shape. Combine both mixtures and cook together for a few minutes. Pour into sterilized jars and seal securely. Makes about 5 quarts.

PINEAPPLE CHUTNEY

1 large pineapple, or 2 cans
  (1 pound, 13 ounces each)
  pineapple
4 cups brown sugar
3 cups cider vinegar
2 cloves garlic
1 pound seeded raisins
1 pound currants
1 pound blanched almonds or
  broken-up walnuts

2 tablespoons peeled and chopped
  green ginger root
1½ teaspoons salt
⅛ teaspoon pepper
½ teaspoon whole cloves
½ teaspoon ground cinnamon
½ teaspoon allspice

Cut pineapple into small pieces. Combine all ingredients in a 4-quart saucepan and boil until thick, about 20 minutes.

Remove garlic and cloves. Pour mixture into hot, sterilized jars and seal with paraffin immediately. Makes 4 8-ounce jars.

Chalfont St. Peter, England—Among the 501 varieties of sandwiches served at a local pub is one called the Mother-in-Law. The ingredients are: cold shoulder, strong pickle, and tongue.

The chutney recipe below yields a product similar to the imported kind and does not have the "jamlike" consistency usually found in American chutneys.

NECTARINE CHUTNEY

Use fully mature unripe fruit—the greener, the better. Unless a good quality of green ginger is available, it is better to use crystallized ginger. When possible, buy it in bulk rather than packaged; it costs less that way.

2 slightly heaping quarts prepared nectarines
¾ cup green ginger (or 5 or 6 ounces crystallized ginger)
2½ to 3 cups sugar
2 cups wine vinegar
4 cloves garlic, minced
¾ cup Worcestershire sauce
1 teaspoon salt
1 cup finely chopped onion
¾ teaspoon ground ginger
1 small pod chili or cayenne pepper
1½ cups lime juice

Wash, rinse, drain, peel and cut fruit in about ½-inch chunks; measure; cover with a brine of 2 tablespoons salt to each quart water. Let stand 24 to 36 hours.

If using green ginger, scrub and cut in small pieces before measuring, then cook until tender in water to barely cover; reserve water.

Mix sugar, vinegar, garlic, Worcestershire sauce and 1¼ cups of the water in which ginger was cooked. (If using crystallized ginger, use plain water plus ½ teaspoon ground ginger.) Cook until sugar dissolves.

Add drained fruit and cook until clear, as with preserves. Remove fruit and add all other ingredients to sirup. Cook until onions are soft and mixture is as thick as desired. Add fruit again, heat to boiling point. Taste and add seasoning if needed. Pour boiling hot chutney to within ⅛ inch of top of tapered ½-pint fruit jars. Put lid on, screw band tight. Makes 5 or 6 ½-pint jars.

PEACH CHUTNEY

Substitute peaches for nectarines and then proceed the same way.

PLUM CHUTNEY

3 pounds damson or tart red plums
1 pound tart green apples
2 cloves garlic
1 large onion
2 cups brown sugar, firmly packed
1 pint vinegar
1 tablespoon ground ginger
2 teaspoons ground cloves
½ teaspoon ground cayenne pepper
1 tablespoon salt

Wash, pit, and quarter plums; peel, core, and quarter apples; mince garlic; peel and chop onion.

Combine all ingredients in a large preserving kettle; cook slowly until thick (about 2 hours), stirring occasionally. Pour into hot, sterilized jars, filling to top; seal at once. Makes about 5 pints.

IDAHO PURPLE PLUM CHUTNEY

1 cup light brown sugar, firmly packed
1 cup granulated sugar
¾ cup cider vinegar
1½ teaspoons crushed red peppers
2 teaspoons salt
2 teaspoons mustard seed

2 fat cloves garlic, thinly sliced
1 small onion, thinly sliced
½ cup preserved ginger, thinly sliced
1 cup seedless white raisins
3½ cups fresh purple plums, halved and pitted (about 20)

Mix together sugars and vinegar in kettle and bring to boil. Add remaining ingredients, except plums, and mix well.

Then stir in plum halves. Simmer until thickened, about 50 minutes, stirring frequently and gently. Fill hot sterilized jars. Seal. Store in dark place. Makes 3 ½-pint jars.

PUTNEY CHUTNEY

4 pounds apples, cored, pared and sliced
2 pounds raisins
2 pounds brown sugar
3 pints vinegar

4 tablespoons salt
2½ tablespoons white or yellow mustard seed
2 tablespoons ground ginger
Dash cayenne pepper

Mix; simmer until very thick. Pack in jars and seal. Makes about 3 quarts.

RHUBARB CHUTNEY

1 pound rhubarb
1 peeled lemon
½ ounce garlic
½ ounce root ginger
1 pound brown sugar

½ pint vinegar
Dash cayenne pepper
1½ pounds seeded or seedless raisins
½ ounce salt

Slice rhubarb, lemon; crush peeled garlic; bruise ginger and wash raisins. Place all items in enameled saucepan; stir over low heat until sugar is dissolved; then boil, stirring frequently, until thick. Put in hot, sterilized jars and seal. Makes 2 pints.

SOUTH SEA CHUTNEY

2 pounds apples
1 pound pears
¾ pound peeled melon rind
½ cup orange peel
½ cup lemon peel
Water
2½ cups vinegar

1 cup raisins
1 small onion, diced
1 chili pepper, chopped
1 teaspoon salt
1 teaspoon allspice
1 teaspoon cloves

Seed, stem and chop fruits; chop rind and peels; cook in covered kettle with minimum of water until tender. Drain. Add remaining ingredients and boil until clear and slightly thick, stirring frequently. Pour into sterilized jars and seal. Makes about 4 pints.

SUMMER SUN CHUTNEY

5 pounds green mangoes, peeled
   and diced
2 pounds seedless raisins
½ pound preserved ginger
½ pound chili peppers
1½ cups mustard seed

6 cloves garlic
1½ pounds blanched whole
   almonds
1 gallon cider vinegar
1 pound sugar
Salt

Put mangoes, ½ of raisins, ginger, chili peppers, mustard seeds, garlic and ½ of almonds through food chopper, using fine blade. Slice remainder of almonds into slivers, add to mixture. Also add remainder of raisins, the vinegar, sugar and salt to taste, stirring to mix well.

Bottle in small jars and seal well. Place jars where sun will warm them, turning every few days so sun shines on all sides. Continue for 6 weeks, or longer if there are many cloudy days. Makes about 12 pints.

TOMATO-PEAR CHUTNEY

2½ cups quartered tomatoes,
   fresh or canned
2½ cups diced pears, fresh
   or canned
½ cup white seedless raisins
½ cup chopped green pepper
   (1 medium)
½ cup chopped onions
   (1 or 2 medium)

1 cup sugar
½ cup white vinegar
1 teaspoon salt
½ teaspoon ground ginger
½ teaspoon dry mustard
⅛ teaspoon cayenne pepper
¼ cup canned chopped
   pimiento

When fresh tomatoes and pears are used, remove skins; include sirup when using canned pears. Combine all ingredients except pimiento. Bring to a boil; cook slowly until thickened (about 45 minutes), stirring occasionally. Add pimiento and boil 3 minutes longer.

Pack the boiling hot chutney into clean, hot jars, filling to the top. Seal tightly. Store in refrigerator.

If extended storage without refrigeration is desired, this product should be processed in boiling water. Pack the boiling hot chutney into clean, hot jars to ½ inch of top of jar. Adjust jar lids. Process in boiling water for 5 minutes; start to count processing time when water in canner returns to boil. Remove jars and complete seals if necessary. Set jars upright, several inches apart, on a wire rack to cool.

NOTE: If a less spicy chutney is preferred, the amount of cayenne pepper may be reduced or omitted.

TOMATO CHUTNEY

7 pounds ripe tomatoes	5 ounces sliced shallots
5 pints vinegar	(10 tablespoons)
2½ ounces garlic	Cayenne pepper to taste
2½ ounces black pepper	Juice of 3 lemons
2½ ounces salt	1 teaspoon anchovy sauce

Bake tomatoes until tender, then pass through a coarse sieve. Add vinegar, garlic, salt, pepper and shallots; season with cayenne to taste. Simmer for 2 hours. Add lemon juice and anchovy sauce and pass through sieve again. Boil until as thick as double cream; cool until cold and pour into jars. This chutney must be cooked thoroughly in order to keep well. Makes 6 to 8 pints.

INDIAN TOMATO CHUTNEY

4 pounds ripe tomatoes	2 pounds seedless or seeded raisins
1 quart vinegar	4 pounds sugar
1 pound green ginger	½ pound salt
2 ounces garlic	1 ounce red pepper

Roast tomatoes in pan in oven until skins split; then peel and stem. Boil in 1 pint of the vinegar for about 15 minutes.

Make a thick paste of the ginger, garlic and raisins, moistening with a little of the remaining vinegar.

Boil the sugar with remaining vinegar to make thick sirup. Mix all together, adding salt and pepper to taste, and cook until chutney is thick. Makes about 8 pints.

TOMATO-APPLE CHUTNEY

3 quarts tomatoes (about 6
pounds), pared and chopped
3 quarts apples (about 5 pounds),
pared and chopped
2 cups white seedless raisins
2 cups chopped onions
(4 medium)
1 cup chopped green peppers
(2 medium)

2 pounds brown sugar
1 quart white vinegar
4 teaspoons salt
Spice bag:
  1 teaspoon ground ginger
  ¼ cup whole mixed pickling
  spice

Combine all ingredients except the whole spices. Place spices loosely in a clean, white cloth; tie with string, and add to mixture. Bring to a boil; cook slowly, stirring frequently, until mixture is thickened, about 1 hour. Remove spice bag.

Pack boiling hot chutney into clean, hot pint jars to ½ inch of top of jar. Adjust jar lids. Process in boiling water for 5 minutes; start to count processing time when water in canner returns to boiling. Remove jars and complete seals if necessary. Set jars upright, several inches apart, on a wire rack to cool. Makes 7 pints.

OTHER CHUTNEY COMBINATIONS

Apples, onions, raisins, ginger, brown sugar, mustard seed, cayenne pepper, allspice, cider vinegar.

Gooseberries, raisins, onion, crushed mustard seed, mixed spices.

Plums, onions, raisins, brown sugar, a few apples, chili pepper.

Green or ripe tomatoes, a few apples, onions, raisins, allspice, cinnamon, cloves and peppercorns.

Dates, raisins, shallots, chili peppers, vinegar and sugar.

Also see Around the World chapter for other chutney recipes.

Mincemeat

Mincemeat pie is a traditional holiday dessert, and this is a tradition that celebrates the antiquity of the dish, since *meat* mincemeat is one of the few recipes that are fairly similar to the pie filling that was served 500 and more years ago.

Unless you leaf through the recipes of that time, especially the English ones, it is difficult to realize that such strong combinations of meat or fish and sweet seasonings were the order of the day. It took an armor-plated stomach, inside as well as out, to consume the dishes of the Dark Ages—especially after sugar was imported from the East, and was thought to be a medicine good for practically every ailment.

More and more people, it seems, are prejudiced against the mixture of meat and sweet, so for them there are a number of fruit-and-vegetable-only recipes.

By the way, do you know who is credited with first calling pie "custard coffin"? It was that great quotation-writer, William Shakespeare.

MAMA'S MINCEMEAT

4 pounds lean beef
5 pounds apples, cored, peeled and chopped
2 pounds seedless raisins
1 pound currants
1½ pounds brown sugar
2 tablespoons salt

2 tablespoons cloves
2 tablespoons cinnamon
1 tablespoon mace or nutmeg
Juice and thin skin of 1 lemon
3 pints liquor from cooking beef (or apple cider)

Cook beef slowly in water to cover until tender. Cool in liquid; remove, reserving liquid, and chop fine.

Cook all ingredients together over low flame for 2 hours. Remove to hot, sterile jars or stone crock. Makes 8 to 10 pints.

OLD-TIME MINCEMEAT

2 boiled calves' tongues
2 pounds sugar
1 pound raisins
1 pound currants
¼ pound citron, cut fine
3 pounds chopped apples
½ tablespoon cloves
½ tablespoon cinnamon
½ tablespoon allspice
1 nutmeg, grated
1¼ pounds suet

¼ pound almonds, chopped fine
½ tablespoon salt
Rind and juice of 2 oranges
¼ pound candied orange peel,
    cut fine
Rind and juice of 2 lemons
¼ pound candied lemon peel,
    cut fine
1 pint brandy
1 quart whiskey

Trim, then chop the calves' tongues very fine; add sugar, raisins, currants and citron. Mix all together.

Chop apples fine (do not mash) and add to tongues. Add spices and suet, almonds and salt; mix thoroughly. Pour over this the fruit juices, rind and peel, and the brandy and whiskey. Mix well. Put mixture into a crock with a lid. Place a cloth over the top of the crock and put on lid. Put in cool place for 3 weeks.

Then add more salt and spices if needed. Let stand at least 4 weeks before using. When using as filling for pies, always bake between 2 crusts. Makes 8 pints.

MINCEMEAT BY THE CROCK

1 large fresh beef tongue or
    3 calves' tongues
4 whole cloves
1 stick cinnamon
1 tablespoon salt
3 pounds beef suet, chopped
Juice and rind of 4 oranges
Juice and rind of 4 lemons
4 pounds tart apples, cored
3 pounds seedless raisins
2 pounds light brown sugar
2 pounds dark brown sugar
2 pounds dates, chopped
1 pound almonds, unpeeled

1 pound figs, chopped
1 pound currants
1 pound citron, sliced
½ pound candied orange and
    lemon peel
2 tablespoons salt
1 tablespoon pepper
2 tablespoons allspice
2 tablespoons cinnamon
2 tablespoons clove
2 tablespoons mace
2 tablespoons nutmeg
1 quart Madeira
1 cup brandy

Tongue must be fresh. Bring to boil with cloves, cinnamon and water to cover. Lower heat and simmer 1 hour; then add salt and cook until meat is very tender. Cool in same liquid. Remove skin and gristle, put through meat grinder. Grind suet and orange and lemon rind. Add remaining ingredients, mix well, and keep in well-covered stone crock for 3 weeks before using. Keeps indefinitely in cool place. Makes 2½ gallons.

In making pies, if mixture is too thick, moisten with cup of brandy. If shtill too thick, keep addig braddy.

WASHINGTON IRVING MINCEMEAT

2 pounds lean beef, ground
1 pound suet, ground
2 pounds sugar
5 pounds tart apples, pared, cored and chopped
2 pounds muscat raisins
1 pound currants
1 pound sultana raisins

½ pound citron, chopped
½ pound orange peel, chopped
1 tablespoon salt
1 teaspoon cinnamon
1 teaspoon allspice
1 teaspoon mace
Boiled cider (about 1 quart)
Brandy

Mix beef, suet, sugar, fruit, salt, spices and cider in a large kettle. Cover and simmer, stirring often, for 2 hours. Add more cider if needed. Stir in brandy to taste. Pack into sterilized 1-quart jars, seal securely, store in a cool place, and allow to mellow at least 1 month before using. Makes 5 quarts.

CITRUS GROVE MINCEMEAT

1 pound stewing beef
2 pounds tart apples, cored and peeled
1 pound suet, cooked and cooled
2 candied orange peels
2 candied lemon peels
2 pounds seedless raisins
2 cups sugar

1 cup apple juice
Juice and grated rind of 2 oranges
Juice and grated rind of 2 lemons
1½ teaspoons salt
1 teaspoon crushed allspice
1 teaspoon grated nutmeg

Simmer beef in water to cover until almost in shreds. Cool. Put through food chopper with suet, apples, candied peels and raisins. Mix with remaining ingredients. Simmer 1 hour, stirring occasionally to prevent burning; seal in hot, sterilized jars. Makes about 6 pints.

COUSIN CELIA'S MINCEMEAT

2 pounds lean beef, cooked tender
  and put through food chopper
½ pound beef suet, chopped fine
5 pounds tart apples, chopped
3 pounds raisins, chopped

1 tablespoon salt
2 cups brown sugar
1 quart sweet cider
1 cup meat stock

Allow the above mixture to come to a boil; simmer for 1 hour, stirring occasionally. Then add:

2½ pints grape juice
1 teaspoon mace
½ teaspoon pepper
2 teaspoons cloves
2 teaspoons nutmeg
2 teaspoons cinnamon
2 teaspoons allspice

1 cup molasses
Juice and thin peel, chopped,
  of 1 orange
Juice, zest (thin peel), chopped,
  of 1 lemon
¼ pound citron, chopped
¾ cup vinegar

Bring mixture to boil and boil 10 minutes. Pack into hot, sterilized jars to within 1 inch of top of jar. Put on cap, screwing band tight. Process in water bath for 30 minutes. Makes about 8 pints.

MOOSE MINCEMEAT

If you haven't a haunch of moose about, shoot an elk—or at least a deer.

4 pounds moose meat, cooked
1 pound moose suet, cooked,
  cooled and chopped
6 pounds apples, cored but not
  peeled, chopped
1 quart apple juice
5½ pounds sugar
1½ tablespoons salt
2 pounds seedless raisins,
  washed and chopped
2 pounds light currants, washed
½ cup chopped candied citron
1 cup chopped candied orange
  peel

½ cup chopped candied lemon
  peel
¼ cup chopped candied ginger
1 teaspoon white pepper
1 tablespoon ground cinnamon
1 tablespoon allspice
1 tablespoon cloves
1 tablespoon mace
1 pint apple brandy or
  applejack
1 pint sherry

Grind meat and suet through fine blade of food chopper. Mix all the ingredients, except the brandy and sherry, and bring to a slow boil. Simmer until mixture thickens. Add brandy and sherry; cook until fruit is tender and mixture thick. Store in crock or hot sterilized jars.

PORK MINCEMEAT

2 pounds cooked pork, ground	½ tablespoon pepper
4 pounds apples, ground	1½ pounds raisins
1 pint molasses	1 pound currants
½ pound suet, ground	1 pound sugar
3 cups vinegar	1 pound dried peaches, ground
1 pint grape juice	½ pint gooseberries
½ tablespoon allspice	3 oranges, ground
½ tablespoon nutmeg	1 quart meat broth
½ tablespoon cloves	1 tablespoon salt

Mix all together; simmer in kettle 1 hour; pour into hot, sterilized jars; seal. Makes 5 pints.

PEAR MINCEMEAT

2 quarts pears	1 box currants
1 box raisins	1 cup candied orange peel
3 cups apples	2 teaspoons ground cinnamon
⅓ pound beef suet	2 teaspoons ground cloves
3 lemons	2 teaspoons ground allspice
3 cups brown sugar	2 teaspoons ground nutmeg
1 cup white sugar	2 cups sweet pickle juice
1 cup dark molasses	or fruit juice

Wash, quarter and core enough pears to make 2 quarts after they are ground. Cover with water and boil 10 minutes.

Wash and grind raisins; chop apples and suet; use grated rind and juice of the lemons. Add all ingredients to pears. Simmer 45 minutes. Pack into sterilized jars and seal while hot. Process in water bath for 20 minutes. Makes 5 to 6 pints.

*The Cooperative Extension Service of the University of Massachusetts
at Amherst is celebrated for its devotion to the cause of pickling. It has
published many leaflets about food and some of them are so excellent
that they are distributed by the extension services of other states.*
Here follows one of their recipes:

AMHERST GREEN-TOMATO MINCEMEAT

4 quarts green tomatoes (24 to 28 medium-sized)

2 quarts tart apples (8 to 10 medium-sized)

1 pound raisins

8 tablespoons minced candied citron

1 tablespoon ground cinnamon

2 teaspoons salt

¼ teaspoon ground allspice

¼ teaspoon ground cloves

2½ cups firmly packed brown sugar

2½ cups granulated sugar

¾ cup vinegar

¼ to ½ cup lemon juice

2 cups water

Fine-chop the tomatoes; core and pare the apples and chop fine. Combine all ingredients and cook mixture slowly until tender and slightly
thickened. Stir frequently to prevent sticking. Pour at once into hot,
sterile jars. Fill jars to top, and seal. Store in cool, dry place. Makes about
3 quarts.

Lemon or orange peel or a mixture of both can be substituted for the
citron. If desired, increase brown sugar to 5 cups and omit granulated
sugar. The vinegar may be increased to 1 cup and the lemon juice
omitted.

*The next mincemeat formula is recommended by the Ball Brothers
glass jar people of Muncie, Indiana.*

GREEN TOMATO MINCEMEAT

2 quarts chopped green tomatoes

1 orange

2½ quarts chopped apples

1 tablespoon salt

1 pound seeded raisins

3½ cups brown sugar

2 teaspoons cinnamon

1 teaspoon cloves

½ teaspoon ginger

1 teaspoon nutmeg

½ cup vinegar

Wash and drain tomatoes, orange and apples. Core, chop, measure and
sprinkle tomatoes with salt. Let stand 1 hour. Drain tomatoes, cover with
boiling water; let stand 5 minutes, drain well.

Grate rind and chop pulp of orange. Core, pare, chop and measure apples.

Mix all ingredients and boil slowly until tomatoes and apples are tender. Pour, boiling hot, into hot, sterilized jars; seal at once.

1½ cups chopped suet may be added to the above recipe. If suet is used, cook mincemeat only until boiling hot. Pack, and process pints and quarts for 25 minutes. Makes 3 to 4 quarts.

MEATLESS MINCEMEAT

6 quarts tart apples, chopped	2 cups molasses
6 quarts green tomatoes, chopped	3 tablespoons salt
1 pound suet, chopped	1 tablespoon ground cloves
4 pounds brown sugar	1 tablespoon powdered nutmeg
2 pounds raisins	1 tablespoon powdered cinnamon

Dust suet with flour before chopping. Put all ingredients in preserving kettle and cook slowly until apples are tender. Pour into hot, sterile jars and seal. Makes about 12 quarts.

ORANGE MINCEMEAT

½ cup orange juice	¼ cup orange marmalade
3 cups apples, chopped	2 teaspoons cinnamon
1 cup raisins, chopped	1 teaspoon ginger
2 cups sugar	1 teaspoon cloves
½ cup chopped mixed nuts	½ teaspoon salt

Combine ingredients; cook 15 minutes; pour into hot, sterilized jars and seal. Use for pies by adding 2 ounces melted butter for each pie. Makes about 2 pints.

Fruit Butters

A few fruit butters have been included, but only those that use vinegar or lemon juice in their preparation.

Use only enough spices to give the butter a delicate flavor without killing the natural fruit taste. If you want a light-colored butter, use whole spices in a spice bag.

Fruit butters are done and ready to be poured into jars when a small amount, poured on a cold plate, leaves no rim of liquid separated around the edge.

CONCORD GRAPE BUTTER

6 pounds Concord grapes
6 cups sugar
1 cup cider vinegar
1 tablespoon powdered cinnamon

1½ teaspoons powdered cloves
¾ teaspoon grated nutmeg
½ teaspoon salt

Wash grapes, drain and remove from stems. Squeeze pulp from skins into preserving kettle, saving skins. Cook pulp without water until soft, about 10 minutes, stirring frequently. Put through sieve to remove seeds.

Heat remaining ingredients together in kettle. Return pulp, plus skins, which have been put through food chopper, to kettle and simmer over low heat for about 20 minutes, stirring slowly and constantly. When thickened like jam, pour into hot sterile jars or glasses and seal at once. Makes 4 to 5 pints.

PEAR BUTTER

10 pounds pears
10 cups sugar
2 cups vinegar

Wash and cook the pears until soft. Force them through a sieve or collander, discarding skins and seeds. Put pulp in an enameled pan and add the sugar and vinegar, mixing thoroughly. Place in a slow (300°F) oven and bake for 4 hours. During the last hour stir mixture occasionally with a wooden spoon. Test by placing a small quantity on a dish. When juice no longer separates from pulp, the pear butter is done. Pour into hot, sterilized pint jars and seal. Makes about 10 pints.

PRUNE BUTTER

2 pounds prunes
Water
2 cups sugar
1 cup cider or white vinegar
1 teaspoon powdered cinnamon

1 teaspoon powdered allspice
½ teaspoon grated nutmeg
½ teaspoon powdered cloves
¼ teaspoon pepper

Wash prunes, cover with water and bring to boil; then simmer for 50 minutes, or until tender. Cool, drain, remove pits and cut into quarters. Add remaining ingredients, mix and boil for 6 minutes. Put into hot, sterilized jars or jelly glasses and seal. Makes about 3 pints.

TOMATO BUTTER

12 cups tomato pulp
7 cups sugar
¼ cup lemon juice

½ teaspoon ginger
1 teaspoon cinnamon
¼ teaspoon cloves

Wash and core firm, ripe tomatoes. Cook until soft. Press through sieve or food mill. Drain off juice and use for other purposes. Measure pulp and mix with other ingredients. Boil until thick. Pour, hot, into hot jars. Process 10 minutes in boiling water bath. Makes about 4 pints.

RED PEPPER JAM

7 cups chopped red sweet peppers
2 tablespoons salt

6 cups sugar
4 cups cider vinegar

Wash and drain thick-walled peppers; remove seeds and ribs; chop fine and measure. Mix with salt. Let stand 3 to 4 hours; drain. Add sugar and vinegar. Boil until thick (the consistency of jam). Pour, boiling hot, into hot, sterilized jars; seal at once. Makes 3 to 4½ pints.

Put up and Put in
the Refrigerator

FRESH PICKLING

Since the chief object of pickling is to preserve the vegetables and fruits for lengthy periods, to pickle when the product will be eaten immediately or kept for a week or so, or stored in the refrigerator, is comparatively simple.

No need to be precise about heating the garden or orchard stuff and no need to process the jars.

Fresh pickling is the answer to that sudden craving for a pickled product when there is nothing on the shelves. And it's also an answer to the question, What to do with leftovers from pickling cucumbers and other produce?

Richardson Wright, a most delightful writer on subjects epicurean (see his *Bed-Book of Eating and Drinking*), once tried to make his Connecticut farm provide most of the family food. He planted too many cucumbers and the vines shot off in all directions, playing hob with everything from the snap beans to the compost heap. And "try as we did, we could never eat as fast as those vines produced." Pickling and gifting the neighbors failed to stem the tide.

So, to vary the guises under which the Wrights consumed cucumbers, he researched the subject and came up with:

"Cut fine and mixed with cream and gelatine, they make an excellent mousse. Peeled and seeded, they can be steamed, stuffed with sweet corn cooked in milk and mixed with cream, butter and an egg and sprinkled with bread crumbs for their final 20-minute baking in a 350° oven."

He also recommended that seeded slices be boiled in salted water for 15 or 20 minutes and served cold with a butter-flour-pimiento-tarragon sauce, adding a squirt of lemon juice. Another unusual combination was cubed cukes, with cubed jellied consommé and hard-boiled eggs, served with shredded red cabbage and mayonnaise. And he found that the lowly cucumber blends well with pineapple in a jellied salad—or with onions, tomatoes and sour cream in tossed salads.

Here are other easy fresh pickling ideas.

PICKLED CABBAGE

1 head white cabbage	8 peppercorns
½ cup salt	1 chili pepper
12 very small onions	Vinegar
10 cloves	

Trim and wash a white (or red) cabbage; drain and slice it into a bowl. Sprinkle with salt and let stand 24 hours, turning cabbage occasionally. Drain and place in glass jar with peppercorns, cloves, onions and chili pepper well mixed in and strong vinegar to cover. Let stand for another 24 hours. Drain; arrange in a bowl or flat dish. One head makes 10 or more hors d'ouvre servings.

FRESH CANTALOUPE PICKLE

Peel a large unripe cantaloupe; remove seeds; cut into small pieces. Cover with white vinegar, then pour off all the vinegar and measure it.

To every pint of vinegar add 1¾ cups brown sugar (firmly packed), 8 whole cloves, ½ teaspoon cinnamon, and ¼ teaspoon mace. Bring the mixture to a boil.

Add melon and cook over a low heat until tender and almost transparent. With a slotted spoon, transfer cantaloupe to a bowl. Continue to boil pickling liquid for about 12 minutes. Pour over melon. Cool completely before using. Makes about 1 quart.

Miss Llewellyn Miller is a notable author, especially on subjects relating to the home. In her own home in New York City she serves delectable dinners to her guests. As a preliminary there are cocktails and, frequently, crunchy cocktail carrots which she prepares in advance.

LLEWELLYN MILLER'S COCKTAIL CARROTS

Very thin-sliced long carrot sticks, to fill 4 ½-pint jars	1 tablespoon mustard seed
	Salt to taste
1 cup dill vinegar	Dash Tabasco or small piece
2 cups water	red pepper
1 cup sugar	

Fill jars with carrot sticks. Combine remaining ingredients in saucepan, stir to dissolve sugar and bring to boil. Pour over carrots. Let stand 2 or 3 days before using. Keep refrigerated.

COCKTAIL CELERY STICKS

Substitute thin-sliced sticks of celery for carrots in above recipe and proceed in same manner.

COCKTAIL CAULIFLOWER

Break head of cauliflower into small flowerets and proceed as above, only let stand almost a week.

BLENDER BANANA CHUTNEY

2 ripe bananas
4 tablespoons rum
1 cup mango chutney

Blend chopped bananas and rum in blender until smooth. Add to chutney and stir until smooth. Heat gently. Makes 2 cups.

Serve as condiment with curries or as sauce for fish or lamb.

INDIAN MINT CHUTNEY

¼ pound fresh mint leaves
1 small onion
Salt to taste
1 teaspoon black pepper

1 teaspoon cayenne pepper
1 slice lemon or tamarind
Water

Wash mint and pound in a mortar. Slice onion and add, pounding to pulp. Add other spices and mix well; then pound all to pulp. Sprinkle in a little water if chutney is too dry. It is ready to use when it is a thick paste. Makes 1 cup.

QUICK CHUTNEY

2 large tomatoes
1 large green pepper
1 large sweet red pepper

½ medium onion
1 cup lemon juice

Stem tomatoes, stem and seed peppers, and peel onion; chop vegetables and combine with juice, stirring well. Stir occasionally at room temperature during next hour. Chill. Serve cold. Makes 2 pints.

AROMATIC CUCUMBERS

Sliced cucumbers
Chopped fresh thyme
Peppercorns
Garlic

Currant leaves (if available)
Salt
Water

Place 1 teaspoon chopped fresh thyme, 4 peppercorns, 2 or 3 black currant leaves and ¼ chopped garlic clove in a bowl. Moisten with salt water, cover with sliced cucumbers. Repeat layers of aromatic mixture and cucumbers. Let stand covered 10 days in cool place. Then remove cucumbers from aromatic mixture to serving dish.

FRESH CUCUMBER DELIGHT

3 quarts sliced cucumbers
½ pound salt
9 pints water
1 pound brown sugar

¼ ounce mustard seed
½ ounce celery seed
½ ounce black pepper
1 quart cider vinegar

Use only fresh green cucumbers for making this pickle. Slice into rounds; place immediately in a weak salt solution, ½ pound salt to 9 pints water; allow to stand overnight.

Next morning drain, pack into jars and cover with a cold, sweet liquor made by mixing remaining ingredients. Pack into jars. Seal tightly and store in a cool, dark, dry place. Makes 3 quarts.

CUCUMBER CATSUP

6 6-inch cucumbers
1 medium onion
¾ teaspoon freshly ground
   pepper

1 teaspoon salt
1 cup cider vinegar

Cover cucumbers with cold water and let stand 2 hours. Drain, peel and grate into a bowl or glass jar. Grate onion, and with pepper, salt and vinegar add to cucumbers. Mash and mix well. Make a purée by pressing through a sieve or by running briefly in electric blender. Chill. Makes about 3 ½-pints.

PICKLED EGGS, BOHEMIAN STYLE

12 hard-boiled eggs
¼ cup salt
1 cup dry yellow onion skins

2 teaspoons caraway seeds
4 cups water

Cool eggs under running cold water and tap shells all over to crack, but do not peel. Place in bowl or Pyrex deep dish. Boil other ingredients for 5 minutes and pour, hot, over eggs. Let cool; chill 12 hours. Peel and serve halved or quartered.

STUFFED PICKLED EGGS

6 hard-boiled eggs
1 cup beet juice
2 small cooked beets
1 cup vinegar
¾ teaspoon salt
¼ teaspoon pepper

½ teaspoon cloves
¼ teaspoon allspice
¼ teaspoon mace
2 teaspoons lemon juice
Mayonnaise
Parsley

Cut eggs in half lengthwise. Remove yellows.

Combine beet juice, beets, vinegar, salt, pepper, cloves, allspice and mace. Place egg whites in the juice and soak until whites are dyed red (about 1 hour).

Remove and drain dry. Mash yellows. Combine with lemon juice and enough mayonnaise to moisten. Fill centers with the mashed yellows. Top with small sprig of parsley. Makes 12 egg halves.

PICKLED HERRING

2 salt herrings
1 cup vinegar
½ cup sugar

Small onion, minced
5 peppercorns, black or white

Clean herring, soak in cold water overnight.

Remove skin and bones, cut into ½-inch slices, crosswise, and arrange on shallow serving dish. Mix other ingredients and pour over herring. Chill in refrigerator 6 hours or more before serving.

FRESH MUSHROOM PICKLES

1 pound button mushrooms
2 teaspoons salt
⅔ cup olive or salad oil
½ cup sliced celery
2 tablespoons sliced green olives
2 tablespoons sliced ripe olives

2 tablespoons lemon juice
1 tablespoon capers
1 tablespoon chopped fresh parsley
1 tablespoon wine vinegar
1 clove garlic, split

Wash mushrooms and leave whole. Cook 10 minutes in 1 inch of boiling water containing 1 teaspoon of the salt. Drain, add remaining ingredients and toss lightly.

Refrigerate overnight or for several days. Makes 3 ½-pints.

PICKLED OYSTERS

1 quart large oysters	1 tablespoon whole allspice
1 quart oyster liquor	Salt
1 lemon, cut in thin slices	Vinegar
1 tablespoon whole black pepper	Cayenne pepper

Put oysters and liquor in top of double boiler over hot water. Heat just enough to curl edges of oysters. Drain; reserve liquor. Wipe oysters with a clean cloth; arrange in bowl with lemon slices.

Boil liquor with spices until a strong infusion is made, about 30 minutes.

Pour over oysters and sliced lemon. Add salt, vinegar and cayenne to taste. Let stand in refrigerator for at least 24 hours. Oysters will keep in refrigerator for about 3 weeks.

QUICK PICKLED PEARS

2 pounds fresh or 1 1-pound, 14-ounce can pear halves	3 tablespoons cider vinegar
	1 3-inch stick cinnamon
Whole cloves	¼ cup sugar
1 cup apple cider	Currant jelly (optional)

Drain pears well, reserving ¼ cup sirup. Stud each pear half with several cloves.

In saucepan, combine reserved pear sirup (or fresh pear juice), cider, vinegar, cinnamon and sugar. Slowly bring to boil; add pear halves; simmer gently 5 minutes. Remove from heat and saucepan. Refrigerate, covered, at least 1 hour. Serves 6.

Serve as garnish for meat or poultry. Centers can be filled with jelly.

SWEET-FROM-SOUR PICKLES

1 quart whole sour pickles	1 teaspoon whole cloves
2 cups sugar	2 tablespoons olive oil
1 tablespoon whole allspice	

Drain liquid from large sour pickles; slice them crosswise in ¼-inch slices. Mix sugar and spices. Return pickle slices to jar, sprinkling each layer with sugar-spice mixture. Pour olive oil over; seal and stand in refrigerator for at least a week before using.

Original liquid from pickles used can be mixed with cut cabbage as an unusual coleslaw.

If you have a large family, or run a delicatessen-type restaurant, or someone gives you a wagonload of cucumbers and a barrel—or if you just love fresh cucumber pickles, here's what to do with them:

FRESH PICKLES BY THE BARREL

1 50-gallon barrel suitable for pickling
5 bushels medium cucumbers
10 pounds salt
2 pounds mixed pickling spices
2 pounds coarse-ground garlic
1 pound stale rye bread slices
Bunch of fresh dill or dill seasoning
Water to cover

Lay down a layer of cucumbers; sprinkle with salt, spices, garlic, bread and dill. Repeat until ingredients have been used, then cover with water. Place wooden lid over, so it is submerged and holds down cucumbers; weigh down with glass jar filled with water. After 1 week, fish out pickles as needed. Rinse and use. Do not hold too long, as they are perishable.

If you care to continue a pickling career, the brine can be saved for the next batch of cucumbers. Add 5 pounds of salt.

This recipe is the one used by Mickey Greenberg, one of New York's most skillful creators of delicatessen food.

JIFFY PICKLES

½ large cucumber
1 large Bermuda onion
1 cup cider vinegar
Salt and pepper

Pare cucumber and slice thin. Peel onion and slice into thin rings. Cover both with vinegar, to which salt and pepper have been added. Chill in refrigerator. At meal time, remove cucumber and onions from vinegar and serve as a pickle.

REFRIGERATOR DILLS

20 to 22 firm, fresh cucumbers, 3½ inches long (4 to 5 pounds)
3 tablespoons white vinegar
3 cloves garlic, peeled
2 teaspoons mixed pickling spices
1 teaspoon mustard seed
3 bay leaves
3 bunches fresh dill
¾ cup pickling salt
3 pints water

Wash and drain cucumbers and pack in 3 hot, sterile quart jars, lengthwise. Add ⅓ of the garlic, spices, mustard seed, bay leaves and dill to each jar.

Make brine of salt and water, heat to a boil and pour over cucumbers to within ½ inch of top; seal immediately. Store in refrigerator 1 week and use within next week or 2 after. Makes 3 quarts.

LAZY HOUSEWIFE PICKLES

4 quarts small cucumbers
1 cup dry mustard
1 cup sugar

1 cup salt
1 gallon vinegar

Wash the cucumbers; then pack in glass jars. Mix mustard, sugar and salt together; then add the vinegar slowly, stirring well.Pour this brine over pickles and seal. Let stand for at least a week before using. The brine is not heated. Makes 4 quarts.

PICKLED PIGS' FEET

Boiled pigs' feet
Vinegar
Whole cloves

Whole allspice
Black peppercorns

Drain pigs' feet, place in jar and cover with hot vinegar. For each quart of vinegar add 8 cloves, ¼ teaspoon allspice and ½ teaspoon peppercorns. Cover, place in refrigerator and let stand for 3 days.

REFRIGERATOR RELISHES

FRESH CABBAGE AND PEPPER HASH

1 sweet red pepper
2 green peppers
1 tablespoon onion juice
2 cups shredded cabbage
¾ cup vinegar

2 tablespoons brown sugar,
  or to taste
1 teaspoon salt
1 teaspoon whole mixed spices
1 clove garlic

Blister skins of peppers over flame, then plunge into cold water. Drain and remove skins, seeds and stems; chop or shred. Mix with onion juice and cabbage.

In pan bring vinegar, sugar and salt to boil; add spices and garlic. Cover and cool. Pour through strainer over vegetables. Chill before serving. Makes about 3 cups.

CELERY-PEPPER RELISH

6 stalks celery
2 green peppers
1 canned pimiento
2 tablespoons prepared horse-
radish

1 cup tiny pickled onions
½ teaspoon dried oregano
Prepared mustard

Chop celery and seeded peppers very fine; mince the pimiento, combine and add the other ingredients. Mayonnaise seasoned with dry mustard may be substituted for the prepared mustard if desired. Makes 3½ to 4 cups.

HURRY-UP CORN RELISH

1⅓ cups cooked, whole-kernel
corn
½ cup diced celery
1 tablespoon chopped green
pepper
3 tablespoons wine vinegar

2 tablespoons brown sugar
½ teaspoon salt
⅛ teaspoon pepper
⅛ teaspoon turmeric
1 tablespoon chopped pimiento

Combine all ingredients, except pimiento, in saucepan and mix well. Heat thoroughly. Add pimiento. Cool and refrigerate. Makes 2 cups.

One of the first native foods to attract the colonists off the Mayflower was the cranberry, a larger, coarser version of the northern European lingonberry. Another native food they relished was the wild turkey. Ever since, cranberries and turkey have been going together.

Ever wonder how the cranberry got its name? The settlers noticed that the berries were a favorite food of the cranes and originally called them "craneberries." Somehow, the "e" got lost in the shuffle.

The late Pierre de Rohan, a delightfully informative writer on food, found the following recipe for cranberries on Cape Cod. "It is wonderful with turkey, goose, duckling, chicken, hot or cold ham, pork chops, game or cold cuts," he wrote in the New York Post. *"It also makes a delightful salad."*

CRANBERRY RELISH-SAUCE DE ROHAN

1 whole unpeeled orange
2 cups raw cranberries

1 cup sugar
15 marshmallows

Cut orange into 8 pieces, remove all seeds. Run it and cranberries through meat grinder, using medium blade. Add sugar and mix well.
Cut marshmallows into small pieces with kitchen scissors dipped in cold

water. Mix into fruit, store in refrigerator several hours or overnight to "marry" the flavors. Makes over 1 pint.

One of the most famous and one of the busiest restaurants in Atlantic City is Hackney's, which can seat 3,000 diners at one time. While the diners are waiting for their seafood orders, they can munch on Hackney Pepper Hash. We are indebted to Mr. William H. Jepson of Hackney's for the recipe:

HACKNEY PEPPER HASH

1 head of cabbage	Sugar
½ sweet red pepper or pimiento	Salt
1 tablespoon celery seed	
White vinegar diluted with equal amount of water	

Put cabbage through grinder, using finest blade. Chop pepper into medium-sized bits, combine with celery seed and moisten with diluted vinegar. Season with salt and sugar to taste. Blend well. Makes 2 to 2½ pints.

DINTY MOORE'S CABBAGE RELISH

While you wait for your order to be served at Dinty Moore's fine old eating establishment off Broadway in New York, you are given small portions of chopped cabbage, with just a bit of shredded carrot, marinated in white wine vinegar and sprinkled with dill and caraway seeds. Brings the digestive juices rushing out.

READY RELISH

This relish can be used immediately after preparing.

8 small white onions	1 tablespoon salt
6 green peppers	2 tablespoons sugar
1 red pepper	1 cup vinegar
6 tart apples, cored	¼ teaspoon celery seed
8 medium green tomatoes	¼ teaspoon mustard seed
8 medium red tomatoes	

Peel and dice onions; seed and stem peppers; cut fine or put through food chopper. Grate unpared apples. Cut tomatoes fine or put through food chopper, using coarse blade. Mix all vegetable ingredients and apples.

Put salt, sugar and vinegar over medium heat for 4 minutes; then add celery and mustard seeds. Combine this mixture with vegetables. Makes about 6 pints.

ONION RELISH

24 small white onions
⅓ cup olive oil
⅓ cup wine vinegar
1⅓ cups water
1 clove garlic
½ teaspoon salt
½ teaspoon mustard

½ teaspoon mustard seed
½ teaspoon pepper
1 clove
1 teaspoon sugar
⅓ cup light raisins
Minced parsley or dill

Boil onions 5 minutes, drain and rub off skins. Add next 10 ingredients; simmer until onions are just tender. Add raisins. Simmer 3 minutes more. Chill and sprinkle generously with parsley or dill. Makes about 6 servings.

FRESH TOMATO RELISH

3 quarts peeled, chopped red
  tomatoes
1½ cups chopped celery
1 cup chopped onions
¾ cup chopped green pepper
1 tablespoon salt

4½ tablespoons sugar
5 teaspoons mustard seed
½ teaspoon cinnamon
¼ teaspoon mace
¼ teaspoon powdered cloves
1½ cups 4% cider vinegar

Mix all items until well blended. Pour into sterile jars, seal and place in refrigerator. Use within 15 days. Makes 3 quarts or 6 pints.

GARDEN SALAD

6 medium red ripe tomatoes
3 medium sweet onions, such
  as Bermudas
3 sweet green or red peppers

2 tablespoons olive oil
1 tablespoon cider vinegar
Salt and pepper

Peel and core tomatoes, peel and rough-chop onions, seed peppers and remove ribs. Drain tomatoes and put all vegetables through medium knife of food grinder. Stir in oil and vinegar and season to taste. Chill 2 or more hours before serving.

This Midwest recipe can be used as a hot-weather vegetable or as a relish on hot dog sandwiches.

PICKLED SALMON

2 pounds center-cut fresh salmon
4 tablespoons salt
2 tablespoons sugar

Fresh-ground pepper
4 sprays fresh dill

Remove bone from fish, cut into 2 fillets, mix salt and sugar and rub into flesh of fillets, put dill between them and place together so that thin side of one rests against thick side of other. Place in dish with weight or heavy plate on top and chill in refrigerator for 8 to 10 hours. If salmon is too salty for taste, soak in milk for 1 hour before serving. Serves 4 as main course, with boiled new potatoes and salad.

BARBECUE SAUCE

1 can (1 pound, 3 ounces) tomatoes
1 medium onion, chopped
1 clove garlic, chopped
1 tablespoon brown sugar
1 tablespoon butter
½ cup catsup
½ cup Worcestershire sauce
½ cup vinegar
1 teaspoon salt
¼ teaspoon pepper
Dash cayenne
¼ teaspoon dry mustard

Pour tomatoes into a saucepan, breaking up large chunks with a fork. Add all remaining ingredients and cook to boil; then reduce heat and simmer slowly for about 45 minutes. Makes about 2 cups.

CATSUP-BASED BARBECUE SAUCE

1 cup catsup
1 cup vinegar
2 cups water
2 cups butter or margarine
2 tablespoons brown sugar
1½ tablespoons salt
1½ tablespoons chili powder
1½ tablespoons paprika
1 tablespoon Worcestershire sauce
1 tablespoon Tabasco sauce
1 tablespoon black pepper
¼ teaspoon cayenne pepper
1 medium onion, minced
1 clove garlic, minced

Mix all items well and simmer over low heat for 30 minutes.

Use to baste broiling chickens, applying every 5 minutes until tender, from 45 minutes to 1 hour, depending on size. Makes about 2 pints.

TEXAS BARBECUE SAUCE

2 cups water
½ teaspoon pepper
4 tablespoons brown sugar
1 teaspoon garlic salt
2 teaspoons salt
1 cup vinegar
1 5-ounce bottle Worcestershire sauce
4 tablespoons butter

Add pepper to water and simmer for 5 minutes; add remaining ingredients and ½ of the Worcestershire sauce. Simmer 5 minutes and add remaining Worcestershire sauce. Makes about 1½ pints.

UNCOOKED BARBECUE SAUCE

2 crushed garlic cloves
1½ teaspoons salt
1 teaspoon fresh-ground black
  pepper
¼ cup fine-chopped scallions
2 teaspoons prepared mustard

1 teaspoon dry mustard
Juice of 1 lemon
1½ cups tomato catsup
½ cup tomato juice
1 teaspoon tarragon

Combine and shake vigorously. Makes 2½ cups.

UNCOOKED CHILI SAUCE

4 pounds ripe tomatoes
½ cup chopped onions
½ cup cooked celery
2 green peppers
¼ cup salt
½ cup sugar

1 cup vinegar
4 tablespoons white mustard
  seed
¼ teaspoon cinnamon
½ teaspoon brown cloves
½ teaspoon black pepper

Chop all vegetables, dissolve salt and sugar in vinegar, mix all ingredients thoroughly and seal in cold, sterilized jars. Makes 3 pints.

CHUTNEY SAUCE

1 cup chutney
1 glass currant jelly

1 wineglass sherry
1 teaspoon Worcestershire sauce

Combine and mix well. Serve cold. Makes about 2 cups.

FISH COCKTAIL SAUCE

1 cup tomato catsup
5 tablespoons chili sauce
4 tablespoons bottled (or 1½
  tablespoons grated) horse-radish

4 tablespoons lemon juice
½ teaspoon celery salt
8 drops Tabasco sauce

Combine ingredients and blend well; chill. Makes almost 1 pint.

DILL AND MUSTARD SAUCE

2½ tablespoons dry mustard
5 tablespoons sugar
½ teaspoon salt
2 tablespoons olive oil
1 tablespoon vinegar

½ cup commercial sour cream
2 tablespoons chopped fresh dill
  or 1 tablespoon dried dill,
  freshened in hot water

Blend together mustard, sugar, and salt. Add oil and vinegar alternately. Stir slowly until blended, then beat hard. Fold in sour cream and dill. Serve with cold fish and shellfish. Makes about 1·cup.

FRANKFURTER SAUCE

2 tablespoons butter or
margarine
1 tablespoon flour
2 tablespoons dry mustard
2 tablespoons sugar
½ teaspoon salt

½ cup water
¼ cup vinegar
2 tablespoons mayonnaise
¼ cup chopped dill pickle
½ teaspoon Tabasco sauce

Melt butter in saucepan over low heat. Remove from heat and blend in the flour, mustard, sugar and salt. Combine with the water and vinegar and return to medium heat. Cook and stir until mixture thickens and boils. Remove and stir in mayonnaise, dill pickle and Tabasco. Makes 1 cup.

REMOULADE SAUCE FOR PAN-FRIED FISH

½ cup chopped sour pickles
2 tablespoons chopped capers
1 tablespoon prepared mustard

1 tablespoon mixed chopped
parsley, tarragon and chervil
2 cups mayonnaise

Combine and mix well. Makes 2½ cups.

TARTAR SAUCE

6 finely chopped ripe olives
1 teaspoon chopped chives

Add to remoulade sauce.

SEAFOOD SAUCE

¼ teaspoon Tabasco
1 teaspoon vinegar
½ cup mayonnaise
½ cup sour cream
1 tablespoon minced onion

1 tablespoon chopped parsley
1 tablespoon chopped green
olives
2 tablespoons chopped pickle

Combine and mix well. Makes 1¼ cups.

Here is an old American recipe from that beautiful and unique volume The American Heritage Cookbook.

OVERNIGHT PICKLED SHRIMP

2 pounds raw shrimp	2 teaspoons celery seed
¼ cup mixed pickling spices	1 teaspoon salt
½ cup celery leaves	¼ teaspoon black pepper
1 cup salad oil	Few drops Tabasco
¾ cup white vinegar	1 large onion, chopped

Combine unshelled shrimp, pickling spices and celery leaves in a saucepan and add enough water to cover. Cover tightly, bring to a boil, reduce heat, and simmer 3 to 5 minutes. Do not overcook. Cool shrimp in the liquid, then remove shells and devein.

Mix together salad oil, vinegar, salt, pepper, celery seed and Tabasco.

Arrange layers of shrimp and chopped onion in a jar or bowl, add the oil-vinegar mixture, cover and refrigerate overnight. Serves 4.

PICKLED SHRIMP

2½ pounds shrimp	1¼ cups salad oil (or olive oil)
Boiling water to cover	¾ cup white vinegar
½ cup chopped celery tops	1½ teaspoons salt
3½ teaspoons salt	2½ teaspoons celery seed
¼ cup mixed pickling spices	2½ tablespoons capers,
2 cups thin-sliced white onions	with juice
7 bay leaves	Tabasco sauce to taste

Wash the shrimp; place in a heavy kettle; cover with boiling water; add the celery tops, salt and pickling spices; cook 12 minutes. Drain; cool; peel, removing dark vein. In a casserole, alternate the shrimp and sliced onion, adding bay leaves over each layer.

Make a marinade by combining in a bowl the oil, vinegar, salt, celery seed, capers and juice, and Tabasco. Pour over the shrimp and onions. Cover. Marinate in refrigerator 24 hours, stirring several times. Serve cold. This will keep about 2 weeks in the refrigerator. Makes 10 or more servings.

PICKLE SAUCE

For an excellent sauce for fish or meat, mix 2 tablespoons of pickle relish, mixed relish, piccalilli, chili sauce or catsup to 1 cup of medium white sauce.

CURRANT PICKLE SAUCE

½ cup currant jelly
¼ cup fine-chopped dill pickles
1 tablespoon prepared horse-
  radish

2 teaspoons prepared mustard

Combine all ingredients; cook over low heat until jelly is melted.
Serve hot or cold with pot roast or roast leg of veal. Makes about ¾
cup sauce.

DILL PICKLE SAUCE

3 tablespoons butter
¼ onion
3 tablespoons flour
1 cup soup stock

1 dill pickle
1 teaspoon chopped parsley
½ cup sour cream
Salt and pepper

Fine-chop onion and sauté in butter until light yellow; blend in flour,
gradually add stock, or hot water in which bouillon cube has been
melted, and cook 15 minutes. Remove and force through strainer. Reheat.

Chop pickle and add along with parsley. Bring to a boil. Add sour
cream and reheat, almost to boiling point. Season and remove from heat.
If fresh dill is available, add 1 teaspoon, chopped, just before serving.
Makes 1½ cups.

FRENCH PICKLE SAUCE

Mix ¼ cup mustard pickle relish with ¾ cup French dressing for a
tangy sauce which goes well with ham slices or assorted cold cuts.

Pickles and Condiments for Reducers

With the exception of the sweet pickles and relishes, almost every recipe in this book is a low-calorie one, since such basic materials as cucumbers and tomatoes are among the least fattening vegetables.

However, for dieters with a sweet tooth, here are a number of recipes using Sucaryl (sodium cyclamate and calcium cyclamate) and saccharin. In using large quantities of either sweetening agent, it is a good idea to taste the pickling solution as you go along.

The usual function of pickles, relishes and catsups is to sharpen the appetite. However, few dieters need such a stimulus. But here are some aids to dieting which add zest and variety to otherwise restricted meals.

DILL PICKLES
(14 calories per cucumber)

1 teaspoon garlic powder
1 teaspoon whole peppercorns
6 whole cloves
½ cup whole dill seed
2 quarts cider vinegar

1 quart water
1 cup salt
Cucumbers (3 to 4 inches) for
    4 quarts

Sterilize 4 quart jars. Combine all ingredients except cucumbers. Bring to a boil. Scrub cucumbers, but do not peel. Fill quart jars with the cucumbers. Cover with boiling vinegar. Seal. Makes 4 quarts.

CUCUMBER SLICES
(40 calories per pint)

10 pounds medium cucumbers
1 cup salt
2¼ quarts vinegar

2 tablespoons Sucaryl solution
¼ cup mixed pickle spices

Wash and cut cucumbers into slices about ¼ inch thick. Mix cucumbers and salt. Let stand overnight. In the morning drain and press out all the juice possible. Rinse once in cold water. Combine vinegar, Sucaryl and spices. Boil 1 minute. Add cucumbers, and simmer 5 minutes. Pack cucumbers into clean, hot, sterile jars to within 1 inch of top. Fill jars with hot liquid to top; seal tightly. Makes about 12 pints.

MIXED GARDEN PICKLES
(53 calories per pint)

3 cucumbers (6 or 7 inches)
2 medium green peppers
1 cup cauliflower flowerets
¼ pound fresh snap beans

8 small white onions
Salt
1 quart cider vinegar
2 tablespoons mixed pickling spice

Score cucumber rinds with a fork but do not peel. Cut into fourths lengthwise and then into ¾-inch chunks. Seed and cut peppers into ¾-inch pieces. Cut cauliflower into 1-inch pieces. Cut beans into 1-inch lengths. Peel onions. Combine all vegetables and cover with salt. Let stand 24 hours. Drain and rinse.

Heat vinegar and pickling spice. Add vegetables and simmer until just tender—about 15 minutes. Place in sterilized jars and seal. Makes 4 pints.

SPICED PICKLES
(15 calories per pickle)

100 small (3¾ inches) pickles
1 ounce whole cloves
1 ounce cinnamon
3 tablespoons Sucaryl solution

½ cup salt
1 ounce yellow mustard
1 pint cider vinegar

Scald pickles in boiling water. Drain. Mix cloves and cinnamon together. Place a layer of pickles in a 5-gallon crock and sprinkle with the spice mixture. Repeat until crock is full.

Combine Sucaryl, salt, mustard and vinegar, and bring to a boil; cook about 5 minutes. Pour brine over the pickles, filling the crock. More brine may be needed, depending on size of pickles. Cover crock and let stand in a cold place.

THE ETIQUETTE OF PICKLES:

According to expert Helen Linn, when pickles are served with sandwiches, they are eaten with the fingers; when served with meat, a fork is used.

MUSTARD PICKLES
(115 calories per pint)

2 heads cauliflower
3 pounds small white onions
½ dozen green pepper shells
  (1 pound)
3 pounds green tomatoes
3 quarts white wine vinegar
2 to 3 tablespoons Sucaryl
  solution, or to taste

¼ pound dry mustard
2 tablespoons mustard seed
2 tablespoons celery seed
1 tablespoon turmeric
3 pints sweet spiced gherkins

Separate cauliflower into flowerets. Peel onions and slice pepper shells very fine. Slice tomatoes and combine all 4 ingredients. Cover with salt and let stand overnight. Drain. Cover with boiling water and cook until vegetables are soft. Drain.

Heat vinegar, add Sucaryl, and pour over the thoroughly mixed mustard, celery seed and turmeric. (A thicker mustard sauce can be made by adding flour.) Blend well.

Add gherkins to the cooked vegetables. Pour all the liquid over them and cook about 10 minutes, or until mixture thickens. Pour into sterilized jars and seal. Makes about 12 pints.

SWEET SPICED GHERKINS
(40 calories per pint)

5 pounds very small cucumbers
½ cup coarse salt
3 cups water
1 pint mild vinegar
1 pint water

5 tablespoons Sucaryl solution,
  or to taste
1 teaspoon cinnamon
¼ teaspoon ground allspice
¼ teaspoon ground cloves

Scrub cucumbers with a brush, then soak for 24 hours in brine made of salt and 3 cups water. Remove from brine and pour boiling water

---

While cucumbers are by weight 1 per cent carbohydrate, when they are transformed into dill or process pickles, they lose even this small amount, but gain in mineral content and vitamin A.

Pasteurized dills have almost the same percentage of carbohydrate, but more minerals and vitamin A.

over. Drain quickly. Pack cucumbers closely, while hot, in sterilized jars. Cover at once with boiling mixture made from vinegar, 1 pint water, Sucaryl and spices. Seal jars at once. Makes about 5 pints.

CHILI SAUCE
(7 calories per tablespoon)

18 tomatoes
2 green peppers
2 medium onions
3 tablespoons Sucaryl solution, or to taste

2 teaspoons salt
1 teaspoon ground cinnamon
½ teaspoon ground cloves
1 teaspoon allspice
2 cups vinegar

Peel, core, and chop tomatoes. Chop peppers and onions fine. Combine all ingredients. Boil slowly 4 hours, or until sauce reaches desired thickness. Pour, boiling hot, into hot, sterilized ½-pint containers; seal. Makes about 6 ½-pint jars.

PEPPER-ONION RELISH
(4 calories per tablespoon)

1 quart finely chopped onions
2 cups finely chopped sweet red peppers
2 cups finely chopped green peppers

2 tablespoons Sucaryl solution, or to taste
1 quart vinegar
4 teaspoons pure granulated salt

Combine all ingredients and bring slowly to boil. Cook until slightly thickened. Pour into clean, hot, sterile jars. Fill jars to top; seal tightly. Makes about 5 pints.

FRANKFURTER RELISH
(19 calories per serving)

3½ pounds sweet red peppers
3 pounds green peppers
3 pounds onions
1 quart vinegar
1 tablespoon Sucaryl solution

1 teaspoon mustard seed
1 tablespoon dry mustard
1 tablespoon celery seed
2 tablespoons salt

Wash peppers; remove cores and seeds. Peel onions. Put peppers and onions through food chopper, using medium blade. Cover with boiling water; let stand 5 minutes; drain. Add vinegar, Sucaryl, spices and salt. Cook until vegetables are tender—about 15 minutes—stirring occasionally. Pour, boiling hot, into hot, sterilized jars; seal. Makes about 8 pint jars.

PICKLED RED CABBAGE
(10 calories per ounce)

Shred red cabbage rather fine and sprinkle generously with salt. Set aside in a cool place for 3 hours. Drain all moisture from cabbage; place it in the sun, allowing it to remain for several hours.

In a saucepan place sufficient vinegar to cover the cabbage, adding 2 teaspoons Sucaryl solution for every quart of vinegar and a small amount of celery seed, pepper, mace, allspice and cinnamon. Boil this together for 7 minutes; pour over cabbage. Put in stone crocks, cover and store in a cool place.

SEASONINGS FOR SAUERKRAUT
(32 calories per cup)

Sauerkraut, especially crisp and raw, gains much flavor when caraway or dill seeds or juniper berries are mixed with it. Also try a sliced or shredded raw carrot mixed with the kraut.

JIFFY CATSUP
(12 calories per tablespoon)

5 saccharin or Sucaryl tablets	½ teaspoon paprika
3 tablespoons cider vinegar	⅛ teaspoon ground cloves
¾ cup tomato paste	¼ teaspoon dry mustard
1 teaspoon salt	⅛ teaspoon nutmeg
¼ teaspoon celery salt	¼ teaspoon garlic powder

Dissolve sweetening in vinegar. Stir in the other ingredients. Stir well. Cover; store in refrigerator. Makes about 1 cup.

A regular 6-ounce can of tomato paste contains ¾ cup.

MUSHROOM CATSUP
(3 calories per tablespoon)

1 cup (8-ounce can) tomato purée	⅛ teaspoon allspice
6 ounces chopped broiled mushrooms	¼ teaspoon dry mustard
	¼ teaspoon celery salt
2 tablespoons vinegar	½ teaspoon Kitchen Bouquet
⅛ teaspoon cinnamon	Sucaryl to taste

Blend all ingredients except Sucaryl until smooth—about 30 seconds—in electric blender or mixer. Pour into saucepan, sweeten to taste and bring to boil. Simmer, covered, over low heat 15 minutes. Makes 2 cups.

HORSE-RADISH RELISH
(8 calories per tablespoon)

Grate sound horse-radish roots. Measure about ½ as much vinegar as horse-radish, add ¼ to ½ teaspoon salt for each cup of vinegar, and pour over grated horse-radish. Pack at once into clean, hot, sterile jars. Fill jars to top; seal tightly.

SACCHARIN PICKLES

½ cup granulated sugar
1 cup salt
1¼ cups dry mustard
3 quarts vinegar

1 quart cold water
1 ounce saccharin
150 small cucumbers

Mix other items together and pour over pickles in crock. Stir every other day for a week. Makes about 10 pints.

Around the World in a Pickle Barrel

Pickles are not only an ancient food, they are a universal one. No matter how different the eating habits of the world may be, in almost every culture there is a department devoted to the preserving of food with salt and vinegar, not only to make perishable foods last, but also to add spice and savor to meals.

Here is a collection of recipes for pickling and for pickle products as ingredients in other dishes, ranging from reindeer and bear marinade from the frozen north of Canada, to olives as they are prepared in desert-hot Iraq.

This is only a sampling of the recipes that exist around the world, but they are from 26 different countries and will give you an idea of the international pickle picture. And, if the nations of the world are not united in any other way, they are in their common regard and enjoyment of "vegetables under acid."

ARAB COUNTRIES

PICKLED TURNIPS (Kabees el Lift)

Turnips to fill quart jar	1 cup vinegar
1 small beet, peeled	Garlic cloves
2 cups water	2 teaspoons salt

Wash turnips well and cut slice from tops and bottoms. Slice lengthwise into ¼-inch slices to within ½ inch of bottom of turnip. Do not separate the slices entirely from each other. Soak in water overnight. Wash well in morning.

Place in glass jar with the beet to give color. Cover with cold pickling solution made of remaining ingredients. Store in cool place. Ready for eating after 3 days. Makes 1 quart.

PICKLED CAULIFLOWER (Kabees el Qarnabette)

1 large cauliflower	2 teaspoons salt
1 cup vinegar	1 small peeled beet (optional)
2 cups water	

Wash cauliflower and separate into small flowerets. Place in boiling water and boil until not quite tender.

Mix vinegar, water and salt.

Pack cauliflowerets into clean jars, cover with vinegar solution. Add beet for color, if desired. Let stand for 3 or 4 days before using.

AUSTRALIA

DOWN UNDER CUCUMBERS

Grape leaves	Brine (2 tablespoons salt to each
Medium cucumbers	quart of water)
Chili peppers	

Put thick layer of grape leaves in bottom of wide-mouthed crock and then a layer of well-washed cucumbers; cover with a sprinkle of small peppers. Repeat until crock is 1½ inches from full. Cover with grape leaves and pour brine in to cover leaves. Place dish or wooden disk over, cover and let stand for 15 days.

CANADA (YUKON)

BIG GAME MARINADE

3 onions, minced	2 teaspoons salt
1½ cups diced carrots	1 teaspoon fresh-ground black
1 cup chopped green onions	pepper
¾ cup tarragon vinegar	2 bay leaves
5 cups dry white wine	⅔ cup diced celery
1 clove garlic, crushed	

Combine all items in saucepan and cook 5 minutes, covered. Cool.

Use to tenderize steaks or fillets of reindeer, moose, elk, bear. Pour over meat and marinate in cool place 3 or 4 days, turning meat daily and keeping submerged. Makes over 4 pints.

CHINA

CHINESE PICKLED CUCUMBERS (P'ao Ts'ai)

2 cucumbers
1 large cauliflower
½ cabbage
6 green peppers
3 red chili peppers

1 carrot
2 cups white vinegar
½ cup sugar
1 teaspoon salt

Remove seeds from cucumbers, cut cauliflower and cabbage into coarse pieces, remove seeds and ribs of peppers and cut into squares; peel and dice carrot.

Boil cauliflower in a deep saucepan for 10 minutes, drain water, then add all other ingredients, except vinegar, sugar and salt.

Boil the vinegar, sugar and salt and pour over vegetables; soak in boiled vinegar for 20 minutes. Then turn the vegetables over and cover the saucepan with the lid. Allow to stand for 5 hours. Serve cold.

For Chinese kraut see Japanese section of this chapter.

DENMARK

DANISH PICKLE

12 large cucumbers
12 small white onions
½ cup salt
3 cups cider vinegar

1½ cups water
1 cup sugar
1 ounce mixed pickling spices
(2 tablespoons)

Peel cucumbers, cut in half lengthwise and remove seeds.

Blanch onions in boiling water for 2 minutes; plunge into cold water and drain. Cut off thin slice from root end and slip skins off. Sprinkle salt over vegetables and let stand overnight.

Rinse thoroughly in cold water to remove salt; pat dry with clean towel; cut cucumber halves into 3 chunks each.

Boil vinegar, water, sugar and mixed spices, which have been placed in spice bag. Add onions and as many cucumber chunks as can be covered by liquid; simmer gently for 6 minutes, or until cucumbers are transparent. Remove cucumbers and repeat until all cucumbers have been cooked. Leave onions in throughout.

Pack vegetables into hot, sterilized jars; cover with boiling liquid and seal at once. Makes about 8 pints.

ENGLAND
ANCHOVY CATSUP

1 quart ale	½ teaspoon fine white sugar
¼ pound anchovies	½ teaspoon ground ginger
3 fine-chopped shallots	¼ teaspoon ground mace
3 tablespoons mushroom catsup	2 cloves

Simmer all ingredients together very gently for 1 hour, then strain. Do not bottle until quite cold. Makes about 1 pint.

BEEFSTEAK SAUCE

7 pounds large, ripe tomatoes	Spice bag:
3 pounds sugar	1 ounce cinnamon stick
1 pint cider vinegar	½ ounce cloves

Tomatoes can be skinned or not. Simmer all for 6 hours. Bottle in hot, sterilized jars. Makes 3 or 4 pints.

Beetroot is the English word for our beets. Here is how they pickle it.

BEETROOT

Wash the roots carefully, taking care not to break the skin, and either boil in salt water for about 1½ hours, or else bake them in a moderate oven, until tender. When cold, peel the roots and either cut into slices about ¼ inch thick or else cut into small cubes. Pack into jars and cover the beetroot well with cold plain or spiced vinegar. If the beetroot is to be kept for long, it is safer to put the sliced or diced beetroot while still hot into warmed jars; add boiling vinegar to fill the jar and seal at once with an airtight cover. Glass-covered preserving jars are very suitable for this.

ENGLISH CHUTNEY

6 large ripe tomatoes	1 pound light brown sugar
6 large sour apples	1 quart cider vinegar
4 medium onions	3 tablespoons salt
4 red peppers	1 teaspoon fresh-ground cinnamon
1 pound seeded raisins	

Cut fruit and vegetables into small pieces. Combine all ingredients and cook slowly for 3 hours. Pack into jars. Process in a boiling water bath at 212°F for 10 minutes. Makes 4 or 5 pints.

FRANCE

For a fresh French pickle, see aromatic cucumbers in the Refrigerator chapter.

GERMANY

From Germany we have Senfgurken or mustard gherkins, but this time the mustard is in seed form, not paste. Here are two varieties.

SENFGURKEN CHUNKS

14 large yellow cucumbers
1 cup pickling salt
9 cups water
1 gallon distilled white vinegar or wine

8 cups sugar
⅓ cup white or yellow mustard seed
1 cup mixed pickling spices in bag

Peel cucumbers, cut into quarters, lengthwise, and trim off all seeds; cut into chunks like watermelon rind.

Make brine of salt and water and soak cucumbers overnight (or 12 hours); drain.

Sterilize and have ready 10 or 11 quart jars.

Dissolve sugar in vinegar and add mustard seed. Heat enough of the vinegar mixture to cover bottom of large pan to depth of ½ inch. Add spice bag. When it comes to boil, cover bottom of pan with cucumber slices and bring to boil again. Immediately, remove cucumbers to jar, filling to within ½ inch of top. Cover with boiling liquid to within ¼ inch of top and seal at once. Repeat until all cucumbers and liquid have been used. Store in dark, cool place and allow pickles to ripen at least 6 weeks before using. Makes 10 to 11 quarts.

Serve very cold with meat dishes.

SHREDDED SWEET SENFGURKEN

8 medium ripe cucumbers
1 cup pickling salt
9 cups water
1 quart white vinegar
1 quart water

8 cups sugar
½ cup mustard seed
½ cup mixed pickling spices in bag

Peel cucumbers, cut into quarters, lengthwise, and trim away seeds; put through shredder or shred by hand to get long shreds looking like thin onion rings.

Make brine of salt and 9 cups water, and soak cucumber shreds overnight; drain well.

Sterilize and have ready 6 pint or 12 ½-pint jars.

Dissolve sugar in vinegar and water; add mustard seed and spices in bag. Heat enough of the liquid to cover bottom of large pan to depth of ½ inch. When it comes to boil, add enough cucumber shreds so that they are just under liquid; bring to boil again. Remove shreds immediately, pack in jar to within ½ inch of top; cover with boiling liquid to within ¼ inch of top; seal at once.

Continue until all cucumber shreds and liquid have been used. Store in dark, cool place. Ready to eat in 3 or 4 weeks. Makes about 6 pints.

Great for the relish tray.

HAWAII

The following is an appetizer for a luau.

PICKLED FISH (Lomi Lomi)

1½ pounds salmon	2 teaspoons lemon juice
8 green onions	1 teaspoon sugar
8 ripe tomatoes	1 cup fine-cracked ice

Soak fish overnight, drain, wash well, skin, bone. Pat dry with paper towels and cut into small bits.

Blend white part of onions, sliced as thin as possible, with tomatoes, which have been peeled, seeded and chopped. When a paste has been formed, knead this into the fish by hand. After 5 minutes, add lemon juice and sugar; knead again so that fish absorbs paste. Cover bowl, place in refrigerator for 1 to 1½ hours to give fish time to ripen.

When ready to serve, blend in ice. Serves 6.

HOLLAND

DUTCH DILL PICKLES

10 quarts water	4 tablespoons pepper
2 cups salt	4 stalks of dill
1 quart vinegar	Cucumbers

Make solution of first 4 ingredients and bring to a boil. Fill crock with cucumbers, placing dill between layers. Add the hot solution. Cover crock and let stand several days before using.

If preferred, onions or garlic may be added and cucumbers may be preserved in jars rather than crock.

DUTCH SAUERKRAUT

2 tablespoons shortening
1 onion
1 quart sauerkraut

1 teaspoon caraway seeds
1 raw potato, grated

Melt the shortening, chop the onion, combine and cook until brown. Add the sauerkraut and cook for 8 minutes. Add the caraway seed and potato, cover with boiling water and cook 30 minutes in an uncovered pot over a slow fire. Cover the kettle and cook 50 minutes longer. Serves 4.

Brown sugar or an apple may be added to give different flavor.

INDIA

This country has a long history of pickling in its food culture. Of course Indian chutneys are famous, but India also pickles grapes, zucchini, eggplant, bananas, pineapple, artichokes and mushrooms.

PICKLED GRAPES

4 pounds Thompson seedless
  grapes
1 cup distilled white vinegar
3 cups sugar
½ teaspoon mace

½ teaspoon ginger
½ teaspoon cinnamon
½ teaspoon cardamom seeds
¼ teaspoon sweet basil

Wash and dry grapes, remove from stems and cut in half, lengthwise.

Put remaining items into pan, bring to boil and boil 6 minutes. Add grapes and cook 3 minutes until fruit is not quite tender. Pack in hot, sterilized jars, making sure liquid covers fruit; seal. Let stand 3 days before using. Makes 5 pints.

INDIAN MUSTARD

¼ pound dry mustard
¼ pound flour
½ ounce salt
Hot water
4 chopped shallots

2 ounces vinegar
4 tablespoons mushroom catsup
2 tablespoons anchovy essence or
  sauce

Put mustard, flour and salt into a bowl and mix into smooth paste with small amount of hot water. Boil the shallots in the vinegar with the remaining ingredients for 10 minutes. Add the paste; stir and simmer for another 2 or 3 minutes. Bottle when cold. Makes about ½ pint.

Technically, the next recipe has no business in a book of pickles, but since we have some 40 chutneys, here is an Indian curry to accompany them.

INDIA CHICKEN CURRY

1 4- to 5-pound fowl, cut up
5 cups boiling water
1 teaspoon salt
¾ cup finely chopped onion
3 tablespoons peanut oil
1 whole clove
1½ teaspoons curry powder
1½ teaspoons turmeric
1½ teaspoons ginger
1 teaspoon cardamom

1 teaspoon marjoram
⅓ teaspoon thyme
1 small bunch parsley, finely chopped
½ cup chopped carrot
¼ cup celery leaves
4 chili peppers, chopped
1½ cups chicken broth
1½ cups coconut water

Cook chicken in boiling salted water until tender, about 2 hours. Remove pieces from pot and reserve broth.

Sauté onion in oil until tender, being careful not to burn. Add all the seasonings and blend well. Add chicken broth and coconut water, stirring well.

Remove chicken from bone and cut into small pieces. Add to sauce and simmer for 15 minutes. Remove chicken, serve with rice and pineapple chutney. Makes 8 portions.

NOTE: Make coconut water by soaking 1 cup coconut in 1¾ cups water for several hours and drain; use water, not coconut milk.

ITALY

ITALIAN MUSTARD

½ pint white wine
1 small onion
6 cloves

Pinch of salt
4 ounces dry mustard

Put wine in small saucepan; stick cloves into onion and add; also salt. Simmer over very low fire for 15 minutes. Remove and strain liquid through sieve. Stir in mustard, a little at a time. When smooth and thick, place in a small (½-pint) jar.

In the Fiji Islands, hot little red Spanish peppers are called "Goddammits."

HOMEMADE ANTIPASTO

1 pound celery
1 pound small or pearl onions
1 pound carrots
1 pound cauliflower
½ water, ½ vinegar solution
3 pints tomato sauce
(or 6 8-ounce cans)
3 cups tomato juice
2 cups olive oil
1 tablespoon peppercorns
1 pound wax beans
(or 1 No. 2 can)

1 pound artichoke hearts
(or 1 No. 2 can)
1 pound green ripe olives
(or 1 No. 2 can)
10 ounces button mushrooms
1 bottle capers, drained
1 pint small sour gherkins
1 12-ounce jar peperoncini sott'
aceto (small pickled peppers)
2 quarts red wine vinegar
2 cans tuna (solid) in oil

Cut celery in 1-inch pieces, slice carrots, break cauliflower into pieces. Cook all raw vegetables in ½ water and ½ vinegar for 10 minutes; drain well overnight.

Next day, mix tomato sauce, juice, olive oil, and pepper and cook together 10 minutes, stirring well. Add all remaining ingredients except tuna. Boil 10 minutes, then pack into hot, sterilized jars. Divide chunks of tuna among the jars, pushing pieces under the sauce in each jar just before sealing. Seal while hot. Hot water may be mixed with sauce to fill jars full. Let stand 1 month before using. Makes about 10 to 12 pints.

DILLED GREEN BEANS, CAPRI STYLE

3 pounds green beans (3 quarts)
6 cups vinegar
2 cups water
1 cup salt

6 bunches dill
6 very small hot red peppers
6 small cloves garlic

Wash beans after removing stem ends.

Heat vinegar, water and salt to boil.

In each sterilized jar place a piece of dill, pod of pepper, and clove of garlic. Pack beans in jars to within 1 inch of top. Pour vinegar solution over the beans. Seal and store at least 3 weeks before using. Makes 6 pints.

John Bass Dabney, writing to his family in Boston from the Azores, where he was the first United States Consul-General, hated Portuguese cooking: "It often happens that everything on the table is sour except the pickles."

JAPAN

Pickles are a standard dessert in Japan.

PICKLED VEGETABLES, JAPANESE STYLE

Many vegetables, especially mushrooms, lend themselves to this method of Japanese salad making. For mushrooms, use 8 ounces; take 6 ounces of turnips and 1½ tablespoons of dried bonito fish, called katsuobushi, which should be finely shaved. Make a sauce of 1½ teaspoons salt, ½ teaspoon soy sauce, 2 tablespoons sake, 2 tablespoons dashi—a soup stock which can be purchased or made—and 2 tablespoons lemon juice.

The mushrooms are stemmed and roasted on long metal skewers.

The turnips are boiled until soft and cooled and the turnip greens are cut into 1-inch lengths. The roots are also sliced.

The mushrooms and turnips are served in small individual bowls, each being filled with the sauce. The lemon juice and fish shavings are then added to complete the recipe.

To make dashi, you need ½ cup of katsuobushi shavings, ¾ square inch of tangle (seaweed), ⅛ teaspoon of a Japanese seasoning known as Aji-no-Moto, and 4⅓ cups of water. The tangle should be placed in the water and taken out when the water starts to boil. The shaved katsuobushi is placed in the water and removed when the water boils. The clear liquid left is dashi.

JAPANESE PICKLED RADISH (Takuanzuke)

16 ounces radish (or turnip, cabbage or cucumber)
1½ tablespoons salt

Soak the Japanese radish in a weak solution of bleaching powder, then wash well. The highly edible leaves should be chopped and sprinkled with salt, the salt being rubbed well into the greens. The leaves should then be put into a bowl and the radish, cut into strips, should be added. Place cover atop entire mixture and place heavy weight on cover. The pickling is done in 4 to 5 hours. The leaves and strips should be served with soy sauce—shoyu—and flavored with vinegar, chopped ginger, some red pepper and, if desired, a dash of lemon juice.

JAPANESE VINEGARED MACKEREL

1 pound mackerel
¾ cup vinegar
¾ tablespoon salt
8 ounces radish, grated
Powdered ginger

4 tablespoons lemon juice or
  vinegar
1¼ tablespoons salt
½ teaspoon soy sauce

Scale, skin and clean the fish. Wash, salt and cut into 4 slices, or 1 for each person. Allow fish to stand in vinegar and salt for 3 hours. Then slice thin and serve individually with a side dish of radish, seasoned with ginger, vinegar, soy sauce and a pinch of salt; dip the fish into this mixture before eating.

The Japanese eat their fish raw but Occidentals prefer to boil or steam it. If the fish is steamed, it should be done before it is allowed to stand in the vinegar and salt mixture.

JAPANESE SOUR LOBSTER, SHRIMP OR PRAWNS

3 ounces of lobster, shrimp or
  prawns, seasoned with ½ teaspoon salt, ½ tablespoon sweet
  sake
4 small cucumbers, seasoned with
  ¾ tablespoon salt

2 egg yellows
¾ tablespoon sugar
¼ teaspoon salt
1½ tablespoons vinegar
½ tablespoon sweet sake

Seafood should be cleaned and washed in salted water and then lightly boiled. Cut into pieces and allow to stand in sake. Peel and seed cucumbers, slice into 1-inch lengths. Combine seasoned fish with cucumber, sprinkle with salt and set aside.

Make sauce of last 5 ingredients. Boil the eggs for 15 minutes; use only the yellows, mash and mix with vinegar, sake, sugar and salt. Shellfish and cucumbers may then be rolled in egg-yellow sauce, or may be eaten separately. Serves 1.

JAPANESE VINEGARED SCALLOPS OR CLAMS

4 scallops or 24 clams
1½ tablespoons vinegar
1 cucumber—season with ¼ teaspoon salt and 1¼ tablespoons vinegar
  and a sauce made with 2 tablespoons vinegar or lemon juice, ½ teaspoon soy sauce, 3 tablespoons sake and ¾ tablespoon sugar

Clean and carefully wash the scallops or clams. Slice meat thin and soak in vinegar. Set aside to be served in small bowls. The shellfish may be served either raw, boiled or steamed. Slice cucumber thin from end to end and sprinkle with salt and vinegar. Let strips stand for some time in this vinegar mixture and then serve alongside the scallops or clams. Over the entire mixture pour the sauce of vinegar, soy sauce, sake and sugar.

CHINESE KRAUT

A favorite Japanese (sic) dish known as O'Shinko. For this you need 20 pounds of Chinese lettuce, and 12 ounces of salt. The lettuce is cut into quarters and washed very carefully. Layer of salt is placed in an earthenware jar or cask and then the lettuce is laid flat on the bottom. Sprinkle all the leaves liberally with more salt. Continue to do this until all the leaves have been inserted flat into the cask. When the container is full of lettuce, it is filled ½ full with water and a cover placed on the leaves. A weight of at least 40 pounds—double the amount of the lettuce —should be placed on top.

Pickling is achieved, the Japanese say, after the water has risen. In summertime, they claim the process takes from 6 to 8 hours; in the fall a full day; and in the winter from 2 to 3 days. Remove, drain and serve with soy sauce.

Turnip greens and spinach may be similarly prepared and pickled.

CABBAGE AND RADISH
KOREA PICKLE KINGS

SEOUL, Korea (Reuters). *Bumper harvests of cabbage and radish have assured South Korean housewives of a good pickling season for kimchi— a malodorous but indispensable dish in this country.*

Kimchi, a spicy pickled cabbage and radish with the pungent smell of garlic and onion, is practically a trademark of Korea in the eyes of the United States servicemen and visitors.

In October and November each year, South Korean housewives prepare enough kimchi to last until March of the next year. It is eaten by Koreans three times a day throughout the winter.

In 1965 housewives were expected to pickle about 118,000 tons of kimchi to feed a population of 25,000,000.

Most foreigners dislike the smell of kimchi and many Koreans themselves agree that it is unpleasant, although they like the taste.

Korean girls working in American offices or military clubs chew gum constantly in an attempt to kill the smell of kimchi. Mouthwash is as important as white shirts for officials of the Korean Foreign Ministry.

MEDITERRANEAN SPECIALTIES

OLIVES   In the U.S. we eat about 10 million gallons of imported olives, plus 2 million cases of the domestic ripe variety a year.

We eat them mostly as they come to us, or as an obstacle in a martini, but there are many interesting ways to prepare and serve them which are almost unknown in this country. *Here are ways of serving from Iraq, Italy, Greece, Turkey and Spain.*

CRACKED OLIVES AS APPETIZERS   I am indebted to *The New York Times* food writer, Craig Claiborne, and its home economist, Mrs. Ruth P. Casa-Emellos, for the following recipes using olives as appetizers which begin by cracking—but not crushing—the olive and its seed. This allows the flesh to absorb the flavors of herbs, spices and seeds more readily.

IRAQI PICKLED OLIVES

3 cloves garlic
¼ teaspoon coriander seed
2 tablespoons parsley
¼ teaspoon nutmeg
2 pounds large green olives
¼ teaspoon ginger

¼ teaspoon freshly ground
   black pepper
1½ teaspoons turmeric
¾ cup olive oil
3 tablespoons vinegar
1 tablespoon water

Crush garlic and coriander. Chop parsley fine. Grate nutmeg. Drain olives and crack them lightly with a hammer or mallet or make lengthwise cuts in each olive and place them in a large bowl. Combine remaining ingredients and add to olives. Mix well and pour into sterilized jars. Seal and keep in a cool place until ready to serve. Makes 12 servings.

A Sicilian specialty is composed of cracked olives mixed with vegetables and spices. It is called:

OLIVE SCHIACCIATE

2 pounds green olives
3 stalks celery
1 cup capers
2 cloves garlic
1 small onion
1 carrot
2 large pickled peppers

Freshly ground black pepper
   to taste
Salt to taste
½ teaspoon fennel seed
1 tablespoon wine vinegar
1 cup olive oil

Crack the olives with a mallet or hammer. Chop celery, onion, garlic, carrot and peppers. Place in a bowl, add remaining ingredients and let stand covered, for a day or so. Pack in sterilized jars and store in refrigerator.

Use as an appetizer or as an ingredient in green salads. Makes 12 to 18 servings.

MIXED ITALIAN OLIVES

½ pound green olives
½ pound black olives
3 stalks celery
1 green pepper
1 red pepper

¼ cup olive oil
Freshly ground black pepper
   to taste
Oregano to taste

Crack the olives and combine with remaining ingredients. Let stand at room temperature for 2 days. Store in refrigerator. Makes 8 to 10 servings.

Here is a recipe for Elies Laderes, or:

BLACK OLIVES, GRECIAN STYLE

2 pounds small, pointed black
   Greek olives
Vinegar to cover

Lemon slices
Celery stalks, coarsely chopped
Olive oil to cover

Crack the olives and cover them with vinegar. Let stand for 2 days. Drain and pack in jars, arranging olives in alternate layers with lemon slices and celery. Cover with olive oil and keep in a cool place until ready to serve. Makes 12 to 18 servings.

OLIVES WITH DILL (Turkey)

1 quart large green olives
3 cloves garlic, crushed
2 red chili peppers
2 sprays fresh dill or teaspoon
   dried dill seed

1 bay leaf
¼ cup olive oil
¼ cup vinegar

Drain the olives and crack them with a hammer or mallet. Combine them with remaining ingredients and let stand a day or so in a cool place. Place in sterilized jars, seal and store in the refrigerator. Makes 8 to 10 servings.

SPICED SPANISH OLIVES

1 cup Spanish green olives
¼ cup vinegar
¼ cup olive oil
2 tablespoons chives

1 clove garlic
1 teaspoon paprika
½ teaspoon peppercorns

Crack olives with a hammer or mallet. Chop chives and garlic fine. Combine with remaining ingredients and let stand at room temperature for 4 hours. Chill in the refrigerator. Makes 4 to 6 servings.

EGGPLANT

In every country bordering the Mediterranean there is some version of Caponata, the relish which has eggplant as its base. In Nice it is called Ratatouille. In Palermo it is Caponatina alla Siciliana.

Just to give you an idea of what the recipe sounds like in Italian, here is a literal translation. However, the U.S. measures are given in parentheses.

CAPONATINA ALLA SICILIANA

12 fresh eggplants
Olive oil
12 white celeries
200 grams olives (1 pint)
200 grams capers (1 pint)
1 large onion
300 grams tomato sauce
 (2½ cups)

50 grams sugar (½ cup)
1 glassful vinegar (1 cup)
8 eggs
300 grams shrimps (2½ cups)
8 octopuses
100 grams tunafish (1 cup)
10 anchovies

Peel and dice the eggplants, salt them and drip them, or else dip them in fresh water, so as not to let them become hard and sour. Fry them in abundant oil. At the same time cut in strips the celeries and fry it. Remove the stones from the olives; boil and unsalt the capers. Fry in oil large onion cut in thin slices, add the tomato sauce and the sugar dissolved in a glassful of vinegar. Let it thicken, stir constantly; add the eggplant, the celery, the olives and the capers. Cook until all the vinegar has evaporated; then put everything in a serving dish. Mince the yellows and whites of 3 boiled eggs separately and place these on the caponatina, alternately with the shrimp and octopus, 5 hard-boiled eggs, tunafish and anchovy fillets, all placed crownwise around the edge of the serving dish.

MALAYA

TOMATO CHUTNEY

3 large tomatoes
1 cooking apple
1 large onion
1 clove garlic
Peanut oil

1 tablespoon paprika
1 tablespoon sugar
2 bay leaves
Salt to taste

Cut tomatoes, apple, onion and garalic, after trimming and peeling. into small pieces.

Deep-fry onions and garlic in oil. Remove to saucepan, add tomatoes, apple, paprika, sugar, bay leaves and salt to taste. Cook over medium heat until apple is cooked. Remove bay leaves.

This recipe is also a favorite in Australia.

MOROCCO

MOROCCAN PICKLE STEW

12 prunes
3 pounds lamb shoulder
3 tablespoons flour
2 tablespoons melted shortening
1½ cups sliced onions

2 teaspoons salt
Dash thyme
2 cups water
¼ cup sweet pickle relish
12 apricots, pitted

Soak prunes overnight in cold water; drain; slit 1 side with a sharp knife and remove pits. Cut lamb into 1-inch cubes; dredge with flour. In a large, deep skillet, brown meat in shortening. Add onions and cook until soft, or about 5 minutes. Add salt, thyme and water. Cover with a tight-fitting lid, bring to a boil and simmer 1 hour. Add relish, prunes, pitted apricots, and cook 30 minutes, or until tender. Makes 6 to 8 servings.

Colonial correspondence preserved from the year 1634 shows that a major purpose of the early settlers' kitchen gardens was to provide pickles. And pickles were highly regarded by all of the pioneering generations because, under frontier conditions, pickles were the only zestful, juicy, green food available for many months of the year.

NEW ZEALAND

The kiwi berry or Chinese gooseberry is a New Zealand fruit which is imported to the Pacific Coast via refrigerated lockers aboard ships from the Antipodes. It has a distinctive flavor which might be described as partway between gooseberry and guava.

KIWI CHUTNEY

12 kiwi fruit
3 medium onions
1 lemon
4 tablespoons preserved ginger
1 teaspoon ground ginger

6 ounces raisins
½ teaspoon salt
¼ teaspoon cayenne pepper
1 cup brown sugar
1½ cups vinegar

Peel kiwi fruit, cut into quarters. Peel and cut onions into fine pieces; slice lemon very thin, discarding seeds. Cut or chop raisins coarsely; chop preserved ginger into small pieces.

Put all ingredients into large saucepan and simmer gently for 1½ hours, stirring frequently to break down to a pulp. Cool slightly; put into small jars; seal and store in a cool place. Makes about 3 ½-pints.

ROUMANIA

ROUMANIAN FRESH PICKLED PEPPERS

Skin sweet green peppers by holding against high flame until skins blister, then plunge into cold water and remove skins with knife. Drain well, then make slit in top or side of peppers with paring knife, core and remove seeds. Pack peppers into quart jars.

Make solution of 1 part water to 2 parts white vinegar; boil; cool; then pour over peppers. To each quart jar add 1 carrot quartered the long way, 1 clove garlic, 1 bay leaf, 1 small hot red pepper, 10 peppercorns, ½ teaspoon salt and 1 tablespoon brown sugar. Cover; let stand at least an hour before serving. Will keep a week or longer in refrigerator.

RUSSIA

SAUERKRAUT SOUP (Shchi)

1½ pounds beef
12 cups water
1 large onion, minced
1 pound fresh sauerkraut,
    chopped

¼ cup washed barley
½ teaspoon salt
2 solid tomatoes, sliced, or 2 apples,
    cored, peeled and sliced
½ cup sour cream

Place beef and cold water in kettle, bring to boil; add onion, sauerkraut and barley; cook for 2 hours. Skim when necessary. During last ½ hour, add tomatoes or apples. When ready, salt to taste and divide sour cream among soup plates. Serves 6.

SCOTLAND

Serve the pickle below with cold meats and fowl.

SCOTCH APPLE PICKLE

20 medium apples	1 pound brown sugar
½ onion	½ pound seeded raisins
Spice bag:	2 tablespoons salt
½ ounce white mustard seed	1½ pints cider vinegar
6 chili peppers	

Peel, core and slice apples. Peel and chop onion. Put apple, onion, spice bag, sugar, raisins, salt and vinegar in enameled pan over low flame and bring slowly to a boil. Stir until sugar dissolves, then simmer until apple is tender. Remoce spice bag and place apple mixture in hot, sterilized jars; seal. Makes 4 or 5 pints.

SWEDEN

PICKLED HERRING (Inlagd Sill)

1 large salt herring	5 tablespoons sugar
1 red onion, sliced	5 white peppercorns
6 allspice, crushed	5 whole allspice
¾ cup white vinegar	2 bay leaves
¼ cup water	2 tablespoons chopped dill

Clean fish, remove head, soak in cold water overnight.

Remove bones, cut into fillets and then into small slices. Arrange slices in glass bowl or dish like whole fillets. Cover with onion slices and sprinkle with crushed allspice.

Blend vinegar, water, sugar, peppercorns, whole allspice and bay leaves in saucepan. Bring to boil, remove, chill and strain. Pour liquid over herring and let stand overnight in refrigerator. Before serving, garnish with chopped dill. Serves 4.

SYRIA

PICKLED CAULIFLOWER, SYRIAN STYLE

1 large head cauliflower
Salt
1 cup vinegar

1 small beet, cooked and
peeled (optional)

Wash cauliflower and separate into small flowerets. Cook in salted water to cover until not quite tender.

Mix vinegar with 2 cups water and 2 teaspoons salt.

Pack cauliflower in hot, sterile jars, cover with vinegar mixture. Add beet to color product, if desired. Store a week before using. Makes 1 quart.

SYRIAN PICKLED MUSHROOMS

4 pounds small sound
  mushrooms
1 tablespoon salt
Juice of 2 lemons

1 tablespoon fresh-ground pepper
1 quart distilled vinegar
1 cup olive oil
½ teaspoon thyme

Clean mushrooms, trim stems; place in pan or kettle with salt, lemon juice; add water to cover; bring to boil; then simmer 6 minutes. Drain; dry mushrooms; pack in 4 hot, sterile pint jars. Divide pepper among 4 jars.

Put vinegar, oil and thyme in pan, heat to boil and pour over mushrooms. Seal at once. Store 1 week to 10 days before using. Makes 4 pints.

Dishes with Pickles or Relishes as Ingredients

In addition to eating pickles by themselves or using a relish along with another dish, these foods frequently blend into other dishes and add piquancy and taste. They "punch up" otherwise prosaic entrees and are especially great additions to salads, as you will see when you read the following chapter.

PICKLE GARNISHES

Pickle relish will add a fillip to cole slaw.

Try chopped pickles in corned beef hash.

Spread sweet pickle relish on cold sliced turkey sandwiches.

Add pickle relish to the yellow when making deviled eggs.

Creamed potatoes may be garnished with chopped pickles.

Cut thin slice from stem end of large dill pickle; hollow out center with apple corer. Stuff with softened cream cheese or smoked Cheddar spread. Chill well and slice.

ADDING ZING TO FOODS WITH PICKLES

In Stew: Dice or slice sour or semisour pickles into beef stew. Or add to pot roast while it cooks. Makes the gravy taste better.

In Salads: Use sour pickles instead of fresh cucumbers with sour cream. And add 1 teaspoon of pickle juice to 2 tablespoons sour cream for a "pickler" flavor. Refrigerate for 2 hours.

Above can be blended with chopped fresh tomatoes, chopped celery, diced carrots and minced scallion (optional), for a garden salad.

Or sour cream and pickles can be blended with cottage cheese for a light luncheon platter.

In Soup: Cheese soup has become quite popular, both homemade and canned. Try cross-cutting a dill or sour pickle so that when you slice it, small dice will fall into the soup before heating it. Stir well when serving so that the pickle dice will be evenly distributed.

APPETIZERS

PICKLE FANS

Cut sweet or dill pickles into thin parallel slices almost the length of each pickle. Spread carefully into a fan shape; then press the uncut end between the thumb and forefinger so the fan will hold its shape.

FLUTED CUCUMBERS

Hold the whole, peeled or unpeeled (whichever you prefer), cucumber in the left hand and score it heavily lengthwise with the tines of a fork on all sides; then cut it crosswise into thin slices.

CHERRY POINSETTIAS

With a sharp knife, make 6 to 8 cuts in each maraschino cherry from the pitted end to within ⅛ inch of round end. Flatten cherry, outside up, on paper towel. Press flat in center and carefully separate petals.

QUICK TRICKS WITH PICKLES

Wrap pickled sour onions in ½-slices of bacon. Fasten with toothpicks. Broil until bacon is done.

Cut sharp Cheddar cheese or canned luncheon meat into ½-inch cubes. Spear with toothpicks; top with pickled sour or sweet onions or ½-inch slices of sweet gherkins.

Wrap midget gherkins or sweet pickle slices in anchovies or smoked salmon.

Join slices of Vienna sausages or frankfurters with slices of sweet gherkins.

Onion Cheese Balls: Roll pickled sweet onions in softened cream cheese. Serve with toothpicks.

Pickle Cheese Balls: Combine softened cream cheese with sweet or fresh cucumber relish; form into small balls.

Dill Liverwurst Balls: Combine mashed liverwurst with minced celery and green pepper. Form into small balls; roll in minced dill pickles. Serve with toothpicks.

Vienna Tidbits: For a tasty appetizer, cut Vienna sausages in half lengthwise. Spread inside of each half with prepared mustard. Place thin slice of dill pickle in center to form sandwich. Cut in half; fasten with toothpicks.

OLIVES IN OIL

Drain olives (use an assortment of large black, green, ripe, mottled and stuffed) and marinate for 1 hour at room temperature in 1 cup olive oil, 3 tablespoons wine vinegar and minced clove of garlic. Marinade should cover, and olives should be stirred occasionally.

NUTTY CHUTNEY CANAPES

Mix fine-chopped nutty chutney with peanut butter, spread on rounds of toast and top with small strips of bacon. Heat in oven until bacon is crisp and serve hot.

GEFILTE PICKLES

Large sour pickles
Hard-boiled chopped egg

Mayonnaise
Grated sharp Cheddar cheese

Using an apple corer, remove centers of pickles—or cut them in halves and scoop out shallow wedges of centers. Chop pickle pulp, mix with equal amount of egg, moisten with mayonnaise, add some cheese to mixture and stuff centers of pickles with mixture. Wrap in Saran or other plastic film and chill until ready to serve. Then slice.

SOUPS

PICKLE VICHYSSOISE

2 tablespoons butter or
  margarine
½ cup sliced onions
½ teaspoon salt
Dash cayenne
5 medium-sized potatoes

3 cups chicken bouillon
2 cups light cream
1 cup milk
½ cup fine-chopped sweet fresh
  cucumber pickles
Chopped chives

Melt butter or margarine and add onions; cook over medium heat until onions are tender. Add salt, cayenne, potatoes, which have been pared and thinly sliced, and chicken bouillon; cover and cook until potatoes are tender. Force through food mill or sieve; cool. Add cream, milk and pickles. Chill thoroughly. Serve with chopped chives. Makes about 2 quarts.

BLACK BEAN AND DILL SOUP

1 10½-ounce can condensed black bean soup
¼ cup chopped dill pickles

Combine soup and dill pickles. Prepare according to directions on can. Serve garnished with thin slices of dill pickles, if desired. Serves 4.

SALADS AU GO-GO

ASPARAGUS SALAD, VINAIGRETTE

1 pound fresh asparagus, cooked and drained
3 tablespoons vinegar
¼ teaspoon salt
½ cup olive or salad oil
2 tablespoons fine-chopped chives
1 tablespoon chopped parsley
¼ cup chopped sweet gherkins
Crisp lettuce

Cook, then drain asparagus; chill. Meanwhile, combine vinegar, salt, olive or salad oil, chives, parsley and gherkins; mix well. Pour over asparagus and chill 30 minutes. Serve on lettuce. A 10-ounce package of frozen asparagus spears may be used instead of the fresh vegetable. Serves 4.

BEAN AND CHEESE SALAD

1 can beans in tomato sauce
½ cup julienne cheese
1 cup chopped celery
1 can drained, sliced Vienna sausage (4 ounces)
2 hard-boiled chopped eggs
1 tablespoon minced onion
½ cup sweet relish
2 tablespoons mayonnaise
¼ teaspoon salt

Drain excess sauce from beans. Combine beans and remaining ingredients. Mix well; chill. Serve on lettuce. Makes 4 servings.

GREEN BEAN SALAD

1½ pounds green beans
½ cup thinly sliced pickled sour onions
¼ cup liquid from pickled sour onions
2 tablespoons salad oil
½ teaspoon salt
⅛ teaspoon paprika

Wash beans, cook in boiling salted water until tender. Drain; cool; cut lengthwise into thin strips. Combine with other ingredients. Refrigerate about 3 hours. Heap in lettuce cups; garnish with pimiento. Serve with mayonnaise. Makes 3 to 4 servings.

AUNT SALLY'S PICKLE ASPIC

1 pint pickles and juice
1 package (½ ounce) unflavored gelatin
1½ pints boiling water

Use your favorite pickles, sweet, sour or bread and butter; drain.

Save juice and seasonings and in them soak gelatin 5 minutes.

Save some slices of pickle to decorate bottom and sides of 1-quart mold or ring; chop balance and place in mold.

Combine softened gelatin, juice and boiling water, stirring until gelatin is fully dissolved. Pour liquid carefully into mold; cool and place in refrigerator to harden (about 2 hours). When ready to serve, remove from mold onto lettuce leaves. Makes 1 quart.

Another method: Hold out chopped pickles until mixture in mold just begins to jell, then pour pickles in for more even distribution through aspic.

KIDNEY BEAN SALAD

1 can drained kidney beans (16 ounces)	½ cup chopped dill pickles
2 tablespoons salad oil	¼ cup minced onion
1 tablespoon vinegar	2 hard-boiled chopped eggs
¾ teaspoon salt	Dash pepper
½ cup chopped celery	2 tablespoons mayonnaise
	Grated cheese

Combine first 4 ingredients; chill at least 1 hour. Add celery and remaining ingredients, except cheese; chill. Serve on leaf lettuce. Garnish with grated cheese. Makes 4 servings.

KIDNEY BEAN AND TONGUE SALAD

1 can drained kidney beans (16 ounces)	2 tablespoons chopped pimiento
1 cup julienne cooked tongue	1 cup chopped sweet pickles
1 cup chopped celery	3 tablespoons mayonnaise
2 tablespoons chopped green pepper	1 teaspoon salt
	Dash pepper

Combine ingredients. Let stand in refrigerator 1 hour to blend flavors. Serve on lettuce. Makes 4 to 6 servings.

ROAST BEEF SALAD

3 cups cubed cooked beef
½ cup chopped kosher dill
  pickles
½ cup chopped celery
⅓ cup fine-chopped onion

⅓ cup mayonnaise
1 teaspoon prepared mustard
1 teaspoon Worcestershire sauce
1 teaspoon salt

Combine first 4 ingredients. Blend mayonnaise and remaining ingredients. Mix lightly with meat mixture; chill. Serve in lettuce cups; garnish with pimiento or green pepper. Makes 4 to 6 servings.

HEARTY BEET SALAD

2 cups cubed cooked beets
  (1-pound can)
½ cup cubed cooked potato
  (1 medium)
½ cup chopped celery

½ cup chopped sweet pickles
½ cup diced cucumber
1 teaspoon salt
¼ cup French dressing
3 hard-boiled sliced eggs

Combine all ingredients except eggs; marinate 1 hour. Serve in lettuce cups; garnish with egg slices and mayonnaise. Makes 6 servings.

STUFFED BEET SALAD

For an eye-catching salad, scoop out centers of canned small whole beets with melon-ball cutter. Fill beets with a mixture of 1 part India or sweet relish, 2 parts dairy sour cream and a dash of salt. Serve 3 or 4 stuffed beets on crisp greens with French dressing. Garnish with parsley or water cress.

CABBAGE SLAW WITH CREAM DRESSING

½ cup dairy sour cream
3 tablespoons chili sauce
1 tablespoon minced onion

¼ teaspoon salt
Dash pepper
1 quart shredded cabbage

Combine first 5 ingredients; toss with cabbage. Makes 4 to 6 servings.

CAROL G'S SALAD

½ cup mayonnaise
2 tablespoons pickle juice
¼ cup vinegar
1 tablespoon Worcestershire
  sauce
3 hard-boiled minced eggs
1 tablespoon minced onion

¼ cup minced sweet pickles
1 large head lettuce, broken
  into bite-sized pieces
1 cup julienne cooked chicken
1 cup julienne cooked ham
1 medium tomato, cut into
  thin wedges or strips

Combine first 4 ingredients. Stir in eggs, onion and pickle. Allow to stand in refrigerator at least 1 hour. Toss lettuce with dressing; serve on individual plates or salad bowls. Top with chicken, ham and tomato. Makes 6 main-dish salads.

½ cup barbecue relish may be substituted for the pickles and juice.

SPICY CELERY SALAD

1 package lemon-flavored gelatin (3 ounces)	1 cup cold water
	2 cups chopped celery
1 cup hot water	½ cup hamburger relish

Dissolve gelatin in hot water. Add cold water. Chill until it starts to thicken. Stir in celery and relish. Pour into individual molds. Chill until firm. Unmold onto bed of endive or lettuce. Garnish with mayonnaise. Makes 6 servings.

CUCUMBER CHEESE RINGS

1 package cream cheese (3 ounces)	3 tablespoons chopped candied dill strips
1 teaspoon minced onion	Dash cayenne pepper
1 teaspoon Worcestershire sauce	2 medium cucumbers
1 tablespoon chopped pecans	

Blend all ingredients except cucumbers. Peel cucumbers; cut in half, crosswise; remove center of cucumber with apple corer. Sprinkle cavities with salt and pepper; pack cheese mixture firmly into cavities. Wrap in waxed paper; chill until firm, about 4 hours. Cut into ¼-inch slices; arrange on lettuce leaves. Garnish with paprika. Serve with French dressing or one of its spicier variations. Makes 4 to 6 servings.

ALMOND CHICKEN SALAD

3 cups cubed cooked chicken	½ cup mayonnaise
⅔ cup chopped sweet pickles	½ teaspoon salt
½ cup blanched, quartered toasted almonds	1½ teaspoons vinegar
	Lettuce
⅓ cup seedless white grapes	Water cress

Combine first 4 ingredients. Blend mayonnaise, salt and vinegar. Mix lightly with chicken mixture. Chill. Spoon into lettuce cups; garnish with water cress. Makes 4 to 6 servings.

SNAPPY CHICKEN SALAD

2 hard-boiled eggs, sliced
3 cups cubed cooked chicken
⅔ cup chopped sweet pickles
1 cup chopped celery

1 teaspoon salt
1 teaspoon lemon juice
½ cup mayonnaise

Select 3 or 4 center slices of eggs for garnish; chop remaining eggs. Mix chopped eggs lightly with remaining ingredients. Mound on lettuce. Garnish with egg slices and sprinkle with paprika. Makes 6 servings.

WALDORF CHICKEN

Substitute ½ cup diced red apples for hard-boiled eggs. If apples are sweet, more lemon juice may be added.

OLIVE CHICKEN

Omit pickles; add ½ cup sliced ripe olives.

PINEAPPLE CHICKEN SALAD

Omit eggs and pickles. Add ½ cup drained, chopped pineapple and ⅓ cup chopped English walnuts.

HOT CHICKEN SALAD

⅔ cup mayonnaise or
  salad dressing
2 teaspoons cider vinegar
1 teaspoon salt
¼ teaspoon celery seed
⅛ teaspoon pepper
2 cups diced cooked chicken

1 cup chopped celery
¼ cup blanched, slivered
  almonds
¼ cup sweet relish
2 teaspoons chopped onion
1 cup crushed potato chips or
  1 cup grated American cheese

Heat oven to 350°F (moderate). Blend mayonnaise, vinegar, salt, celery seed and pepper. Combine chicken and next 4 ingredients; toss with dressing. Place in baking dish (10 x 6 x 2-inch) or individual casseroles. Sprinkle with potato chips and/or cheese. Bake for 20 minutes or until cheese is melted. Garnish with parsley or pickle fans. Makes 5 to 6 servings.

CONTINENTAL SALAD

3 cups shredded cabbage
1 cup julienne salami
½ cup chopped green peppers
3 hard-boiled chopped eggs

3 tablespoons tomato catsup
3 tablespoons mayonnaise
1 teaspoon vinegar
¼ teaspoon salt

Toss ingredients together. Garnish with tomato. Makes 6 to 8 servings.

CONFETTI SALAD

1 envelope unflavored gelatin	1 tablespoon lemon juice
¼ cup cold water	1 tablespoon minced onion
¼ cup sugar	½ cup carrots
½ teaspoon salt	¼ cup radishes
1 cup boiling water	1 tablespoon green pepper
¼ cup pickle juice	½ cup celery
½ teaspoon Worcestershire sauce	¼ cup dill pickles

Soften gelatin in cold water 5 minutes. Add sugar, salt and boiling water; stir until gelatin dissolves. Add pickle juice, Worcestershire sauce, lemon juice and onion. Cool.

Shred carrots and radishes, mince onion and green pepper, dice celery, chop pickles and add when gelatin mixture begins to thicken. Turn into a 9 x 5 x 3-inch loaf pan. Chill until firm. Unmold; slice and serve on crisp salad greens. Makes 6 servings.

"COOL AS A PICKLE" SALAD

1 tablespoon unflavored gelatin	¼ cup juice drained from
¼ cup cold water	crushed pineapple
¾ cup boiling water	1 cup diced sweet pickles
¼ cup sugar	1 cup canned crushed
½ teaspoon salt	pineapple, drained
¼ cup cider vinegar	

Soften gelatin in cold water. Dissolve in boiling water. Add sugar, salt, vinegar, pineapple juice. Chill until slightly thickened; add pickles and pineapple. Pour into individual molds. Chill until firm. Unmold on lettuce beds. Serves 5.

CORN SALAD

1 can drained whole kernel	Dash pepper
corn (1 pound)	2 tablespoons salad oil
⅓ cup finely chopped celery	3 tablespoons vinegar
¼ cup chopped green pepper	¼ cup finely chopped dill
2 tablespoons chopped pimiento	pickles
2 tablespoons minced onion	¼ teaspoon prepared mustard
¾ teaspoon salt	

Combine ingredients. Chill several hours or overnight. Serve as a salad or relish. Makes 6 servings.

CRAB LOUIS

¾ cup mayonnaise
¼ cup chili sauce
2 tablespoons minced parsley
2 teaspoons vinegar

½ teaspoon Worcestershire sauce
¼ teaspoon prepared horse-radish
1 pound fresh or canned crab meat

Blend first 6 ingredients. Toss lightly with crab meat. Chill. Serve in lettuce cups or as a filling for avocado halves. Makes 4 servings.

HAWAIIAN CRAB MEAT

2 cups fresh or canned crab meat
1 cup chopped celery
1 tablespoon horse-radish relish
¼ cup mayonnaise
¼ cup tomato catsup

1 teaspoon onion juice
1 tablespoon lemon juice
1 can sliced pineapple (1 pound, 4 ounces), drained

Combine crab and celery.

Combine horse-radish relish with next 4 ingredients. Mix ½ this sauce with crab; reserve other ½ for top of salad. Place crab mixture between 2 slices of pineapple, sandwich style, or mound crab on pineapple ring and garnish with pineapple sections. Serve on lettuce, top with dressing. Makes 5 servings.

DELICATESSEN SALAD

¼ pound julienne bologna
¼ pound julienne salami
½ cup sliced ripe olives
½ cup chopped kosher dill pickles

⅓ cup chopped green pepper
⅓ cup sliced celery
⅓ cup sour cream
1 medium, unpared, coarsely chopped apple

Lightly mix ingredients; chill. Serve in lettuce cup; garnish with unpared apple slices. Makes 4 to 6 servings.

DILL PICKLE FRAPPE

1 tablespoon unflavored gelatin
¼ cup cold water
2 cups vegetable juice cocktail
1 cup dill pickle liquid

½ teaspoon celery salt
3 dill pickles, cut in lengthwise strips

Soften gelatin in water. Combine vegetable juice, pickle liquid and celery salt; mix well and heat to boiling point. Add softened gelatin and stir until dissolved. Cool. Freeze until mushy, stirring occasionally. Turn into glasses and garnish with pickles. Makes 6 servings.

EGG SALAD DELUXE

1 teaspoon unflavored gelatin	⅓ cup mayonnaise
1 can undiluted condensed consommé (10½ ounces)	2 hard-boiled eggs, chopped
¾ teaspoon salt	½ cup chopped celery
⅛ teaspoon pepper	1 tablespoon minced onion
2 teaspoons vinegar	1 tablespoon chopped pimiento
	2 tablespoons sweet relish

Soften gelatin in 2 tablespoons cold consommé. Heat rest of consommé just to boiling; add to gelatin and stir until gelatin is dissolved. Add salt, pepper and vinegar. Chill until slightly thickened.

Combine mayonnaise and remaining ingredients and fold into gelatin mixture. Pour into 4 individual molds. Chill until firm. Unmold on lettuce. Garnish with tomato wedges and water cress. Makes 4 servings.

DEVILED EGG SALAD

6 hard-boiled eggs, chopped	⅓ cup chopped celery
¼ cup hot dog relish	½ teaspoon salt
3 tablespoons mayonnaise	

Combine ingredients; chill. Spoon onto bed of lettuce. Makes 3 to 4 servings.

EGGS A LA RUSSE

6 hard-boiled eggs, sliced	1 tablespoon minced onion
¾ cup mayonnaise	1 tablespoon minced green pepper
3 tablespoons chili sauce	

Arrange egg slices on shredded lettuce, allowing 1½ eggs for each serving. Blend mayonnaise and remaining ingredients. Spoon mixture over eggs. Makes 4 servings.

PICKLE EGG MOUSSE

1 tablespoon unflavored gelatin	½ cup celery
¼ cup cold water	2 tablespoons green pepper
½ cup boiling water	¼ cup sweet pickle relish
1 cup mayonnaise	¾ teaspoon salt
4 hard-boiled eggs	

Soften gelatin in cold water. Add boiling water and stir until gelatin is dissolved; cool slightly. Add mayonnaise and beat until smooth. Dice eggs, chop celery and pepper. Add remaining ingredients; mix well. Pour into 9 x 5 x 3-inch pan, or 4 to 6 individual molds. Chill until firm. Unmold and serve on crisp salad greens, as desired. Makes 4 to 6 servings.

EMERALD GARDEN SALAD

1 envelope unflavored gelatin	⅓ cup liquid from sweet pickles
¼ cup cold water	1 tablespoon lemon juice
2 tablespoons sugar	½ cup finely shredded cabbage
½ teaspoon salt	¼ cup chopped sweet pickles
1 cup boiling water	3 radishes, sliced paper-thin
Green food coloring	½ cup chopped celery

Soften gelatin in cold water. Add sugar, salt and boiling water; stir until gelatin is dissolved. Add enough food coloring to make gelatin an attractive green. Stir in pickle liquid and lemon juice. Chill until gelatin begins to set. Fold in cabbage and remaining ingredients. Pour into 4 individual molds. Chill until firm. Unmold on lettuce and serve with mayonnaise or French dressing. Makes 4 servings.

SALAD FAGOTS

2 or 3 dozen large lettuce leaves	⅛ teaspoon powdered dry
1 tablespoon sweet pickles	mustard
3 stuffed olives	Dash red pepper
1 cup dry cottage cheese	2 or 3 tablespoons mayonnaise

Wash and dry lettuce. Crisp in refrigerator.

Fine-chop pickles and olives. Mix with remaining ingredients. Spread on the lettuce leaves; roll like little jelly rolls; fasten with toothpicks. Chill. Serve on dish with carrot and celery sticks.

FISH SALAD

2 cups flaked, cooked fish	3 tablespoons chili sauce
2 tablespoons dill pickle liquid	½ teaspoon salt
1 cup diced cucumber	⅛ teaspoon ground marjoram,
¼ cup chopped dill pickle	if desired
3 tablespoons mayonnaise	Dash pepper

Sprinkle fish with pickle liquid; chill at least 30 minutes. Lightly mix in cucumber and remaining ingredients. Serve in lettuce cups. Garnish with mayonnaise or salad dressing. Makes 3 to 4 servings.

FRANKFURTER SALAD

1 tablespoon prepared mustard	6 cooked frankfurters, sliced
3 tablespoons chili sauce	diagonally
1 teaspoon vinegar	2 cups diced cooked potatoes
1 teaspoon salt	¼ cup minced onion
⅓ cup mayonnaise	½ cup chopped cucumber

Blend first 5 ingredients. Toss lightly with remaining ingredients. Chill. Serve in lettuce cups; garnish with green pepper rings. Makes 6 servings.

HOT FRANKFURTER POTATO SALAD

4 strips bacon	¼ cup water or milk
½ pound sliced frankfurters (4)	2 tablespoons vinegar
½ cup sliced onion	2 tablespoons sweet relish
1 can undiluted condensed cream	3 cups diced cooked potatoes
of celery soup	(5 medium)

Fry bacon in deep skillet over low heat until crisp. Remove from skillet; drain and crumble. Cook frankfurter slices and onion in bacon drippings until onion is tender. Add soup, water, vinegar and relish; mix well. Add potatoes, toss lightly; heat. Serve hot with crumbled bacon sprinkled over top. Makes 4 to 6 servings.

GOLDEN SLAW

4 hard-cooked fine-chopped eggs	2 teaspoons vinegar
¾ teaspoon sugar	¼ cup mayonnaise
¾ teaspoon salt	2 cups shredded cabbage
2 teaspoons prepared mustard	⅓ cup chopped sweet pickles

Combine all ingredients, tossing lightly. Chill. Serve on lettuce; garnish with chopped parsley. Makes 4 servings.

HAM AND EGG SALAD

½ pound cooked chopped ham	¼ cup diced cucumber
(1½ cups)	⅓ cup mayonnaise
½ cup chopped celery	3 tablespoons hot dog relish
2 hard-boiled eggs, chopped	

Combine ingredients. Chill. Serve on lettuce. Garnish with parsley. Makes 4 servings.

SHREDDED LETTUCE SALAD

½ cup dairy sour cream	1 small head lettuce, coarsely
¼ cup India, sweet or fresh	shredded
cucumber relish	2 green onions, sliced
1 teaspoon prepared mustard	1 cup shredded carrots
½ teaspoon salt	

Combine first 4 ingredients. Toss lightly with vegetables in salad bowl. Makes 6 to 8 servings.

LIMA BEAN SALAD

2 cups cold, drained cooked lima
beans
2 tablespoons sweet pickle relish
1 tablespoon minced onion

½ teaspoon salt
¾ cup chopped celery
3 tablespoons mayonnaise
2 hard-boiled eggs, sliced

Combine ingredients except eggs. Mix lightly, but well. Serve on salad greens; garnish with egg slices and extra mayonnaise if desired. Sprinkle with paprika. Makes 4 to 6 servings.

TART LOBSTER SALAD

2 grapefruit, cut into small
sections
2 cups diced, cooked lobster

1 tablespoon grapefruit juice
⅓ cup tomato catsup
⅓ cup mayonnaise

Combine grapefruit with lobster. Serve on lettuce, endive or water cress in a sea shell or salad plate. For sauce, mix grapefruit juice with catsup and mayonnaise. Makes 4 servings.

MACARONI SALAD

1½ cups elbow macaroni
1½ cups chopped celery
⅓ cup minced onion
6 radishes, thinly sliced
2 tablespoons minced parsley
½ cup minced dill pickles

¾ cup grated sharp cheese
(optional)
1 cup mayonnaise
2 tablespoons vinegar
2 teaspoons prepared mustard
1½ teaspoons salt
⅛ teaspoon pepper

Cook macaroni in boiling salted water until tender; drain, rinse. Combine with next 6 ingredients. Blend mayonnaise and remaining ingredients. Combine with macaroni mixture. Chill. Serve on lettuce. Garnish with grated cheese or parsley. Makes 6 servings.

"At this moment your body contains a pound or more of salt. To keep up this vital stock-pile of salt, you normally require ten grams of salt daily. Under conditions of heat, violent exercise, or hard work, which induce perspiration, you need a great deal more. When your body needs more salt, it's wise to get in a pickle. A medium size Dill Pickle provides half of the normal daily salt requirements in palatable form—and other essential nutritive elements as well. A tip to hardworking people!"

—Pickle Packers Association

GERMAN MACARONI SALAD

¾ cup elbow macaroni
¼ pound cubed liverwurst
½ cup chopped sweet pickles
½ cup sliced celery

⅓ cup mayonnaise
2 tablespoons chili sauce
½ teaspoon salt

Cook macaroni in boiling salted water; drain; rinse. Combine with liverwurst, pickles and celery. Blend remaining ingredients; toss with macaroni mixture. Garnish with tomato wedges, green pepper rings or egg slices. Chill. Makes 4 servings.

MEDLEY PICKLE SALAD

1 package lemon-flavored gelatin
1½ cups boiling water
6 sweet gherkins, sliced lengthwise
½ cup sweet mixed pickles,
  coarse-chopped

1 cup cottage cheese (8 ounces)
1 teaspoon grated onion
1 teaspoon salt
½ teaspoon horse-radish

In a bowl, pour boiling water over gelatin; stir until completely dissolved. Pour ½ cup gelatin mixture in an oiled 1-quart mold; arrange gherkins, cut side up, in gelatin. Chill until firm. Combine remaining ingredients with remaining gelatin mixture; mix well. Pour on top of firm gelatin layer; chill until firm. Unmold on crisp salad greens. Makes 6 servings.

PEAR–WATER CRESS SALAD

8 fresh or canned pear halves
1 bunch water cress

1 package softened cream cheese
  (3 ounces)
2 tablespoons chili sauce

Cut each pear half into 4 lengthwise strips; arrange on bed of water cress. Top with dressing made by combining cheese and chili sauce. Makes 8 servings.

PORK AND APPLE SALAD

2 cups diced cooked pork
2 cups diced unpared red apples
1 cup diced celery
¼ cup sweet relish

1 tablespoon lemon juice
¼ teaspoon onion juice
Dash salt
⅓ cup mayonnaise

Combine ingredients; chill. Serve on lettuce. Makes 4 servings.

STUFFED PEPPER SALAD

2 medium green peppers
1 package softened cream cheese
(8 ounces)

2 tablespoons mayonnaise
¼ cup minced sweet pickles
1½ teaspoons minced onion

Remove stems and seeds from peppers. Blend cheese and remaining ingredients. Fill peppers with cheese mixture, packing firmly; chill until firm. Slice peppers crosswise. For each salad, arrange 2 to 3 slices on lettuce, garnish with tomato wedges and carrot curls. Serve with French dressing. Makes 4 to 6 servings.

PINE-NUT SALAD

½ cup water
2 tablespoons cornstarch
1 can pineapple tidbits
(1 pound 4 ounces)
½ cup tomato catsup

2 tablespoons butter or
margarine
2 cups diced cooked chicken,
veal or pork
1½ cups sliced celery
½ cup coarsely chopped walnuts

In saucepan, gradually mix water with cornstarch; add pineapple, pineapple juice, catsup and butter. Cook, stirring, over low heat until mixture comes to boil and thickens. Combine pineapple mixture with meat and celery. Chill. Serve in lettuce cups. Sprinkle with nuts. Makes 5 to 6 servings.

PICNIC POTATO SALAD

3 cups diced cooked potatoes
(4 medium)
½ cup chopped celery
¼ cup chopped onion
4 sliced radishes

¼ cup French dressing
1 teaspoon salt
2 hard-boiled eggs, chopped
¼ cup hot dog relish
¼ cup mayonnaise

Combine first 6 ingredients. Chill several hours. Add remaining ingredients; chill. Garnish with radish roses and parsley. Makes 4 to 6 servings.

For a main dish salad, add 1½ cups julienne salami, bologna or cooked ham or 2 cups canned salmon or tuna.

SAUERKRAUT SALAD

1 cup sauerkraut
6 tablespoons French dressing

1 teaspoon chopped onion
2 teaspoons chopped parsley

Drain sauerkraut well and slice through several times. Add other ingredients and mix well. Rub bowl beforehand with cut clove of garlic, if desired. Chill before serving. Makes 4 small portions.

Here is a more elaborate sauerkraut salad.

SAUERKRAUT SALAD

1 pint sauerkraut	1 cup chili sauce
1 green pepper, chopped fine	1/3 cup brown sugar
1 small onion, chopped fine	1 teaspoon paprika
3 stalks celery, chopped fine	3 tablespoons fresh lemon juice

Drain sauerkraut and place in a salad bowl. Toss in green pepper, onion and celery. Set aside. Blend together chili sauce, brown sugar, paprika and lemon juice. Pour over salad mixture and toss well. Serves 4 to 6.

SAUERKRAUT AND APPLE SALAD

1 pint sauerkraut, drained	2 tablespoons lemon juice
2 apples, thinly sliced	Mayonnaise (optional)

Combine the ingredients. Serve on lettuce leaves. Garnish with mayonnaise, if desired.

SAUERKRAUT AND BEET SALAD

1 quart sauerkraut, drained	Lettuce
1 cup diced cooked beets	Mayonnaise or French dressing
1/4 cup minced onion	

Mix sauerkraut with beets and onion. Allow to stand for 1/2 hour. Serve on lettuce with mayonnaise or French dressing. Serves 6.

SAUERKRAUT AND CARROT SALAD

2 cups sauerkraut	1/4 teaspoon salt
2 cups grated raw carrot	1 cup mayonnaise or salad
1/4 cup chopped green pepper	dressing
1 cup chopped nut meats (peanuts, hickory nuts, etc.)	

Chop the kraut slightly. Mix all ingredients lightly and serve on lettuce. Serves 6 to 8.

SAUERKRAUT AND GREEN SALAD

Sauerkraut, drained, may be added to any green salad and tossed along with the other ingredients.

SAUERKRAUT AND FISH SALAD

1 cup flaked cooked fish (mullet mackerel, flounder, red snapper)
1 tablespoon chopped pickle or a few stuffed olives
1 cup drained sauerkraut
½ cup diced celery
2 tablespoons onion juice

Combine ingredients. Serve with mayonnaise or cooked dressing. Makes 3 or 4 servings.

SHRIMP SALAD

¼ cup mayonnaise
2 tablespoons chili sauce
1 tablespoon horse-radish relish
¼ teaspoon salt
1 pound shrimp (½ pound cooked, shelled and cleaned), coarsely chopped
1 cup chopped celery

Blend mayonnaise with next 3 ingredients; add shrimp. Chill for at least 1 hour. Just before serving, add celery. Serve on lettuce. Garnish with parsley. Makes 4 servings.

VEGETABLE-PICKLE SALAD

1 cup chopped dill pickles
½ cup chopped celery
1 No. 2 can kidney beans, drained
2 hard-boiled eggs, chopped
1 tablespoon grated onion
¾ teaspoon salt
¼ cup mayonnaise

In a large bowl, combine all ingredients; mix thoroughly. Chill. Makes 4 to 6 servings.

TONGUE SALAD

2 cups chopped cooked tongue
1 cup diced cooked carrots
½ cup chopped celery
¼ cup chopped green pepper
¼ cup French dressing
¼ cup minced dill pickle
¼ teaspoon salt
2 teaspoons prepared mustard
3 tablespoons mayonnaise

Combine first 6 ingredients. Chill at least 1 hour. Blend salt and mustard with mayonnaise. Toss with meat mixture. Serve on lettuce or romaine with radish roses. Makes 4 servings.

TUNA SALAD

1 can flaked tuna (7 ounces),
  drained
½ cup chopped celery
2 hard-boiled eggs, chopped

3 tablespoons hot dog relish
⅛ teaspoon salt
⅓ cup mayonnaise

Combine ingredients. Serve in lettuce cups. Makes 3 or 4 servings. 1 cup boned, drained, flaked salmon may be substituted for tuna.

HEARTY TUNA SALAD

2 cups cubed cold boiled
  potatoes
2 cans flaked tuna (7 ounces
  each), drained
¼ cup French dressing

¾ cup chopped sweet pickles
½ teaspoon salt
¾ cup chopped celery
¾ cup mayonnaise

Marinate potatoes and tuna separately, each with 2 tablespoons French dressing; let stand in refrigerator about 1 hour. Mix potatoes and tuna lightly with pickles and next 3 ingredients. Serve on lettuce. Sprinkle with paprika and fine-chopped parsley. Makes 4 to 6 servings.

TOMATOES STUFFED WITH COMBINATION SALAD

6 medium tomatoes
2 cups cubed cooked potatoes
⅔ cup chopped dill pickles
8 sardines, flaked
2 tablespoons chopped parsley
1 tablespoon prepared mustard

1 teaspoon salt
Freshly ground pepper
1 teaspoon onion salt
2 tablespoons mayonnaise
French dressing

Wash, core and scoop out tomatoes. Invert on a plate and chill. In a bowl, combine remaining ingredients, using enough French dressing to moisten salad. Chill. Fill tomatoes with salad mixture, garnish with pickle slices and serve on crisp salad greens. Makes 4 to 6 servings.

SALMON AND COTTAGE CHEESE SALAD

1 can drained, boned, flaked
  salmon (1 pound)
¾ cup chopped sweet pickles
½ cup chopped celery

1 teaspoon salt
1 to 1¼ cups cottage cheese
½ cup mayonnaise

Mix ingredients lightly. Chill. Serve in lettuce cups. Garnish with radish roses, pickles, sieved egg yellow or carrot sticks. Makes 6 servings.

SOME SALAD DRESSINGS

RUSSIAN DRESSING

1 cup mayonnaise
1 sour cucumber pickle, chopped
3 tablespoons chili sauce
3 tablespoons fine-chopped
    green pepper

2 tablespoons fine-chopped sweet
    red pepper or pimiento
½ teaspoon grated onion
2 drops Tabasco

Combine and mix well. Makes 2 cups.

TAJ MAHAL DRESSING

1 cup mayonnaise
½ cup whipped cream
6 tablespoons pineapple chutney

Combine. Serve on fruit salads. Makes almost 2 cups.

THOUSAND ISLAND DRESSING

1 cup mayonnaise
1 hard-boiled egg, chopped
1 chopped pimiento

2 tablespoons chopped sweet and
    sour pickles or chow-chow
⅓ cup chili sauce or catsup
⅓ cup whipped cream

Mix well. Serve on lettuce. Makes 2 cups.

A FEW FISH DISHES

PICKLE-TUNA CUPS

8 slices enriched bread
2 tablespoons butter
2 tablespoons minced onion
1 can cream of mushroom soup
    (10½ ounces)
¼ cup water

1 can tuna (7 ounces), drained
⅓ cup sweet pickle relish
2 tablespoons chopped pimientos
¼ teaspoon salt
Pepper
Dash of ground cloves

Trim off crusts of bread and press slices into molds of muffin tin to form cups; bake in hot oven (425°F) 5 to 10 minutes, or until golden brown.

In a saucepan melt butter over low heat; add onion and sauté for 2 minutes. Add soup and water; heat thoroughly. Stir in remaining ingredients. Remove from heat and serve in toast cups. Makes 4 servings.

PICKLE-HALIBUT CASSEROLE

1 pound halibut	½ teaspoon salt
2 cups soft bread crumbs	Freshly ground pepper
1 cup light cream	Dash of Tabasco
½ cup diced dill pickles	4 egg whites

Trim and bone halibut; chop into small pieces. In a bowl, combine fish, bread crumbs and cream; mix thoroughly. Add pickles, salt, pepper and Tabasco.

In a bowl, beat egg whites until stiff. Fold into fish-pickle mixture. Turn into greased 9 x 5-inch loak baking dish. Bake in moderate oven (350°F) 45 to 50 minutes, or until firm. Serve with mustard sauce. Serves 4.

MUSTARD SAUCE

2 tablespoons butter	½ teaspoon dry mustard
1 tablespoon flour	½ teaspoon salt
1 cup milk	1 tablespoon lemon juice
2 egg yellows	

In a saucepan melt butter over low heat. Add flour and blend. Add milk and slightly beaten egg yellows; simmer until thick, stirring constantly. Remove from heat and add mustard, salt and lemon juice. Makes 4 to 6 servings.

MEAT DISHES

PICKLE BEEF STEW PAYSANNE

1 can beef stew (1 pound, 8 ounces)	¼ cup dry red wine
	1 cup biscuit mix
½ cup diced sweet mixed pickles	⅓ cup milk

Combine beef stew, pickles and wine. Mix well and turn into greased 1-quart casserole.

Combine biscuit mix and milk. Mix lightly and turn out on lightly floured surface. Knead gently 10 times. Roll out to ½ inch thickness. Cut into 4 2½-inch rounds with floured biscuit cutter. Place on top of pickle stew. Bake in hot (425°F) oven 20 to 30 minutes, or until biscuits are browned. Serves 4.

BEEF PICKLE ROULADES

1½ pounds round steak
  (¼ inch thick)
Salt
2 tablespoons melted butter or
  margarine
1 cup soft bread crumbs
¼ cup chopped dill pickles
1 tablespoon fine-chopped onion

½ teaspoon salt
Dash of crushed red pepper
Dash of black pepper
All-purpose flour
Fat
1½ cups tomato juice
½ teaspoon salt

Cut steak into 4 pieces. Sprinkle with salt. Combine butter (or margarine), bread crumbs, pickles, onion, salt, pepper; mix well. Place stuffing on steak. Roll up and fasten with toothpicks. Dredge with flour. Brown in small amount of fat. Add tomato juice; sprinkle with salt, cover and cook over low heat until meat is tender, about 1 hour. Serves 4.

DILL PICKLEBURGERS

1 cup chopped dill pickles
1 pound lean ground beef
3 tablespoons onion or
  ½ teaspoon onion salt

1 teaspoon salt
Freshly ground pepper
8 round buns

In a bowl, combine pickles, beef, grated onion, salt and pepper; mix thoroughly.

With sharp knife, split buns crosswise. Toast uncut side of buns, in broiler, until golden brown. Remove from broiler. Spread untoasted side of buns with dill pickle–beef mixture. Broil on broiler rack 3 inches from heat, 5 to 8 minutes, or until meat is cooked and browned. Serve immediately. Makes 4 to 6 servings.

DILL-STUFFED PORK CHOPS

4 pork chops (¾ to 1 inch
  thick)
2 tablespoons butter
2 cups soft bread crumbs

3 tablespoons milk
½ cup dill pickles
Salt and pepper
½ cup warm water

Have butcher cut pocket in pork chops from side next to bone.

In a skillet, melt butter over low heat; add bread crumbs and brown. Remove from heat and add milk, pickles, salt and pepper; mix thoroughly.

Salt and pepper the chops; stuff pocket loosely with dressing. In the skillet, add a little fat; brown the chops on both sides. Remove from heat and add water to browned chops. Cover skillet; bake in moderate oven (350°F) 1 hour, or until chops are thoroughly cooked. Remove chops and make gravy with drippings. Makes 4 servings.

SPARERIBS AND SAUERKRAUT

3 pounds spareribs
Water to cover
2½ to 3 cups sauerkraut
1 tart apple

1 tablespoon sugar (optional)
1 teaspoon caraway seed
   (optional)

Cut spareribs into serving-sized portions and wipe with damp cloth. Place in kettle and barely cover with water and juice from kraut; simmer until very tender, about 1 hour. If preferred, bake at 350°F for 1 hour, Add sauerkraut, pushing it down into meat stock. Apple, sliced, may be put in with the kraut and, if desired, sugar may be added. Cook 10 to 30 minutes longer, depending on kraut flavor desired, or cook until most of the liquid has evaporated. A teaspoon of caraway seed may be sprinkled over the kraut just before serving.

    If desired, spareribs may be browned in a Dutch oven and then simmered or baked. Slices of pork shoulder, pork chops or leftover roast pork may be used in place of the spareribs. Makes 6 servings.

HAM-PINEAPPLE RINGS

2 eggs, slightly beaten
1 pound ground cooked ham
½ cup sweet pickle relish
Freshly ground pepper

2 cups mashed sweet potatoes
   (1½ pounds)
½ teaspoon salt
6 slices pineapple rings

    In a bowl, combine egg, ham, relish; season with pepper; form into 6 patties.

    In a bowl, combine sweet potatoes and salt; form into 6 patties. With a sharp knife, slice each pineapple ring in half horizontally.

    In bottom of greased 18 x 8-inch casserole, place 6 half-slices pineapple; top each with sweet-potato patty, then ham patty, next, remaining pineapple slices. Bake in moderate oven (350°F) 30 minutes. Garnish with dill-pickle strips. Makes 4 to 6 servings.

PIGS' KNUCKLES WITH SAUERKRAUT AND DUMPLINGS

5 pigs' knuckles
2½ pounds sauerkraut
1 egg
1½ tablespoons butter

½ cup water
1 cup flour
½ teaspoon salt
Dash nutmeg

Clean, scrape and wash the pigs' knuckles thoroughly. Combine with the sauerkraut and cover with cold water. Cook slowly until knuckles are tender.

Beat the egg well, melt the butter, and combine with water.

Sift the flour, salt and nutmeg together and combine with egg mixture. Beat thoroughly. If necessary, add more flour to make batter stiff enough to drop from spoon.

20 minutes before serving, drop the batter by spoonfuls into the hot sauerkraut. Cover pot tightly and serve as soon as dumplings are cooked.

SKILLET CHICKEN PICKLE CURRY

1 4-pound dressed stewing chicken
½ cup flour
2 teaspoons salt
¼ teaspoon pepper
½ cup fat or salad oil

⅔ cup onion
3½ cups boiling water
1½ tablespoons curry powder
¼ cup sweet pickles

Cut cleaned chicken into serving pieces, dredge with a mixture of flour, salt and pepper. (Toss them together in a paper bag.)

Heat fat or salad oil in a large heavy skillet; add onion and chicken; brown quickly on both sides. Add boiling water; cover and simmer 1½ hours, or until chicken is tender. Stir in curry powder and sweet pickles; cook, uncovered, until thickened. Serve with buttered egg noodles. Makes 4 to 6 servings.

PICKLE-BAKED CHICKEN

1 young chicken (3 to 3½ pounds, ready to cook)
⅓ cup enriched flour
⅓ cup fat
1 cup tomato juice
⅓ cup chopped sweet mixed pickles

2 teaspoons Worcestershire sauce
1½ teaspoons salt
¼ teaspoon dry mustard
1 bay leaf

Disjoint chicken or have butcher do it; roll pieces in flour and slowly brown on both sides in ½ inch of hot fat. Place chicken, skin side up, in shallow baking pan.

Combine remaining ingredients in skillet and heat just to boiling point. Mix thoroughly and pour over chicken. Bake uncovered in moderate (375°F) oven 45 minutes, or until tender. Spoon sauce over chicken before serving. Serves 4 to 6.

PICKLE BARBECUED CHICKEN

1 3-pound frying chicken
Flour
Salt and pepper
⅓ cup fat
1 6-ounce can tomato paste
1 cup chopped dill pickles
¼ cup chopped onion

2 tablespoons cider vinegar
2 tablespoons Worcestershire sauce
¾ teaspoon chili powder
1 teaspoon salt
Dash Tabasco
1⅓ cups water

Cut cleaned chicken in serving pieces; dredge in flour, salt and pepper. Brown in ½ inch hot fat.

In a bowl, combine remaining ingredients for barbecue sauce. Place browned chicken in casserole; pour barbecue sauce over chicken. Cover. Bake in moderate oven (350°F) 1 hour, or until chicken is tender. Serve piping hot. Makes 4 to 6 servings.

SOUTHERN TURKEY PICKLE CASSEROLE

2 eggs
3 cups cooked turkey
¼ cup pimientos
½ cup sweet fresh cucumber pickles
1 cup turkey broth

½ cup milk
1½ cups bread crumbs
1 tablespoon melted butter
1 teaspoon salt
Freshly ground pepper

In a bowl, beat eggs slightly. Chop turkey, pimientos and pickles. Add other ingredients; mix well. Pour into 1-quart baking dish. Bake in moderate oven (350°F) 45 to 50 minutes. Makes 4 servings.

Vinegar weighs more in winter because it expands in warm weather and the capacity of the container is lessened.

Of course, this only matters if you are buying your vinegar in bulk.

COMBINATION DISHES

HAM AND PICKLE FONDUE

5 slices bread
1 cup diced cooked ham
⅓ cup chopped sweet mixed
 pickles
¾ cup grated American cheese

3 eggs
1¾ cups milk
1 teaspoon salt
Dash paprika
1 tablespoon grated onion

Remove crusts from bread, cut bread into cubes, arrange ½ in greased 1½-quart casserole. Combine ham and pickles; place over bread cubes. Add cheese and top with remaining bread cubes.

Beat eggs; add milk, salt, paprika and onion; beat thoroughly. Pour over ingredients in casserole. Place in pan of hot water. Bake in moderate oven (350°F) 1 hour. Makes 4 servings.

PICKLE CHEESE GNOCCHI

1 cup corn meal
1 cup cold water
1 teaspoon salt
3 cups boiling water
½ cup sweet pickle relish
¼ cup butter or margarine
1 egg, well beaten

3 tablespoons butter or
 margarine
3 tablespoons all-purpose flour
2 cups milk
½ teaspoon prepared mustard
2 cups grated Cheddar cheese
 (about ½ pound)
¾ cup diced sweet gherkins

Combine corn meal and cold water; mix well. Add mixture and salt to boiling water, stirring constantly. Cook over medium heat, stirring occasionally, until thickened. Add pickle relish and ¼ cup butter or margarine. Cover and cook over low heat 10 minutes.

Add a small amount of corn meal mixture to egg; mix well and add to remaining hot mixture. Turn into greased 8-inch square pan. Chill until firm. Cut into squares and arrange in greased shallow baking dish.

Meanwhile, melt 3 tablespoons butter or margarine and blend in flour. Gradually add milk and cook over low heat, stirring constantly, until thickened. Add remaining ingredients and stir until cheese is melted. Pour over ingredients in baking dish. Bake in moderate oven (350°F) 45 minutes, or until browned. Serves 4 to 6.

PICKLE QUICHE LORRAINE

½ pound Swiss cheese
½ cup sweet gherkins
1 9-inch unbaked pastry shell
4 eggs, beaten
1 tablespoon all-purpose flour
½ teaspoon salt

Dash cayenne
1 tablespoon melted butter or margarine
2 cups light cream
Radish and sweet gherkin slices

Slice cheese thin, chop gherkins. Arrange in pastry shell.

Combine eggs, flour, salt, cayenne, butter (or margarine) and cream; beat well. Pour over cheese and pickles. Bake in moderate (375°F) oven 40 to 50 minutes or until knife inserted in center comes out clean. Garnish with radish and gherkin slices. Makes 6 servings.

3-IN-1 CASSEROLE

1 pound bulk sausage
1 quart sauerkraut
2 cups mashed potatoes

1 tablespoon butter
Paprika

Shape sausage into cakes and cook until light brown. Place in bottom of casserole and cover with a thick layer of sauerkraut. Top with fluffy mashed potatoes, dot with butter and sprinkle with paprika. Bake 30 minutes in a moderate oven. Serves 6.

KRAUT CHEESETTE

1 quart sauerkraut
½ cup grated onion
1 pound frankfurters
½ cup grated sharp cheese

Mashed potatoes (optional)
Melted butter (optional)
Paprika (optional)

Mix together sauerkraut and onion. Place ½ of mixture in a greased casserole. Cut frankfurters in slices and arrange ½ on top of the kraut. Sprinkle with grated cheese and repeat layers.

If desired, top the casserole with mashed potatoes, brush with melted butter and sprinkle with paprika.

Bake in moderate (350°F) oven 30 minutes. Serves 6.

EARL WILSON'S PEARLS:

They've discovered cucumber juice is good for the skin, noted Taffy Tuttle at the Sea-Fare—which means we'll be seeing a lot of pickle-pusses.

SAUERKRAUT SAUSAGE PIE

1 quart sauerkraut	12 small pork sausages
2 tablespoons flour	Baking powder biscuit dough

Place ½ of kraut in bottom of baking dish; sprinkle with 1 tablespoon flour. Add remainder of kraut. Sprinkle with remaining flour.

Brown sausages and place on top of kraut; reserve drippings.

Add 1 cup hot water or kraut juice.

Cover with crust made of baking powder biscuit dough. Bake ½ hour at 425°F. Serve with brown gravy made with sausage drippings.

SAUERKRAUT ESCALLOPED WITH CHEESE

2 tablespoons **butter**	⅛ teaspoon paprika
2 tablespoons **flour**	2 cups sauerkraut
2 cups milk	1 cup grated cheese
½ teaspoon salt	½ cup buttered crumbs

Make a white sauce by melting butter, adding flour and then milk. Allow to boil and then add seasoning.

Spread a layer of ½ of the sauerkraut on the bottom of a buttered baking dish. Cover it with ½ the white sauce; then add a layer of ½ the grated cheese. Make a second layer of sauerkraut, sauce and cheese. Cover the top with a layer of buttered crumbs and place in the oven. Bake until the sauce bubbles through the crumbs. Serve hot in the baking dish. Serves 6.

Danny Kaye's daughter, Deena, would rather eat pickles than dessert. Here is a specialty that is dedicated to her.

DEENA'S PICKLE RABBIT

Cut sour pickles lengthwise in pieces ¼ inch thick. Place on same-sized strips of rye bread. Top with a slice of Cheddar or Muenster cheese. Place under broiler and heat until cheese melts.

Strips may be cut into bite size and served as canapés.

PICKLE TOMATO RABBIT

2 tablespoons **butter or** margarine	2 teaspoons prepared mustard
1 tablespoon all-purpose flour	⅓ cup chopped sweet gherkins
1 cup milk	Salt and pepper to taste
2 cups grated Cheddar **cheese** (about ½ pound)	Tomato wedges
	Toast points

Melt butter (or margarine) and blend in flour. Gradually add milk and cook over low heat, stirring constantly, until thickened. Add cheese, mustard and gherkins. Cook, stirring constantly, until cheese is melted. Season with salt and pepper. Serve over tomato wedges and toast points. Serves 4.

VEGETABLES

MARINADE OF DILL

The spicy brine from dill pickles may be used as a marinade for relish vegetables such as sliced cucumbers, onions, or beets. 2 hours of marinating will impart a good dill flavor.

HOW TO SERVE SAUERKRAUT

Serve kraut cold or hot. It is one of the least expensive sources of vitamin C available. 1 cup of kraut funishes about ½ the daily requirement of vitamin C. Kraut is an excellent emergency food for quick meals. When served cold it may be an appetizer, either plain or with a dash of celery seed, caraway seed or pineapple chunks. Sauerkraut juice mixed half and half or less with tomato juice is also a good appetizer for a meal.

Full-flavored sauerkraut, served hot, offers a spicy contrast to meat, fish and fowl. Combinations such as frankfurters and sauerkraut are pleasing. The amount of sharp flavor when the kraut is served hot depends on how long it has been cooked. To preserve the tang and crispness, just heat it through. For milder blended flavor, cook kraut longer.

SAUERKRAUT WITH APPLES

3 or 4 tart cooking apples 3 tablespoons butter
1 quart sauerkraut   3 to 4 tablespoons sugar
Water to cover

Peel apples, core and cut in eighths. Alternate layers of kraut and apples in a saucepan. Add water to barely cover, heat to boil; then reduce heat, cover and simmer until apples are very tender (20 to 25 minutes). Most of the liquid should be evaporated. Add butter and sugar, stir to blend and cook rapidly until all liquid has evaporated. Stir frequently to prevent burning. Turn into a hot serving dish and serve immediately. Serves 6.

If apples have tender red skins, leave skins on for color. Chopped parsley may also be sprinkled on for color.

SAUERKRAUT AND TOMATOES

¼ cup chopped onion	2 cups tomatoes
2 tablespoons bacon fat	¼ cup honey or brown sugar
2 tablespoons flour	1 quart sauerkraut

Brown the onions in the bacon fat. Add the flour and mix until smooth. Press the tomatoes through a food press or sieve to remove the seeds. Add to the onion-flour mixture. Add honey or brown sugar. Simmer 15 minutes. Add the sauerkraut and simmer 15 to 30 minutes.

SAUERKRAUT WITH GRAPES

1 pound sauerkraut	⅓ cup boiling water
¼ cup diced onions	1 cup seedless grapes
1⅓ tablespoons butter	

Wash sauerkraut in cold water; drain. Sauté onions in butter 2 to 3 minutes; add sauerkraut and boiling water. Cover and simmer for 12 minutes. Add grapes and cook 1 minute longer. Serves 4.

This is a dish which goes well with duck or game.

EGGS

PUFFY OMELET

4 eggs, separated	4 tablespoons water
½ teaspoon salt	1 tablespoon butter
Freshly ground pepper	

Beat egg whites until stiff but not dry; then beat egg yellows until thick and lemon-colored; add salt, pepper and water. Gently fold in whites.

Heat butter in skillet; add egg mixture. Cook slowly for 3 minutes, or until omelet puffs up and is firm on the bottom. Place skillet in moderate oven (350°F) for 10 minutes, or until top of omelet is dry and does not retain an impression when pressed lightly. Make a deep crease across the center without cutting all the way through. Pour half of Spanish pickle sauce on omelet; fold omelet in half without breaking. Serve with remaining sauce. Makes 4 servings.

SPANISH PICKLE SAUCE

2 tablespoons butter
⅔ cup chopped onion
2 tablespoons chopped green
  pepper
¼ cup chopped sweet mixed
  pickles

1 No. 2 can tomatoes
6 cloves
1 tablespoon sugar
1½ teaspoons salt
Freshly ground pepper

Melt butter in heavy pan; add onions and pepper; sauté 5 minutes until soft. Add chopped sweet pickles and remaining ingredients and simmer over low heat for 30 minutes, or until sauce thickens slightly.

PICKLE-STUFFED EGGS ON SPINACH

4 hard-boiled eggs
¼ cup sweet pickle relish
2 tablespoons minced onion
⅛ teaspoon celery seed

2 tablespoons mayonnaise
3 cups cooked salted spinach
2 tablespoons butter

Cut eggs in half lengthwise and remove yellows. In a bowl, mash yellows and combine with relish, onion, celery seed and mayonnaise. Refill whites with yellow mixture. Place spinach in individual casseroles or a shallow baking dish; dot with butter. Arrange stuffed eggs on top of spinach. Bake in a hot oven (400°F) 8 to 10 minutes. Serve immediately. Makes 4 servings.

SANDWICHES

PETER PIPER SANDWICHES

4 slices bread
Butter
4 sweet gherkins

4 slices American cheese
2 strips bacon

Toast bread on 1 side. For each sandwich, spread untoasted side with butter. Slice 1 pickle lengthwise and place on buttered side. Lay slice of cheese over pickle slices. Cut ½ bacon strip into small pieces and place on top of cheese. Broil slowly on broiler rack, 3 to 4 inches from heat, until bacon is slightly browned and crisp. Serve immediately. Makes 4 open-faced sandwiches.

PICKLE SANDWICH LOAF

1 5-ounce can deviled ham
2 tablespoons piccalilli
¼ cup minced pimientos
3 tablespoons mayonnaise
3 hard-boiled eggs, chopped
¼ teaspoon salt
1 teaspoon fine-cut chives
1 3-ounce package cream cheese, softened

½ cup sweet pickle relish
1 loaf unsliced day-old white bread
1 8-ounce package cream cheese, softened
2 tablespoons milk
½ cup grated cucumber

In 3 small bowls, combine the different fillings.
1. Deviled ham, piccalilli, pimientos and 1 tablespoon mayonnaise.
2. Eggs, salt, chives and remaining 2 tablespoons mayonnaise.
3. 3-ounce package cream cheese and sweet pickle relish.

Remove crusts, cut loaf of bread lengthwise into 4 equal slices. Spread 3 slices with 3 fillings and place them on top of each other in order given. Cover with unspread slice to form a loaf. Wrap tightly in waxed paper, then in damp cloth. Chill. When ready to use, frost top and sides with 8-ounce package cream cheese mixed with milk and cucumber. Garnish with pickle fans. Makes 8 to 10 servings.

BROILED CHICKEN PICKLE SANDWICHES

1 8-ounce package cream cheese
½ cup chopped sweet gherkins
½ teaspoon Worcestershire sauce

1 cup chopped, cooked boned chicken
6 to 8 slices bread

In a bowl, soften cream cheese. Add pickles, Worcestershire sauce and chicken; blend well. Toast bread slices on 1 side. Spread cheese-chicken mixture on untoasted side; be sure to cover edges of bread. Place open-faced sandwiches on broiler rack. Toast in broiler, approximately 3 inches from heat. Remove from broiler. Garnish sandwiches with pickle slices. Serve immediately. Makes 6 to 8 sandwiches.

EGG AND PICKLE SALAD SANDWICHES

3 eggs
¼ cup sweet pickle relish
3 tablespoons mayonnaise

Salt
Bread
Butter

Place eggs in a small pan with enough cold water to cover them. Bring slowly to a boil. Remove from heat; cover and let stand 20 minutes. Cool quickly; remove shell and chop coarsely. In a bowl, combine chopped egg, sweet pickle relish and mayonnaise. Add salt to taste and mix well.

Spread bread with softened butter. Divide filling among half of the slices of bread; spread to corners; top with remaining slices of bread. Cut diagonally in quarters. Serve with dill-pickle sticks or mixed sweet pickles. Makes 4 to 6 sandwiches.

CHUTNEY SANDWICH

Toast lightly 2 slices of white bread. On 1 slice spread a layer of chutney or a fruit chili relish. Cover this with a slice of ham or sliced cooked shrimps. Over the meat place a thin slice of yellow cheese. If you prefer, place the slice of cheese on top of the chutney and then the slice of meat. Butter second slice of bread on both sides. Place on top of the slice of cheese. Sprinkle grated cheese and paprika on top of second buttered slice. Heat in slow broiler until cheese is melted and sandwich is hot inside. Serve immediately.

PICKLE SPREAD

1 cup grated American cheese	2 tablespoons mayonnaise
½ cup chopped fresh cucumber pickle	4 teaspoons tomato catsup

Mash cheese with fork; blend in drained, chopped pickle; add mayonnaise and mix, along with catsup. Serve on rye bread or crackers. Makes 1½ cups.

BAKED GOODS

PICKLE-RELISH BISCUITS

For every 2 cups of flour in your favorite baking powder biscuit recipe, add ½ cup of pickle relish or chopped chutney to the dry ingredients, mixing well, then proceed as usual.

Can also be made with ready-mixed baking powder biscuits.

PICKLE-BEEF YORKSHIRE PUDDING

¾ pound ground beef round
½ cup drained sweet pickle
relish
1 tablespoon grated onion
2 tablespoons fine-chopped celery
1 small clove garlic, fine-chopped
1 teaspoon salt
⅛ teaspoon pepper
1 cup sifted all-purpose flour
¼ teaspoon salt
1 cup milk
2 eggs
Dash nutmeg
Dash mace
Dash cayenne

Combine beef, relish, onion, celery, garlic, 1 teaspoon salt and pepper; mix thoroughly.

Sift flour and ¼ teaspoon salt together. Add milk and blend. Add eggs, 1 at a time, beating after each addition, Add nutmeg, mace and cayenne; mix well.

Pour ½ of batter in hot greased 8-inch pie pan. Spoon pickle mixture over batter; top with remaining batter. Bake in hot (400°F) oven about 30 minutes, or until firm. Makes 4 servings.

DESSERTS

While no one has yet figured out an acceptable dessert utilizing pickles, here are two old American recipes using vinegar, one for candy and the other for pie. They will have to do until some reader writes in with a recipe for a dessert embodying pickles or relishes and it can be included in my next edition.

According to the American Heritage Cookbook, *Rebecca Sophia Clarke (Sophie May) of Norridgewock, Maine, wrote more than 40 books for children, including the 6-volume series, published from 1867 to 1869, called the* Dotty Dimple Stories. *Miss Clarke's books were distinguished by their lack of plot, overweening presence of moralizing, cute naughtiness and baby talk. They were distinguished, too, by talk of this candy, which became as popular with children as did the books and was, unlike the stories, enduringly cherished by children.*

DOTTY DIMPLE'S VINEGAR CANDY

Combine 3 cups sugar with 1½ cups vinegar and cook over a low heat, stirring constantly, until sugar is disolved. Continue cooking until sirup reaches the soft-crack stage (270° to 290°F or until a few drops tested in cold water separate into threads which are hard but not brittle). Pour onto a large buttered platter and let cool until candy can be handled comfortably. Butter your hands and pull the taffy until it is white and almost firm. Stretch into a rope about 1 inch in diameter and snip off pieces with scissors.

VINEGAR PIE

Pastry for 1-crust pie	2 egg whites
¼ cup flour	1 cup sugar
½ teaspoon nutmeg	1 cup commercial sour cream
½ teaspoon cinnamon	3 tablespoons melted butter
½ teaspoon allspice	3 tablespoons cider vinegar
½ teaspoon cloves	1 cup coarsely chopped walnuts
Dash of salt	or pecans
4 egg yellows	1 cup raisins

Prepare pastry and line a 9-inch pie pan. Chill while making filling. Sift together flour, spices and salt. Set aside.

Beat egg yellows thoroughly. Wash and dry the beater, then beat the 2 whites until they stand in peaks. Gently fold sugar into egg whites and stir into yellows. Add flour mixture alternately with the sour cream.

Combine butter, vinegar, nuts and raisins and stir into the filling. Pour into pie shell and bake in a preheated 450°F oven for 10 minutes. Reduce heat to 400° and bake 5 minutes. Then turn heat to 350°, and continue baking for about 15 minutes or until filling is set. Cool. May be served with whipped cream.

Showing Your Pickles

Very few people realize how many contests there are that award blue ribbons and prizes for excellence in pickle and relish making. From the local church food festival to the great state fairs, the country is dotted with competitions that pit pickler against pickler. A majority of these pickle festivals are in the fall, after harvest time.

Anyone with pride in her (or his) workmanship in the kitchen can enter. Here is a good way to learn what the world outside of your family and neighbors thinks of your preserving skills.

A good way to go about it is to think of this as a branch of show business, for you must present your productions in the most showmanly manner. In some instances pickles are judged by appearance in the jars only, so uniformity of contents, color, clarity and arrangement are the only factors taken into consideration. So not only does it involve talent and competence to put up prize-winning entries, but the manner in which you display your work counts in impressing the judges.

In England, where there are national competitions which attract contestants from all over the British Isles, sizable money prizes are awarded the principal winners. But in the United States competition is mainly for the honor and recognition it brings, although long-time winners, such as Laura Hamilton Holman of Illinois and Clara Levinson (no relation) of New Jersey, have won impressive sums over the years in county and state competitions.

If you raise the produce you preserve yourself, you have a double pride when you win. And you have better control over the ingredients, too.

Entering your pickles and relishes in competition is very good experience, for whether you win or not, you can see what others have been doing. Exchanging ideas with other contestants is one of the most valuable aspects of these competitions.

Of course, it is important to read the entry requirements of any competition you plan to enter. And to follow these rules. And there are surprises, occasionally, when prizes are awarded for products not listed in the catalogues.

Follow labeling instructions carefully, as outlined in the prospectus or rules issued. Usually in competitions all identifications outside of the classification are removed before judging. Each entry is given an identifying number designating the owner; this number is covered up and revealed only after the judges have made their decisions. This is done to eliminate any possible favoritism on the part of the judges. In state and country fairs, judging is done by committees appointed by the state or county and is strictly impersonal.

Cleanliness is so important that a contestant will be wise to bring along not only materials for a final polish, but also extra supplies so that she won't lose points or place because of a last-minute accident.

Be sure that you get your jars into the right class, with the right information on them. Give yourself plenty of time to get your entries set up. Read the rules. Follow instructions carefully to avoid disqualification. Be sure you know what the show requires—and follow those requirements as best you can.

Usually 2 identical jars of the product are required in entering pickles and relishes. The size of the jars will be indicated in the instructions issued in advance, which are obtainable upon request of the agency conducting the competition. These instructions will also list the prizes.

The procedure at the judging is to open 1 jar for the purpose of judging and to retain the other jar unopened for display. Most competitions do not pay large sums for individual awards because the entries are many and would require huge expenditures. The reward is the prestige and satisfaction of recognition in winning.

In recent years the difficulty in obtaining fresh produce has proved to be a deterrent to many city dwellers entering these competitions. Good quality can not be obtained with produce that is not vine-ripened and fresh. The time lag from field to city market materially affects the excellence of the produce, especially if it has been picked green, or has spent too much time in reaching the consumer. This calls for enterprise on the part of the city dweller who pickles for competition.

For chutneys: clarity is important; be sure the product is homogeneous and does not separate; use whole rather than ground spices when feasible and make sure vegetables and fruits are sufficiently well cooked, *but not mushy.*

Pickles: should have vinegar free of sediment and impurities. Strain or run through filter paper before using. Also, vinegar should cover contents by at least ½ inch.

Do not bring newly made entries to the shows. Flavor and color are both important and entries can have good flavor only when the product has stood in the jars long enough to absorb flavor from its various components.

If produce is used that can only be obtained late in the season, your time may be limited, but you should not enter anything in competition right off the fire, as the over-all quality will not be good. It takes time to clear up and age, so try not to enter anything that has not been able to stand for at least a week, or, if possible, longer.

Don't involve yourself with any entry you do not consider your very best.

TYPICAL COUNTY FAIR SCORE CARD

FOR FRUIT PICKLES

Appearance—firm texture of fruit, uniformity of size and shape,
    attractive color, color of liquid, plump fruit 50
Flavor—spicy, sweet-sour 40
Package—uniform size, clean, neatly labeled 10

FOR VEGETABLE PICKLES

Appearance—firm and crisp texture, uniform size and shape, attractive
    color, color of liquid 50
Flavor—tart, pungent 40
Package—uniform size, clean, neatly labeled 10

FOR RELISHES

Appearance—characteristic of ingredients, bright attractive color,
    firm texture, finely chopped 50
Flavor—highly seasoned, sweet or hot 40
Package—uniform size, clean, neatly labeled 10

Index

Alabama corn chow-chow, 124–25
All-day apple chutney, 221
Allspice, 30, 47
Almond chicken salad, 293
Almonds, blanching, 173
Amber relish, 140
Amherst green-tomato mincemeat, 242
Anchovy catsup, 271
Anchovy sauce, 213
Anise, 47
    sweet, 49
Antipasto, 276
Appetizers, 288–89
Apple catsups, 208
Apple chili sauce, 215
Apple chutneys, 220–21, 234
Apple mélange, 160
Apple and pork salad, 301
Apple relish, 147
Apple and sauerkraut salad, 303
Apples, 159–60, 164–65
    measuring, 37
    pickled crab apples, 164
    pickled lady apples, 160
    pickled little, 159
    pickled Scotch, 285
    sauerkraut with, 315
    spiced crab apples, 165
    spiced sliced, 159
    verjuice of, 214
    for vinegar, 55, 57
Apricots, measuring, 38
Arab countries, 268–69
Arkansas piccalilli, 130
Arkansas Tabasco sauce, 217
Aromatic cucumbers, 248–49
Artichoke pickles, Jerusalem, 181
Artichoke relish, Jerusalem, 130–31
Asparagus salad, 290
Aspic, pickle, 291
Aunt Annetta's pickled tongue, 202
Aunt Annie's dill pickles, 98
Aunt Betsy's sweet pickles, 100
Aunt Ella's dill pickles, 99

Aunt Jennie's barbecue sauce, 213
Aunt Katie's relish, 150
Aunt Mary's dill pickles, 98–99
Aunt Rachel's dill pickles, 99
Aunt Sally's pickle aspic, 291
Aunt Sally's radish relish, 138
Australia, 269

Baked goods, 319–20
Balm, 47
Banana chutneys, 221–22, 248
Banana relish, 147
Bananas, measuring, 37
Bananas, pickled, 161
Barbecue marinades, 65–67
Barbecue sauces, 65, 213, 257–58
Barbecued chicken, 311
Barrels, 14, 171
    pickling in, 33, 252
Basic spiced vinegar, 95
Basil, 47
Basil vinegar, 61
Bay leaf, 47
Beans, 76, 77, 182–83. See also Lima beans
    brining, 82–83
        salt-brined, 87
        vinegar-brined, 182
    dill, 102, 182–83, 276
    and dill soup, black, 290
    dry-salting, 79–80
    measuring, 37
    mustard, 120
    salads, 290, 291
    sour, 182
    washing of, 102
Beef, corned, 201
Beef dill pickleburgers, 308
Beef marinades, 64–65
Beef pickle roulades, 308
Beef salad, roast, 292
Beef stew, pickle, 307
Beef Yorkshire pudding, 320
Beefsteak sauce, 271
Beet and cabbage chutney, 222

Beet relishes, 132
Beet salads, 292, 303
Beets and beet tops, 82–83, 183–84
  English-style (beetroot), 271
  faded color in, 32
  honey pickled, 184–85
  measuring, 37
  sweet pickled, 184
Benne, 52
Berries. *See also* Strawberries; etc.
  measuring, 37
  spiced, 169
  for vinegar, 57
Biscuits, pickle-relish, 319
Black bean and dill soup, 290
Blackberries, pickled, 161
Blackberry catsup, 209
Blanching, defined, 28
Blender banana chutney, 248
Blueberries, spiced, 162, 169
Blueberry chutney, 222
Boiling, defined, 28
Borage, 48
Bordeaux sauces, 140
Bottled sauces, 213–18
Bottles. *See* Jars
Bouquet garni, 48
Brandied peaches, 171
Brandy, cherry, 162
Brass, 27
Bread and butter pickles, 22, 109–12
  Billy Mills', 109
Brine, Mrs. Beeton's, 63
"Brine stock," 16, 19
Brining, 82–85, 86. *See also* specific vegetables
Broccoli, measuring, 37
Brussels sprouts, measuring, 37
Burnet, 48
Butters, fruit, 244–45

Cabbage, 185–87, 247. *See also* Sauerkraut
  and beet chutney, 222
  low-calorie, 266
  measuring, 37
  mustard, 122
  relishes,
    with beets, 132
    with peppers, 253, 255
  with radish (Korean), described, 279
  with tomato, 140
  slaws, 292, 299
  stuffed peppers, 192–93
California olive process, 90–91
Canada, 269
Canapés, nutty chutney, 289
Candied chips, 22
Candy, vinegar, 320–21
Cantaloupe. *See also* Melon
  measuring, 37
  pickled, 247
Capers, 48

Caponatina alla Siciliana, 282
Caraway, 48
Cardamom, 48
Carnacina relish, 141
Carol G's salad, 292–93
Carrot relish, 133
Carrot and sauerkraut salad, 303
Carrots, 82–83, 184
  cocktail, 247
  measuring, 37
  sweet pickled, 187
Cassia, 48
Catsup-based barbecue sauce, 257
Catsups, 48, 205–12
  anchovy, 271
  garden, 207
  jiffy, 266
  low-calorie, 266
  tomato, 205–7, 208
    seasonings for, 53
  vegetable and fruit, 208–12, 249, 266
Cauliflower, 82–84, 187–88, 269
  cocktail, 248
  dill, 102
  measuring, 37
  Syrian, 286
Cayenne, 51
Celery, 30, 48
  cocktail, 248
  measuring, 37
  relishes, 134, 138, 254
    pepper-, 254
    tomato-, 138
  salad, 293
  salted, 81–82
  vinegar, 62
Cheese and bean salad, 290
Cheese cucumber rings, 293
Cheese onion balls, 288
Cheese pickle balls, 288
Cheese pickle gnocchi, 312
Cheese rabbits, 314–15
Cheese and salmon salad, 305
Cheese sandwiches, Peter Piper, 317
Cheese with sauerkraut, 314
Cheese soup, pickles in, 287
Cheesette, kraut, 313
Cherries, 162–64
  cold pickled, 163
  Kimmel, 162
  measuring, 38
  olive, 163
  quick pickled, 163
  salted, 164
Cherry brandy, 162
Cherry poinsettias, 288
Chicken, 310–11
  curries, 275, 310
  pickle-baked, 310–11
  pickle barbecued, 311
  pickle sandwiches, 318
  salads, 293–94

Chili pepper, 51
Chili powder, 48
Chili sauces, 213–14
  apple, 215
  Heinz's, 214
  kitchenette, 213
  low-calorie, 265
  Mrs. Nellis', 215
  Texas, 216
  uncooked, 258
Chili vinegars, 61
Chinese gooseberry (kiwi) chutney, 284
Chinese kraut, 279
Chinese pickled cucumbers, 270
Chiquita Banana relish, 147
Chiquita chutney, 222
Chives, 48
Chock-full-of-nuts peaches, 173
Chow-chow, 22, 122–27
  Alabama corn, 124–25
  college-bred, 125
  curried, 126
  green tomato, 123
  Pennsylvania, 124
  Pottsfield, 125
  raw-raw, 125
  relish, 127
  sour, 123
  sweet mixed-pickle, 124
Chunk pickles, 70
Chut-nut, 228
Chutney sauce, 258
Chutney sandwich, 319
Chutneys, 48, 219–36, 248. *See also* specific
    fruits
  combinations for, 236
  detecting ingredients in, 229–30
  dried fruit, 223
  English, 271
  hints on, 219–20
  just plain, 219
  nutty, 229
    canapés of, 289
  putney, 233
  quick, 248
  South Sea, 234
  summer sun, 234
Cinnamon, 48–49
Clams, Japanese vinegared, 278–79
Cleopatra's cucumber chips, 112–13
Cloudiness in jarred pickles, 36
Clove-starred peaches, 172–73
Clove-starred prunes, 178
Cloves, 47, 49
Cocktail sauce, 258
Cocktail vegetables, 247–48
Coconut, measuring, 38
College-bred chow-chow, 126
Colonial America, 15, 283
Color, 25, 32. *See also* specific fruits and
    vegetables
Combination dishes, 312–15

Combination relishes, 140–47
Combination salad, in tomatoes, 305
Commercial pickle-packing, 15–22
Commercial tomato catsup, 208
Company mustard pickles, 120
Confetti salad, 295
Continental salad, 294
"Cool as a pickle" salad, 295
Copper, 25, 27, 28, 33, 35, 57
Copper sulfate, 25
Coriander, 49
Corn, 78, 81–82
  chow-chow, 124–25
  measuring, 38
  relishes, 133–34
    Billy Mills', 108–9
    hurry-up, 254
  salad, 295
Corned beef, 201
Cousin Celia's mincemeat, 240
Crab apples. *See* Apples
Crab Louis, 296
Crab meat, Hawaiian, 296
Cranberries, 254
  measuring, 38
  spiced, 166, 169
Cranberry catsups, 209
Cranberry chutneys, 222–23
Cranberry relish-sauce, 254–55
Crappies, pickled, 204
Cress, 49. *See also* Water cress
  Indian, 50
Crisp little cucumbers, 94
Crisp lunch pickles, 112
Crocked brandied peaches, 171
Crocks, 33
Cucumber catsup, 209, 249
Cucumber cheese rings, 293
Cucumber delight, 249
Cucumber relish, 131–32
Cucumbers, 41–42, 103–15, 156, 195. *See
    also* Pickles
  aromatic, 248–49
  Chinese, 270
  Cleopatra's pickles, 112–13
  commercial packing of, 16–22
  crisp lunch pickles, 112
  curing of, 68–70
  curry chunks, 115
  dictionary of, 21–22
  dill. *See* Dill pickles
  Down Under, 269
  8-day chunks, 113
  84-hour chunks, 114
  fluted, 288
  golden glow pickles, 104
  Grandmother's pickles, 114
  ice water pickles, 105
  icicle pickles, 105
  harvesting, 19, 42, 173
  low-calorie pickles, 262–63
  measuring, 38

mustard pickles. *See* Mustard pickles
oil pickles, 105
olivettes, 106
and onions, 113, 117, 120–21
overnight pickles, 113
Peter Piper pickles, 114–15
quick process pickles, 93–95
ripe pickled, 103–4
sizes of, 20
sun glow pickles, 103
sweet pickles, 69–70. *See also* Sweet
    pickles
uses for, 246
Cumin, 49
Curing, 68–92
    containers for, 33, 68ff.
Currant pickle sauce, 261
Currants, measuring, 38
Currants, spiced, 166, 169
Curried chow-chow, 126
Curried mustard pickle, 121
Curries, chicken, 275, 310
Curry pickle chunks, 115
Curry powder, 49
Curry relish, 141
Cutting, 28

Dad's vischnik, 162
Danish pickle, 270
Dates, measuring, 38
Dates, pickled, 167–68
Deena's pickle rabbit, 314
Delicatessen salad, 296
Deluxe cucumber pickles, 93
Denmark, 270
Desserts, 320–21
Deviled egg salad, 297
Dictionary, pickle, 21–22
Dieting, 18, 262–67
Different dill tomatoes, 101
Dill, 49
Dill marinade, 315
Dill and mustard sauce, 258–59
Dill pickle(s), 19, 20, 46, 96–102
    Aunt Annie's, 98
    Aunt Ella's, 98–99
    Aunt Mary's, 99
    Aunt Rachel's, 99
    and black bean soup, 290
    burgers, 308
    cauliflower, 102
    defined, 21, 22
    Dutch, 273
    frappe, 296
    fresh-pack, 96
    green beans, 102, 182–83, 276
    kosher, 98, 99
    liverwurst balls, 288
    long method, 97
    low-calorie, 262
    okra, 189
    Polish-style, 22

quick, 96
refrigerator, 252
sauce of, 261
17th-century, 97
short method, 98
stuffed, 287
-stuffed pork chops, 308–9
sweet, 22, 100
tomatoes, 99–101, 102
zucchini slices, 198
Dinty Moore's cabbage relish, 255
Dixie relish, 142
Dotty Dimple's vinegar candy, 320–21
Double-sweet watermelon rind, 153
Down East ripe cucumber pickle, 104
Down Under cucumber, 269
Dozen vegetable relish, 138–39
Dried fruit chutney, 223
Dry salting, 79–82, 85, 86
Dumplings with pigs' knuckles, 310
Dutch dill pickles, 273
Dutch sauerkraut, 274

Egg and ham salad, 299
Egg mousse, pickle, 297
Egg and pickle salad sandwiches, 318–19
Egg salads, 297, 299, 318–19
Eggplant Caponatina, 282
Eggplant pickle, 188
Eggs, 316–17
    pickle-stuffed, on spinach, 317
    pickled, 200–1, 249–50
    puffy omelet, 316
    à la Russe, 297
8-day pickle chunks, 113
84-hour cucumber chunks, 114
11-day sweet pickle chunks, 157
Elderberries, spiced, 168, 169
Elderberry relish, 148
Emerald garden salad, 298
English recipes, 271
Equipment, 33–35
Eschalot. *See* Shallot
Extra-sweet pickles, 27
Eyes, tired, 20

Failures, 31–32
Farmer-style relish, 142
Fennel, 49
Fenugreek, 49
Figkles, 167
Figs, measuring, 38
Figs, pickled, 167
Finocchio, 49
Fish barbecue marinades, 67
Fish cocktail sauce, 358
Fish dishes, 306–7
Fish pickles, 203–4
    Hawaiian, 273
Fish salads, 298, 304
Fish sauces, 259
Fondue, ham and pickle, 312

4-day sweet gherkins, 155
14-day sweet pickles, 157
France, 272
Frankfurter relish. *See also* Hot dog relishes
low-calorie, 265
Frankfurter salads, 298–99
Frankfurter sauce, 259
French pickle, 143
French pickle sauce, 261
Fresh packing, 20, 22. *See also* Fresh pickling; Quick pickles
dill pickle recipe, 96
Fresh pickling, 246–61
Fruit butters, 244–45
Fruit catsups, 208–12
Fruit pickles and spiced fruits, 159–80. *See also* specific fruits
choosing for, 40
shriveling of, 32
spices for, 53
Fruit relishes, 147–50

Galvanized utensils, 33, 57
Game, marinades for, 66–67, 269
Garden catsup, 207
Garden salad, 256
emerald, 298
Garden special, 143
Garlic, 30, 49
Garlic vinegar, 62
Garnishes, 287
Gefilte pickles, 289
Genuine dill pickles, 19, 21
Geranium, 49
German macaroni salad, 301
German Senfgurken, 272–73
Gherkins, 49, 156
Ginger, 49–50, 230
Ginger pears, 175
Ginger tomatoes, 198
Gnocchi, pickle-cheese, 312
Golden glow mix, 104
Golden slaw, 299
Gooseberries, measuring, 38
Gooseberry catsups, 210
Gooseberry chutneys, 223–24
Chinese (kiwi), 284
Grandmother's pickles, 114
Grape-apple catsup, 208
Grape butter, 244
Grape leaf, using, 28
Grapefruit, measuring, 38
Grapes, measuring, 38
Grapes, pickled, Indian style, 274
Grapes, sauerkraut with, 316
Grapes, spiced, 168–69
Grapes, for vinegar, 57
Greek-process olives, 92
Greek-style black olives, 281
Green beans. *See* Beans
"Green stock," 16–17, 20

Greens. *See also* Beets and beet tops; etc.
brining, 82–83
cutting, 28
pickled (Chinese kraut), 279
Guava catsup, 210
Guava chutneys, 224
Guava relish, 149
Guava sweet pickle, 169

Hackney pepper hash, 255
Halibut casserole, pickle, 307
Ham and egg salad, 299
Ham and pickle fondue, 312
Ham-pineapple rings, 309
Hawaii, 273
Headspace, defined, 29
Health, pickles and, 15, 18, 264
Hearty beet salad, 292
Hearty tuna salad, 305
Heinz, H. J., Co., 15–16, 54
Heinz's chili sauce, 214
Heinz's ketchup, 206
Herb vinegars, 58–59ff.
Herbs, 47ff.
defined, 50
Herring, pickled, 250
Swedish, 285
Holland, 273–74
Hollow pickles, 32
Honey vinegar, 57, 58
Horse-radish, 50
Horse-radish relishes, 134, 267
Horse-radish vinegar, 62
Hot dog relishes, 144. *See also* Frankfurter relish
Huckleberries, spiced, 168
Hurry-up corn relish, 254
Hurry-up vegetable hash, 139
Husbands, preserving, 85

Ice water pickles, 104
Icicle pickles, 105
bread and butter, 112
India and Indian recipes, 274–75
chicken curry, 275
mint chutney, 240
mustard, 274
pickled grapes, 274
tomato chutney, 235
India relish, 128–29
Indian cress, 50
Indiana peach chutney, 230
Ingredients, 40–67
Iraqi pickled olives, 280
Iron, 27, 28, 33, 35, 57
Italian recipes, 275–76, 280–81, 282

Jam, red pepper, 245
Japan, 277–79
Jarred brandied peaches, 171

Jars, 24, 26–27ff., 33, 35
  for curing, 71ff.
  liquid content of, 21
Jerusalem artichoke pickles, 181
Jerusalem artichoke relish, 130–31
Jiffy catsup, 266
Jiffy pickles, 252
Juniper berry, 50
Just plain chutney, 219

Kale, brining of, 82–83
Kegs, 33
Kennebunk pickle, 144–45
Ketchup. *See* Catsup
Kettles, 33
Kidney bean salads, 291
Kimmel cherries, 162
Kiwi chutney, 284
Korea, 279
Kosher pickles, 98, 99
Kraut. *See* Sauerkraut
Kumquat chutney, 225

Lamb marinade, 66
Lamb stew, Moroccan pickle, 283
Lancaster relish, 145
Land cress, 49
Lazy housewife pickles, 253
Leek, 50
Lemon balm, 47
Lemon catsup, 210–11
Lemon pickle, spicy, 169
Lemon verbena, 53
Lemons, 50
  measuring, 38
Lettuce kraut, 75, 76, 79–80
  Chinese, 279
Lettuce salad, shredded, 299
Lima beans, 77, 78, 81–84
  measuring, 38
  mustard pickles with, 119
  salad of, 300
Limes, 50
  measuring, 38
Liquid content of jars, 21
Little pickled apples, 159
Liverwurst balls, dill, 288
Llewellyn Miller's cocktail carrots, 247
Lobster, Japanese sour, 278
Lobster salad, tart, 300
Loquat chutney, 226
Louisiana pickled figs, 167

Macaroni salads, 300–1
Mace, 50
Mackerel, Japanese vinegared, 278
Maine catsup, 207
Malaysia, 283
Mama's mincemeat, 237
Mango chutneys, 226–27
Mango relish, 148

Mangoes, 38, 220
  pickled, 170
  seasonings for, 53
  spiced, 169
Marinades, 64–67
  barbecue, 65–67
  beef, 64–65
  cooked, 64
  dill, 315
  fish, 67
  game, 66–67, 269
  lamb, 66
  poultry, 60
Marinated mushrooms, 188–89
Marjoram, 50
  wild, 51
"Marmalade," 177
Maryland peach chutney, 231
Measures, 36–40
Meat dishes, 307–11
Meat pickles, 201–3
  seasonings for, 53
Meatless mincemeat, 243
Mediterranean specialties, 280–82
Medley pickle salad, 301
Melon. *See also* Watermelon
  cutting, 28
  pickled, 153, 247
Mexican barbecue sauce, 66
Mexican marinade and barbecue sauce, 65
Mills, Billy, 107–9
Mincemeat, 237–43
  by the crock, 238–39
  Citrus Grove, 239
  Cousin Celia's, 240
  Mama's, 237
  meatless, 243
  moose, 240–41
  old-time, 238
  orange, 243
  pear, 241
  pork, 241
  spices for, 50
  tomato, 242–43
  Washington Irving, 239
Mint, 28, 46
Mint chutneys, 227, 248
Mint vinegar, 58–59, 62
Minted onion rings, 190–91
Missouri piccalilli, 130
Mixed-pickle chow-chow, sweet, 124
Mixed pickles, 22, 116–17. *See also* specific
    ingredients
  golden glow, 104
  low-calorie, 263
  mustard, 107, 118
  rummage, 117
  simple, 116
Mock olives, 178
Molasses, measuring, 38
Moose mincemeat, 240–41
Moroccan pickle stew, 283

Mother of vinegar, 57
Mousse, pickle egg, 297
Mrs. Beeton's brine, 63
Mrs. Jack Grimes' relish, 141
Mrs. Nellis' chili sauce, 215
Mushroom catsups, 211, 266
Mushrooms, 50, 189
    fresh pickled, 250
    Japanese, 277
    marinated, 188–89
    measuring, 38
    Syrian, 286
Mustard, 30, 50
    and dill sauce, 258–59
    home-prepared, 118
    Indian, 274
    Italian, 275
    measuring, 39
    seasonings for, 53
Mustard greens, brining of, 82–83
Mustard pickles, 106–7, 118–22
    beans, 120
    cabbage, 122
    chow-chows, 122–27
    cucumber-onion, 120–21
    company, 120
    curried, 121
    eggs, 201
    fresh cucumber, 106
    German, 272–73
    with lima beans, 119
    low-calorie, 264
    medley, 121
    mixed, 107, 118
    North Carolina, 70
    sweet, 119
Mustard sauce, 307
Myrtle, 50

Nasturtium, 50
National Pickle Packers Association, 13
Nectarine chutney, 232
New England rhubarb relish, 150
New Zealand, 284
9-day wonder sweet pickles, 156
9 seasons vinegar, 59
North Carolina mustard pickle, 70
Nut meat. *See also* specific kinds
    measuring, 39
Nutmeg, 51
Nutty chutney, 229
    canapés, 289

Off-the-cob relish, 133
Okra, 81–84, 189
    dill, 189
Old-fashioned pickled red cabbage, 186
Old-time mincemeat, 238
Old Vermont sweet pickles, 94
Olive cherries, 163
Olive chicken salad, 294
Olive oil pickle slices, 106

Olive plums, 87
Olives, 280–82
    California green-ripe process, 90–91
    curing, 87–92
    dill, 281
    Greek-process, 92
    Greek-style black, 281
    Iraqi pickled, 280
    measuring, 39
    mixed Italian, 281
    mock, 178
    in oil, 289
    Schiacciate, 280–81
    Spanish-process, 91
    spiced Spanish, 282
Olivettes, 105
Omelet, puffy, 316
Onion cheese balls, 288
Onion relishes, 135, 256
    low-calorie, 265
Onion vinegar, 63
Onions, 51, 190
    brining of, 83–84
    chopping of, 28
    and cucumbers, 117
        mustard-pickled, 120–21
    measuring, 39
    minted rings, 190–91
    and tomatoes, 117, 196–97
Orange-flavored pickle strips, 152
Orange mincemeat, 243
Orange slices, spicy preserved, 170
Oranges, measuring, 39
Oregano, 51
Overnight cucumber slices, 113
Overnight dill pickles, 21
Overnight pickled shrimp, 260
Oysters, pickled, 203, 251

Papaya pickles, sweet spiced, 170
Paprika, 51
Parsley, cutting, 28
Parsley, pickled, 191
Pasteurize, defined, 29
Pasteurized dills, 20
Pawpaw chutney, 228
Peach catsup, 212
Peach chutneys, 228, 230–31, 232
Peaches, 171–75
    brandied, 171
    chock-full-of-nuts, 173
    clove-starred, 172–73
    color of, 24
    measuring, 39
    peeling, 24
    picnic, 172
    pickled, 174–75
    spiced, 175
    sweet and spicy, 165
    for vinegar, 57
Pear butter, 244–45
Pear mincemeat, 242

Pear relishes, 148–49
Pear-tomato chutney, 234–35
Pear-water cress salad, 301
Pears, 175–77
    color of, 24
    ginger, 175
    measuring, 39
    pickled, 176–77
        quick, 257
    spiced, 177
    sweet and spicy, 165
    for vinegar, 57
Peas, 77, 78, 81–82, 83–84
Peeling, 24, 28
Pennsylvania chow-chow, 124
Pennsylvania pepper relish, 136
Pepper jam, red, 245
Pepper pot relishes, 137
Pepper relishes, 135–37
    with cabbage, 253, 255
    with celery, 254
    low-calorie, 265
    with onion, 135, 265
    with pears, 149
    Pennsylvania, 136
    quick, 135
Pepper sauce, pickled, 215
Pepper salad, stuffed, 302
Peppercorns, 47
Peppered pickled eggs, 201
Peppers, 191–93, 275
    brining of, 83–84
    cabbage-stuffed, 192–93
    measuring, 39
    pimiento, 193. *See also* Pimientos
    Roumanian, 284
    salted, 76
    to season dills, 46
Persimmon chutney, 227
Peruvian sauce, 216
Peter Piper pickles, 114–15
Peter Piper sandwiches, 317
Peter's pickled pumpkin, 194
Philadelphia relish, 145
Piccalilli, 22, 30, 51
    recipes, 129–30
Pickerel, pickled, 204
"Pickle," etymology of, 29
Pickle aspic, 291
Pickle Packers International Inc., 13
Pickle fans, 288
Pickle quiche Lorraine, 313
Pickle rabbits, 314–15
Pickle salad, medley, 301
Pickle sandwich loaf, 318
Pickle sauce, 260–61, 317
Pickle spread, 319
Pickle-vegetable salad, 304
Pickle vichyssoise, 289
Pickleburgers, 308
Pickles, 51. *See also* Cucumbers; Dill
    pickles; etc.; specific fruits and vege-
tables. For pickles in combination,
    see other ingredients
commercial packing of, 16–22
Danish, 270
gefilte, 289
history, background of, 13–18
homemade, 23–92
measuring, 39
Picnic peaches, 172
Picnic potato salad, 302
Pie, vinegar, 321
Pigs' feet, pickled, 202, 253
Pigs' knuckles with sauerkraut, 310
Pike, pickled, 204
Pimento, 30, 47, 51
Pimientos, 30, 51
    pickled, 193
    preserved, 193
Pine-nut salad, 302
Pineapple, 28, 39
    chicken salad, 294
    chutney, 231
    pickle bits, 180
    rings, ham-, 309
    spiced, 179–80
Plum chutneys, 232–33
Plums, measuring, 39
Plums, for mock olives, 178
Plums, olive, 87
Polish-style dills, 22
Pop's hot dog relish, 144
Pork and apple salad, 301
Pork chops, dill-stuffed, 308–9
Pork mincemeat, 241
Pot roast marinade, 64–65
Potato salad, hot frankfurter, 299
Potato salad, picnic, 302
Pottsfield pickle, 125
Poultry marinade, 66
Powwow sauce, 216–17
Prawns, Japanese sour, 278
Precooking, defined, 29
Processed dills, 19, 21
Processing, 30
    defined, 29
    utensils for, 33
Prune butter, 245
Prunes, measuring, 39
Prunes, spiced, 178–79
Pudding, pickle-beef Yorkshire, 320
Puffy omelet, 316
Pumpkin, pickled, 194
Putney chutney, 233

Quiche Lorraine, pickle, 313
Quick pickles, 93–95, 96. *See also* Fresh
    packing; specific fruits and vege-
    tables
Quinces, spiced, 177

Radish, Japanese pickled, 278
Radish relish, 138
    Korean, described, 279

Rainbow trout marinade, 67
Raisin relish, 150
Raisins, measuring, 39–40
Raspberries, spiced currants and, 166
Raspberry vinegar, 59
Raw-raw chow-chow, 125
Ready relish, 255
Recipes, use of, 25, 27
Red hot sauce, 217
Reducing. *See* Dieting
Refrigerator pickles, 246–61
  relishes, 253–61
Relish biscuits, 319
Relishes, 128–50. *See also* specific vege-
    tables and fruits
  amber, 140
  Aunt Katie's, 150
  Carnacina, 141
  combination, 140–47
  chow-chow, 127
  curry, 141
  defined, 22
  Dixie, 142
  dozen vegetable, 138–39
  farmer-style, 142
  French pickle, 143
  fruit, 147–50
  garden salad, 256
  garden special, 143
  hot dog (frankfurter), 144, 265
  hurry-up vegetable hash, 139
  India, 128–29
  Kennebunk pickle, 144–45
  Lancaster, 145
  Mrs. Jack Grimes', 141
  Philadelphia, 145
  piccalilli, 129–30. *See also* Piccalilli
  ready, 255
  refrigerator, 253–61
  savory autumn, 146
  sweet, 146, 148
  sweet pickle, 129
  three Cs, 131
  tropical, 149
  vegetable, 130–39. *See also* specific vege-
    tables
Remoulade sauce, 259
Rhubarb, 40
  chutney, 233
  relish, 150
  sauce (Victoria), 218
Robert's barbecue marinade, 65
Rose geranium vinegar, 58–59
Rose vinegar, 63
Rosemary, 51
Roumanian pickled peppers, 284
Rummage pickles, 117
Russia, 284–85
Russian dressing, 306
Rutabaga kraut, 76, 79–80
Rutabagas, brining of, 82–83

Saccharin, measuring, 40
Saccharin pickles, 267
Saffron, 52
Sage, 52
Salad Burnet, 48
Salad dressings, 306
Salad fagots, 298
Salads, 287, 290–305. *See also* specific in-
    gredients
  Carol G's, 292–93
  confetti, 295
  continental, 294
  "cool as a pickle," 295
  delicatessen, 296
  emerald garden, 298
  garden, 256
Salmon and cottage cheese salad, 305
Salmon, pickled, 256–57
Salt, 25, 27, 40, 43, 52, 300
  tables, 85–86
"Salt stock," 16, 17
Salting stations, 19
Salting of vegetables, 76–92. *See also* spe-
    cific vegetables
Sandwich loaf, 318
Sandwiches, 317–19
Sauces, 213–18, 257–61
  anchovy, 213
  barbecue, 65, 213, 257–58
  beefsteak, 271
  Bordeaux, 140
  chili. *See* Chili sauces
  chutney, 258
  cocktail, 258
  cranberry relish, 254–55
  currant, 261
  dill and mustard, 258
  dill pickle, 261
  frankfurter, 259
  French pickle, 261
  green tomato, 217
  mustard, 258, 307
  Peruvian, 216
  pickle, 260–61, 317
  pickled pepper, 215
  powwow, 216–17
  red hot, 217
  remoulade, 259
  seafood, 259
  Spanish pickle, 317
  Tabasco, 217
  tartar, 259
  Victoria, 218
Sauerkraut, 71–76, 79–80, 315–16
  with apples, 315
  cheesette, 313
  Chinese, 279
  Dutch, 274
  escalloped with cheese, 314
  with grapes, 316
  low-calorie, 266
  with pigs' knuckles, 310

salads, 302–4
sausage pie, 314
seasonings for, 53
soup, 284–85
and spareribs, 309
3-in-1 casserole, 313
and tomatoes, 316
Sauerruben. *See* Turnips and turnip greens
Sausage casserole, 3-in-1, 313
Sausage pie, sauerkraut, 314
Savory, 52
Savory autumn relish, 146
Scalding, defined, 28
Scallops, Japanese vinegared, 278–79
Scotch apple pickle, 285
Seafood. *See* Clams; Oysters; etc.
Seafood sauce, 259
Sealing, defined, 29
Seasoned tomato purée, 207
Seasonings, 46–54
Senfgurken, 272–73
Sesame, 52
Shallot, 52
Shallot vinegar, 63
Shredded lettuce salad, 299
Shredded sweet Senfgurken, 272–73
Shrimp, 260
  Japanese sour, 278
  marinade, 67
  salad, 304
Shriveling of pickles, 31–32
Simmering, defined, 29
Sizes, commercial pickle, 20
Skillet chicken pickle curry, 310
Smooth gooseberry chutney, 224
Snap beans. *See* Beans
Snappy chicken salad, 294
Softening of pickles, 31
Soups, 289–90
  black bean and dill, 290
  pickle vichyssoise, 289
  pickles in cheese, 287
  sauerkraut, 284–85
Sour beans, 182
Sour chow-chow, 123
Sour cucumber pickles, 69
Sour cucumber slices, fresh, 95
Sour pickles, 19, 21–22. *See also* specific recipes
Sour relish, 22
South Sea chutney, 234
Southern turkey pickle casserole, 311
Soy sauce, 52
Spanish olives, spiced, 282
Spanish pickle sauce, 317
Spanish-process olives, 91
Spareribs and sauerkraut, 309
Spearmint vinegar, 58–59
Speed, in home pickling, 24
Spice bags, 28, 47

Spiced pickles. *See also* specific ingredients
  fruits, 159–80
  low-calorie, 263
  seasonings for, 53
Spiced vinegars, 60–61, 69, 202
  basic, 95
Spices, 25, 28, 40, 47ff.
  defined, 52
Spinach, for Chinese kraut, 279
Spinach, pickle-stuffed eggs on, 317
Spoilage, 24ff.
  of sauerkraut, 74
Spread, pickle, 319
Steam pressure canners, 35
Sterilizing, 35
  defined, 29
  utensils for, 33
Stews, 287
  lamb, 283
Storage, 31
Strawberries, measuring, 40
Strawberries, pickled, 179
Sugar, 25, 27, 43, 52
  for chutney, 220
  measuring, 40
Summer savory, 52
Summer sun chutney, 234
Sun glow spears, 103
Swedish pickled herring, 285
Sweet anise, 49
Sweet basil, 47
Sweet fennel, 49
Sweet marjoram, 50
Sweet mixed-pickle chow-chow, 124
Sweet pickle relish, 129
Sweet pickles, 20, 22, 46, 151–58. *See also* specific fruits and vegetables
  chips, 151
  11-day, 157
  4-day, 155
  14-day, 157
  from-sour pickles, 251
  low-calorie, 264
  mustard, 119
  9-day wonder, 156
  old Vermont, 94
  orange-flavored, 152
  rounds, 152
  seasonings for, 53
  23-day, 158
  yellow cucumber, 153
Sweet relishes, 22, 129, 146
Sweets and sours, 199
Syria, 286

Tabasco sauces, 52, 217
Taj Mahal dressing, 306
Tarragarlic vinegar, 59
Tarragon, 52
Tart lobster salad, 300
Tartar sauce, 259
Texas A. & M. spiced vinegar, 61

Texas barbecue sauce, 257
Texas chili sauce, 216
Thousand Island dressing, 306
Three Cs relish, 131
3-in-1 casserole, 313
Thyme, 52
Times, processing, 30
Tin, 27
Tomato butter, 245
Tomato catsups, 205-7, 208, 211
  seasonings for, 53
Tomato chow-chow, 123
Tomato chutneys, 221, 234-36, 283
Tomato mincemeat, 242-43
Tomato purée, seasoned, 207
Tomato rabbit, 314-15
Tomato relishes, 137-38
  with cabbage, 140
  with celery, 138
  fresh, 256
  green, 137
  with pears, 149
  uncooked, 137
Tomato sauce, green, 217
Tomatoes, 194-98
  cherry pickled, 195
  chunks, 198
  cocktail, 195
  dilled, 99-101, 102
  ginger, 198
  measuring, 40
  and onions, 117, 196-97
  peeling of, 24, 28
  Rachel, 197
  ripe pickled, 198
  sauerkraut and, 316
  sliced pickled, 196-97
  spiced, 196
  stuffed with combination salad, 305
Tomolives, dill, 101
Tongue, pickled, 202-3
Tongue salad, 304
  kidney bean, 291
Tropical relish, 149
Trout, marinade for, 67
Trout, pickled, 203
Truffles, 52
Tuna cups, pickle, 306
Tuna salads, 305
Turkey pickle casserole, 311
Turkish olives, 281
Turmeric, 52
Turnips and greens, 75-76, 79-80, 283
  brining of, 82-83
  for Chinese kraut, 279
  Japanese, 277
23-day sweet pickles, 158

Utensils, 33-35

Vanilla, 53
Vegetable chop, 139

Vegetable and fruit catsups, 208-12
Vegetable-pickle salad, 304
Vegetable relishes, 22, 130-39. *See also*
  specific vegetables
Vegetables, 181-99, 315-16. *See also* spe-
  cific vegetables
  choosing of, 40
  Japanese pickled, 277
Verbena, 53
Verjuice of apple, 214
Vichyssoise, pickle, 289
Victoria sauce, 217
Vienna tidbits, 288
Vinegar, 25ff., 40, 53, 54-63
  -brined beans, 182
  candy, 320
  for chutney, 220
  making, 56-63
  pie, 320-21
  seasonings for, 53, 58-59
  spiced, 60, 61, 69, 202
    basic, 95
  weight in winter, 311
Vischnik, Dad's, 162
Vitamins, 18, 264
Vitriol, 25

Waldorf chicken salad, 294
Walnut catsup, 212
Walnuts, measuring, 40
Walnuts, pickled, 178
Wash-boilers, 33
Washing, in home pickling, 24
Washington Irving mincemeat, 239
Water, 25, 43-46
Water bath, 29, 30
Water cress, 53
Water cress-pear salad, 301
Watermelon pickles, 153-55
  measuring rind for, 40
Weights and measures, 36-40
  of salted vegetables, 78-79
Wild marjoram, 51
Wine, 53
Winter relish, 146-47
Winter savory, 52
Wintergreen vinegar, 58-59
Wire baskets, 24-25
Worcestershire sauce, 53
Words, 29-30. *See also* Dictionary, pickle;
  specific words
Wright, Richardson, 246

Yellow cucumber sweet pickles, 153
Yorkshire pudding, pickle-beef, 320
Yukon, 269

Zesty cranberry catsup, 209
Zinc, 26, 27, 33, 57
Zucchini, measuring, 40
Zucchini pickles, 198-99

The Author and His Book

LEONARD LOUIS LEVINSON *was born in Pittsburgh, Pennsylvania, and educated in the public schools of Pittsburgh, Portland, Oregon, and San Diego and Los Angeles, California. He completed his formal studies at the University of California at Los Angeles. A writer since he was sixteen years old, he is the author or editor of a number of other cookbooks, over five hundred radio scripts, about two hundred and fifty television shows, many short stories and magazine articles, and a number of musical plays and revues, including two for Broadway. For several years he collaborated with Don Quinn on the scripts for "Fibber McGee and Molly" and then created "The Great Gildersleeve." He has directed radio programs and motion pictures, and created and produced a revolutionary series of cartoon shorts with his company Impossible Pictures, Inc. He has been a newspaperman in Hollywood, Los Angeles, San Francisco, and Houston. During World War II, he served in the Office of War Information. His first cookbook,* The Brown Derby Cookbook *(Doubleday, 1949; Dolphin, 1962) was followed by* The Complete Book of Low Calorie Cooking *(Hawthorn, 1956), which has since been published in a new and revised edition (Hawthorn, 1964). In 1959, Mr. Levinson edited* A Cookbook for Diabetics *for the American Diabetes Association, and in 1962 he spent six months in Italy for his forthcoming culinary book,* The Best of Italian Cooking. *He also wrote the chapter on "Immigrant Influences" and the profile on the Delmonico family for* The American Heritage Cookbook *(Simon and Schuster, 1964). Among the books of humor he has written are* The Left Handed Dictionary *(Collier Books, 1963),* How to Tell a Joke *(Collier Books, 1964),* Impossible Greeting Cards *(Pyramid, 1956); of a more serious nature are* Wall Street: A Pictorial History *(Ziff-Davis, 1961) and two volumes on an eighteenth-century adventurer:* The Affairs of Casanova *(Pyramid, 1958) and* The Memoirs of Casanova, *edited by Leonard Louis Levinson (Collier Books, 1962).*

THE COMPLETE BOOK OF PICKLES AND RELISHES *(Hawthorn, 1965) was set in type by the Harry Sweetman Typesetting Corp., New York City. It was printed by the Meadow Printing Co., New York City, and bound by the Book Press, Brattleboro, Vermont. The type face used for the text is Baskerville, a modernized reproduction of the type faces cut in 1760 by John Baskerville.*